Publications on Russia and Eastern Europe
of the School of International Studies
University of Washington
Volume 10

Sponsored by the Russian and
East European program of
the School of International Studies
University of Washington

WITNESSES
TO THE ORIGINS
OF THE COLD WAR

Edited by
THOMAS T. HAMMOND

University of Washington Press

SEATTLE AND LONDON

TO NANCY WITH LOVE

This book has been published with the assistance of a grant from the Andrew W. Mellon Foundation.

Library of Congress Cataloging in Publication Data

Main entry under title:

Witnesses to the origins of the cold war.

(Publications on Russia and Eastern Europe of the School of International Studies, University of Washington; v. 10)

Includes index.

Contents: Introduction/Thomas T. Hammond—The view from Russia/George F. Kennan—The view from Yugoslavia/Michael B. Petrovich—[etc.]

1. World politics—1945- —Addresses, essays, lectures. 2. Europe, Eastern—Politics and government—1945- —Addresses, essays, lectures. 3. United States—Foreign relations—1945

I. Hammond, Thomas Taylor. II. Series.

D843.W53   947   81-21810

ISBN 0-295-95892-8   AACR2

Contents

Acknowledgments

Many people assisted in the creation of this volume. The person most deserving of thanks is Professor Peter F. Sugar of the University of Washington, who first had the idea of preparing such a book, recruited one of the contributors, helped edit one of the chapters, made many useful suggestions, and offered encouragement from start to finish. Others who helped in one way or another include John C. Campbell, Leslie C. Tihany, Richard W. Tims, Wayne Vucinich, Ambassador Burton Y. Berry, Ambassador James W. Riddleberger, Walter Schwinn, Norman Graebner, John L. Gaddis, and Robert James Maddox.

Essential financial assistance was provided by the Earhart Foundation, and I am happy to express my appreciation to the Board of Trustees and to the President, Mr. Richard A. Ware. I am also grateful to them for giving me absolute, unsupervised freedom in my work.

The highly efficient secretaries of the History Department at the University of Virginia, Mrs. Lottie M. McCauley, Mrs. Ella M. Wood, Mrs. Elizabeth C. Stovall, and Mrs. Kathleen C. Miller, typed and retyped the various chapters in their usual prompt and meticulous manner. Mr. Paul I. McNamara, Director of the Nantucket Cottage Hospital, kindly allowed me to use his copying facilities when no others were available.

My wife, Nancy Bigelow Hammond, did an expert job of editing and proofreading several chapters, compiled most of the index, freed me from many household duties, and aided my morale in ways that cannot be measured.

My research assistant, Gennady Shkliarevsky, checked the footnotes and helped with several other details.

I wish, of course, to express my appreciation to the contributing authors for finding the time to write their chapters and for not only tolerating my many suggestions, but even thanking me for making them.

WITNESSES
TO THE ORIGINS
OF THE COLD WAR

THOMAS T. HAMMOND

Introduction

The Great Debate over the
Origins of the Cold War

The term "the Cold War" is usually taken to mean the intense conflict between the Communist world and the non-Communist world, especially between the Soviet Union and the United States, that started after World War II. It has been called "cold" because it has not involved fighting between Soviet and American troops nor the use of nuclear weapons. But it has involved war between the USSR and the United States by almost every means other than direct armed conflict. It has witnessed wars by proxy, that is, American troops fighting against allies of the USSR (as in Korea and Vietnam), states supported by the United States fighting against states supported by Russia (as in the Middle East), Soviet use of armed force to install Communist regimes in neighboring countries (as in Poland, North Korea, etc.), American attempts to overthrow pro-Soviet regimes in Latin America (as in Guate-

Thomas T. Hammond is a graduate of the Russian Institute of Columbia University and received his Ph.D. in Russian history from Columbia. He has taught at Columbia University, the University of Wisconsin, and Emory University, and for some years has been Professor of History at the University of Virginia. His publications include *The Anatomy of Communist Takeovers* (Yale University Press, 1975), *Soviet Foreign Relations and World Communism* (Princeton University Press, 1965), *Lenin on Trade Unions and Revolution* (Columbia University Press, 1957), and *Yugoslavia Between East and West* (Foreign Policy Association, 1954). On the subject of the Cold War he has written "'Atomic Diplomacy' Revisited," *Orbis* (Winter 1976), and "Revisionism Reconsidered," *Slavic Review* (March 1974). He is a past president of the Southern Conference on Slavic Studies and is presently a member of the Executive Council of the Conference on Slavic and East European History of the American Historical Association.

mala, Cuba, and Chile), Soviet invasions of countries attempting to oust pro-Soviet regimes (as in Hungary, Czechoslovakia, and Afghanistan), and civil wars in which Russia and America supported opposing camps (as in the Congo and Angola).

The Cold War conflict between Russia and America has taken almost every conceivable form short of direct armed clashes. It has involved a massive propaganda war, sometimes becoming quite virulent. It has of course meant a frantic race to see which side could develop the most terrible weapons of destruction. The Cold War has seen competition throughout the world for friends and allies, in the hope that one side or the other could tilt the balances of power in its favor. It has been, indeed, a war on almost all fronts, a war for influence throughout the world, in which both sides have used radio broadcasts, propaganda pamphlets, espionage, subversion, and sabotage.

Along with the other forms of warfare, the Cold War has also spawned a war among the historians, a controversy over how the Cold War got started, whether or not it was inevitable, and (above all) who bears the main responsibility for starting it. Leading Western statesmen like Churchill, Truman, Byrnes, and others,[1] followed by scholars like Herbert Feis,[2] initially dominated the field of battle. They presented what came to be known as the orthodox, traditional, or liberal viewpoint, arguing that, if blame is to be attributed for the outbreak of the Cold War, Russia deserves more blame than any other country. As the years passed, however, many authors presented "revisionist" views of one kind or another, arguing that the United States was the primary

1. A few of the most important memoirs by Western statesmen that deal with the origins of the Cold War are: Winston S. Churchill, *The Second World War* (Boston: Houghton Mifflin, 1948-53, 6 vols.); Harry S. Truman, *Memoirs* (Garden City, N.Y.: Doubleday, 1955-56, 2 vols.); Cordell Hull, *The Memoirs of Cordell Hull*, vol. 2 (New York: Macmillan, 1948); Edward R. Stettinius, Jr., *Roosevelt and the Russians* (Garden City, N.Y.: Doubleday, 1949); James F. Byrnes, *Speaking Frankly* (New York: Harper, 1947); Dean Acheson, *Present at the Creation* (New York: Norton, 1969); Charles E. Bohlen, *Witness to History, 1929-1969* (New York: Norton, 1973); Anthony Eden, *The Memoirs of Anthony Eden* (Boston: Houghton Mifflin, 1965); W. Averell Harriman and Elie Able, *Special Envoy to Churchill and Stalin* (New York: Random House, 1975); George F. Kennan, *Memoirs 1925-1950* (Boston: Little, Brown, 1967); Henry L. Stimson and McGeorge Bundy, *On Active Service in Peace and War* (New York: Harper, 1947).

2. The main works by Feis on the Cold War are: *The Atomic Bomb and the End of World War II* (Princeton: Princeton University Press, 1966); *Between War and Peace: The Potsdam Conference* (Princeton: Princeton University Press, 1960); *Churchill, Roosevelt, Stalin* (Princeton: Princeton University Press, 1957); *From Trust to Terror: The Onset of the Cold War* (New York: Norton, 1970). Among the earliest histories of the origins of the Cold War, and still one of the best, is William Hardy McNeill, *America, Britain, and Russia: Their Cooperation and Conflict, 1941-46* (New York: Oxford University Press, 1953).

villain, while the Soviets deserved little or none or less of the blame.[3]

This battle of the books has been waged without surcease for many years, with new volumes and articles on the subject appearing almost every month. The revisionists initially were few in number and attracted relatively little attention, but in the 1960s and 1970s, partly as a result of Vietnam and the increased tendency of Americans to criticize their country's foreign policies, the revisionists became more numerous and more influential. Their books are often reviewed sympathetically in scholarly journals and are widely used as texts in college courses.[4]

In recent years the controversy over the origins of the Cold War has reached a third stage, sometimes called the postrevisionist stage. A number of writers, particularly younger ones who are not emotionally involved through personal memories of the events they describe, have written works that cannot be accurately defined as either traditionalist or revisionist, but attempt to take the best from both approaches, modifying some of the traditional arguments, accepting some of the revisionist positions, and thereby producing a synthesis of the two camps.[5] These authors credit the revisionists for their diligence in dig-

3. A few characteristic revisionist works are: Gar Alperovitz, *Atomic Diplomacy: Hiroshima and Potsdam: The Use of the Atomic Bomb and the American Confrontation with Soviet Power* (New York: Vintage Books, 1965); Barton J. Bernstein, ed., *Politics & Policies of the Truman Administration* (Chicago: Quadrangle Books, 1970); D. F. Fleming, *The Cold War and its Origins, 1917-1960*, 2 vols. (Garden City, N.Y.: Doubleday, 1961); Lloyd C. Gardner, *Architects of Illusion: Men and Ideas in American Foreign Policy, 1941-1949* (Chicago: Quadrangle Books, 1970), and *Economic Aspects of New Deal Diplomacy* (Madison: University of Wisconsin Press, 1964); David Horowitz, *The Free World Colossus* (New York: Hill and Wang, 1965); Gabriel Kolko, *The Politics of War* (New York: Random House, 1968); Joyce and Gabriel Kolko, *The Limits of Power* (New York: Harper & Row, 1972); Walter LaFeber, *America, Russia, and the Cold War, 1945-1966* (New York: John Wiley, 1967); Thomas G. Paterson, ed., *Cold War Critics: Alternatives to American Foreign Policy in the Truman Administration* (Chicago: Quadrangle Books, 1970); and William A. Williams, *The Tragedy of American Diplomacy* (rev. and enl. ed. New York: Dell, 1962).

4. For criticism of the revisionists see: Robert James Maddox, *The New Left and the Origins of the Cold War* (Princeton: Princeton University Press, 1973); J. L. Richardson, "Cold War Revisionism: A Critique," *World Politics*, vol. 24, no. 4 (July 1972); Charles Maier, "Revisionism and the Interpretation of Cold War Origins," *Perspectives in American History*, vol. 4 (1970); Thomas T. Hammond, "Revisionism Reconsidered," *Slavic Review*, vol. 33, no. 1 (March 1974); Arthur M. Schlesinger, Jr., "Origins of the Cold War," *Foreign Affairs*, vol. 46 (October 1967); and Robert W. Tucker, *The Radical Left and American Foreign Policy* (Baltimore: Johns Hopkins University Press, 1971).

5. Among the best of the recent books that might be placed in the postrevisionist category are: John L. Gaddis, *The United States and the Origins of the Cold War, 1941-1947* (New York: Columbia University Press, 1972); Lynn Etheridge Davis, *The Cold War Begins: Soviet-American Conflict over Eastern Europe* (Princeton: Princeton University Press, 1974); Martin J. Sherwin, *A World De-*

ging out new documents and opening up new and important perspectives, but sometimes feel that the revisionists have been overburdened
with ideological baggage and have carried their revisions too far. At the
same time these new authors have no hesitation about criticizing the
biases and assumptions of the traditionalists. They feel, one might say,
that the traditionalists bent the stick too far to the right, and the revisionists bent it too far to the left, while they have straightened it out.

The purpose of this introduction is to summarize the chief issues in
this Cold War controversy—at least the issues that have to do with
Eastern Europe, the area dealt with in this book. By delineating these
controversies we hope to make the significance of the rest of the book
more apparent. While the memoirs that follow are interesting in their
own right, they become more so when viewed against the background
of the Cold War controversy. This chapter, then, will describe the
chief arguments and counterarguments about the role of Eastern
Europe in the origins of the Cold War, thereby setting the stage for the
accounts by the witnesses to the events.

WHO STARTED THE COLD WAR?

The principal issue in the Cold War controversy, the one that de-
fines the revisionist and traditional camps, is the question of which side
is more to blame for the Cold War. Some authors, surprisingly, have
overlooked this fundamental issue. Michael Leigh in his article, "Is
There a Revisionist Thesis on the Origins of the Cold War?"[6] takes
three issues in the Cold War debate (just *three* and not necessarily the
most important ones), compares the views of six revisionists with those
of three traditionalists, and finds that there is considerable disagreement among the revisionists on these issues and quite a bit of agreement
between revisionists and traditionalists. On the basis of this he concludes:

The term "revisionism" does not provide a useful demarcation within the literature . . . there is little consensus on the boundaries between "revisionist" and

---

stroyed: The Atomic Bomb and the Grand Alliance (New York: Knopf, 1975);
Gier Lundestad, *The American Non-Policy Towards Eastern Europe, 1943-1947:
Universalism in an Area Not of Essential Interest to the United States* (Tromsö,
Norway: Universitetsforlaget, 1978); Daniel Yergin, *Shattered Peace: The Origins
of the Cold War and the National Security State* (Boston: Houghton Mifflin, 1977);
Bruce R. Kuniholm, *The Origins of the Cold War in the Middle East: Great Power
Conflict and Diplomacy in Iran, Turkey, and Greece* (Princeton: Princeton Uni-
versity Press, 1980); and Vojtech Mastny, *Russia's Road to the Cold War: Diplo-
macy, Warfare, and the Politics of Communism, 1941-1945* (New York: Columbia
University Press, 1978).

6. *Political Science Quarterly*, March 1974, pp. 101-16.

and "non-revisionist" historiography . . . . Even if it were found that there is close agreement among the "revisionists" themselves, it would not follow that they constitute a separate "school"; to do so their conclusions would have to differ significantly from the conclusions of the "orthodox" or at least "non-revisionist" historians. [p. 102]

By asking the wrong questions, Leigh gets the wrong answers. The issue that unites the revisionists and that separates them from the traditionalists is the question of which side is more guilty, the Soviet Union or the United States, a question absent from Leigh's list. Without this emotion-generating issue, the Cold War debate would never have become so extensive and so heated; indeed, one wonders if there would have been much of a debate at all. To argue as Leigh does is about like arguing that, since Baptists, Episcopalians, and Catholics disagree on many important issues, there is no such thing as Christianity, and Christianity, in any case, is difficult to distinguish from other religions.[7] Leigh is right, however, in pointing out that there is a broad spectrum of both traditional and revisionist views, some of the authors being more extreme than others, and with members of the same camp criticizing one another.

The revisionists are above all critical of American leaders (especially Truman) and American foreign policy, but tend to be much less critical, or not critical at all, of Stalin and Soviet foreign policy. Indeed, most revisionists are highly critical of the United States in general, including its economic system. They concentrate on the things that the United States did (or failed to do) that helped to bring on the Cold War, while the traditionalists do just the opposite—focusing attention on the sins of the Soviets. It is also worth noting that most of the revisionists are specialists on American foreign policy, but have comparatively little expertise in Soviet foreign policy, and this explains in part why their accounts tend to be one-sided. Vojtech Mastny makes this point in his book, *Russia's Road to the Cold War,* which is based on sources in Russian, Polish, Czech, Slovak, Hungarian, Ukrainian, Serbo-Croat, and several other languages.

In their zeal to try and condemn the United States in the court of history, the revisionists tended to obfuscate the role of the other defendants; they especially tended to exonerate the Soviet Union by default. . . . Relentlessly dissecting and censuring the American policies, they were conspicuously less adept at progressing beyond mere assumptions about the Soviet ones. Usually these experts

7. Leigh also makes the questionable suggestion (p. 115 n) that "the term 'revisionism' might be redefined to designate the gamut of scholars who view American foreign policy as dictated by other than purely altruistic motives." Since there is probably no scholar who views American foreign policy as dictated by "purely altruistic motives," this would place all scholars in the revisionist camp.

and dilettantes in the field of United States foreign relations could not read Russian, much less the more exotic eastern European languages. In neglecting the Soviet side of the story, they could always rationalize that the pertinent sources remained out of reach.[8]

A typical example of the revisionist view was provided by D. F. Fleming when he wrote that "from the first it was the West which was on the offensive, not the Soviets."[9] An equally extreme example of the traditional view was provided in rather blunt terms by a recent writer.

> Those of us who were in close and constant touch with the Russians both before V-E Day, and for years after that, know precisely who initiated the cold war, and how. From the moment the Red Army crossed into Poland and into the Baltic, Balkan and Central European countries, it conducted a campaign of murder, rape, pillage and sabotage that would have outraged Genghis Khan. After the Red Army made contact with its Western "Allies" on the River Elbe, it added such refined excesses as political kidnappings and assassinations. It also broke almost every agreement made with its "Allies," and positioned its soldiers on the Elbe in formations ready to move into Western Europe.[10]

In a somewhat more subtle form, the debate about the origins of the Cold War is not over which *leaders,* American or Russian, bear the most responsibility, but which political and economic *system* was responsible. Some revisionists, for example, say that the existence of a capitalist economic system in the United States and the domination of the American government by representatives of capitalism had several unfortunate effects on American foreign policies during and after World War II: (a) the leaders of the American government were bitterly hostile toward communism and the Soviet Union; (b) American capitalists and their governmental cohorts were determined to keep Eastern Europe open to American business interests; (c) the U.S. government opposed all leftists, whether Communist or not, and supported only rightists, thereby coming into conflict with the democratic aspirations of the masses in Eastern Europe.[11] (More on this below.)

By contrast, some of the traditionalists argue that it was the Soviet system, combined with the inherited attitudes and policies of the tsarist regime, that made the Cold War inevitable. They argue that Russia was

8. Mastny, *Russia's Road to the Cold War*, p. xiv. I cannot think of a single professional scholar whose specialty is Soviet foreign policy and who has written a book on the origins of the Cold War from the revisionist point of view.

9. Fleming, *Cold War and Its Origins*, 1:31.

10. Peter Blake, letter to the editor, *New York Times Magazine* (July 6, 1980), p. 47.

11. Such arguments can be found for example, in Williams, *Tragedy of American Diplomacy;* Kolko, *Limits of Power;* Kolko, *Politics of War;* and Horowitz, *Free World Colossus.*

(and is) inherently expansionist, due to a combination of many factors: (a) Marxism-Leninism-Stalinism, which preaches that to spread communism is a sacred duty; (b) tsarist tradition, which justifies Russian expansion in the past; (c) Russian paranoia, nurtured by numerous invasions over the centuries by enemies from Asia and Europe; (d) Russian messianistic thought, which taught, both before and after the revolution, that Russia must conquer the world in order to save it; (e) Russian national interests, which led its rulers to covet the lands and resources of other states; and (f) the lack of powerful neighbors, which made Russian expansion easy. This general view was voiced, for example, by Arthur M. Schlesinger, Jr., one of the most influential of the traditional writers: "Thoughtful observers . . . concluded that classical Russian imperialism and Pan-Slavism, compounded after 1917 by Leninist messianism, confronted the West at the end of the Second World War with an inexorable drive for domination."[12]

This attitude was also expressed in 1946 by Clark Clifford in a memorandum prepared at the request of President Truman. Clashes with Russia, said Clifford, were unavoidable because "the Soviet government believes in the inevitability of a conflict with the capitalist world and prepares for that conflict by building up its own strength and undermining that of other nations."[13] According to Clifford, Soviet ideology made Russia intrinsically hostile and expansionist:

As long as the Soviet government maintains its present foreign policy, based upon the theory of an ultimate struggle between communism and capitalism, the United States must assume that the USSR might fight at any time for the twofold purpose of expanding the territory under Communist control and weaking its potential capitalist opponents. The Soviet Union was able to flow into the political vacuum of the Balkans, Eastern Europe, the Near East, Manchuria and Korea because no other nation was both willing and able to prevent it. Soviet leaders were encouraged by easy success and they are now preparing to take over new areas in the same way.[14]

The ways in which the American and Soviet political systems function also contributed to the start of the Cold War, in the view of some writers. They point out, for example, that some American con-

---

12. "Origins of the Cold War," p. 24. Schlesinger also emphasizes Stalin's paranoia as a cause of the Cold War.

13. Arthur Krock, *Memoirs* (New York: Funk & Wagnalls, 1968), as reprinted in *The Origins of the Cold War*, ed. Thomas G. Paterson (Lexington, Mass.: Heath, 1974), p. 25. The memo was dated September 24, 1946.

14. Ibid., p. 27. In preparing this memorandum, Clifford read, among other things, the cables from Moscow by George F. Kennan, and apparently was influenced by them. Similar ideas can be found in Kennan's cables and in his famous "X" article in *Foreign Affairs*, vol. 25 (July 1947).

gressmen had to take strong stands against Soviet actions in Eastern
Europe for fear they would be voted out of office.[15] Similarly, the
internal dynamics of the Soviet political system, combined with
Marxism-Leninism and deeply ingrained suspicion of the outside world,
may have compelled Stalin and his lieutenants to impose Communist
regimes on their neighbors in Eastern Europe. As Vojtech Mastny put
it, "the evils of the Soviet system were the ultimate cause of the Cold
War."[16]

Following this line of thought, some writers say that it is a mistake
to try to place blame on one side or the other. They see the Cold War
as inevitable, like a Greek tragedy whose unhappy unfolding could
not have been prevented by Stalin, Roosevelt, Churchill, or anyone
else. Louis J. Halle said,

> In the Cold War various historical circumstances . . . put Russia in the role of
> challenger—superficially, at least, in the role of aggressor. But the historical circum-
> stances, themselves, had an ineluctable quality that left the Russians little choice
> but to move as they did. Moving as they did, they compelled the United States
> and its allies to move in response. And so the Cold War was joined.
> This was not fundamentally a case of the wicked against the virtuous . . . and
> we may properly feel sorry for both parties, caught, as they are, in a situation of
> irreducible dilemma.[17]

EASTERN EUROPE AS A SOVIET SPHERE OF INFLUENCE

A second point of contention between the revisionists and the
traditionalists—one that we are particularly concerned with in this
book—has to do with Eastern Europe. Both sides tend to see the
conflict between Russia and the West over Eastern Europe as the
most important factor in triggering the Cold War, but they differ
completely as to which side was more at fault.

The revisionists argue that for reasons of military security the
Soviet Union had an obvious right to establish a sphere of influence
in Eastern Europe. They argue further that this right was recognized
in the Churchill-Stalin percentages agreement of October 9, 1944, as
modified on the following day by Molotov and Eden, which assigned
Russia 90 percent "predominance" in Rumania, 80 percent in Bulgaria

---

15. One conspicuous example of this was Senator Arthur Vandenberg, the
influential Republican from Michigan, who had many Poles and other East Europeans among his constituents. The role of Vandenberg and the importance of
American politics generally in the origins of the Cold War are described with
great skill in Gaddis, *The United States and the Origins of the Cold War, 1941-
1947.*

16. Mastny, *Russia's Road to the Cold War*, p. 312.

17. Louis J. Halle, *The Cold War as History* (New York: Harper & Row, 1967),
p. xiii.

and Hungary, and 50 percent in Yugoslavia, while assigning Britain 90 percent "predominance" in Greece.[18] If Roosevelt never formally approved of this agreement, say the revisionists, neither did he reject it, and his silence seemed to imply consent.[19]

It was this Churchill-Stalin agreement, the revisionists continue, that governed Allied actions in the Balkans, rather than the vague phrases of the Yalta Declaration on Liberated Europe. In addition, if the Yalta declaration pledged the three Allies to assist in the establishment of "democratic governments" chosen in "free elections," Stalin had a right to interpret these words in a Soviet sense, and the Western leaders should have known that he would do so. Nor did the West have any grounds for objecting to unilateral Soviet actions in Eastern Europe, since the Western powers acted unilaterally in Italy, France, and Japan. One of the revisionists further argues that, although Roosevelt realistically acquiesced in the establishment of a Soviet sphere of influence in Eastern Europe, Truman and Byrnes reversed his policy and waged a campaign "to force Soviet withdrawal from Eastern Europe."[20]

The traditionalist writers respond by arguing that the Western leaders were quite willing for Russia to have a sphere of influence in Eastern Europe, and indeed considered such a development inevitable. They thought that such a sphere might develop along the lines of what happened in Finland. But a "sphere of influence" to them did not mean that the Soviets were authorized to use military force, police terror, mass arrests, and murder to impose Soviet-style dictatorships, subservient to Stalin. When the Russians behaved so brutally and violated so flagrantly the Yalta Declaration on Liberated Europe, the Western powers could not fail to protest, even though their protests accomplished little. While Secretary Byrnes recognized Russia's "special security interests in those countries," he objected to Moscow's apparent determination to "deny their neighbors the right to be friends with others," that is, he opposed "exclusive spheres of interest."[21]

18. Churchill, *The Second World War* 6:226-35; Sir Llewellyn Woodward, *British Foreign Policy in the Second World War* (London: H. M. Stationery Office, 1962), pp. 307-8.

19. For good discussions of the percentages agreement, see Martin F. Herz, *Beginnings of the Cold War* (Bloomington: Indiana University Press, 1966), pp. 112-30, Robert Lee Wolff, *The Balkans in Our Time* (Cambridge, Mass.: Harvard University Press, 1956), pp. 259-64, and Mastny, *Russia's Road to the Cold War*, pp. 207-12.

20. Alperovitz, *Atomic Diplomacy*, p. 235. Similar statements can be found on pp. 13, 127-28, 131, 203, 204, 205, and 240.

21. Speech of October 31, 1945, *Department of State Bulletin* (November 4, 1945), p. 710. Emphasis added.

Traditionalists also argue that neither Truman nor Byrnes attempted to "force Soviet withdrawal from Eastern Europe." Instead they tried for a short while to preserve some semblance of democracy and some minimum Western influence in those countries. But they soon realized that even these modest objectives could not be accomplished short of war, so they reluctantly granted diplomatic recognition to the Soviet-dominated regimes of Eastern Europe and gave up the struggle.[22]

Having seen what the Soviets had done in Eastern Europe, say the traditionalists, the Western leaders naturally and justly took measures to prevent Western Europe, Greece, Turkey, and South Korea from suffering the same fate. There followed the justifiable defensive measures by the West: the Truman Doctrine, the Marshall Plan, the creation of NATO, and the defense of South Korea—in general, what came to be known as the policy of "containment."

WAS THE SOVIET UNION EXPANSIONIST OR DEFENSIVE?

Intimately related to Soviet policies in Eastern Europe is the question of what lay behind Stalin's moves to establish his control over that region. Did this mean that the USSR was expansionist? Or were these merely defensive actions, designed to protect the Soviet Union from future attacks?

The revisionists (and many others) argue that the Soviet desire to have friendly states along its borders was the most natural thing in the world, especially since Russia had been invaded time after time throughout its history. E. H. Carr, the well-known British scholar, wrote as early as 1944 that the USSR would feel it had a right to guarantee the security of its European borders and that "it would be foolish, as well as somewhat hypocritical, to construe insistence on this right as the symptom of an aggressive policy."[23]

While the revisionists have interpreted Soviet moves in Eastern Europe as defensive, the traditional writers have seen them as part of a general Soviet policy of expansion. For example, Joseph M. Jones, an American official writing about the background of the Truman Doctrine, stated that the Soviet Union "had demonstrated beyond any doubt that it was aggressive and expanding, and that its immediate

22. For further elaboration of these points see Thomas T. Hammond, "'Atomic Diplomacy' Revisited," *Orbis* 19, no. 4 (Winter 1976): 1425-27.

23. Quoted in Norman A. Graebner, "Cold War Origins and the Continuing Debate: A Review of Recent Literature," *The Journal of Conflict Resolution* 13, no. 1 (March 1969): 127. This excellent survey of the Cold War controversy has been of great help in the preparation of this chapter.

design for dominon included as much of Europe and Asia and North Africa as it could get away with short of war with its Western allies."[24]

As proof of Soviet expansionist aims the traditional authors have pointed not only to Eastern Europe but also to northern Iran, where the Soviets sponsored the establishment in 1945 of two puppet states, the "Autonomous Republic of Azerbaijan" and the "Kurdish People's Republic," apparently as a step toward detaching these areas from Iran.[25]

Having seen the Soviet army occupy Eastern Europe and help to establish Communist regimes in those countries, the traditionalists feared that Stalin had similar aims for Western Europe. As justification for their fears they pointed not only to Soviet acts, but also to such statements as that contained in a letter from Stalin to Tito: "The Soviet army came to the aid of the Yugoslav people, crushed the German invader, liberated Belgrade and in this way created the conditions which were necessary for the CPY [Communist Party of Yugoslavia] to achieve power. *Unfortunately the Soviet army did not and could not render such assistance to the French and Italian CPs.*"[26]

Whether justified or not, Western leaders feared that, unless they took defensive measures, the Soviet Union would try to spread communism to Western Europe also. Averell Harriman, the American ambassador to Russia, expressed this traditional view in 1945 and has continued to do so ever since. In his first meeting with Truman after Roosevelt's death, he told the new president that the West was faced with "a new barbarian invasion of Europe."[27] Later, in his memoirs, he wrote of himself: "Harriman's opinion . . . was that Stalin's insistence upon a belt of weak, easily dominated neighboring states might not be limited to Eastern Europe. Once the Soviet Union had control of bordering areas, he said, it would probably attempt to penetrate the next layer of adjacent countries."[28] As for Stalin's argument that he had to have a ring of friendly states to protect Russia from

24. Joseph Marion Jones, *The Fifteen Weeks* (New York: Viking, 1955), p. 41.

25. Rouhollah K. Ramazani, "The Autonomous Republic of Azerbaijan and the Kurdish People's Republic: Their Rise and Fall," in *The Anatomy of Communist Takeovers*, ed. Thomas T. Hammond (New Haven: Yale University Press, 1975), pp. 448-74.

26. *The Soviet-Yugoslav Dispute* (London: Royal Institute of International Affairs, 1948), p. 51. Emphasis added. The letter was dated May 4, 1948. It was not intended for publication, but it and others were published by the Yugoslavs after they were ousted from the Cominform.

27. Harriman and Abel, *Special Envoy*, p. 448.

28. Ibid., p. 449.

future German aggression, Harriman said that this was "only a cover for other plans."[29]

Over the years, some revisionist authors (and others) have defended Soviet invasions of other countries with the argument that these were defensive moves, designed to protect the USSR from foreign enemies. This argument was used to justify the Soviet takeover of Eastern Europe in the 1940s, the Soviet invasion of Hungary in 1956, of Czechoslovakia in 1968, and of Afghanistan in 1979. In each case it was said that the Soviet Union was not following a program of expansion, but was merely trying to defend its vital interests, that it was intervening to forestall or to counter intervention by other states. (One might call it, I suppose, "defensive aggression.")

Traditionalist authors have rejected this explanation, pointing out that Hitler too justified his expansionist moves as steps needed to defend Germany from its enemies. The Soviet Union, say some traditionalists, could impose satellite Communist regimes on every one of its neighbors on the basis of such "defensive" arguments. And when would the process come to an end? Would the USSR then invade the neighbors of its satellite states to defend the satellites from possible attack? When would the Kremlin feel secure? Only after all of Europe, Asia, and the Middle East had come under its control? As one writer recently put it, "There has never been anything more offensive than a Russian on the defensive. The Soviet quest for absolute security has, with good reason, generated insecurity on the part of other nations. Will the U.S.S.R. be less paranoid and therefore less predatory now that it has attained the status of superpower? Recent history is not encouraging."[30]

DID THE SOVIET UNION PURSUE MODERATE POLICIES IN 1944-46?

As we have seen, the traditionalists argue that the Cold War was caused largely by Stalin's actions in imposing Communist-dominated regimes on most of Eastern Europe. Countering this argument, many of the revisionists claim that in fact Stalin did not at first communize Eastern Europe, but instead tolerated the continued existence of bourgeois political parties, free elections, civil liberties, and capitalist economies under regimes known as "People's Democracies." Only later, they say, after the Western powers had demonstrated their hostility toward the Soviet Union and had tried to eliminate Soviet influence from Eastern Europe, did Stalin impose Communist regimes

29. U.S. Department of State, *Foreign Relations of the United States, 1945* (Washington: Government Printing Office, 1967), 5:232.

30. Strobe Talbott, "What Every Happened to Detente?" *Time* 115, no. 25 (June 23, 1980):34.

on these states. Thus, they argue, the sovietization of the region was not the result of a preconceived Soviet plan, but was rather a reaction to hostile moves on the part of the West, such as the Truman Doctrine.

Gabriel Kolko, for example, says that "the Russians . . . had no intention of Bolshevizing Eastern Europe if—but only if—they could find alternatives."[31] Barton J. Bernstein offers a similar argument, saying that "Stalin was pursuing a cautious policy and seeking accommodation with the West." "Soviet intentions," he declares, "were conservative."[32] According to Gar Alperovitz, "Stalin's approach [in Eastern Europe] seems to have been cautiously moderate" during 1945-46 and "changed to the harsh totalitarian controls" only after 1946.[33]

To support their position, the revisionists cite the free elections Stalin allowed in Hungary in 1945, which resulted, according to Bernstein, in "the overthrow of the Communist Party in Hungary."[34] In addition, as Alperovitz points out, free elections and democratic governments were permitted in Czechoslovakia, Austria, and Finland. Capitalism cotinued to exist, and multi-party coalitions governed throughout the region. During these early years, the revisionists recall, Stalin criticized Tito for being excessively radical and for not allowing King Peter to return to Yugoslavia.[35]

The traditionalist writers reply that Stalin's policies in most of Eastern Europe in 1944-46 could not in any realistic manner be described as "moderate," "cautious," or "conservative." In Poland, Romania, East Germany, and Bulgaria—long before 1947 and the Truman Doctrine—the Soviets used brute force and terror to install regimes that were completely dominated by the Communists, even though a few non-Communists were allowed, for cosmetic reasons, to occupy posts in the governments. In Hungary, they say, free elections were tolerated in 1945, but this had no long-term significance because the country was occupied by the Red Army and the Communists controlled the police. The non-Communist parties in Hungary were systematically harassed and restricted throughout 1946, and soon thereafter they were destroyed.[36] The Communist party of Hungary, despite Bernstein's assertion, was certainly not "overthrown" in 1945.

31. *Politics of War*, p. 619.

32. *Politics and Policies of the Truman Administration*, pp. 38, 39.

33. *Atomic Diplomacy*, pp. 13-14. See also pp. 131-32.

34. Bernstein, *Politics and Policies*, p. 38.

35. Horowitz, *Free World Colossus*, pp. 90-93. See also Isaac Deutscher, *Russia After Stalin* (London: Hamilton, 1953), pp. 74, et seq., and his *Stalin* (London: Oxford University Press, 1949), pp. 542-43.

36. Hugh Seton-Watson, *The East European Revolution* (London: Methuen, 1950), pp. 190-202. This is the classic account of how the Communists gained

The traditionalists say that to describe Stalin's policies in Eastern Europe in 1945-46 as moderate or conservative one would have to ignore much of what was going on during those years. They point, for example, to Stalin's actions in Poland, where he behaved from the beginning with absolute ruthlessness. As early as 1944, they argue, Stalin refused to aid the Warsaw uprising, and also hindered Western attempts to come to its aid, much to the dismay of Roosevelt and Churchill. At Yalta, they point out, Stalin agreed to reorganize the Polish government by the addition of non-Communist ministers, but for months afterwards obstructed every effort to carry out this agreement. At Yalta also, they say, Stalin promised that Polish elections would be held "in about one month," but then prevented them from taking place until almost two years later, after the Communists had consolidated themselves in power.[37] Further evidence of Stalin's ruthlessness was provided in March 1945 when sixteen of the top leaders of the Polish anti-German resistance movement were seized by the Soviet secret police, carted off to Moscow, and put on trial.[38]

The traditionalists also cite Romania as a case where Stalin, far from following a "moderate" policy, showed from the first that he was determined to establish a satellite state, without regard to democratic principles or Western opinion. They refer especially to Andrei Vyshinsky, Soviet deputy commissar for foreign affairs, flying to Bucharest only a few weeks after Yalta and issuing King Michael an ultimatum, demanding that he appoint a new government under the leadership of Petru Groza, an ally of the Communists. American officials were "genuinely shocked when the Soviets clamped down on Rumania so soon after Yalta."[39] General C. V. R. Schuyler, the American representative on the Allied Control Commission in Romania, wrote to Truman on May 3, 1945, as follows: "The present Rumanian government is a minority government, imposed on the nation by direct Soviet pressure. This government is dominated by the Rumanian Communist Party which probably represents less than 10% of the Rumanian population."[40]

control of Eastern Europe. A good discussion of the arguments about Stalin's "moderate" policies in Eastern Europe in 1944-46 is contained in Richardson, "Cold War Revisionism," pp. 587-89.

37. Susanne S. Lotarski, "The Communist Takeover in Poland," in *The Anatomy of Communist Takeovers,* ed. Hammond, p. 353.

38. Ibid., p. 351. Zbigniew Stypulkowski, one of the sixteen, described his experiences in *Invitation to Moscow* (New York: McKay, 1951).

39. John C. Campbell, who was a member of the Division of Central European Affairs in the State Department, as cited in Davis, *The Cold War Begins,* pp. 214 f.

40. *Foreign Relations of the United States, 1945* 5:541, as cited in Davis, ibid., pp. 273 f.

As far as Tito and King Peter are concerned, the traditionalists say yes, Stalin did urge Tito to let the king return to Yugoslavia after the war, but he also told Tito that later, after the king was no longer needed, Tito could "slip a knife into his back."[41] This example, say the traditionalists, illustrates an important point that the revisionists over-look—the Communists' use of *gradualism and camouflage.* The Soviets and the East European Communists introduced communism gradually, step by step, to minimize internal opposition, thereby avoiding civil war, and to minimize external opposition, thereby avoiding Western intervention. King Michael was kept on for a while in Romania and President Beneš was tolerated in Czechoslovakia as symbols of con-tinuity with the past, to reassure the people that no radical changes were being made. But, say the traditionalists, this did not reflect any lack of determination on Stalin's part to impose Soviet-controlled Communist regimes on Eastern Europe. Rather this was Stalin's policy of camouflage, of hiding his intentions until the Communists were firmly in control.[42] What the revisionists see as moderate policies, the traditionalists see as simply window-dressing to conceal Soviet and Communist domination. What the revisionists see as conserva-tive policies that might have continued if the West had not been hos-tile, the traditionalists see as temporary tactics designed to fool the non-Communists into inaction.

From the traditionalist point of view the revisionist arguments that the communization of Eastern Europe was a defensive reaction by Stalin to hostile Western moves is to reverse the chronology of events. According to them, the Western powers instituted defensive measures such as the Truman Doctrine, the Marshall Plan, and NATO only after Stalin had established his control over most of Eastern Europe, and had threatened Greece and Turkey; indeed, these measures were adopted because of Stalin's policies. To argue as the revisionists do, they say, is to get the cart before the horse.

ATOMIC DIPLOMACY

Many of the revisionists, particularly Gar Alperovitz in his book, *Atomic Diplomacy: Hiroshima and Potsdam: The Use of the Atomic Bomb and the American Confrontation with Soviet Power,* have argued that the Cold War was caused in large part by American policies re-garding the atomic bomb. They argue that, first of all, Roosevelt con-cealed American work on the bomb from Stalin, while sharing this information with Churchill, thereby strengthening Stalin's fears that

41. Vladimir Dedijer, *Tito* (New York: Simon & Schuster, 1953), p. 233.
42. For more on this point see Hammond, *Anatomy of Communist Takeovers,* pp. 24-27.

the Western powers were ganging up on him.[43] After Truman took over, he and Secretary Byrnes continued to keep the bomb project secret from Stalin; meanwhile they planned to use the bomb as a means of getting their way with the Russians. The bombs were dropped on Japan not solely to bring about a Japanese surrender (which was imminent anyhow), but rather to frighten the Soviets into making political concessions. Once the bombs had been used on Hiroshima and Nagasaki, Truman was ready for a showdown with Moscow. He and Byrnes used "atomic diplomacy" in "a powerful foreign policy initiative aimed at reducing or eliminating Soviet influence from Europe."[44]

The Alperovitz thesis initially was well received. *Atomic Diplomacy* got glowing reviews by Christopher Lasch[45] and others; Walter LaFeber described it as "the best book on the 1945 events,"[46] and the *New York Times* listed it as one of the best paperbacks of the year. Later, however, defenders of the traditional point of view examined the Alperovitz thesis and found it faulty. Adam Ulam, for example, wrote: "*No* attempt was made by the United States to exploit politically the monopoly of this weapon. . . . *Even Soviet sources,* while freely accusing the United States of practicing atomic diplomacy during the Cold War . . . do not accuse the United States of threatening the Soviet Union in 1945. Indeed, the Russians would be hard put to specify what more the USSR would have gotten had the United States *not* had the bomb."[47] Ulam also argues that possession of the bomb actually weakened U.S. foreign policy: "The early monopoly of the new weapon debilitated rather than helped American foreign policy. . . . It encouraged . . . a Maginot Line psychology. . . . Possession of the atomic bomb led to a feeling of national guilt. . . . America hugged the evanescent atom monopoly to its bosom, equally unable to exploit it or to exchange it for something useful."[48]

Meanwhile, Robert James Maddox, a strong opponent of the revisionists, wrote a ten-page critique of Alperovitz's scholarship, demonstrating that he misused his sources, cited quotations out of context, and generally violated the standards of honest writing.[49]

43. This is discussed in detail by a post-revisionist, Martin J. Sherwin, in *A World Destroyed.*

44. Alperovitz, *Atomic Diplomacy*, p. 13 and passim. See also his later collection, *Cold War Essays* (Garden City, N.Y.: Doubleday, 1970).

45. *Nation* (September 6, 1965), p. 123.

46. *America, Russia, and the Cold War, 1945-1966,* 1967 ed., p. 266.

47. Ulam, *The Rivals* (New York: Viking, 1971), p. 82.

48. Ibid., pp. 103-5.

49. "Atomic Diplomacy: A Study in Creative Writing," *Journal of American History* (March 1973), pp. 925-34. This article was reprinted in Maddox's book, *The New Left and the Origins of the Cold War.*

Somewhat later, the present author pointed out that the atom bomb was never used as an explicit threat against the Soviet Union. Byrnes tried to use it as an implied threat at the London Conference of Foreign Ministers in September 1945, but without success. Instead of Molotov being more "manageable," as Byrnes had hoped, he proved to be more tenacious than ever. Thereupon Truman and Byrnes, finding themselves unable to get the Soviets to make any meaningful concessions regarding Eastern Europe, gave up their attempts to use atomic diplomacy and granted diplomatic recognition, one after another, to the Soviet satellite governments.[50]

I also argued that Alperovitz was quite wrong in arguing that the objective of Truman's and Byrnes's atomic diplomacy was "to force Soviet withdrawal from Eastern Europe":[51]

Undoubtedly Truman and Byrnes would have been pleased to see the Soviets withdraw from Eastern Europe, but there is no evidence that they ever pursued such an ambitious goal or that they believed it obtainable, even with the atom bomb. Their aims were much more modest. They did not change the *objectives* of their foreign policy because of the bomb, but for a few months they pursued with greater confidence and determination the objectives they (and Roosevelt) had earlier decided upon. They did not attempt to roll back Soviet power, but rather to contain it. They did not try to get the USSR to give in to new demands but rather to live up to old agreements. Not even full compliance with old agreements was asked for. Token compliance with the Declaration on Liberated Europe—enough to satisfy American public opinion—was all that was required. When even this was not granted in some countries, they settled for less.[52]

AMERICAN ECONOMIC GOALS AND THE OPEN DOOR

William Appleman Williams has probably been the most influential of the revisionists, both through his own writings and through the students he has trained and inspired. In his well-known book, *The Tragedy of American Diplomacy*,[53] Williams argued that one of the main causes of the Cold War was the determination of Roosevelt, Truman, Hull, Byrnes, Stimson, and other American leaders to open up the world to U.S. business for markets, investments, and access to raw materials—that is, to obtain an Open Door for American economic penetration. Such a policy was considered essential to prevent the U.S. economy from sinking into another depression in the postwar period. As Dean Acheson said, "We cannot have full employment and prosperity without the foreign markets."[54]

50. Hammond, "'Atomic Diplomacy' Revisited," pp. 1403-28, especially pp. 1422-25.

51. Alperovitz, *Atomic Diplomacy*, p. 235.

52. Hammond, "'Atomic Diplomacy' Revisited," p. 1426.

53. First ed. (New York: World, 1959; rev. and enl. ed. New York: Dell, 1962).

54. Williams, *Tragedy*, rev. ed., p. 236.

The Cold War arose, Williams maintains, when the United States tried to impose the Open Door in areas of Soviet interest—Eastern Europe and the Far East. "President Truman," he says, "initiated and sustained a vigorous drive to undercut the Stalin-Churchill agreement of October 1944 [the percentages agreement] concerning Eastern Europe, and to replace it with the Open Door Policy."[55] Meanwhile Secretary Stimson insisted, and Truman agreed, that the Open Door for American business must also be established in the Far East, especially in Manchuria.[56] From Williams's point of view, Western demands for free elections in Eastern Europe were motivated not by love for democracy, but by a desire to minimize Soviet influence in the area and thus to maximize freedom for American economic activity. In his opinion, the drive for the Open Door was more important than the atomic bomb in bringing about the deterioration of the East-West relations:"It was not the possession of the atomic bomb which prompted American leaders to get tough with Russia but rather their open-door outlook which interpreted the bomb as the final guarantee that they could go further faster down that path of world predominance."[57]

According to Williams, the combination of the Open Door policy and the use of atomic diplomacy is what caused the hostility between Russia and America to become so intense: "It was the decision of the United States to employ its new and awesome power in keeping with the traditional Open Door Policy which crystallized in the cold war."[58]

Joyce and Gabriel Kolko in *The Limits of Power*[59] differ with Williams on some points but agree with him on the importance of economic factors. The objectives of American foreign policy, they say, "were deceptively simple: Essentially, the United States' aim was to restructure the world so that American business could trade, operate, and profit without restrictions everywhere. . . . American business could operate only in a world composed of politically reliable and stable capitalist nations, and with free access to essential raw materials."[60]

The traditionalists agree that there was great concern among American political and business leaders to be able to buy raw materials, sell their products wherever they wished, and invest in foreign countries. But they feel that Williams, Kolko, and other revisionists exaggerate the importance of the economic factor in American foreign

55. Ibid., p. 244.
56. Ibid., pp. 245-46.
57. Ibid., p. 230.
58. Ibid., p. 206. For similar views see Bernstein, *Politics and Policies of the Truman Administration*, and Gardner, *Architects of Illusion*.
59. Kolko, *Limits of Power*.
60. Ibid., p. 2.

policy in 1944-48. In the words of Robert W. Tucker,

It is scarcely a revelation to be told, as Kolko tells us, that "America's economic war aim was to save capitalism at home and abroad." Surely, no one argues that our economic war aim was to promote socialism. It is another matter to argue, as Kolko does argue, that America's "core objectives were economic" and that "politics was only the instrument for preserving and expanding America's unprecedented power and position in the European and world economy." The argument cannot rest simply upon an economic determinism which takes for granted what needs to be proved.[61]

The traditionalists also point out that American diplomatic documents for this period do not support the notion of a U.S. government obsessed above all with economic expansion. The documents show that American officials in Eastern Europe were concerned with all sorts of matters, but seldom with expanding trade, securing raw materials, or making investments in those countries. When these officials did refer to economic matters, it usually had to do not with the expansion of economic interests, but rather with defensive measures—that is, trying to prevent the confiscation of American-owned property and, when that proved impossible, trying to obtain compensation. (For an example, see the chapter by Louis Mark, Jr.)

In addition the traditionalists argue that Eastern Europe had never been important to the American economy and had little potential for becoming so. What were the raw materials in Eastern Europe that American businessmen coveted so madly? What American products could East Europeans afford to purchase in significant quantities, and what could they export to the United States to pay for them? What golden opportunities were there for American investment in Eastern Europe? Of course Eastern Europe did have some raw materials, it did trade some with the United States, and there was some American investment in those countries. But the figures show that Eastern Europe simply was not very important to the survival and growth of American capitalism. According to the traditionalists, it is a gross oversimplification, therefore, to say that the Cold War was caused primarily by the American desire to keep Eastern Europe open for economic penetration.[62]

THE UNITED STATES, RUSSIA, AND THE LEFT IN EASTERN EUROPE

Gabriel Kolko, one of the most prolific of the revisionists, argues

61. Tucker, *Radical Left and American Foreign Policy*, p. 94.
62. For additional comments on the Open Door theory by one of the leading traditionalists, see Arthur Schlesinger, Jr., "The Cold War Revisited," the *New York Review of Books* (October 25, 1979), pp. 46-47.

that an important cause of the Cold War was the opposition of the United States to leftist forces throughout the world, especially in Eastern Europe. This opposition to the Left, he says, was an integral part of the American objective to dominate the world economically: "American business could operate only in a world composed of politically reliable and stable capitalist nations, and with free access to essential raw materials. Such a universal order precluded the Left from power and necessitated conservative, and ultimately subservient, political control throughout the globe."[63]

Yet, according to Kolko, there was little popular support for conservative, capitalist regimes in Eastern Europe at the end of the war, or for the political parties that had run things in the prewar era. Instead the people of Eastern Europe had moved far to the Left. The masses, he says, "were not always Communist," but they all favored "radical social change."[64] There was, he says, "no serious internal opposition to the Communization of Eastern Europe, that is, no significant civil wars."[65] Thus it is wrong "to suggest that social revolution in Eastern Europe was exclusively a product of Soviet intervention." Rather "the existence of Soviet power in Eastern Europe permitted more or less natural and indigenous forces to take their logical course."[66] In sum, the communization of Eastern Europe came about because the majority of the people wanted it, not because of anything the Soviets did.

Kolko asserts that the Soviet Union would have been willing to tolerate a neutral Eastern Europe or a pro-Soviet one, while the United States wanted only an anti-Soviet one.[67] The American goal to dominate Eastern Europe "set the United States at the end of World War II against the Soviet Union, against the tide of the Left, . . . against history."[68]

The traditionalists argue that Kolko's theories about Eastern Europe are not supported by the facts. In the words of J. L. Richardson, he "is the victim of a myth . . . the myth of a revolutionary Left."[69] While it is true that there was a swing to the Left in Eastern Europe at the end of the war, this did not mean, in most cases, a swing to the Communists. And while there were widespread demands for reform, this did not

63. Kolko, *Limits of Power*, p. 2.
64. Kolko, *Politics of War*, p. 169.
65. Ibid., p. 170.
66. Ibid., pp. 169-70.
67. Ibid., p. 170.
68. Ibid., p. 624. For similar views see Horowitz, *Free World Colossus*, and the works of Gar Alperovitz and William Appleman Williams.
69. "Cold War Revisionism: A Critique," p. 598.

mean demands for the establishment of communism. Although Kolko gives the impression that the masses throughout Eastern Europe were pro-Communist, in fact the Communists were a minority everywhere. They did have considerable popularity in Czechoslovakia, where they won 38 percent of the vote in the elections of 1946, and Tito had a great deal of support in Yugoslavia. But in Poland, East Germany, Hungary, and Romania support for the Communists was small. For example, when free elections were held in Hungary in November 1945, the Communists won only 17 percent of the vote, compared with 57 percent for the Smallholders party.[70] Kolko argues that the East European masses, including the non-Communist ones, wanted "radical social change," but Charles Maier disputes this. "America," he says, "did not really have to rescue Europe from radical social change because no significant mass-based elements advocated a radical transformation."[71]

The traditional authors say that Kolko also gives a highly distorted view of the role of the Soviet Union in the establishment of Communist regimes in Eastern Europe. Its role was hardly that of a bystander, permitting "indigenous forces to take their logical course." Rather the Soviets intervened actively and massively in every one of the East European states except Albania, where the Yugoslav Communists played a similar role. Although the Communists in Yugoslavia and Czechoslovakia were probably strong enough and skillful enough to have seized power without Soviet support, the same cannot be said for the other countries. Rather than allowing "indigenous forces to take their logical course," the Soviet armies of occupation used force to impose Communist regimes on much of Eastern Europe. In Poland, East Germany, Hungary, Romania, and Bulgaria, the leaders of Kolko's "indigenous forces" consisted to a large extent of Communists who had lived for years in the USSR, had been carefully trained by Stalin, and had even in some cases taken Soviet citizenship. Here one thinks particularly of Bolesław Bierut in Poland, Walter Ulbricht in East Germany, Mátyás Rákosi in Hungary, Klement Gottwald in Czechoslovakia, Ana Pauker in Romania, and Georgi Dimitrov in Bulgaria.

70. *Foreign Relations of the United States, 1945* 4:904. Imre Kovacs, ed., *Facts about Hungary* (New York: Waldon Press, 1958), p. 60, says that the Smallholders got 59.9 percent.

71. Maier, "Revisionism and the Interpretation of Cold War Origins," p. 337. For detailed accounts of the postwar events in Eastern Europe from the traditional point of view see: Seton-Watson, *The East European Revolution;* Wolff, *Balkans in Our Time;* Stephen D. Kertesz, ed., *The Fate of East Central Europe* (Notre Dame: University of Notre Dame Press, 1956), and Hammond, *Anatomy of Communist Takeovers.*

(It might be added that the Communist regimes in Estonia, Latvia, and Lithuania were also imposed by Soviet troops, not by indigenous forces.)

Traditionalists also argue that the facts do not support Kolko's statement that there was "no serious internal opposition to the Communization of Eastern Europe, that is, no significant civil wars." They maintain that there was strong opposition to the Communists in every country, with long and bloody civil wars raging in two of them— Yugoslavia and Poland.[72] Other countries also, they say, would probably have seen large-scale armed struggles against the Communists if the Soviet occupation armies had not made such struggles impossible.

Kolko and other revisionists, including David Horowitz, argue that the United States followed reactionary, anti-Left, counterrevolutionary policies throughout Eastern Europe, but the traditionalists dispute this. The United States did oppose the Communists, they say, but not the democratic Left, the various socialist and peasant parties, whom the United States supported. The United States continued to have fairly good relations with Czechoslovakia even after May 1946, when a Communist took over the post of prime minister, since he had been chosen in free elections. It was only in 1948, when democratic procedures were abolished and the true coalition government was replaced by a phony coalition that Washington became hostile toward the regime in Prague.

According to the traditionalists, Kolko's picture of a completely reactionary United States, filled with blind hatred of everything and everybody on the Left, does not accord with the facts. They point out, for example, that in Yugoslavia both Britain and the United States shifted the bulk of their wartime aid from the Chetniks to the Partisans, even though they knew that the Partisans were Communist-dominated.[73]

Another example has to do with Poland. Both the British and the Americans exerted great pressure on the Polish government in exile, located in London, to follow less conservative policies and to try to get along with the Soviets.[74] And when the British and Americans

72. There are many books on the civil war in Yugoslavia; one of the best eyewitness accounts, by a British officer, is Stephen Clissold, *Whirlwind* (New York: Philosophical Library, 1949). On the civil war in Poland see Lotarski, "The Communist Takeover in Poland," pp. 358-62.

73. For an insider's view by a British officer who was influential in bringing about this decision, see Fitzroy Maclean, *Eastern Approaches* (London: Jonathan Cape, 1950).

74. See, for example, Churchill, *The Second World War*, especially vol. 6, passim; Edward J. Rozek, *Allied Wartime Diplomacy: A Pattern in Poland* (New York: Wiley, 1958); and Jan Ciechanowski, *Defeat in Victory* (Garden City, N.Y.: Doubleday, 1947).

finally decided to withdraw diplomatic recognition from the London government, they did so in part because they believed it could not work with Moscow.

One final comment on the Kolko thesis is provided by Louis Mark, who served in the American legation in Hungary after World War II. Speaking of himself and his fellow American colleagues in Budapest, he wrote:

> We did not regard democratic, non-Communist governments and parties as being necessarily anti-Soviet. We thoroughly appreciated the Soviets' need for security along their borders, and would have joined with them in opposing the emergence of any political trend which, even under extreme conditions, might have posed a threat to the Soviet Union. We were convinced that democratic regimes in Eastern Europe by themselves could not possibly endanger the Soviet Union as long as the German question was taken care of. We would even have acquiesced in a dominant Communist role in Hungary, IF the Hungarian people had freely opted for such an arrangement. . . . On a more practical level, we would have had no problem with the emergence of a Social democratic regime such as the one that appeared in Finland, had that been what Hungarians wanted.[75]

THE ORIGINS OF THIS BOOK

In looking over the vast literature on the origins of the Cold War, the editor was struck with the paucity of memoirs by participants on the middle and lower levels. There were reminiscences by the top figures on the American side including Truman, Hull, Byrnes, and Harriman, to name just a few. But what about the American officials who were stationed not in Washington but in Eastern Europe, in the front lines of the Cold War? How did the events of 1944-48 appear to them at the time? What were their attitudes toward the Soviets during the war, and how did those attitudes change later on? Did friendliness change to hostility, and if so, why? From their perspective, what were the causes of the Cold War? Who was to blame—the Soviet Union, the United States, incompetent leaders, or the ineluctible forces of history? Did the Soviet Union seem to them to be acting in Eastern Europe from defensive motives? Or was it engaged in imperialistic expansion? Was the Kremlin driven by revolutionary ideology, or by traditional Russian national interests? As American representatives in Eastern Europe did they use atomic diplomacy? Did they devote much of their time to American economic interests, trying to promote American trade, American access to natural resources, and the protection of American investments? What was their attitude toward the the various political parties in Eastern Europe, including the Com-

75. Quoted from the chapter below by Louis Mark, Jr.

munists and the non-Communist Left? In their view, did unwise American policies help to bring about the Cold War? Should the United States have acted differently? Could the Cold War have been avoided, or was it inevitable? If conflict were foredoomed, need the Cold War have become so intense?

It occurred to the editor that it would be interesting to hear answers to these questions from eyewitnesses, from Americans who were on the spot in Eastern Europe, from primary sources whose knowledge of the subject was not limited to what they had read, but who could draw upon personal recollections. With this in mind, the editor organized a panel at a conference of the American Association for the Advancement of Slavic Studies on the subject of "Witnesses to the Origins of the Cold War." The response to the panel was overwhelmingly enthusiastic, and several members of the audience suggested that more papers be solicited and that they all be published. This is what I have labored to do. Finding the first few contributors was easy, but locating qualified authors to cover all of the countries in Eastern Europe proved to be difficult and time consuming. Many of the participants in these events had, of course, passed away. Few of those remaining had the writing ability, the leisure, the necessary detachment or the inclination to undertake such an assigment. Persistent searching paid off, however, and the authors finally assembled have, in my opinion, written chapters that are both interesting and informative, chapters that add significantly to our knowledge and that help to answer the questions raised above.

GEORGE F. KENNAN

The View from Russia

At the time when the Cold War is generally supposed to have begun—
let us say, between 1944 and 1948—I was serving with the U.S. government, first as Averell Harriman's deputy in the American embassy at
Moscow from 1944 to 1946, and then in Washington, principally as
director of the newly established Policy Planning Staff. I might also
point out that when I arrived in Moscow in 1944, I already had, I suppose, as deep a background in Russian affairs as anyone in our government. I also, to my own surprise, had the longest service in the Soviet
Union of the Moscow diplomatic corps. I should have had, therefore,

George Frost Kennan joined the Foreign Service in 1925 and served in several
European posts before and during World War II, including Berlin, Tallinn, Riga,
Moscow, and Prague. He was Minister-Counselor in Moscow in 1944, Director of
the Policy Planning Staff of the State Department in 1947-49, and Ambassador to
the USSR in 1952. He retired from the Foreign Service in 1953 and became a member of the Institute for Advanced Studies in Princeton, N.J., but came out of retirement from 1961 to 1963 to serve as Ambassador to Yugoslavia. He has taught
at the University of Chicago, Princeton University, and Oxford University, and is
presently Professor Emeritus at the Institute for Advanced Study.

His many books include *Russia Leaves the War, The Decision to Intervene,
Russia, the Atom and the West, Soviet Foreign Policy, 1917-1941, Russia and
the West under Lenin and Stalin, On Dealing with the Communist World, From
Prague after Munich,* and *The Cloud of Danger.* His books have won Freedom
House and National Book Awards, and Bancroft, Francis Parkman, and Pulitzer
Prizes.

He was instrumental in founding the Kennan Institute for Advanced Russian
Studies in Washington, D.C.

whether I did or not, *some* qualifications for judgment as to any new developments or tendencies in our relations with the Soviet Union.

If anyone had told me at the time that what we were then beginning was a wholly new phase in our relations with the Soviet Union, to be known in historical discussion as the "Cold War," and to be sharply distinguished from everything that had gone on before, I would not have known what he was talking about. To this day I have never been able to understand why, when people choose to use the term Cold War to describe our relations with the Soviet Union, they begin with the end of World War II, as though there were some sharp difference between what went on after that time and what had gone on before it. Indeed, one gains the impression that many people are only imperfectly aware that the Soviet Union existed prior to the Second World War.

In what way, I have asked myself, is it conceived that these postwar relations differed from the prewar ones? Is the Soviet government seen as having been more hostile to us after that event than it was before, or we to it? Is it thought that our relations with Russia before the war were pleasant and relaxed and unmarked by conflict? I cannot see the basis for such a view. For fifteen years after the Russian revolutions of 1917 we had no diplomatic relations at all with the Soviet government, so sharp were the conflicts of outlook and aspiration that divided us. And even after relations were established, in 1933, they soon degenerated into a discord and tension quite as disagreeable as anything that was to come later. There was, as I see it, only one notable and significant new factor in our relations. Before the war there had been no arms race and no mutual military fear added to the political disagreements. Moscow had not been in control of half of Europe; there had been no nuclear weaponry; formidable armies, not our own, had stood between us and the Soviet Union; and we had not assumed the responsibilities in Europe that we were forced to take on when the war was over.

But that, as you see, is a difference that made itself felt only somewhat later and is not very well reflected in the term Cold War. And I stress the confusing quality of this term, because I wish to a make it clear that when I returned to Moscow in 1944, after a seven year absence, I was not merely *aware* of (the word is too weak) but had had drilled into me by painful experience over a number of years that the Soviet regime was not an easy one for us to have good relations with: a number of factors, such as the ideological preconceptions of the Soviet leaders, the ingrained Russian habits of secrecy and suspicion of foreigners, the sharp differences between the two governmental and social systems, and not least, the great cruelties the Stalin regime was already guilty of—precluded anything like a fully normal and pleasant

relationship and left only a relatively narrow area in which useful inter-
course and collaboration was even conceivable. And this being the case,
I saw as the war approached its end, despite all the rosy pronounce-
ments of President Roosevelt and others, no reason to expect or to
hope that our relations with the Soviet regime would be any better
after the war than they had been before—if anything, rather the contrary. For it was clear that at the end of the war the Soviet leaders
would be in a very favorable position to become the dominant power
throughout a great deal of Europe. Between them, they and the Nazis
had pretty well destroyed such semblance of indigenous order and
stability as had existed throughout Eastern Europe; there was now
nothing to oppose them there, nothing to stand in their way. Their
greatest military rival in Central Europe, Germany, was now sure to
be eliminated as a factor in the military and political balance. The
sweep of military operations was rapidly carrying them, with our
blessing, into a position of unchallenged control over great areas of the
continent. And it was clear, even as early as 1944, that this was already inducing a certain giddiness with success, whetting their ambitions, leading to a new self-confidence and even arrogance on their
part.

I knew that at some point all this would come into conflict with
our own concepts and expectations. Our government had been prepared, like the British government, to concede to them, as the price of
their great military contribution during the war, the permanent control over those parts of Eastern Europe acquired through their agreement with Hitler in 1939: the Baltic states, eastern Poland, and parts
of Finland and Romania. But our peoople were continuing to indulge
themselves in the comforting illusion that the other Eastern European
countries about to be overrun by the Soviet forces would somehow
escape political domination and continue to lead independent national
lives. I saw no reason to entertain such hopes. And the great day of
disillusionment and reckoning loomed all the more forebodingly in
my eyes, because I could see that our national leaders in Washington
had no idea at all, and would probably have been incapable of imagin-
ing, what a Soviet occupation, supported by the Russian secret police
of Beriya's time, meant for the peoples who were subjected to it.

I don't like to review the memories of that time. I would prefer to
let bygones be bygones so far as we are concerned (for the Russians,
it may be a different thing), and to let our present exchanges relate to
present conditions, not to past ones. But if we are to speak of the
history of the Cold War, we cannot avoid the past. The Stalin era was at
its peak, as was the power of the Stalinist police system. We wonder
today, on the basis of later evidence, whether even Stalin was aware

what dreadful things were being done by that system, in his name and in the name of the Soviet Union, in the occupied territories and elsewhere. But, whether Stalin was aware of it or not, some of us were. We also knew that if those Soviet police and political authorities were going to behave in other areas of Europe as they already had in Poland and the Baltic states, the people of the West would, sooner or later, protest. This, basically, was why I had no confidence in the dreams of close postwar collaboration between the Soviet Union and our country. I did not want bad relations with the Soviet Union. None of us did. On the contrary, I had devoted fifteen years of my life to the hope of achieving something better. But I saw an immense and tragic misunderstanding growing and being cultivated day by day; and I wished that we would begin to face up to the realities of the situation, so that the eventual shock of adjustment would not be too severe. This, incidentally, was why I favored a complete sphere of influence policy.

I say all these things to explain why it never occurred to me at the time to imagine that the emerging difficulties in our relations with Russia could be exclusively, or even mainly, the result of some special prejudice or ill will on the part of the American political establishment. I thought, if anything, that our government was inviting trouble by catering too extravagantly to the Soviet leaders, by trying too hard to please them and curry favor with them, often at the expense of the British, and by giving our own people the impression that earlier tensions had had only trivial causes and that wonderful harmony and collaboration was now in the offing, assuring the future peace of the world. As I saw it, the seeds of further conflict and misunderstanding were built into the situation. Not even the best of will on our part could remove them entirely, and the sooner we faced up to the situation, the better. These are not afterthoughts. I wrote all this at the time. You can find much of it in the State Department's *Foreign Relations of the United States* series, and in the appendixes to my own memoirs.

So much, then, for the general proposition that ill will and prejudice on our part were the main cause of the difficulties that arose in our relations with Russia after the war. Now for two or three of the specific theses that, as I understand it, are carried forward in the revisionist literature.

First, there is the thesis that the Soviet leaders, concerned for their security, wanted only nonreactionary, non-Fascist, "friendly" governments along their western frontier, but that we insisted on trying to foist upon those countries right-wing, anti-Soviet political cliques, and thereby put the Soviet leaders in a position where they had no choice but to clamp down on them generally. The allegation that all the Soviet leaders wanted was friendly liberal governments along their border was one that was frequently heard at that time. I thought it then, and think it today, a highly misleading expression. What was wanted by Moscow in the way of governing personalities in those Eastern European countries was something far more than, and different from "friendly" and also different from "nonreactionary." Beneš and young Masaryk were friendly and far from reactionary, but it didn't save them. What was wanted at that time in the occupied territories, I am afraid, were subordinate political figures, tried and trusted agents of Soviet power, like the first president of the new Poland, Bierut, who had never been heard of by most of us and who was not much better known, I think, to most of the Polish population.

I am not saying things are this way today. I am not saying that all the present leaders of the Warsaw Pact countries are of this ilk. I am saying it was this way in the days of Beriya and Stalin. Those of us who were serving in Moscow knew this, and it was with a skepticism approaching despair that we found ourselves repeatedly assured by well-meaning Westerners that all the Kremlin really wanted in the Eastern European countries were friendly governments.

A second question debated by the revisionists is the termination of Lend-Lease for Russia at the time of the German surrender in 1945. Certainly, the abruptness with which this was done was a mistake. President Truman himself soon recognized this. One could have tried to soften the blow, but this was only part of the story, and the significance of the action has often been exaggerated. Lend-Lease was not generally terminated; the measure applied only to shipments for use in the European theater. Shipments for use in the Far East were permitted to continue, and continue they did, to the tune of hundreds of millions of dollars' worth of goods, the overwhelming bulk of which certainly never played any significant part in the hostilities against Japan.

The Soviet leaders were also perfectly well aware that existing legislation left the president no authority to continue shipments to Europe after the termination of hostilities there. We had not only long been warning the Russians of this, but we had also been urging them, for many months, to conclude a special agreement with us that would permit the shipments to continue, no longer as Lend-Lease, but as long-term credits at a very low rate of interest. To these urgings we had no response. In general, most of the shipments that had been going forward near the end of the war—some of them including entire industrial plants—were obviously not going to play any part in the Russian war effort, and had significance only for postwar reconstruction. It was not unreasonable that a new basis would have to be found for such shipments once the war was over. People serving in Moscow at the time, like myself, regretted the abruptness of the cancellation, thought the blow could have been eased by a little better communication, but also thought it was high time the Russians were made to realize that they could not take aid for granted.

A similar situation existed with respect to the question of a major loan to the Soviet Union. Since we had had no response to our repeated offers to continue the Land-Lease shipments as long-term credits, we were rather surprised to receive, suddenly and without forewarning, in January 1945, just before the Yalta Conference, a most curiously worded little note from Molotov expressing readiness—as though this were an act of special graciousness on the Soviet part—to receive from us a loan of six billion dollars. It is not true that the receipt of this note was never acknowledged as is sometimes alleged; it was. There was at that time, as the Soviet leaders must have known, no legislative authority that would have permitted the president to extend a loan of this nature. The question could not be clarified, in any event, before the question of the Lend-Lease shipments were resolved. A delay was therefore unavoidable. Before the matter could be seriously considered in our government, President Roosevelt died, the war came to an end, and the emerging differences over Poland and other problems made it most improbable that Congress would have been responsive to any such proposal, even if the president had suggested it. Stalin, if my memory is correct, never mentioned the matter either at Yalta or at Potsdam. Altogether, we found it difficult to believe that the Soviet approach of January 1945 was serious. We never learned what was really behind it.

There is also the question of "atomic diplomacy," the suggestion that Messrs. Truman and Stimson held up the Potsdam Conference pending completion of the nuclear weapon testing in order to hold the bomb as an extortion threat. People like myself knew nothing about the preparation of this weapon until its successful testing at the time of the Potsdam Conference; and we had no knowledge of the diplomatic exchanges leading up to that conference, so we could have no views about the question at issue. But I knew well, and was in contact with, several of the people who participated on our side at Potsdam, and I never heard the slightest suggestion of anything like this from any of them. I do not believe today that there was anything in the allegation. I have examined large parts of Gar Alperovitz's book, *Atomic Diplomacy*. I find it, in addition to being of extremely low scholarly quality, quite unconvincing in its main argumentation.

Finally, I mention the suggestion, which seems to me to be either explicit or implicit in much of the revisionist literature, that the American statesmen of those years were prejudiced against the Soviet Union because they were the representatives of American capitalism, lusting for the economic subjugation of Russia and Eastern Europe and angry at the Soviet leaders for denying them this possibility. In retrospect, I can think of nothing sillier than this suggestion. Had I heard it at the time, I would have thought someone had gone out of his mind. Franklin Roosevelt, the anathema of the American business world; Harry Hopkins, this breezy, Iowa-born, New Deal labor intellectual; Averell Harriman, the most selfless and dedicated public servant the United States government and people had during the war; Cordell Hull, the elderly Tennessee politician and lawyer, swimming in dreams of a world-wide system of liberal free trade and spewing clouds of incoherent rhetoric about it at any foreign statesman who came his way; Harry Truman, the earthy and courageous ex-haberdasher from Missouri; General Eisenhower, full of enthusiasm for a happy future of Soviet-American relations, and convinced that his relations with Zhukov would assure it—that such men would be suspected of being the tools of Wall Street, and of being animated in their approach to the Soviet Union by a desire for the economic subjugation of Eastern Europe, is a suggestion of such absurdity that I cannot really treat it seriously.

In short, I can give very little comfort, I am afraid, to the revisionist theses about the origins of the Cold War. I do not mean to say that the United States government of that time made no mistakes in its policy toward the Soviet Union. I was myself in many ways unhappy about that policy at the time. But the attitudes and behavior of the United States government were not the main factor, on our side, in making the Cold War what we have known it to be in the past twenty-five years. Where our government made its really important mistakes was in thinking too militarily about our relations with Russia. Such thinking overcame us in the years from 1950 to 1955 and has distorted our policy ever since. If you want to take that phase of American policy under critical scrutiny, I am with you. But the image of the American statesmen of the 1944-48 period as wicked, ill-motivated characters, deeply prejudiced against the Soviet government for its socialist quality, and striking down the hand of friendship offered by a trusting and liberal Stalin, finds sustenance neither in my memories nor in the historical evidence as I know it today, and I am afraid I can give it no support.

MICHAEL B. PETROVICH

The View from Yugoslavia

1

In 1943 I was a beginning graduate student at Columbia University, trying to forget the indignity of having been rejected for military service because of a punctured eardrum I never knew I had. Before my first semester was over, I was recruited by the Office of Strategic Services (OSS), largely because I was bilingual in English, my mother tongue, and Serbo-Croatian, my "father tongue." After brief training in and around Washington, I was sent for five months to Cairo, where

Michael B. Petrovich is Professor of Russian and Balkan history at the University of Wisconsin-Madison and has been teaching there since 1950. He received his B.A. in 1943 from Western Reserve University in his native Cleveland, and entered Columbia University that same year, but was soon recruited by the Office of Strategic Services. He served in Cairo, Egypt (February-May 1944), Bari, Italy (May-November 1944), and in Yugoslavia (November 1944-February 1946). During most of that time he was with the Research and Analysis Branch of OSS and a member of the Independent American Military Mission to Marshal Tito. Upon returning to Columbia University, he received the M.A. degree in history in 1947, the Certificate of the Russian Institute in 1948, and the Ph.D. in 1955. Most of his scholarly works deal with nineteenth and twentieth-century Russia and the Balkans, notably his book *The Emergence of Russian Panslavism 1856-1870* (Columbia University Press, 1956) and his two-volume *History of Modern Serbia 1804-1918* (Harcourt, Brace, Jovanovich, 1976). Ever since his article "The Central Government of Yugoslavia," in the *Political Science Quarterly*, vol. 62, no. 4 (December 1947), he has written various articles on contemporary Yugoslavia as well, most recently one on "Continuing Nationalism in Yugoslav Historiography," in *Nationalities Papers*, vol. 6, no. 2 (Fall 1978). He has also translated four books by Milovan Djilas: *Land without Justice, Conversations with Stalin, Njegoš,* and *Wartime.*

the Yugoslav government in exile was located at the time, and then for another five months to Bari, Italy, where our base had closer contact with events in Yugoslavia. Having demonstrated my uselessness as a purveyor of "dirty tricks" against the enemy in MO (Morale Operations), I was transferred to the more scholarly Research and Analysis branch, where my job was to write reports of what was going on in Yugoslavia.

In October 1944 I was made a member of what was officially known as the Independent American Military Mission to Marshal Tito. That word "Independent" was included to distinguish us from our British allies, who were still regarded as having a greater stake in Balkan affairs than we.[1] Now the United States was about to share in the burden of that commitment, and I was excited to play some small part in the venture. However, my mission left without me, because Tito's headquarters delayed their approval of my coming; apparently my Serbian surname led them to suspect that I might be some variety of politically undesirable Yugoslav. It took them about two weeks to discover that I was just a nice, harmless American kid of twenty-two. Though I was perturbed by this inauspicious delay, I was also relieved; since Belgrade had been liberated by the Red Army and the Yugoslav Partisans in the meantime, on October 27, I was able to land on the airfield at Belgrade instead of being parachuted into the woods of Serbia. (I had never even worn a parachute up to that time.) On the trip I was reminded that I was in a war zone by the flak our planes encountered over the Dinaric Mountains and by the booming of nearby Soviet and German artillery when we landed at Belgrade. I was to remain in Yugoslavia the next sixteen months—from November 1944 to February 1946.

2

Although I did not realize it at the time, the Cold War began for me even before the Hot War was over. Within various United States' agencies I encountered a difference of opinion even in 1943 as to whether our support should go to the Chetniks of Gen. Draža Mihailović or to the Communist-led Partisans under Tito. As a rather romantic young American who was steeped in his father's Serbian heritage, I was an admirer of Mihailović and his Chetniks. I recall how I thrilled as I sat in a Cleveland movie theater and watched a Hollywood motion picture that depicted the daring exploits of this Serbian hero against the Axis invaders. On the other hand my job in the OSS gave me access to reports that not only told of Partisan fighting against the in-

1. Charles W. Thayer, *Hands across the Caviar* (Philadelphia and New York: J. B. Lippincott, 1952), p. 16.

vaders in Yugoslavia, but pointed to the Chetniks' increasing reluctance to fight the external enemy and of the willingness of at least some Chetnik commanders to collaborate with the enemy in order to fight the Partisans. I had a terrible time giving up my loyalty to the Chetniks, particularly since I was not at all pleased with the Communist domination of the Partisan movement, however much I may have admired the Partisan struggle against our common Axis enemies.

Apparently I was not alone in my quandary. In his book *Hands across the Caviar,* Charles W. Thayer, who was chief of the Independent American Military Mission to Marshal Tito for most of its existence, recalled that the Office of War Information and the OSS "didn't exactly see eye-to-eye on the Yugoslav problem" because "at the moment OWI was rooting for the Chetniks."[2] I do not think that Thayer wished to imply that the OSS was solidly pro-Partisan. However, Thayer and many of us in his mission reflected the policy that the United States should aid those who were fighting the Axis, and if that meant the Partisans more than the Chetniks, so be it. Prime Minister Churchill gave extreme expression to this view when he stated, with all of the desperation of an Englishman with his back to the wall, that he would make a pact with the devil himself to beat the Germans.

My trouble was that I could easily identify with both Chetniks and Partisans: I was an American with a deep attachment to the Serbian heritage of his father, a Serbian Orthodox priest, and a love for the Croatian heritage of his American mother's family. At the same time, I was a child of Roosevelt's New Deal and, as a recent college graduate and an avid reader of *P.M.* and the *Nation,* I was open to something a bit more to the American Left. The authoritarian Communists held no attraction for my young liberal spirit. Apparently I grated on some people's nerves. I offer as a sign of the times that within the same six months in the OSS I was twice challenged to a fistfight—once by an OSS officer of Serbian descent, and once by a Navy Intelligence officer of Croatian descent, both of whom thought I was too pro-Partisan. Luckily I was able to decline their invitations since both men had the advantage over me of at least a foot in height and fifty pounds in weight! At the same time, while in Bari, I was almost dismissed by an OSS superior because he thought that one of my reports was too favorable to the Chetniks.

3

During the early years of the war, relations between the Soviet Union and its Western allies in regard to Yugoslavia were almost totally

2. Ibid., p. 22.

free of the sort of conflicts that later led to the Cold War. This reflected the difficult struggle that the Allies were joined in against common enemies, and all parties agreed that military matters should get
priority over other considerations. This "united for victory" spirit
was manifested in both Western and Soviet policies toward Yugoslavia.
On the one hand, the United States and Britain decided to give their
major support to the Partisans, even though they knew the Partisans
to be Communist-dominated. On the other hand, the Soviet Union
maintained diplomatic relations with the royal Yugoslav government
in exile and refrained from giving support to the Partisans—all to reassure the West that it was not trying to promote communism in
Yugoslavia. Stalin even agreed to Churchill's famous "percentages
agreement" of October 9, 1944, whereby the West and the USSR
would supposedly share influence "fifty-fifty" in Yugoslavia. Secretly,
of course, Stalin was in regular contact with the Partisans by radio, and
he was probably hoping to help install a Communist regime in Yugoslavia at the end of the war. But at this stage of the game he did nothing
openly to antagonize his Western allies, and he even urged the Partisans
to follow moderate policies.

For those of us Americans who were officially concerned with
Yugoslav affairs, the Soviet Union played little visible role in Yugoslavia until the Red Army crossed the frontier on October 1, 1944.
Outwardly Moscow was scrupulously "correct" in its relations with
the royal Yugoslav government. Similarly, while the war was in progress
the Communist leaders of the Partisans made every effort to soft pedal
Communist dominance of their National Liberation Army. It became
almost a game for some Allied liaison officers to try to get any of
Tito's entourage to admit they were Communists. Indeed, in Partisan
refugee camps near Bari, Italy, in 1944, I remember solemn-faced Partisans with red hammers and sickles on their military caps being marched
off to Sunday morning mass! However, there was no attempt to hide
from anyone their adulation of the Soviet Union. For the Communists
the Soviet Union was, of course, the fatherland of the workers of the
world. In addition, for Yugoslav Communists and non-Communists
alike the Soviet Union was Slavic Mother Russia, great mythical protec-
tress of the Balkan Slavs.

I, and probably everybody else on our side, took it for granted that
the Soviet Union returned all this love. It was not until the Tito-Stalin
rift came out into the open in the summer of 1948 that I recalled the
first time I had ever seen a meeting between a Yugoslav Partisan and
a Russian. It was in a Partisan refugee camp near Bari, in mid-1944.
The Yugoslav rushed to a Soviet officer in our group, as excited as an
affectionate puppy, and proudly shouted in Russian: "*Zdravstvui,*

tovarishch!" (Greetings, comrade!). The Soviet officer coldly rejected this greeting with the words, "I am not *tovarishch* but Mister Colonel to you." The Yugoslav reddened, saluted, and withdrew in confusion. At the time I saw in this episode only a display of zeal for military discipline, which is all it may have been. Later, however, I regarded it as symbolic of the whole Soviet attitude of official "correctness" and even aloofness toward the Partisans.

The Soviet government in the early years of the war went to great pains to give the impression that it had no designs against King Peter or his minister of war, Mihailović. Moscow long refused to take sides in the Chetnik-Partisan quarrel, and even gave Mihailović credit for attacks against the Germans that were in fact carried out by the Partisans. Moscow's attitude toward the Chetniks was not the result of ignorance, however. Tito sent a stream of dispatches to Moscow condemning Chetnik collaboration with the enemy and asking for both diplomatic and military support, and for a long time getting neither. Later, after the Tito-Stalin break in mid-1948, Yugoslav Communist leaders were to attribute this attitude to Stalin's reluctance to encourage a strong Communist movement in Yugoslavia that would act independently.[3] Whatever the merits of such an argument, there is ample reason to take seriously, in view of the Soviet Union's grim military situation, Stalin's desire not to strain his alliance with Great Britain and the United States. As Moscow lectured Tito at the beginning of March 1942:

> Defeat of the fascist bandits and liberation from the invader, those today constitute the main task which stands above all other tasks. Take into account that the Soviet Union has treaty relations with the Yugoslav King and Government, and that taking an open stand against these would create new difficulties in the joint war efforts and the relations between the Soviet Union on the one hand and Britain and America on the other. Do not view the issues of your fight only from your own, national standpoint, but also from the international standpoint of the British-American-Soviet coalition.[4]

While both the British and Americans sent officers and supplies to the Partisans, Moscow kept sending warnings and reprimands to Tito and did not honor him with the presence of a Soviet military mission until February 23, 1944. This was almost two and a half years after the first Allied officer, British Capt. D. T. Hudson, made contact with Tito in October 1941. It was also nine months after the first full-fledged Allied military mission, the British one, arrived at Tito's headquarters at the

3. Vladimir Dedijer, *Tito* (New York: Simon & Schuster, 1953), p. 173.

4. Mosha Piyade [Moša Pijade], *About the Legend That the Yugoslav Uprising Owed Its Existence to Soviet Assistance* (London: [no publisher listed], 1950), p. 11.

end of May 1943.[5] Brig. Fitzroy Maclean, who was appointed chief
of that mission in August, later recalled the "frantic excitement" with
which "the devoutly Communist Partisans" greeted the first Russians.[6]
Milovan Djilas, then the top-ranking Yugoslav Communist leader, recalled, however, that the Soviet chief of mission, Lt. Gen. N. V. Korneev, behaved "with an almost cold formality which we attributed to
apprehension that someone . . . might tell the British that the Soviet
mission was acting in collusion with the Yugoslav Communists."
Djilas quickly added, "Later this relationship changed; the mission's
tasks and our ideological fervor became intertwined."[7]

4

As for relations between the American military mission and our
Soviet counterparts, it can be said that in 1944-46 these relations were
not only "correct" but at times even cordial. This personal cordiality
may have arisen in part because the head of the American military
mission, Col. Charles Thayer, a West Pointer, was also a trained diplomat with experience as a Foreign Service officer in the Soviet
Union under George Kennan, and had a knowledge of the Russian
language. As his books attest, Thayer also knew how to mix joviality
and humor with business. On the other hand, the chief of the Soviet
military mission, General Korneev, was one of the few Soviet generals
who had completed the Imperial Military Academy before the Russian
Revolution of 1917, and Thayer found him to be "an intelligent and
cultivated officer."[8] Thayer was no less cordial with Korneev's successor, Maj. Gen. A. F. Kiselev.

My own contacts with Soviet personnel were few but memorable.
I met my first Russian on the morning after my arrival in Belgrade, in
November 1944. I was strolling along Terazije Square getting my first
look by day at the war-torn capital, dressed in my American officer's
uniform with a large American flag on my sleeve. Suddenly coming
at me from the other side was the most gigantic man I had ever seen.
He seemed even taller because of his high fur cap. With enormous arms
outstretched, like some wrestler about to attack, he lunged at me,
grabbed me about the waist—which was considerably more slender
in those days—and threw me into the air repeatedly like a ball, while

5. Walter R. Roberts, *Tito, Mihailović and the Allies, 1941-1945* (New
Brunswick, N.J.: Rutgers University Press, 1973), pp. 28-29, 117.

6. Fitzroy Maclean, *Eastern Approaches* (London: Jonathan Cape, 1949),
p. 433.

7. Milovan Djilas, *Wartime*, trans. Michael B. Petrovich (New York and
London: Harcourt, Brace, Jovanovich, 1977), p. 373.

8. Thayer, *Hands across the Caviar*, p. 60.

jubilantly shouting *"Soiuznik! Soiuznik!"* (Ally!). I was apparently his
first American, and he was overjoyed. He took me into the nearest
bar, but was crushed to learn that I did not drink. We soon solved that
little difficulty; for his every toast to Allied friendship with a tumbler
of vodka, I responded with a toast of ice cream!

That midnight I met my second Russian in Belgrade—under my bed.
This was in the Balkan Hotel, where the American, British, and Soviet
military missions each had a floor. The Russian was trying to make
off with my army boots while I was sleeping. As I heard someone
groping under my bed, I switched on the light, and when I looked
down, there was this face staring up at me, giving off not only surprise
but vodka fumes. He managed to get up, still clutching my boots. He
was not so drunk that he did not recognize the American flag on my
officer's tunic hanging over a chair. When he realized that he was in the
room of an American officer rather than some Yugoslav little brother,
he quickly sobered up from the shock. He knew that if I reported him
to his commanding officer, just up the stairs, he could be taken out and
shot for looting and disgracing his country before its allies. I assured
the man that I would not report him and offered him a cigarette to
calm him down. In the course of our conversation he told me that he
loved Americans, that he admired our superior technical skill (he had
worked in a Douglas airplane factory in Russia), and that he hated the
Stalin regime. He explained that he was one of thousands who had been
sent to Siberia at the time of Stalin's purges because he had served under the ill-fated Marshal Tukhachevskii. One might regard this encounter as unique—and it was; however, Thayer had several nocturnal
visits from quite sober Soviet officers from upstairs—a Jewish major
who complained to him of anti-Semitism in the Soviet Union, and a
colonel from Leningrad who bitterly criticized Stalin for his pact with
Hitler in 1939.[9]

For many Soviet soldiers the jeep was the symbol of America. The
love some Soviet soldiers bestowed on their Lend-Lease American
jeeps seemed to me to be atavistically akin to the near erotic relationship between certain mounted warrior tribes and their horses. I remember in particular one Soviet soldier standing disconsolately in front of
the American military mission building in Belgrade, trying to explain
to one of our guards in Russian, *"Moi Vylis bolen!"* (My Willys is sick!).
We were glad to make it well again.

Not all Soviet soldiers were that fortunate in their dealings with us.
One night one of them, apparently drunk, was shot down by our Partisan guard when he tried to get into our garage. At Thayer's request, I

9. Ibid., pp. 63-69.

immediately called the Soviet military mission to inform them of this tragic and, for us, embarrassing death. I talked on the phone with my counterpart on the Soviet mission, a very amiable young officer called Sakharov. I was still trembling from having seen the bloody corpse, and my voice shook as I explained what had happened. Sakharov comforted me with words that I shall not forget as long as I live: *"Eto nichego, nas mnogo!"* (Never mind, there are lots of us!).

In my few official encounters with Soviet officers, I found them to be at least "correct" and often friendly. I remember the Central Asian sergeant on whose Dodge Lend-Lease truck I hitched a ride into the interior of Serbia. His Muslim religion did not keep him from storing gasoline in one tank and excellent Voivodina wine in the other. Every once in a while he would stop, invite me out, put a hose into the proper tank, and urge me to take a swig. Even when I was once shot at by Soviet planes, I felt that they were very considerate about it. I am referring to the time, in late December 1945, when I decided to hitch a ride on our mission mail plane on one of its flights to Vienna. I needed a Christmas vacation badly, and Thayer, who was then chief of the OSS mission in Austria, invited me. During our flight I looked down and noticed a lake whose contours were unlike those of any lake in northern Yugoslavia, where we were supposed to be. It suddenly struck me that we were over Lake Balaton in Hungary and therefore in the Soviet military zone, where we were *not* supposed to be. But our navigator, "Jonesy," a mountain boy from the Ozarks, paid no heed to silly regulations that contradicted one of the basic rules of geometry, that the shortest distance between two points is a straight line. Suddenly two or three Soviet MIGs came at us out of nowhere and fired. Obviously these were only warning shots because they could have easily demolished our slow shuttle plane. Jonesy was most annoyed, and I was thankful to the God of my fathers for His mercy.

Whatever problems there may have been between the Western Allies and the Soviet Union just after the war, we in the OSS military mission did not feel them in Belgrade, as Thayer's memoirs confirm. At the time I felt that the Russians could well afford to be nice since their obedient Yugoslav satellite took care of being nasty whenever the occasion arose.

5

If relations between the Americans and the Soviets in Yugoslavia in 1944-46 were correct and at times even cordial, relations between the Americans and the Yugoslav Communists deteriorated rapidly as soon as the Partisans knew that they would emerge victorious in Yugoslavia. As far as I was aware, the Soviets themselves did nothing directly in Yugoslavia during my stay that could be looked upon as a cause of the Cold War, but the same could not be said for the Yugoslav Communists. Once the Partisan leaders no longer needed our aid, they showered all their friendship on the Soviet Union, and proceeded to act in ways that angered and antagonized the United States. Since the United States assumed that the Yugoslavs were doing all these disagreeable things with Soviet support, if not on Soviet orders, this increased American ill will toward Moscow and thereby helped to bring on the Cold War.

Almost everything the Communists did in Yugoslavia after they rose to power met with disfavor in Washington. They tried to seize territories from Italy and Austria. They encouraged and supported a Communist rebellion in Greece. They shot down an unarmed American airplane. They established a police dictatorship. They harassed, dispossessed, arrested, or shot those Yugoslav citizens who were known to be friendly toward the United States or Great Britain. They executed thousands of Yugoslavs whose only crime was that they were anti-Communist. They nationalized American properties without compensation. They persecuted the church and preached atheism. They engaged in a massive campaign of anti-American propaganda and vilification. And, having gotten 95 percent of their foreign aid from the West during the early years of the war, they now belittled that aid and gave the credit to the Soviets. What made these Yugoslav actions important was that the United States tended to put much of the blame on the Soviet Union, even though (as we learned later) the Soviets often were not responsible. Thus Yugoslavia contributed significantly to the birth of the Cold War.

It is easy to understand why Western observers, up until 1948, looked upon Tito as a tool of Moscow. He had fought in the Red Army during the Russian Civil War, had served for many years as a Comintern agent, and had been installed by Stalin as the head of the Yugoslav Communist party. As far as one could tell from the public record, Tito had never disagreed with Stalin on anything, but had obediently followed all his orders. Tito made speeches in which he praised Stalin and the USSR in the most eloquent terms. He supported Stalin's foreign policy on every issue, and in Yugoslavia he established a close replica of Stalin's Communist system. We Westerners knew that Stalin had installed stooges as rulers in the other countries of Eastern Europe, and Tito seemed to fit the general pattern. Indeed, Tito appeared to be the most extreme of the East European dictators—more doctrinaire, more ruthless in imposing communism, more defiant toward the West, and more grandiloquent in his glorification of Stalin and the Soviet Fatherland. In fact, at the time Tito and his lieutenants seemed to be almost more Stalinist than Stalin.

This Western view that Yugoslavia and the USSR were acting in unison was largely correct for the period when I was in Yugoslavia, from 1944 to 1946. Although, as we now know, there were secret differences of opinion between the two Communist regimes, they looked upon these at the time as merely friendly disagreements between comrades.

The extent to which the Yugoslav leaders identified with the Soviet Union is illustrated by a conversation I had in 1945 with Edvard Kardelj, who was second only to Tito among the Yugoslav leaders. He received me graciously in the comfortable study of his newly acquired villa on Dedinje Hill, the neighborhood where Belgrade's prewar plutocracy had lived. Perhaps because he had been a schoolteacher and I was, despite my assimilated rank of captain, very obviously a student, Kardelj treated me much as a kindly professor would. At one point in our conversation he leaned back in his easy chair and, staring as though into the future, declared slowly and deliberately, "It is our greatest ambition to become the seventeenth republic of the Soviet Union." I learned later that this was not the only occasion on which Kardelj made such a statement.

The tone of the Yugoslav press in 1945-46 strengthened our impression that the Tito regime was absolutely faithful to the Soviet Union. Day after day the newspapers excoriated the Western powers, while glorifying Russia in the most obsequious way. For example, on June 22, 1945, both of the country's leading newspapers featured full-page spreads on the anniversary of the Soviet Union's entry into World War II. *Borba,* the official organ of the Communist party, published a heroic-size portrait of Stalin, along with the caption, "The Soviet Union—Saviour of the Slavic Race."

6

During my stay in Yugoslavia there were numerous issues that created friction between Belgrade and the West and that helped to create a Cold War atmosphere. While these disputed issues were intertwined, we can conveniently divide them into two categories: international affairs and domestic affairs. The former category included the Italian and Austrian boundary questions; the infringement on Yugoslav air space by American planes; reparations; the return of Yugoslav refugees and persons designated by Belgrade as war criminals; and the Greek civil war. The latter category included differences between the Western Allies and Tito's government over whether or not the Belgrade regime was carrying out the Big Three's recommendations proclaimed at Yalta, that is, the issue of democracy.

In 1945, and for several years to come, the question of Yugoslavia's boundary was a major source of irritation between Yugoslavia and the West. This involved both the borders with Italy (the Istrian Peninsula, the city of Trieste, and the area known as the Julian March) and the borders with Austria (the provinces of Styria and Carinthia). All of these areas contained large numbers of inhabitants who were ethnically Yugoslav, but they had been given to Italy and Austria after World War I, much to the disgust of all Yugoslav nationalists, Communist and non-Communist alike. In mid-1945 each set of allies, Western and Eastern, rushed to occupy as much as possible of these territories before the other did.

The chief prize was the valuable port of Trieste, which was predominantly Italian in population. Tito's troops raced frantically across Yugoslavia in the hope of capturing the city and thereby presenting the Western Allies with a fait accompli. Realizing this, Field Marshal Sir Harold Alexander, supreme allied commander of the Mediterranean theater, ordered his forces to race across northern Italy in the hope that they would get to Trieste first. The Partisans won, but only by a day, and they were unable to prevent the British and American troops from entering the city and sharing the administration with them. Tito had hoped that temporary occupation by the Yugoslavs would lead to permanent possession, and he demanded that Alexander give him an immediate explanation as to why the Western forces had entered this area.[10] The situation became very tense, and for weeks there was a real possibility that armed conflict would break out between the soldiers of the West and the Soviet-backed Yugoslav Communists.

I was in a position to watch both sides of the dispute—in Belgrade and in Trieste. In the capital I followed the full-scale press campaign that proclaimed that the Yugoslavs would not tolerate being cheated out of territories that were theirs by right. On the other hand, I was in Trieste in November 1945 and could feel the hostility of the Western troops against the Yugoslav Communists. I talked with New Zealanders and Americans and could readily see that they were sick and tired of the war and could hardly wait to get home now that Germany was beaten. Besides, while traversing the length of Italy in their fight against the Germans, they had gotten to know the Italians and to like them— especially the girls. The Yugoslavs, on the other hand, were unknown and potentially dangerous people, and Communists besides. In addition, the Partisans had been treating their opponents in Trieste very brutally, and this deeply offended the sensibilities of the Western onlookers. I talked to several American officers in Trieste who were quite prepared to push the Yugoslav Partisans out by force on humanitarian grounds alone.

10. Bogdan C. Novak, *Trieste 1941-1954: The Ethnic, Political, and Ideological Struggle* (Chicago: University of Chicago Press, 1970), p. 162.

Tito also hoped to gain those parts of Austrian Carinthia and Styria that were inhabited by Slovenes, even though a decided majority of the inhabitants had voted to remain in Austria in a 1920 plebiscite. Yugoslav Partisans hastened to occupy as much of southern Austria as they could, and Tito asked the Allies to admit Yugoslavia as a fifth occupying power in Austria. The Soviet government supported the Yugoslavs' request, but the Americans and the British refused.[11]

Meanwhile Field Marshal Alexander found that the Yugoslav troops in the British zone of Austria were trying to set up their own government. He wired General Eisenhower that he could not stop these activities without the use of force, and that open hostilities could break out at any moment.[12] This was one day after President Truman let Churchill know that while he was unwilling to involve the United States in a war against the Yugoslavs, he would approve of using Allied troops to throw back the Yugoslavs if they attacked.[13] Three days later an exasperated Alexander issued an official statement in which he charged, "It is . . . Marshal Tito's apparent intention to establish his claims by force of arms and military occupation. Action of this kind would be all too reminiscent of Hitler, Mussolini, and Japan. It is to prevent such actions that we have been fighting this war."[14] Finally, on May 19, Tito backed down and ordered his troops to withdraw back of the 1937 frontier with Austria.[15] Thus an armed collision was averted.

After protracted negotiations, on May 21 Tito notified the British and Americans that, with respect to the temporary occupation of the Italian frontier areas, he would accept the line of demarcation between Allied and Yugoslav troops proposed by Gen. D. Morgan, Alexander's chief of staff. Alexander himself came to Belgrade to visit Tito and, indeed, was a guest at the celebration of Tito's fifty-third birthday

11. "The Secretary of State to the Ambassador in the United Kingdom (Winant), Washington, April 11, 1945." U.S. Department of State, *Foreign Relations of the United States* (hereafter cited as *FRUS), 1945, 5, Europe* (Washington: Government Printing Office, 1967):1314. "The Chargé in the Soviet Union (Kennan) to the Secretary of State," Moscow, May 15, 1945, ibid., pp. 1321-22.

12. "The Ambassador in France (Caffery) to the Secretary of State, Paris, May 18, 1945," ibid., p. 1324.

13. Winston S. Churchill, *The Second World War*, 6, *Triumph and Tragedy* (Boston: Houghton Mifflin, 1953):557.

14. "Message Issued to Allied Armed Forces in the Mediterranean Theater, May 19, 1945," *New York Times*, May 20, 1945; see also *Voices of History 1945-1946: Speeches and Papers of Roosevelt, Truman, Churchill, Attlee, Stalin, de Gaulle, Chiang and Other Leaders Delivered during 1945*, ed. Nathan Ausubel (New York: Gramercy Publishing Co., 1946), p. 213.

15. "The Ambassador in Yugoslavia (Patterson) to the Secretary of State," Belgrade, May 20, 1945, *FRUS, 1945, 5, Europe:* 1325.

on May 25, 1945. So was I and other members of the Allied military
missions in Belgrade. It was an evening of good cheer, to say the least.
If I may be permitted a trivial but unique recollection of that event,
I am surely the only person that has ever danced, hand in hand, with
both Field Marshal Alexander and Randolph Churchill at the same
time. I found myself between them in the *kolo,* the traditional Yugoslav circle dance. Unfortunately for me, Churchill, who seemed to be
as drunk as the proverbial English lord, kept lurching in the opposite
direction while the imperturbable Alexander bobbed up and down
with superb dignity and decorum. As I was being pulled asunder, I
managed to blurt out a tactless jest to Alexander: "Now I know how
the American colonies felt!" He merely smiled in sympathy.

This festive birthday party was quite untypical, however, of Yugo-
slav-Western relations during the crisis over the Italian and Austrian
borders. I recall vividly the tension that hung over us throughout this
period. The anti-Western campaign reached such proportions that for
several days we surrounded our military mission building with all our
vehicles facing the building, and kept their headlights on all night as
a safety precaution. I also recall with what vehemence one of our
officers said to me, just after getting a letter from his wife and children,
"I don't want to die now, over Trieste!"

One morning I was awakened by a shouting "spontaneous demonstration" of Yugoslav Communist Youth under my bedroom window.
They were painting a huge sign on the pavement below. The white
letters proclaimed "Down with the International Reactionaries!" I
snapped a photo of the scene. Many years later I was visited by the
then Yugoslav consul general in Chicago and his wife, and I showed
them a scrapbook of my photographs from Yugoslavia. Suddenly, as
the consul's wife saw the picture of the group painting that anti-
American sign, she reddened and fairly shrieked, "O my God, I was in
the group that painted that!" Some fifteen years after the event—
and after Yugoslavia's break with Moscow—all that seemed so long
ago. We had a good laugh. But it was no laughing matter in 1945.

It was during this period that the Yugoslavs peremptorily ordered
the American and British military missions to leave Yugoslavia, the
excuse being that their work could be handled by the military attachés.
From the American mission I alone stayed on, with a radio operator,
attached to the American embassy, which had been established in the
meantime. There I continued to monitor the Yugoslav press, to write
reports on political developments, and to serve as an interpreter on
special occasions. Richard C. Patterson, Jr., a businessman who had
been designated ambassador to the Yugoslav government in exile in
London, arrived in Belgrade on March 31, 1945. Patterson's lack of

experience was more than compensated by his able deputy, Counselor Harold Shantz.

The significance of these border disputes for the causes of the Cold War lies in more than the personal fears we Americans in Belgrade felt, however. Much more important was that the Yugoslav Communists, by attempting to seize territories through force of arms, strengthened the impression in the West that Communist states were expansionist and aggressive, and that they were intent on spreading communism wherever they could, by whatever means they could, including military means. Although the Partisans felt that they were occupying territories that on ethnic or other grounds properly belonged to Yugoslavia, the Americans felt that Tito was engaging in naked aggression. And Yugoslav expansionism seemed to be part and parcel of Soviet expansionism. Just as the Soviets used their army to establish hegemony over most of Eastern Europe, the Yugoslavs appeared determined to assert their hegemony over parts of Italy and Austria, not to mention Albania or the Greek and Bulgarian parts of Macedonia. It was Western fears of Communist expansion like this that led to the adoption of the Truman Doctrine, the Marshall Plan, and the policy of containment—that is, to the Cold War.

Other events that helped to create a Cold War atmosphere involved the flights of American airplanes over Yugoslav territory. These were American military transport planes flying between Rome and Vienna; a straight line between these two points goes through the northwest corner of Yugoslavia, and the American pilots were ordered to avoid Yugoslav territory. However, it was easy for pilots to stray in bad weather or to be tempted to hold a straight line to avoid dangerous mountains. In the tense atmosphere of the day the leaders of Yugoslavia looked upon these violations of their airspace as deliberate provocation, intimidation, and humiliation. On August 9, 1946, Yugoslav fighter planes forced down an American transport, wounding a Turkish passenger and interning the eight Americans on board. Then on August 19 the Yugoslavs shot down a second plane, killing all five Americans on board. This killing of unarmed Americans in an unarmed plane greatly excited Western public opinion against Tito's regime. An irate State Department demanded the release of the interned Americans within forty-eight hours or else the United States would refer the matter to the Security Council of the United Nations. The Yugoslavs not only complied but later paid indemnities to the families of the five dead Americans.[16] Still, these events strengthened

16. Robert Lee Wolff, *The Balkans in Our Time* (Cambridge, Mass.: Harvard University Press, 1956), pp. 311-12.

the impression in the United States that Communists, whether Yugoslav or Soviet, were ruthless, irresponsible people. We also assumed that
the Yugoslavs would not have dared to shoot that plane down if they
had not believed that the Soviets would back them up.

Far less explosive but nonetheless galling, to both Belgrade and the
Western Allies, was the question of the repatriation of Yugoslav refugees and prisoners of war as well as the extradition of persons identified by the new Yugoslav government as war criminals. By one report
of August 4, 1945, some 70,000 Yugoslav citizens of one type or
another were in Italy, living in most cases in the open air in the stadiums
and athletic fields.[17] Just between May 23 and 31 the British military
authorities turned over to Tito's Partisans some 12,196 Croats, 5,480
Serbs, 8,263 Slovenes, and 400 Montenegrins—Ustaši, Chetniks, and
Home Guards, many of whom were dubiously classed as "anti-Allied
Yugos."[18] Reports of their mass murder by the Partisans soon reached
the Allies as a few escapees made their way back. Djilas has since reported that between twenty and thirty thousand of these returnees
were killed, and has condemned "these senseless acts of wrathful retribution" done out of "sheer frenzy."[19] The executions by the Yugoslav security police OZNA were for the most part carried out with little
or no judicial procedure and on the basis of local and inconsistent
criteria. They reached such proportions that Tito himself cried out in
disgust at a meeting of the Communist party Central Committee in late
1945, "Enough of all these death sentences and all this killing!"[20] It is
not to be wondered that as evidence of this butchery reached Western
Allied authorities, they refused to hand over any more Yugoslavs, regardless of their past activities. Since the Soviets also followed the
practice of summarily killing returnees who were suspected of having
fought against the Soviet regime, many Americans concluded that
Communists of whatever variety were bloody executioners, indifferent
to notions of justice and due process.

The Yugoslav action that most obviously and directly contributed
to the Cold War was its encouragement of the Greek civil war, which in
turn prompted the Truman Doctrine. When the Communist-dominated
Greek rebels renewed their fight against the government in 1946,
Yugoslavia was their main supporter. Indeed, the Greek Communists
probably could not have staged their rebellion without Yugoslav aid.
Tito sent not only supplies but also military and political advisers. To

17. *FRUS, 1945*, 5, *Europe:* 1246-47, n. 14.
18. "Mr. Alexander C. Kirk, Political Adviser, Allied Force Headquarters, to
the Secretary of State," Caserta, August 4, 1945, ibid., p. 1246.
19. Djilas, *Wartime*, pp. 446-47.
20. Ibid., p. 449.

the West, Yugoslav support of the Greek rebellion seemed to be another example of Tito attempting to spread communism by armed force. It was assumed that he was acting with the full support of Moscow (an assumption that was quite logical at the time), so Russia again was accused of expansionism. Only later, after the Tito-Stalin break, did we learn that the Yugoslavs were acting independently in Greece, pursuing their own national interests, while Stalin had grave doubts about the Greek civil war.[21] But at the time the Communist insurrection in Greece seemed to be just one more chapter in Stalin's grand design to gain control of all of Eastern Europe, and the American response, in the form of the Truman Doctrine, was one of the major events in the development of the Cold War.

7

Yugoslav domestic issues—especially Tito's establishment of a police dictatorship—created no less friction with the West than foreign issues. The British had served as hosts to King Peter and the royal government in exile during the war, and while they were not particularly enthusiastic about the king or his government, they did not want to see them removed except by popular vote. The Americans for their part felt the same way about Yugoslavia as they did about other European countries—that the war had been fought against Fascist dictatorships, and they hoped these would not be replaced by Communist dictatorships. For Yugoslavia this was a vain hope, however, for the Partisans had entrenched themselves in power and, since they had Soviet support, there was absolutely no chance of their being persuaded to give up power, or even to share power. Nonetheless, at Yalta Roosevelt proposed, and got adopted, the Declaration on Liberated Europe, in which the Big Three promised to assist in the holding of free elections and the formation of democratic governments. In addition, they endorsed provisions applying specifically to Yugoslavia, stating that Tito and Dr. Ivan Šubašić, the premier of the government in exile, should immediately put into effect their agreement of November 1, 1944, and form a coalition government. To accomplish this: "(i) The Anti-Fascist Assembly of National Liberation (AVNOJ) should be extended to include members of the last Yugoslav Parliament (Skupschina) who have not compromised themselves by collaborating with the enemy, thus forming a body to be known as a temporary Parliament. . . ."[22]

21. Milovan Djilas, *Conversations with Stalin*, trans. Michael B. Petrovich (New York: Harcourt, Brace and World, 1962), pp. 181-82.
22. "Report of the Crimea Conference," *FRUS: The Conferences at Malta and Yalta, 1945* (Washington: Government Printing Office, 1955), p. 974.

To the best of my knowledge, only after this decision was made did anyone in Washington consider the practicability of "watering Tito's wine" in this way. When the Yalta communiqué was radioed to our military mission in Belgrade, I was assigned the task of finding out just how many members of Yugoslavia's last parliament might be available and eligible. Luckily I discovered a relative in Belgrade, Dr. Uroš Trbojević, who had been very active in prewar Yugoslav politics and who had a reputation—somewhat unsavory, I gathered—for his political expertise. Together we laboriously went through the entire roster of that last parliament. I was able to report the following: "Less than 30 percent of the former deputies are considered even by non-Partisans as eligible for the temporary parliament, while a full 35 percent are definitely compromised; 30 to 45 percent are dead and the remainder are either exiles or prisoners of war or persons who were appointed to the Senate and hence resigned from the Skupschina [the Parliament]."[23] In determining how many were "compromised," I assumed that Tito would determine the criteria. In actual fact, one could hardly blame him for being wary about that parliament; it had been elected in 1938 under Premier Stojadinović's high-handed regime, and it was not representative since the Government party received only 54 percent of the votes but 82 percent of the 374 seats in parliament. I could not help but wonder, as I gathered my data, if the Big Three would have made so much of that last prewar Yugoslav parliament had they known the facts.

At any rate, Tito did nothing about that part of the Yalta agreement until August 1945, when AVNOJ met and, after some dickering, added only thirty-nine members of the old parliament, fewer than a tenth of that body. To make up for this, Tito added sixty-nine members of six non-Communist parties and thirteen distinguished public figures.[24] These additions, however, in no way affected Tito's control over the new legislature or over the rest of the government.

Throughout 1945 the Tito regime showed clearly that it would permit no outside agreements to interfere with its assumption of power. King Peter was not allowed to return to Yugoslavia, and the three regents named to act for him had no power whatever. Besides, though non-Communists, they were all Tito's candidates. The Serb among them, Srdjan Budisavljević, another distant relative of mine, told me that he had no influence at all. Of the twenty-eight posts in the new "coalition" cabinet, inaugurated on March 7, 1945, only five were held by non-Tito representatives. When they tried to conduct election cam-

23. Office of Strategic Services Documents, National Archives, Washington, D.C., OSS Report L53152, February 21, 1945, from Belgrade, dissemination no. A-50879, original report no. GB-3792.
24. *Borba*, August 8, 1945, p. 4.

paigns in the fall of 1945, the first national elections since the war, these non-Communist leaders found it impossible to carry on normal political activities. The police, called the Section for the Protection of the People (OZNA), threatened the safety of anyone who supported the opposition candidates.

The election campaign proceeded in an atmosphere of fear that the government's Popular Front abetted with such slogans as "Ballots for Tito, bullets for Grol" (Milan Grol was the leader of the Democratic party). I myself saw a paperboy who was selling copies of Grol's newspaper *Demokratija* on a Belgrade street burned when his newspapers were doused with gasoline and set on fire by a Communist gang, a gang whose identity the otherwise vigilant authorities allegedly could not determine.

As a signatory of the Yalta agreement, the United States inevitably became involved in these domestic events. The non-Communist opposition in Yugoslavia naturally looked to the United States for support, but we were able to give little more than kind words. While still a vice-premier in the coalition government, Milan Grol asked the Americans whether they planned to secure implementation of the Yalta agreement, and whether he could count on their support if he stayed in office.[25] Apparently he was not satisfied on this point, for he resigned from the cabinet on August 18.[26] On October 8 Ivan Šubašić, former royal premier and later foreign minister in Tito's coalition cabinet, resigned along with his Croatian colleague, Juraj Šutej, giving as their reason the nonfulfillment of the Tito-Šubašić agreement cited in the Yalta recommendations.[27]

In late September 1945, Counselor Harold Shantz reported to Washington: "We believe time has come for our Government to state publicly [the] opinion that present conditions in Yugoslavia make it impossible for elections on November 11 to express [the] free will of the people, and that postponement is necessary until primary freedoms are found to exist." He added: "A relatively small group of Communists, inspired and directed by Moscow, has succeeded in foisting a ruthless totalitarian police regime on the Yugoslavs." "To allow this regime," he said, "to consolidate its position unchallenged is to abandon all prospect for democracy in this country." His final recommendation was: "We owe it to ourselves and the Yugoslav people to state plainly that we do not consider conditions envisioned at Yalta and elsewhere to have been met."[28]

25. "The Ambassador in Yugoslavia (Patterson) to the Secretary of State," Belgrade, April 26, 1945, *FRUS, 1945*, 5, *Europe:* 1224-25.

26. *Borba*, August 21, 1945, p. 1.

27. *Borba*, October 11, 1945, p. 3; *Politika*, October 11, 1945, p. 2.

28. "The Chargé in Yugoslavia (Shantz) to the Secretary of State," Belgrade, September 27, 1945, *FRUS, 1945*, 5, *Europe:* 1259-61.

Washington tried to line up both London and Moscow in a joint démarche to Tito charging nonfulfillment of the Yalta recommendations and calling for postponement of the elections. The Soviet government refused, of course,[29] and surprisingly, the British did also.[30] So the United States by itself sent Tito a note on November 6, reminding him that the Yalta declaration called for not only a coalition government, pending a freely elected constituent assembly, but also for guarantees of personal freedom, freedom from fear, liberty of conscience, freedom of speech, freedom of the press, and freedom of assembly and association. The note added that existing conditions in Yugoslavia were not conducive to free elections that would express the real views of the Yugoslav people.[31] Tito did not bother to reply until *after* the elections.

Thanks to Tito I had an opportunity to observe the election campaign outside of Belgrade—something no other American was able to do. In October I accompanied two members of Congress, Carl Mundt and Frances Bolton, on a visit to Tito in the White Palace. When he saw me, he said: "What, Petrovich, are you still here?"

"Yes, unfortunately," I replied with the candor of youth.

"Why 'unfortunately'?" Tito asked in mock reproach. "After all, this is the land of your fathers, and you ought to stay a while and see more of it."

I thought of the restrictions placed on our travel and replied somewhat boldly: "I would like to, but your Ministry of the Interior thinks otherwise."

Tito thereupon urged me to submit a travel request and assured me that it would be received favorably. "You really should see the country during our first national elections," he said. "As you go around the country, you will find that many people are dissatisfied with how some things are in our country. So are we. The dissatisfied we shall try to satisfy, and the opposition we shall liquidate."

Tito did not say how he distinguished between the dissatisfied and the opposition, but OZNA made it quite clear that the distinction was at best a precarious one.

Election day, November 11, 1945, found me in Lika, Croatia, my late father's native province. In my travels I discovered that, except in a few pockets, the dissatisfied about whom Tito had spoken did not have the nerve to express their dissatisfaction when they actually came to vote. There was little practical reason indeed to stick out one's neck.

29. "The Secretary of State to the Ambassador in the United Kingdom (Winant)," Washington, October 26, 1945, ibid., p. 1274.

30. "The Ambassador in the United Kingdom (Winant) to the Secretary of State," London, October 30, 1945, ibid., pp. 1276 and 1278-79.

31. "The Ambassador in Yugoslavia (Patterson) to the Yugoslav Minister for Foreign Affairs (Tito)," Belgrade, November 6, 1945, ibid., pp. 1281-82.

The opposition candidates decided just before the election that they would abstain, so only the government's Popular Front was in the running. To lend some appearance of legitimacy to an election without an opposing slate, the government furnished each polling place with a non-party ballot box—the "widow's box," as it was wryly dubbed—into which voters opposed to the Popular Front could cast their ballots. True to the original historical form from which ballots get their name, these ballots were quite literally little balls that, despite precautions, often made a noise as the voter inserted his closed fist into both boxes and released the ball in the box of his choice, while voting officials watched. Thanks to this and other reasons, the regime's ballot boxes received 90 percent of the votes cast, whereas the widow's box received only 10 percent. I would have guessed at the time, having traveled up and down the country from the Greek border to Trieste, that the actual national sentiment was more nearly the opposite.

Although those of us in the American embassy had no means of exercising any real effect on political developments in Yugoslavia, Ambassador Patterson could at least give Washington an accurate picture of what was going on. On November 29, 1945, the day when the Federal People's Republic of Yugoslavia was officially proclaimed, Patterson urged the State Department not to recognize the new government. He gave his reasons as follows:

> Contrary to the wishes of the great majority of the people, present ruling clique under Communist control maintains itself by force and secret police as satellite of USSR. Democracy, freedom and civil liberty, as we understand these terms, do not exist. As regards foreign policy, Belgrade is like the capital of a Soviet Republic and regime is hostile to America and Britain, ostensibly [because?] of Trieste affair but really because without Russian support and Russian methods it could not remain in power.[32]

Despite his recommendation, the United States did recognize the newly created Federal People's Republic of Yugoslavia, and Patterson dutifully went to the parliament building to attend the inaugural ceremony. He was accompanied only by a very junior member of the embassy staff—myself. As Tito entered the chamber, he received a standing ovation. I remember that Ambassador Patterson and I also stood, but we did not applaud.

8

It became increasingly evident to me, as it did to other Americans in Belgrade, that we were caught in what was to be called the Cold War. With the German surrender in May 1945, whatever feeling there had

---

32. "The Ambassador in Yugoslavia (Patterson) to the Secretary of State," Belgrade, November 29, 1945, ibid., p. 1292.

been of camaraderie in the joint effort against the Axis quickly faded. True, the Yugoslav Communists had never really trusted us. I will always see as a symbol of our dual relationship of cooperation and suspicion the time Tito visited our military mission for lunch, in early 1945. His coming was a friendly gesture. Yet his staff not only sent two of their own cooks ahead to prepare his meal, but I noticed that both had revolvers in their hip pockets!

After V-E Day, as the new regime was consolidating its political power, often by means of raw terror, the atmosphere became increasingly grim. In the course of 1945 our embassy staff noticed growing signs of official Yugoslav reserve, suspicion, and hostility, in marked contrast with the friendliness of the people. Indeed, some Americans in Belgrade even developed a siege mentality that sometimes produced an emotional and morbid outlook.

Certainly the Yugoslav security police, OZNA, contributed to this atmosphere. Take for example, the following embassy report of May 18, 1945, to Washington: "Visitors tell us they are often questioned after leaving the Embassy; two Embassy employees were arrested during the past week; we asked for an explanation which has not yet been given. Partisans [sic] told a third employee that he should not work for U.S. and warned him against further 'collaboration' with Americans or British." Ambassador Patterson reported in the same dispatch that so many Yugoslavs were being arrested after being seen in the company of British soldiers that the British ambassador protested to Marshal Tito. "Nevertheless," the report continued, "dozens of Yugoslavs have since been arrested after attending parties where American and British soldiers were present. Some were told quite frankly that their arrest was due to their association with British and Americans."[33] American and British personnel were also shadowed by OZNA.[34]

For me there were quite personal signs of this hostile atmosphere. Two stand out in my memory because they involved persons who were very close to me. . . .

I always assumed that my Serbian secretary in the United States Embassy might be under pressure to give the Yugoslav security police information about what I was doing. This did not trouble me too much, for two reasons: first, I was sure of her loyalty; and second, I was not doing anything subversive. Years later, after she had emigrated to America, I discovered how zealous the OZNA had been. She confessed,

33. "The Ambassador in Yugoslavia (Patterson) to the Secretary of State," Belgrade, May 18, 1945, ibid., pp. 1229-30.

34. "The Ambassador in Yugoslavia (Patterson) to the Secretary of State," Belgrade, November 28, 1945, ibid., p. 1291.

with some embarrassment, that she had been regularly interrogated about me every Thursday afternoon, in an empty apartment.

Much more serious, the secret police intervened in the most personal aspect of my private life. Soon after arriving in Belgrade I had met a beautiful Serbian girl named Dušanka Djermanović. We found we had a great deal in common, dated regularly, fell in love, and finally made plans to marry. One night, after we had been out together, she found a police agent waiting for her in the corridor leading to her family's apartment. He told her that I was an "American spy" and that she must never see me again. We felt obliged to stop dating and give up our plans to marry, for fear of what the regime might do to her family. Her father, who had been a banker, was vulnerable to charges of being a "class enemy," while her brother, who was of military age, could have been drafted into the army and sent to one of the front-line units where death rates were high. I left Belgrade a very sad man. (Those who are romantically inclined will be glad to learn that she and I met again, eight years later, and were married.)

Another thing that the Yugoslav Communists did to poison the atmosphere between East and West was to fill their newspapers with criticisms of "the American imperialists." Between 1945 and mid-1948 the government-controlled press presented a most unfavorable picture of the United States, and since one of my duties was to prepare the English-language *Daily Press Review,* I had ample opportunity to observe this trend. The picture of America as presented by Belgrade's newspapers was one of strikes, chronic unemployment, high cost of living, mistreatment of Blacks, control by rich reactionary industrialists, and little else. Ambassador Patterson reported to Washington in late 1945 that the Yugoslav press was "completely sold out to the USSR" and that the "the relatively few articles pertaining to the US and UK are mainly designed to place the politics and economics of both in most unfavorable light possible."[35] The Soviet Union, on the other hand, always received especially favorable treatment.

It would be wrong to suppose that the attempt by Yugoslav Communists to tarnish the public image of a once popular ally was purely the result of differences over Trieste or the fulfillment of the Yalta agreement. In 1945 Yugoslavia had just emerged not only from a world war but from a Communist revolution. The Yugoslav Communists had a deep commitment to the Marxist ideology in its Leninist-Stalinist form, an ideology that dialectically divided the world into "we" and "they" with a quasi-religious fervor. In the immediate postwar period

---

35. "The Ambassador in Yugoslavia (Patterson) to the Secretary of State," Belgrade, December 26, 1945, ibid., p. 1302.

the Yugoslav Communist revolution was still in its ideological stage; only after the 1948 break with Moscow did necessity teach the Yugoslav Communists to be more pragmatic. Before the break, they regarded the Soviet Union with a devotion whose ideological inspiration was but reinforced by the wartime alliance and by primeval myths of Slavic kinship. It was this devotion that caused Yugoslav Communists to excuse even the Stalin-Churchill fifty-fifty agreement over the division of influence in Yugoslavia. "No one in our leadership," Djilas recalled, "saw anything inappropriate or even unpleasant in that at the time. We understood it as the neutralizing of British intervention."[36] Yugoslav Communist adulation of the Soviet Union was so strong that it long overcame doubts raised by all those many cases of Soviet abuse, interference, and economic exploitation that came out into the open after the schism. That same ideological stance of the Yugoslav Communists also contributed to their general distaste for the United States and Great Britain who, after the German surrender, were seen no longer as allies but as bastions of reactionary capitalism. As I look back upon those days in Belgrade, I can see that had there been no such issues as Trieste, Carinthia, and the like, there would have been less cause for the Yugoslav Communists to disparage the Western Allies, but I cannot envisage that even the complete absence of these issues would have made for good relations, given the ideological climate.

We learned only later that it was wrong to attribute the Yugoslav Communist attitude to postwar Yugoslavia being just another Soviet satellite. The Tito regime was not imposed by the Soviet army but emerged by its own efforts, from a double struggle of national liberation and revolutionary civil war. Whatever outside aid the Partisans received during the war came from the Western Allies and not from the Soviet Union. If Tito's Yugoslavia were a loyal Soviet satellite between 1945 and mid-1948, it was by choice and with a sense of Communist solidarity. Moreover, it bears repeating that Soviet troops never "occupied" Yugoslavia, the way they did other East European countries, but merely passed through it in pursuit of the Germans. There is no evidence that Soviet leaders ever had to place any pressure on Yugoslav Communists to oppose the West. On the contrary, in retrospect, one can detect instances in which Soviet leaders exerted a moderating influence on the Yugoslav Communists and kept them from overreaching themselves. After the Tito-Stalin schism, Yugoslav Communist writers often attributed this Soviet restraint to Stalin's unwillingness to allow Tito and his party to become too strong and independent. Whatever truth there is in that assessment, and I do not deny its

36. Djilas, *Wartime*, p. 422.

merits, the Yugoslav Communists were still caught up in the ideological phase of their revolution, a phase that the Soviet Union had long since outgrown and abandoned in favor of *Realpolitik*. The Soviet stance was based on two leading assumptions: that Soviet interests took precedence over Communist international interests, and that Russian interests took precedence over Yugoslav interests. However hard these assumptions were for even disciplined Yugoslav revolutionaries to justify, they made perfect sense from the standpoint of *Realpolitik* and easily found justification by skillful Soviet apologists.

Trieste offers an instructive case in point: None of the Big Three wished to fight over Trieste. "The Allies threw us out of Trieste, and its environs," Djilas recalled, "after the Soviet Central Committee informed us [Yugoslavs] that, after such a terrible war, the U.S.S.R. could not embark on another."[37] However, they could get consolation from what Stalin told Tito, Djilas, and other Yugoslavs at a party in his villa on April 11, 1945. Hitching up his pants, Stalin said, "The war shall soon be over. We shall recover in fifteen or twenty years, and then we'll have another go at it."[38]

In 1944, 1945, and 1946 it was not illogical (and not entirely mistaken) for Americans to view Yugoslav and Soviet policies as being virtually identical. They were. If the Yugoslavs did something that offended us, we assumed that the Soviets approved of it, if they had not in fact instigated it. Yugoslav Communists and Soviet Communists were looked upon as all the same—disagreeable people who destroyed democracy, suppressed freedom, and strove to impose communism upon their neighbors. Thus events in Yugoslavia contributed significantly to the start of the Cold War. Yugoslavia and the Soviet Union were viewed as two parts of a monolithic Communist bloc that was bent on expansion and threatened the interests of the United States. Harold Shantz, counselor of our embassy in Belgrade, summed up the prevailing view when he reported to Washington: "Tito is an agent of Moscow."[39]

As far as I am aware, all outside observers shared Shantz's view at the time, myself included. In 1947, after my return to Columbia University, I told my major professor, Geroid Tanquary Robinson, that for my doctoral dissertation I wished to write about Yugoslavia and its Communist regime during and after World War II. In those days I regarded myself, not entirely with the arrogance of youth, as an expert on Communist Yugoslavia. I had, I assured Professor

37. Ibid., pp. 449-50.
38. Ibid., p. 438.
39. *FRUS, 1945, 5, Europe:* 1260.

Robinson, ample evidence to prove that Tito's Yugoslavia was the most
zealously loyal of all the satellite states in the Soviet sphere. Robinson
dissuaded me from choosing this topic, on the grounds that it was too
recent to treat with historical perspective. Some months later—on June
28, 1948, to be exact—I had reason to be eternally grateful to my
distinguished teacher. It was on that day that the Cominform read
the "Tito clique" out of the Soviet camp and the world Communist
movement. It was little consolation to my professional pride that
almost everyone else was caught by surprise by the Tito-Stalin split.
By that time, of course, the Cold War was in full force.

During the years that followed, Yugoslavia contributed to the intensification of the Cold War in still another way. After June 1948
Stalin embarked on a massive effort to bring Yugoslavia to its knees.
On his orders the Soviet bloc cancelled all economic relations with
Yugoslavia. Loyal Communists throughout the world subjected Tito
and his lieutenants to a scurrilous campaign of vilification—in speeches,
newspaper articles, and radio broadcasts. Soviet agents attempted to
subvert Tito's rule from within. And—most threatening of all—hostile
armies marched along the Yugoslav frontier, making numerous small
incursions across the border and killing Yugoslav soldiers who got in
the way.

These actions further blackened Stalin's reputation in the West.
The view that Stalin was expansionist, aggressive, and warlike found
further confirmation in his treatment of Yugoslavia. If Stalin could
not get along even with a loyal Communist satrap, how could the
capitalist West possibly deal with such a man? The Yugoslav case
seemed to indicate the unlimited nature of Stalin's ambitions. For
him it was not enough that Yugoslavia be Communist; in addition it
must be exploited for the sake of Soviet national interests. For him
it was not enough that Tito run Yugoslavia in a Stalinist manner; he
must in addition be Stalin's slave, obedient to his every whim. From
the Western viewpoint, Stalin the great wartime statesman had become
the big bully who threatened all his neighbors.

The United States eventually came to Yugoslavia's aid, and this
paid off in several ways. Yugoslavia's successful survival of its excom-
munication by Stalin had an effect on the other East European satellites and caused Stalin's successors to adopt a more moderate stance.
Moreover, the polar tension between the United States and the Soviet
Union was mitigated as both superpowers confronted a rising group of
"unaligned" nations of the Third World whose resolve to act independently was supported by Tito's Yugoslavia. The Yugoslav's "independent road to socialism" put a big dent in Moscow's claims to
hegemony in the world Communist movement; it encouraged a poly-

centrism in the Communist camp that forced the Soviet leaders into a more cautious and less strident policy toward the United States and the West. Thus Yugoslavia came to serve, eventually, as one of several important factors that have facilitated the transition from Cold War to Peaceful Coexistence and Détente.

CYRIL E. BLACK

The View from Bulgaria

In discussing the origins of the Cold War in Bulgaria, it is important to keep in mind the background of the high American hopes for a post-war settlement and the limited capabilities for the exertion of U.S. influence under the interim surrender and occupation arrangements that were concluded in the autumn of 1944. Inter-Allied relations in the course of 1944-45 evolved in terms of three main issues: American

Cyril E. Black is Professor of History and Director of the Center of International Studies, Princeton University. His publications include *The Establishment of Constitutional Government in Bulgaria* (1944); (coauthor), *Twentieth Century Europe* (4th ed., 1972); (editor and coauthor), *The Transformation of Russian Society* (1960); (coeditor and coauthor), *Communism and Revolution* (1964); *The Dynamics of Modernization* (1960); and (coauthor), *The Modernization of Japan and Russia* (1975).

In the period covered by this chapter, he served in the Department of State as country specialist in the Office of Special Political Affairs and secretary of the Subcommittee on Territorial Problems of the Advisory Committee on Post-War Problems (1943-44); and Foreign Service Auxiliary Officer, assigned to the U.S. Political Mission in Sofia (1944-45); to the Ethridge Mission to Bulgaria, Romania, and the USSR (October to December, 1945); and to the Division of Southeastern European Affairs, Department of State (1945-46). He lived from 1926 to 1934 in Bulgaria, where his father was President of the American College of Sofia.

NOTE: This paper was written under the auspices of the Center of International Studies, Princeton University. An earlier version was published in the *Review of Politics* 41 (April 1979):163-202. I wish to thank John C. Campbell, Boyan Choukanoff, Martin H. Curtis, L. A. D. Dellin, Thomas T. Hammond, Martin F. Herz, Paul E. Keal, Stephen D. Kertesz, Paul L. Miles, Nissan Oren, Robert C. Tucker, and Wayne Vucinich for their comments on the original draft.

and British participation in the Allied Control Commission; the election crisis of August 1945; and the Ethridge mission.

My own experience with these events extended from the planning of postwar policy in the Department of State in 1943-44 through the first year (1944-45) of American participation in the implementation of the Bulgarian armistice.

HIGH HOPES AND LOW CAPABILITIES

American policy proposals relating to the negotiation of a postwar settlement evolved along essentially separate lines from those concerning interim problems of surrender and occupation. Plans for the postwar reconstruction of Europe and for a new international organization were the responsibility of the State Department's Office of Special Political Affairs, as it was known in 1944 after several reorganizations. Interim policies in regard to surrender and occupation were developed by the State Department in consultation with the Joint Chiefs of Staff, with which it communicated in the last instance through Adm. William D. Leahy at the White House, in his capacity as chief of staff to the commander-in-chief of the Army and Navy, that is, President Roosevelt. These policies were coordinated with the two major U.S. allies through the European Advisory Commission (EAC) in London.[1] Although both interim and postwar policies were in the last analysis determined by the president, they were not treated as part of a single policy process. Questions of surrender and occupation were seen as essentially military matters to be determined on a short-term, pragmatic basis. Negotiation of a European peace settlement was seen as a postwar problem, and one that was subordinated in the president's thinking to achieving a consensus on the new international organization.

From where I sat, virtually at the bottom of the bureaucratic pyramid, after leaving my teaching duties at Princeton University in January 1943, the prevailing view among the department's postwar planning staff was that the political structure of Europe after the war would have a democratic character similar to that anticipated after the First World War. The states of Europe to the west of the Soviet Union would have independent and representative governments as these terms were generally understood in the United States, and would participate in the solution of common problems within the framework of the new international organization.

This view of postwar Europe reflected the goal of "freedom of

1. The organization, scope, and development of this work are described in U.S. Department of State, *Postwar Foreign Policy Preparation, 1939-1945*, Publication 3580, General Foreign Policy Series 15 (Washington: Government Printing Office, 1949).

speech and expression everywhere in the world" set forth by President Roosevelt in his speech on the Four Freedoms (January 1941) and in the pledge of the United Kingdom and the United States in the Atlantic Charter (August 1941) to "respect the right of all countries to choose the form of government under which they will live. . . ." The Soviet Union expressed agreement with the charter in the following month, on the understanding that "the practical application of these principles will necessarily adapt itself to the circumstances, needs, and historic peculiarities of particular countries. . . ."[2] The degree of agreement achieved by the Big Three in the wartime conferences at Moscow (October 19-30, 1943), Tehran (November 28-December 1, 1943), and Dumbarton Oaks (August 21-September 28, 1944), led to an American expectation that cooperation on postwar problems would continue in the same spirit.

The Department of State's research staff was concerned with studying the background of territorial and political problems that the policy makers were likely to face after the termination of hostilities, and with proposing alternative solutions for the consideration of the policy makers. The precedent for this work was the inquiry organized by Col. Edward M. House on behalf of President Wilson in preparation for the Versailles peace conference, and consideration was given to the entire range of problems that might come up at the anticipated peace settlement. The only recommendations of the research staff that reached a policy level in 1944 were those formulated in October in a report of the department's policy committee on American interests and policies in Eastern Europe, with a separate statement regarding Bulgaria.[3]

The aims set forth in this report included the right of peoples to choose the political, economic, and social systems they preferred without outside interference; equality of opportunity and freedom to negotiate in commerce, trade, and transit; the right of access of all countries in matters of press and public information; freedom of activity for American philanthropic and educational organizations; and protection of American citizens and their legitimate economic rights. The recommendations for Bulgaria specifically included withdrawal from occupied Greek and Yugoslav territory, with the subsequent possibility of free port facilities on the Aegean; and American access to Bulgarian tobacco on the basis of free enterprise. This report was not a summary of U.S. policy, but simply a recommendation to the secre-

2. *Postwar Foreign Policy Preparations*, p. 51.
3. U.S. Department of State, *Foreign Relations of the United States* (hereafter cited as *FRUS*) *1945* (Washington: Government Printing Office, 1968), 4: 143, nn. 26, 27.

tary of state based on the views current in 1944 within the department. It clearly assumed the predominance of Anglo-American rather than Soviet influence in Bulgaria.

The work of the research staff reflected an awareness of differences among the allies in outlook and national interests, but the predominant disposition was to anticipate the resolution of these differences by means of multilateral consultation. Thus in preparing recommendations on the creation of representative governments after the termination of hostilities for discussion at the Yalta Conference, it was proposed in January 1945 that an Emergency High Commission for Liberated Europe be established. This body would be an agency of the four governments (now including France) "acting together to assist in establishing popular governments and in facilitating the solution of emergency economic problems in the former occupied and satellite states of Europe." The proposal was accompanied by the text of a Declaration on Liberated Europe, couched in terms of the principles of the Atlantic Charter.

On the eve of the Yalta Conference (February 4-11, 1945), President Roosevelt and his immediate advisers reviewed the proposal and rejected the idea of an emergency high commission. Only the declaration was presented to the conference, and it was adopted with minor revisions. The proposed high commission was rejected in part because of dissatisfaction with the way in which the European Advisory Commission had worked, and in part because of the fear that it might prejudice acceptance of the proposed United Nations organization, which was the president's primary concern at Yalta. The president preferred to have questions regarding the liberated areas handled directly by the foreign ministers.[4]

It is clear that the president was also concerned that the proposed high commission might involve the United States in responsibilities in Eastern Europe that it did not wish to assume. There are numerous indications of the president's views. In September 1943, for example, Archbishop Francis Spellman reported that in a long private conversation on postwar prospects the president had expressed the view that the world would be divided into spheres of influence. Britain and the Soviet Union would take the responsibility for Europe and Africa, and the United States would concentrate on the Pacific.[5] In a note to Acting Secretary of State Edward R. Stettinius, Jr., in February 1944, the president stated more explicitly that "I do not want the United

4. *Postwar Foreign Policy Preparation*, pp. 372-73; 394-95; the texts of the proposal and of the final declaration are on pp. 655-57 and 663-64.

5. Robert I. Gannon, *The Cardinal Spellman Story* (New York: Doubleday, 1962), p. 222.

States to have the post-war burden of reconstituting France, Italy and the Balkans. This is not our natural task at a distance of 3,500 miles or more."[6] In this case he referred to Britain alone as the interested and responsible party. Pursuant to the president's views, the plans of the Operations Division of the U.S. Army in the summer of 1944 provided that the American political role in Europe should be limited to measures strictly necessary for the defeat of Germany. In the case of Austria, Hungary, Bulgaria, and Romania, no U. S. forces were expected to be used for occupational duty, nor would civil affairs or relief and rehabilitation responsibilities be undertaken.[7]

It was in the context of this restricted view of the U.S. role in southeastern Europe that the question of the Bulgarian surrender arose in the summer of 1944. Bulgaria had been at war with the United States and the United Kingdom, but not with the USSR, and armistice terms became a matter for negotiation between the two Western allies and between them and representatives of the indecisive Bulgarian governments headed by Dobri Bozhilov (September 14, 1943-June 1, 1944), and Ivan Bagrianov (June 1-September 2, 1944). Bulgaria had as a member of the Tripartite Pact occupied the territories of Macedonia and Thrace, to which it had long laid claim in neighboring Yugoslavia and Greece, while avoiding military action and remaining at peace with the USSR. Apart from the Allied bombing of Sofia and other cities in the winter of 1943-44, Bulgaria had suffered little from the war. Bagrianov had hoped to secede from the Tripartite Pact and adopt a policy of neutrality, while keeping the occupied territories. The allies pressed for a declaration of war on Germany and withdrawal from these territories. When the Soviet armies launched their offensive against Romania, the Bulgarian government announced on August 26 its withdrawal from the alliance with Germany and the adoption of a policy of neutrality. This gesture was rejected as inadequate by both the Western allies and the USSR, however, and within a week Soviet troops had reached the Danube.

Bagrianov now resigned, and on September 2 a pro-Western cabinet headed by Konstantin Muraviev took office. It was composed of moderate Agrarians and Democrats who had opposed the alliance with Germany, but it did not include members of the more radical Fatherland Front coalition. These latter did not join because they expected to seize power themselves in a few days. Muraviev's government finally decided on September 5 to break relations with Germany. On the same

6. Maurice Matloff, *Strategic Planning for Coalition Warfare, 1943-1944* (Washington: Department of the Army, 1959), p. 491.

7. Matloff, *Strategic Planning*, pp. 504-6.

day it also discussed the possibility of declaring war on Germany, but apparently decided to delay the decision at the request of the minister of war, Gen. Ivan Marinov. Marinov has since stated that he found the military situation in a state of disarray, and that it took him until September 7 to reorganize the general staff, and to prepare the Bulgarian forces to take action against the German troops that had not yet been disarmed and interned.[8]

Meanwhile, on September 5, the Soviet government took the initiative by declaring war on Bulgaria, without previous consultation with its allies and giving them only an hour's notice. It seems likely that the USSR took this action on very short notice, fearing that otherwise it would be left out of the armistice negotiations that would follow a Bulgarian declaration of war on Germany. The fact that General Marinov was later awarded an ambassadorship while his colleagues in the Muraviev government received prison sentences as war criminals, has led many observers to conclude that the general had played a key role in this Soviet maneuver by delaying a declaration of war until the Soviets were ready to move and by assisting the takeover by the Fatherland Front. Bulgaria finally declared war on Germany on the same day that Soviet troops began to occupy Bulgaria, September 8, and thus was briefly at war with both Germany and the USSR as well as with the United States and the United Kingdom. That evening the Soviet government agreed to a cease-fire, and the following day the Muraviev government was overthrown by the Fatherland Front.[9]

Armistice negotiations were now resumed with active Soviet participation, on the basis of the precedents established in Italy and Romania. In 1943 an Allied Control Commission (ACC) had been established in Italy under joint American and British command and with no formal participation by the USSR. An Allied Advisory Commission for Italy was also established, with Soviet participation, but it had no executive authority. These arrangements in Italy, which reflected the view that occupation policy was the exclusive prerogative of the governments exercising military control, served as the precedent for the armistice terms in Eastern Europe, and later for the unilateral U.S. control of Japan. In September 1944 the United States and the United Kingdom

8. Ivan Marinov, "Pet dni v pravitelstvoto na K. Muraviev" [Five days in the government of K. Muraviev], *Istoricheski pregled* 24 (May-June 1968):81-102.

9. Developments in Bulgaria in the summer and autumn of 1944 are discussed in Marshall Lee Miller, *Bulgaria during the Second World War* (Stanford: Stanford University Press, 1975), pp. 174-216. The most recent Bulgarian account is Vitka Toshkova, *Bulgariia i Tretiiat Raikh, 1941-1944* [Bulgaria and the Third Reich, 1941-1944] (Sofia: Nauka i Izkustvo, 1975), pp. 182-234. The U.S. role in the armistice negotiations is covered in *FRUS, 1944*, 3:300-395.

agreed to armistice terms with Romania in which the Soviet representative on the ACC was to exercise exclusive executive authority. It was explicitly understood that, by analogy with the Soviet status in Italy, the role of the American and British representatives in Romania would be limited to maintaining liaison between the ACC and their governments.[10]

In the Bulgarian case, particular attention was given to Article 18, which dealt with the respective roles of the three allies on the ACC. As negotiated by British Foreign Secretary Anthony Eden and Soviet Foreign Minister V. M. Molotov in Moscow on October 12, this article provided that for the whole period of the armistice the ACC would be under the chairmanship of the Soviet representative with the "participation" of the British and American representatives. The term "participation" was not defined, but it was understood to mean no more than liaison, as in Romania. The execution of the armistice terms would be under the general direction of the Soviet high command.[11]

In the days immediately following this agreement, Eden and Molotov had several oral and written exchanges in which the former sought to increase the role of the British and American representatives after the defeat of Germany. The only concession that Molotov would make, on October 15, was that in this second period the role of the Soviet high command would be "to some extent restricted in favor of British and American representatives."[12]

Eden finally accepted this Soviet position, feeling that Soviet military occupation of the country prevented the British and American representatives from insisting on a more influential role. Perhaps the best explanation of these events is that of U.S. Ambassador John G. Winant, reporting from London on October 12: "A casual evaluation of the conversations in regard to Bulgarian armistice terms, on the evidence I have seen, might suggest that our friend Eden was having his pants traded off. But when you stop to realize the advance of Russian troops into Yugoslavia, it is clear that the primary British purpose was to continue their relationship with Greece and to maintain a sufficient degree of control in Yugoslavia to protect British Mediterranean interests."[13]

It is significant that the armistice terms for Bulgaria were considered in Moscow only a few days after Churchill's famous percentage deal with Stalin of October 9, in which the USSR was assigned a 75 percent interest in Bulgaria and "the others" 25 percent. This agree-

10. *FRUS, 1944*, 4:230.
11. Ibid., 3:449-50.
12. Ibid., p. 463.
13. Ibid., p. 452.

ment was revised on the following day by Eden and Molotov to give the USSR an 80 percent interest. To be sure, this agreement, like the armistice itself, was applicable only to the period up to the conclusion of peace, and did not signify a postwar division into spheres of influence. Yet the attitudes reflected by these arrangements were bound to cast a long shadow into the future. It is also significant that in the case of both Churchill's negotiations with Stalin and Eden's with Molotov, the United States was not represented and U.S. Ambassador W. Averell Harriman participated only as an observer at some of the meetings. President Roosevelt was opposed to bilateral British-Soviet talks, not wishing to be committed to any agreements that Churchill and Stalin might reach, and preferring to regard their talks as preliminary to agreements to be reached later by all three heads of state.[14] Whatever the president's motives, it seems most likely that Stalin and Molotov gained the impression that the United States was not particularly concerned with developments in southeastern Europe and was leaving these matters to its British and Soviet allies. The State Department, for its part, was not fully informed about the details of the British-Soviet agreements at the time and did not regard them as binding on the United States.

The negotiations on the Bulgarian armistice terms now reverted to London and were concluded in the EAC on October 18. In its final form, Article 18 provided that, during the period prior to the conclusion of hostilities against Germany, the Allied Control Commission would be under the general direction of the Allied (Soviet) high command, as it was called. This was generally understood to mean that the Soviet commander would have unrestricted authority, as in Romania. The arrangements for the second period, from the termination of hostilities to the conclusion of peace, were left vague. So far as the British and Soviet governments were concerned, the arrangement giving the Soviet commander continuing but somewhat modified authority during the second period had already been agreed to in Moscow on October 15. The U.S. government, however, did not accept this agreement as binding. In a formal letter to its two allies on October 22, it restated its position that the three governments should have an

14. Llewellyn Woodward, *British Foreign Policy in the Second World War* (London: H. M. Stationery Office, 1962), pp. 307-8; and Albert Resis, "The Churchill-Stalin Secret 'Percentages' Agreement on the Balkans, Moscow, October, 1944," *American Historical Review* 83 (April 1978):268-87. On the U.S. role, see W. Averell Harriman and Elie Abel, *Special Envoy to Churchill and Stalin, 1941-46* (New York: Random House, 1975), p. 354; Vojtech Mastny, *Russia's Road to the Cold War* (New York: Columbia University Press, 1979), pp. 207-12; and *FRUS, 1944* 3:455.

equal role on the ACC during the second period, and reserved its right to raise the issue again at a later date. The armistice was finally signed in Moscow on October 28, by Marshal F. I. Tolbukhin and Lt. Gen. J. A. H. Gammel of the British Mediterranean Command, the latter signing also on behalf of the United States. On the same day, Molotov rejected the American interpretation of Article 18, and reasserted the Soviet view that since only Soviet troops were on the territory of Bulgaria, the Soviet high command should preserve its leading role in the second period, although in a somewhat modified form.[15]

THE ALLIED CONTROL COMMISSION

This is how matters stood when the American officials arrived in Sofia. Maj. Gen. John A. Crane, who had served as military attaché in Istanbul and Sofia before the war, was chief of the United States military representation on the Allied Control Commission. Maynard B. Barnes, with the personal rank of minister, was head of the American mission as American representative in Bulgaria. He had served in Bulgaria in 1930-34 and was well acquainted with the local political scene.

Their assignments in Bulgaria in the 1930s had overlapped, and Barnes had urged the War Department to assign Crane to Bulgaria in 1944 so as to be assured of a congenial colleague. Under Soviet and British practice, the military representatives on the ACC had full authority and the political representatives served as their advisers. In the case of the United States, however, the president had issued an executive order in 1942 placing all American representatives in a foreign country under the political representation. As this applied to the ACC in Bulgaria, General Crane took the initiative only in matters relating strictly to the armistice terms, while Barnes spoke for the United States on political matters. This arrangement gave Barnes much more authority than his Soviet and British counterparts, and accounts for some of the initiatives that he was able to take.[16]

I left the United States with Barnes on November 4 and arrived in Sofia ahead of him on November 14, having hitched a ride from Italy on the plane of Brig. Gen. Egmont F. Koenig. Koenig was chief of the American delegation on the Allied Joint Military Mission for Bulgaria, and had the task of verifying the withdrawal of Bulgarian armed forces from Macedonia and Thrace. His mission was easily accomplished, and on November 25 he joined his signature to those of his Soviet and British colleagues to the protocol declaring that Bulgaria had complied

15. *FRUS, 1944* 3:396-479; and Miller, *Bulgaria during the Second World War*, pp. 204-20.

16. Maynard B. Barnes, "The Current Situation in Bulgaria," Lecture, National War College, Washington, D.C. (June 3, 1947), p. 11.

with all prearmistice requirements. This particular inter-Allied task was of a purely technical character. It did not involve any contention for influence, and was carried out without controversy. In the meantime, Barnes arrived on November 19 and Crane joined him a few days later.

The terms of the armistice agreement gave full authority to the Soviet Commander, Marshal F. I. Tolbukhin, represented locally by Col. Gen. S. S. Biriuzov and his deputy Maj. Gen. A. I. Cherepanov. Lacking clear instructions, as well as any knowledge of the British-Soviet negotiations in Moscow, it was difficult for Barnes and Crane to believe that they should not at least be informed of major decisions of the ACC and be given an opportunity to comment on them. Not only were there no provisions for such minimal participation apparent when they arrived, but their personal movement was restricted to the city limits of Sofia. They could not go beyond these limits without a Soviet officer accompanying them—and it often took a day or more before such an officer was made available. Since the airport was outside these limits, and severe restrictions were placed on the movements of personnel, supplies, and even mail pouches from Italy, their resulting frustration where they represented the victorious powers in a defeated country can be readily imagined.

More significant than these relatively minor inconveniences was that important decisions were relayed to the Bulgarian government in the name of the ACC without the knowledge of the American and British members. By November the ACC had military representatives in all district administrative centers and in the main seaports, who worked in close support of the local Fatherland Front committees. They brought the Soviet garrisons to the assistance of local Communist efforts "to liquidate fascism," to use the then current euphemism, by suppressing all opposition to Communist influence and by organizing demonstrations. More often than not we learned of such activities only from the press or from members of the Bulgarian government. This was humiliating enough in dealing with officials of what was an occupied enemy country. It was all the more frustrating when such decisions of the ACC were directed against the political self-determination that the United States was trying to foster.

The initial frustrations were somewhat relieved as a result of an extended dinner meeting on December 26 attended by Biriuzov and Cherepanov as guests of Barnes and Crane. Biriuzov confirmed the American conjecture that the restrictions imposed by the ACC on the Western Allies were primarily directed against the British, whom at this point they tended to suspect as the inspirers of all anti-Communist activity in Bulgaria. In the ensuing months these matters were handled more subtly. A greater effort was now made to communicate with the

British and American members of the ACC, although without in any way restricting Soviet authority.

The outlook of General Biriuzov and his colleagues was that Soviet influence in Bulgaria could best be implemented by a government dominated by the Communist party (known officially as the Bulgarian Workers party) in coalition with Agrarian and Socialist elements that fully supported Communist policies within the framework of the Fatherland Front that had come to power on September 9. He saw the current political situation as a conflict between "popular-democratic" forces (i.e., those groups adhering to Communist policies) and "bourgeois" forces (in effect, all others), which he regarded as "reactionary" and aiming at the restoration of "fascism." As he later wrote in his memoirs, "We did not have the right to withhold assistance to the efforts of the Bulgarian people to crush this reptile." And, with reference to his American and British colleagues on the ACC, "We had no doubt that they would try to interfere with the establishment of a democratic order in Bulgaria. We had to strike from the hand of our 'partners' the spoke which they were constantly trying to put in the wheel of history." [17]

An important role in these plans was played by the series of trials organized by the new government, as least nominally in implementation of the provision of the armistice terms that "Bulgaria will cooperate in the apprehension and trial of persons accused of war crimes." No article of the armistice was implemented with greater enthusiasm. Many hundreds of individuals around the country were sentenced to death by local people's courts, in what was probably the most extensive postwar purge of any of the European countries. The crucial trial was that of the heads of previous governments that opened in Sofia on December 21. The defendants included the three former regents (Prince Kiril, brother of the late King Boris III; Bogdan Filov, the leading pro-German political figure; and Gen. Nikola Mihov), and all of the cabinet members, royal counselors, and members of the National Assembly from 1941 to September 9, 1944.

The public prosecutor asked for fifty-two death penalties, and on February 1 the defendants prepared to hear the sentences standing in a square in the courtroom surrounded by armed militiamen. The prince

17. S. S. Biriuzov, *Surovye gody* [Bitter years] (Moscow: Nauka, 1966), p. 486. See also pp. 522-30. On the domestic activities of the ACC, see Stoyan Tanev, "Pomoshtta na suvetskoto voenno komanduvane za politicheskoto ukrepvane na narodnodemokratichnata vlast v Bulgariia (Septemvri 1944-1947 g.)" [The assistance of the Soviet military command in political support of the national democratic power in Bulgaria (September 1944-1947)], *Voennoistoricheski sbornik* 40 (July-August, 1971):65-81.

looked haughty and defiant, Filov was restless and uneasy, and the others talked and joked nervously with each other while waiting for the judges to appear. The clerk read the sentence in a loud and clear voice: death for twenty-five regents and ministers, eight counselors, and sixty-seven members of the National Assembly—a round one hundred. They were shot that evening in batches of twenty.

Light prison sentences were meted out to members of the pro-Western government of Konstantin Muraviev, which had come to power on September 2 in an effort to conclude peace with the United States and the United Kingdom. Muraviev had in fact decided to break relations with Germany on September 5 but, as already noted, the Soviet Union had declared war on Bulgaria on the same day so that the opportunity for Bulgaria to negotiate with the Western Allies was preempted. Muraviev's government was overthrown on September 9 by the Fatherland Front, which arranged a cessation of hostilities with the Soviet Union on the same day.

The one-hundred death sentences, almost twice the number that the public prosecutor had demanded, were generally regarded as an arbitrary figure designed to strike terror into the hearts of all who might contemplate further opposition to the new government. The lighter sentences handed out to the Muraviev government served to eliminate from the political scene the centrist parties, including the moderate Agrarians and the Democrats. Their only war crime had been their refusal to join the Fatherland Front in the course of 1944. This trial is as good an example as any of how the Soviet high command, through the ACC and in implementation of the armistice terms, could clear the way for the the eventual elimination of all rivals to the Communists.

There remained now the Fatherland Front itself. The government that took power on September 9 was headed by Kimon Georgiev, who, along with Damian Velchev (minister of war) and Petko Stainov (minister of foreign affairs), led the Zveno National Union. Zveno was an elite group of antidynastic officers and technocrats who saw it as their role to form a link (zveno) uniting the diverse parties and interest groups. They had strong influence in the army and the bureaucracy, but little general support. There were in addition two nonparty cabinet members, known in the contemporary jargon as "independent intellectuals."

A much more important component of the Fatherland Front government was formed by the representatives of the radical Agrarians and the Social Democrats. The radical Agrarians—or more accurately the Pladne Agrarians from their newspaper *Pladne* (Noonday) founded in 1928—were distinguished from the moderate or Vrabcha l Agrarians, from their street address, who were led by Dimitur Gichev and Konstantin Muraviev. The radical Agrarians within the Fatherland Front government were led by Nikola Petkov, who had headed the party throughout the war, and three other cabinet members. The principal leader of the party was Dr. G. M. Dimitrov, who returned to Bulgaria from exile on September 23, 1944, and was elected secretary-general of the party on October 15. The broad popular support of the radical Agrarians was reflected in the large public meetings they held in Sofia, Lovech, Stara Zagora, and Plovdiv in the autumn of 1944. The Social Democrats had a much more limited following among trade union members and civil servants. They were led by Grigor Cheshmedjiev until his death (of natural causes) in September 1945, and thereafter by Konstantin Lulchev.

The Communists themselves were represented by Anton Yugov (minister of interior, controlling the militia, the ubiquitous police force), Mincho Neichev (minister of justice, administering the courts), and two other members. The National Committee of the Fatherland Front, headed by Tsola Dragoicheva, was more openly dominated by the Communists at this time than the government. Traicho Kostov, secretary-general of the party, and most of his colleagues, remained outside the government. The veteran Communist leaders Georgi M. Dimitrov and Vasil Kolarov remained in the USSR for the time being, either hesitating to return until their party's position was more firmly consolidated, or more likely restrained by the Soviet government for fear of alarming their allies.[18]

A new council of regency was also appointed, including one Communist, one member of Zveno, and one independent. The council of regency had been established when King Boris III died in August 1943 and was succeeded by his six-year-old son Simeon II. Its original members, as already noted, were arrested in September 1944 and executed in February of the following year. The new regents remained in office until September 1946, when Bulgaria was declared a republic and the young king and his family went into exile.

When it came to power, the Fatherland Front could properly be

18. The political situation in Bulgaria in late 1944 and early 1945 is discussed in Nissan Oren, *Revolution Administered: Agrarianism and Communism in Bulgaria* (Baltimore: Johns Hopkins University Press, 1973), pp. 79-102. On the role of the radical Agrarians, see also Charles A. Moser, *Dimitrov of Bulgaria: A Political Biography of Dr. Georgi M. Dimitrov* (Ottawa, Ill.: Caroline House, 1979), pp. 187-203. Both the Agrarian and the Communist leaders were named Georgi M. Dimitrov—with middle names of Mihov and Mihailov, respectively. Since the Agrarian was a physician by training, he was generally known as Dr. G. M. Dimitrov. His political nickname was "Gemeto"—literally, "the G. M."

said to have represented a solid majority of the politically active population, in view of the wide popular support of the radical Agrarians and Social Democrats and the narrower but substantial support of the Communists among urban workers and some minority groups. Ten days after taking office, the government announced a program of reforms that included further socialization of the already extensively socialized economy and society, legalization of trade unions and civil marriages, credits for the peasants, and guarantees of civil liberties. This was essentially the established Agrarian program, and it was well received by the general public so far as one could gather in the confused situation existing at the time. Bulgaria also became a cobelligerent with the Russians, but this status was not recognized by the United States or the United Kingdom. In the course of the winter its armed forces lost some 32,000 lives fighting with the Soviet armies from Bulgaria to Hungary—the farthest from its borders that a Bulgarian army had ever ventured.

At the same time, the Communists from the beginning controlled the police and the courts directly. The Bulgarian army was fully counterbalanced by the Soviet occupation forces. Some sixteen general officers of Bulgarian origin who had served with the Soviet armed forces were appointed to leading positions in the army, one of them becoming chief of staff. Suspect officers were soon purged, and the Zveno minister of war was effectively isolated—his adjutant was killed, it being rumored that he was found in his office one morning with his skull crushed, as a gentle reminder to the minister that he should not meddle in army affairs.

By February 1945 there remained as potential opponents of Communist control only the radical Agrarians and the Social Democrats. They had worked closely with the Communists in the Fatherland Front opposition group during the war, in contrast to the moderate Agrarians and other centrist parties who had preferred a Western connection, and Nikola Petkov in particular had been confident in the early weeks after September 9 that the Agrarians would be able to share power with the Communists and the Social Democrats. All three parties had a heritage of independent and frequently conflicting policies dating back to the early 1900s; but since 1923, and especially during the war, they had shared the common experience of being in opposition to prevailing government policies. The task confronting the Communists in the spring of 1945 was thus to consolidate their exclusive control of the government, while keeping up the appearance of collaboration with the radical Agrarians and Social Democrats.

During the early months of the occupation Barnes and Crane were working on the assumption that Biriuzov and his colleagues were overstepping their rights in promoting extensive political changes within the country without reference to their allies on the ACC. The moment of truth finally came on January 18, when Barnes and Crane learned for the first time from their British colleagues of the Eden-Molotov negotiations of October 12-15, which limited the role of the American and British members of the ACC in effect to that of liaison.The State Department responded to Barnes's queries rather ambiguously, by asserting that the Eden-Molotov deal was not binding on the United States and urging Crane to press for frequent meetings of the ACC with prior information about important decisions; and at the same time acknowledging that the Soviets would have full authority in the first period. For the second period, after the conclusion of its hostilities with Germany, the department noted that it had reserved its rights to press for a more active role.[19]

The question of the American and British roles on the ACC continued to be a matter of active concern. There were extended messages from Barnes and Crane documenting the limitations under which they were working, and equally eloquent responses from the department expressing its concern and determination. Yet the defeat of Germany on May 8 came and went with no change in the situation, despite new communications from Barnes and Crane that were in due course brought to the attention of President Truman.[20] After the Potsdam Conference, the Soviet government proposed some alterations in ACC procedures, but these did not change matters substantially. The principal change was that Western journalists were now admitted to Bulgaria, with the result that the election crisis received wide publicity.

THE ELECTION CRISIS

The Yalta Declaration on Liberated Europe (February 11, 1945) had come at a time when the Fatherland Front was beginning to prepare for elections. Within the country the issue of free elections centered on the Communist insistence that the candidates of the four parties in the Fatherland Front run on a single government list, and that other candidates could run only as individuals. In other words, the Communists would use their control of the police and the courts to bargain before the elections for a larger share of the candidates than they could expect to win if they ran in competition with the other parties. At the same time they sought to split their two main competitors, the radical Agrarians and the Social Democrats, by isolating their leaders and limiting participation in the Fatherland Front to splinter elements of these

19. *FRUS, 1945*, 4: 144-54.
20. Ibid., pp. 191-211.

parties. On January 20, 1945, the leader of the radical Agrarians, Dr. G. M. Dimitrov, who had returned to the country from Cairo in September, was forced to resign his position, and on April 23 he was placed under house arrest. His close relations with the British both before and during the war made him particularly vulnerable in Soviet eyes. Nikola Petkov, who had led the radical Agrarians during the war and was at this time considered by the Communists to be more amenable to their influence, again became head of the party.

After the publication of the Yalta declaration in the Bulgarian press, Barnes queried the department: "Does the U.S. really intend to make its influence felt in this part of the world and, in particular, will it actually seek to assure a free expression of Bulgarian opinion in the forthcoming elections?"[21] The department responded to this query that it expected "to see with respect to the former Axis satellite countries full implementation of the Crimea Declaration on Liberated Europe, announcing mutual agreement among the three principal allies to concert their policies in helping these former enemy states . . . to form interim governmental authorities broadly representative of the democratic elements."[22]

Pursuant to this policy, Ambassador Harriman was instructed at the end of March to inform the Soviet government of American concern about Bulgaria's electoral plans and to propose that the parties forming the Fatherland Front have full freedom to present separate lists of candidates to the electorate. The proposal was also made that this procedure be supervised by a tripartitie commission in Sofia, independent of the ACC, composed of the Soviet, British, and American political representatives.[23] Molotov was not attracted to this idea, however, replying that he had no information about Bulgarian elections in the near future, that foreign intervention in eventual elections would not be justified, and that successful elections had been conducted in Finland without foreign interference.[24]

While the forthcoming elections had for some time been the main political topic in Bulgaria, Molotov's reply was correct in the technical sense that the date for elections had not yet been set. In the Finnish elections, held on March 18, the People's Democratic party, formed by the Communists running on a single ticket with the Farmers' party and dissident Social Democrats (a grouping analogous to the Fatherland Front) had won a quarter of the seats in the assembly. The Social Democrats, running independently, had won another quarter, with

21. Ibid., p. 163.
22. Ibid., p. 169.
23. Ibid., pp. 179-81.
24. Ibid., p. 186.

the balance going to the Agrarians and other parties. The government resulting from this election was recognized by the United States after the Potsdam Conference as broadly representative of the democratic forces in the country.

In Bulgaria, the radical Agrarians and the Social Democrats were becoming increasingly aware that if the elections were carried out as planned the two parties would very shortly be shorn of all political influence. In this context the dramatic escape of Dr. G. M. Dimitrov from house arrest sharpened the issue of political freedom and of the American role in supporting representative government. Dr. Dimitrov escaped from house arrest on May 23 and sought asylum with a member of the British mission. The British representatives, after communicating with London, informed him that they could not offer him asylum. Barnes agreed to take him in, pending instructions from the U.S. government, and at 4:00 A.M. on May 24 he was driven to Barnes's residence about four miles outside Sofia.[25]

Dr. Dimitrov was now under American protection. Foreign Minister Stainov and other high officials were out of town celebrating a national holiday, so Barnes spent the day consulting Exarch Stefan, head of the Bulgarian Orthodox church, and several political leaders, as to the legal and political aspects of his problem. In the afternoon Barnes finally got in touch with the Senior Regent Venelin Ganev and Prime Minister Georgiev, and discovered that neither of them had yet been informed of Dr. Dimitrov's escape. The prime minister agreed that the police search—now proceeding full force—should be called off, and promised that the government would take no action until Barnes had received instructions from the United States. In the evening, Barnes had another long session with the prime minister and Minister of Interior Yugov. The latter agreed to withdraw the large militia detachments that had been thrown around Barnes's villa, and said he would leave only a few unobtrusive agents to guard the place.

In the meantime I spent the evening of May 24 alone with Dr. Dimitrov at the villa. Not knowing that Washington might decide to do, or what sudden steps the militia or the Soviet authorities might take, he was not a little nervous. We closed all the downstairs shutters as soon as it got dark, and then after dinner went upstairs to be out of sight of militia who might enter the grounds. We talked until twelve-thirty, when Barnes finally returned from Sofia with the news that the situation was at least for the time being under control.

In the course of the first two days of negotiations Barnes did not

25. Moser, *Dimitrov*, pp. 215-48, provides a full account of Dimitrov's escape and subsequent events.

know what Washington's response to this incident would be. Finally, on the morning of the 26th, we received the cable that gave the department's view. "Your action," it said, "has the Department's entire approval. We consider that through your prompt notification to the Bulgarian authorities and your action in obtaining their declaration of intention to work out a solution for Dimitrov's safety you have kept within reasonable limits as regards the application of the principle of asylum, and at the same time have placed the ultimate responsibility for the protection of Bulgarian political leaders on the Bulgarian Government where it belongs." [26] Barnes replied on the following day: "I don't believe any more welcome telegram has ever been received in the history of the Service." [27]

In the course of these developments, we learned that Mrs. Dimitrov had been arrested, and severely beaten while under interrogation.When her plight became known, the British made a strong protest, and in about two weeks she was released and interned in her husband's native village with her two children and her mother. The fate of Mara Racheva was more tragic. She had been the private secretary of Dr. Dimitrov, and subsequently of Nikola Petkov, and it was to her apartment that Dr. Dimitrov went first before seeking refuge with a member of the British mission. She was apprehended as soon as his escape was discovered, and was severely tortured. Her death four days later was attributed by the police to suicide by jumping out of a prison window. When her remains were returned to her parents for burial, however, the results of extensive mutilation were quite evident. Apart from the personal tragedy, this incident contributed further to the prevailing atmosphere of terror.

The situation on May 29 could be described roughly as follows: The U.S. view was that (1) the security of Dr. Dimitrov must be guaranteed; (2) Barnes was authorized to take such steps as he saw fit to assure Dr. Dimitrov's security; (3) the matter was considered to be one for negotiation primarily between the United States and Bulgaria; (4) no pledge given by the Bulgarian government for Dr. Dimitrov's safety would be respected; and (5) a decision of the Allied Control Commission would be accepted only if it were reached on a tripartite basis.

The Bulgarian view was that (1) Dr. Dimitrov should be surrendered to the Bulgarian government; (2) if the United States desired to negotiate directly with Bulgaria, then the ordinary rules of international law should apply, and these required the United States to return

26. *FRUS, 1945*, 4:224.
27. Ibid., pp. 230-31.

Dimitrov; and (3) if the United States desired to negotiate with Bulgaria as an occupied country, then the matter should be handled by the Allied Control Commission.

The Russian position was that (1) Dr. Dimitrov was a "defeatist" and that the official Bulgarian position was justified; (2) this was primarily a matter for negotiation between the U. S. and Bulgarian governments; and (3) the Allied Control Commission remained under Soviet authority and could not make decisions on a tripartite basis.

The British mission in Sofia—headed by Maj. Gen. Walter H. Oxley, with William E. Houstoun-Boswall as political representative, reflecting the spirit of the October negotiations in Moscow and aware of the analogous British position in neighboring Greece—was reluctant to challenge Soviet authority and was prepared to accept the single electoral list of the Fatherland Front. The British felt that any approach to the Bulgarian government through the ACC would have to be on a tripartite basis, and that the Soviet representative would clearly not cooperate. London's refusal to grant asylum to Dr. Dimitrov was consistent with this policy.

The issue remained deadlocked at this point throughout June and July and into August. Dr. Dimitrov remained in Barnes's villa, in good health and excellent spirits considering his situation. Barnes frequently had visitors for drinks or meals, and Dr. Dimitrov participated as a permanent guest—like "the man who came to dinner," or rather "to breakfast" in this case.

Meanwhile in May, the Communists had undercut Petkov's leadership of the radical Agrarians by organizing a splinter party led by Alexander Obbov as the officially recognized radical Agrarians. They similarly set up a splinter Social Democratic party under Dimiter Neikov, replacing Cheshmedjiev, who refused to accept Communist predominance. Obbov and Neikov were induced to accept Communist control by a combination of bribes and threats that depended for their effectiveness on the pervasive employment of terror against opponents of exclusive Communist controls.

The single Fatherland Front electoral list remained the central issue, since it guaranteed a plebiscitary form of elections based on a representation of parties negotiated in advance on Communist terms. Announced in early July, the list made provision for ninety-five Communists, ninety-five Agrarians, forty-six members of Zveno, thirty-one Social Democrats, and nine independents, which was a clear enough indication that the Communists expected to do much less well in a free competition. Apart from this basic limitation on free elections, throughout the summer of 1945 opposition political workers, especially Agrarians, were continually harassed by restrictions on newsprint and printing facilities, and by beatings and arrests.

In the midst of these developments, it became clear that the main Soviet objective at this time was to obtain American and British recognition of postwar governments in Romania, Bulgaria, and Hungary. Stalin sent a forceful note in May to Truman and Churchill urging recognition, and pursued the subject vigorously at the Potsdam Conference (July17-August 2). Truman and Byrnes, for their part, sought during several extended confrontations at Potsdam to press for more open electoral procedures and also for a larger role for the American and British representatives on the ACC now that hostilities with Germany were concluded. These issues remained essentially deadlocked at Potsdam, however, and the only significant Soviet concession was agreement to lift restrictions on the access of Western journalists.[28]

Petkov now emerged as the leader of the opposition within the Fatherland Front, and on July 26 he wrote a letter to the prime minister urging postponement of the elections until they could be held on a more democratic basis under Allied control.[29] He was forthwith forced to resign from the cabinet, and in mid-August he was soon followed by the remaining independent Agrarians and Social Democrats in the Fatherland Front. For Petkov this was a critical step. Both his father and his brother had been prominent political leaders who had lost their lives by assassination. Perhaps because of this family history, he himself had not been noted for aggressive leadership. In 1944 he had been convinced that cooperation with the Communists would be possible without sacrificing Agrarian independence, but during the winter of 1944-45 he reached the conclusion that this would not be possible. When on May 9 the Communists replaced him with Obbov as leader of the radical Agrarians (as they had replaced Dimitrov with Petkov in January), he felt that he had no choice but to oppose Communist policies. Thenceforth, until his execution in September 1947, he used all the resources at his disposal to prevent unilateral domination by the Communists.

Events moved rapidly as the election day approached. On August 13, Secretary of State James F. Byrnes instructed Barnes to convey the American criticisms of the electoral procedure to the Bulgarian government, and on August 18 Byrnes issued a public statement to the same effect. It asserted that the United States was prepared to

28. Curtis H. Martin, "United States Diplomacy and the Issue of Representative Government in the Former German Satellite States 1943-1946: A Study of Foreign Policy and the Foreign Policy Process" (Ph.D. diss., Tufts University, 1974), pp. 234-311, provides a detailed account of the discussion at Potsdam of the complementary issues of free elections and recognition.

29. The text of Petkov's letter is in FRUS, Conference of Berlin (Potsdam), 1945 (Washington: Government Printing Office, 1960), 2:724-25; and for related comments see pp. 722-23, 728-32.

establish diplomatic relations "with a provisional government which
would be representative of all important elements of democratic
opinion," but added that it was not satisfied that the elections being
prepared would ensure effective participation of all democratic elements.[30] The British now took a similar position, and pressure was
exerted on the Soviet authorities by the regents and by influential
Bulgarians outside the government to postpone the elections. On
August 14 the USSR had strengthened its support of the Fatherland
Front by granting diplomatic recognition to the Bulgarian government.
On August 22, however, Foreign Minister Stainov held a press conference at which he stated that it was up to the ACC to determine
whether the elections should be postponed. Taking advantage of this
hint, Crane and Oxley pressed successfully for a meeting of the ACC
on the following day, at which they presented a comprehensive proposal outlining the conditions under which acceptable postponed elections might be held. The political representatives then joined the
generals from midnight to 5:15 A.M. After repeated statements of their
opposing positions, the meeting ended in a deadlock and Biriuzov
said that he would have to consult Moscow.

   At midnight on August 24, Barnes was able to telegraph Washington
that the "battle of elections" had been won. The decision was doubtless made in Moscow, but the form it took was a request from the
Bulgarian government to the Allied Control Commission for permission to postpone elections. Barnes now recommended that the United
States award Biriuzov a decoration, and that arrangements be completed for a Bulgarian political representative to be sent to the United
States. The Bulgarian government was now in a state of sufficient
shock that it agreed to let Dr. Dimitrov leave the country, and on
September 5 he departed with his wife for Italy. Their two children
were left behind with their maternal grandmother.

   It is ironic that on the same August 24 on which the elections were
postponed, Washington informed Barnes that it was not making representations to Moscow in regard to the elections and could not support the proposals for postponement that Crane and Barnes had made
to the Allied Control Commission. The department had not contemplated requesting postponement of the elections, and felt that "the
formation of a representative democratic government in Bulgaria
is a matter for Bulgarians to undertake in absence of pertinent provisions in armistice not for consideration by ACC." It added that
Barnes had exceeded his authority, and should have consulted the
department before proposing postponement.[31] This was certainly

30. Ibid., 4: 284-94, 302-6.
31. Ibid., pp. 308-9.

a sharp reprimand, and in his reply Barnes referred to it as a "censure." He explained his action on the ground that postponement had seemed to him to follow from the logic of his instructions, and that "obviously the purpose of expressing the view of the U.S. government was to forestall rigged elections and formation of a government that [the] U.S. could not recognize."[32] This telegram again crossed with one expressing the department's gratification at the postponement of elections and authorizing Barnes to convey to the Bulgarian government the American hope that this decision "When appropriately implemented . . . will ensure to the Bulgarian people full freedom of choice in the establishment of a representative government."[33]

THE ETHRIDGE MISSION

The postponement of the elections scheduled for August 26 revealed to the Communist party in Bulgaria that Soviet support had its limits, and it now recognized that some concessions would have to be made to the American position. New elections were scheduled for November 18, and the electoral procedure was revised to permit opposition candidates to run on separate party lists. Greater freedom was also permitted to the opposition press, although the government retained its monopoly of the radio.

Meanwhile the Council of Foreign Ministers had held its first meeting in London (September 11 to October 3, 1945), and reached a deadlock on the question of implementing the Yalta declaration in Bulgaria and Romania.[34] In the course of these discussions Molotov maintained that Byrnes was not well informed about conditions in these countries. Byrnes also apparently felt that American public opinion was insufficiently informed to give him the support he would need if recognition were to become a major issue. He therefore announced the appointment on October 10 of Mark Ethridge, publisher of the *Louisville Courier-Journal* and a liberal Democrat, to make a fresh appraisal in Bulgaria and Romania of the extent to which the conditions of the Yalta declaration were being met. Ethridge had no knowledge of southeastern Europe, but with his journalistic experience and keen mind he soon proved to be an able investigator. He never mispronounced a name once he heard it, and he quickly grasped the frequently subtle differences between groups and individuals. As a publisher he had had long experience in negotiating with labor unions, and he had a sympathetic understanding of left-wing attitudes.

32. Ibid., pp. 311-12.
33. Ibid., pp. 312-13.
34. The London meeting and its aftermath are discussed in Martin, *United States Diplomacy*, pp. 365-449.

I had left Bulgaria with Barnes and Dimitrov on September 5, and was on the point of resuming my academic career at Princeton University. When the State Department asked me to delay my resignation and accompany Ethridge on his mission, however, it looked like an offer that I could not refuse. We covered 13,000 miles between October 18 and December 3, spending two weeks in Bulgaria, one in the Soviet Union, and ten days in Romania. In Bulgaria, Ethridge talked with some forty-five political leaders, and with the Soviet and British representatives. The inteviews were freely conducted, and included all the leading members of the government and the opposition. The opposition leaders reported the extensive use of violence by the militia in the recent electoral campaign, and also the methods that might be used in a future election to stuff the ballot boxes.

In two lengthy talks, Nikola Petkov defended his position that he would not participate in elections unless the Fatherland Front parties could run on separate lists. He also insisted that the Communists relinquish the Ministries of Interior and Justice in a reconstructed government before the elections. He did not believe that the Communists would be able to govern the country without the independent participation of the other Fatherland Front parties. He based this view partly on the international situation, no doubt influenced by the recent postponement of elections, and also on his belief that the Communists did not have enough popular support to govern the country alone. Petkov recognized, at the same time, that the United States did not intend to press for the postponement of the new elections scheduled for November 18. Since there was no chance of the Communists meeting his conditions, he would not compete in the new elections.

Prime Minister Georgiev, for his part, pointed out in his talks with Ethridge that the electoral procedure had been revised since the postponed elections to permit opposition parties, instead of individual opposition candidates, to run on separate tickets—although the Fatherland Front itself would run again on a single ticket, including the dissident Agrarians and Social Democrats. The prime minister felt that he had achieved some success in getting the Communists to take their governmental responsibilities more seriously, and implied that his efforts would be jeopardized if Petkov and the other Fatherland Front leaders insisted on challenging the government rather than helping him exert constant pressure on it from within. He acknowledged that Petkov was an exceptional personality in Bulgarian politics because of his great integrity, but he strongly disagreed with his tactics. Other Zveno leaders also advocated a policy of gradualism in containing the Communists, and seemed to feel that this goal could be achieved better by administrative means than through an elected parliament.

In some ways the most interesting talk was with the veteran Communist leader Georgi Dimitrov. He returned to Bulgaria on the eve of November 7, 1945, the twenty-eighth anniversary of the Russian Revolution, for his first visit since 1923. In the course of the past year he had been sending instructions to his Bulgarian colleagues by telegram, some of which were published in the press, and had come to be known as "Telegram George." He was reported to be in poor health, and indeed his color seemed very high. He looked like an aging actor at the end of a long performance, who had not yet had time to remove his makeup. He was accompanied by an unidentified individual who never left his side. We assumed that he was a Soviet watchdog.

Dimitrov maintained firmly that he considered one area of discussion closed. There could be no further postponement of elections, and no reorganization of the Fatherland Front government before the currently scheduled elections were held. He foresaw the possibility, however, that when the government was reorganized after the forthcoming elections the admission of opposition Agrarians and Social Democrats might be discussed. Under such circumstances, however, the opposition would have to come to terms with the government rather than vice versa. In reviewing the recent history of the Fatherland Front, Dimitrov also sought to assure Ethridge that the Communists had no intention of monopolizing political power and wished instead to cooperate with the other parties within the framework of the Fatherland Front. Ethridge, for his part, reiterated the conclusion he had reached in the course of his visit that the Fatherland Front was no longer representative in the sense that it had been in September 1944, and that the forthcoming elections were not likely to change the situation.

Among the numerous social events in the course of the mission was a lunch tendered by Mr. and Mrs. Barnes for Generals Biriuzov and Cherepanov, Prime Minister Georgiev, Foreign Minister Stainov, Soviet Political Representative Kirsanov, and their spouses. This event was notable not only for its relaxed and friendly atmosphere, but also for a menu that included two roast suckling pigs sent to Barnes by peasants from the Pleven district in gratitude for his efforts on behalf of Dr. Dimitrov.

In the meantime the electoral campaign was proceeding without the participation of the radical Agrarians and Social Democrats. It was clear that it would not result in a government that the United States could recognize if it continued to be guided by the Yalta formula of one that was "broadly representative of all democratic elements of the population." Adherence to this formula called for reorganization of the Fatherland Front government, either as a result of elections or by negotiation, to include the radical Agrarian and Social Democratic leaders who had resigned in August.

It was clear that the local situation was now firmly deadlocked, and that no change was likely without an initiative from Moscow. Barnes now came up with the suggestion that Ethridge himself go to Moscow to report his findings to the Soviet government. Secretary Byrnes gave his approval to this idea, and instructed Ethridge to recommend that the Yalta powers "take appropriate steps immediately (1) to provide for the submission to the electorate of lists of opposition candidates, postponing the election scheduled for Nov. 18, for sufficient time to accomplish this purpose, and (2) in the meantime to reorganize the Government by the inclusion of opposition representatives. A necessary condition for the achievement of a basis for this course would appear to be the reorganization of the militia to preclude its use as an instrument of force and intimidation."[35]

Ethridge flew to Moscow on November 11, and two days later had a long talk with Andrei Vyshinsky, vice-commissar of foreign affairs. Ambassador Harriman accompanied us, and the interpreter on the American side was Robert C. Tucker of the embassy staff—with whom I had studied Russian at Harvard University before the war and who was later to become my colleague at Princeton. The exchange was pleasant enough, but it did not bring the two sides any closer together. After listening to Ethridge's extensive report on the ways in which representative government was being restricted in Bulgaria, Vyshinsky replied that the reports he had received presented a different picture. He had no reason to believe that the Fatherland Front was not representative or that the elections would not be free. In response to a direct question, Vyshinsky replied that postponement of the elections would be an unjustifiable intervention in Bulgarian affairs. If the Bulgarian government should ask for Soviet advice on this question, however, the matter would be considered in the light of existing circumstances.[36]

Ethridge now recommended that the State Department issue another statement such as that of August 18, expressing the view that there was no reason to believe that elections held under existing conditions would represent the free expression of the popular will, and this was done on November 14.[37] This time the elections were held as planned, and the Fatherland Front won the overwhelming victory that was anticipated in view of the absence of opposition

35. *FRUS, 1945*, 4:364.
36. Ibid., pp. 374-75.
37. Ibid., pp. 376-77.

candidates. In the meantime Ethridge made a further recommendation from Moscow on November 14, along lines already discussed with Barnes, that in the event the elections were held, the United States should press for a reorganization of the government to include the leaders who had resigned in the course of the spring, neutralization of the Ministries of Interior and Justice, and the holding of new elections with single or separate lists as the parties might wish. He also suggested that the national assembly issuing from the November 18 elections should have a limited competence pending the reorganization of the government.[38] It is perhaps significant that Ethridge's trip from Sofia to Moscow had been in a plush Soviet plane, but he was sent back to Bucharest via Odessa in a crowded bucket-seat transport plane.

After ten days in Romania we returned to Washington on December 4 to report to Byrnes. My own direct participation in these events came to an end shortly thereafter. I stayed on in the department's Division of Southeastern European Affairs into February, when I resumed my teaching position at Princeton.

Ethridge's report to Byrnes included separate accounts of the developments in the two countries he had visited, a "Summary Report on Soviet Policy in Rumania and Bulgaria," dated December 7, and a briefer letter to Byrnes, dated the following day, intended for publication.[39] Ethridge had a lengthy talk with Byrnes on December 8 and on the following day received a phone call from the secretary to explain that he had decided not to publish the letter but instead would take it with him to the forthcoming meeting of the Council of Foreign Ministers in Moscow. Ethridge agreed to this change in plans.

The subsequent development of events can best be understood in terms of Bulgaria's relation to the changing international context. When he became secretary of state in July 1945, Byrnes had inherited a situation arising from the adoption of two related but conflicting policies during the preceding months. One was the short-term policy, initiated by the United States and the United Kingdom in Italy, favoring the administration of liberated satellite states by the armies of the countries that occupied them at the end of the war. The other was the longer term policy of a tripartite sponsorship of free elections leading to representative governments along the lines of the Yalta formula. The conflict between these two policies, in view of the differences in ideology and interests between the USSR and the Western democracies,

38. Ibid., pp. 377-78.
39. The latter two documents are published in ibid., 5:633-41; see also Mark Ethridge and C. E. Black, "Negotiating on the Balkans, 1945-1947," in *Negotiating with the Russians*, ed. R. Dennett and J. E. Johnson (Boston: World Peace Foundation, 1951), pp. 171-206, for a more general account of the mission.

were in the early postwar months treated as isolated episodes subject to local settlement. With the termination of hostilities in the Pacific, however, political leaders felt increasing pressure to conclude the peace treaties and move on to postwar reconstruction.

In this atmosphere the difficulties experienced with tripartite cooperation made the alternative of compromise by division into spheres of influence more attractive. In the course of the American-Soviet negotiations preparatory to the December meeting of the Council of Foreign Ministers, the USSR had demanded a more active role in the control arrangements for occupied Japan and this question became linked to that of Romania and Bulgaria. The USSR could not very well be excluded completely from a voice in occupation policy in Japan in view of American complaints about ACC procedures in Romania and Bulgaria, but on the other hand there was no need to give them greater voice than we had received in the Balkan countries. This linkage argued for accepting Russian dominance in the Balkans in return for a similar U.S. role in Japan.[40]

A policy of compromise in the Balkans was strongly urged at this time by the British. The view was advanced by Sir Orme G. Sargent, British deputy undersecretary for foreign affairs, that the best approach to breaking the stalemate in Romania and Bulgaria would be a negotiated "dilution" of the existing governments. Further freedom within these countries might then be achieved by "nagging" to a point where recognition would be possible. Once peace treaties were signed, Soviet troops would be withdrawn and this in turn might lead to a relaxation of Communist controls.[41]

Reorganization of the Bulgarian government had already been broached, as an alternative to or in connection with new elections with separate lists, as a solution to the stalemate. Byrnes now seized on this device. Publication of the Ethridge report would have made such a compromise more difficult, so instead he took it to Moscow to show to Molotov and Stalin.

Byrnes's position was made all the more difficult by the division within the American foreign policy establishment between the advocates of compromise and firmness. Those who advocated compromise were the heirs of the New Deal and Atlantic Charter themes of Roosevelt's policies. For them cooperation with the Russians, especially in view of the forthcoming first meeting of the United Nations General Assembly scheduled for January 1946, was a higher priority than the form of government in the countries bordering Russia in southeastern

40. Martin, *United States Diplomacy*, p. 480.
41. *FRUS, 1945*, 4:405-6, 409-10.

Europe. In this view Byrnes was strongly supported by his principal assistant, Benjamin V. Cohen, now serving as counselor of the Department of State, by Joseph E. Davies, former ambassador to the USSR, and by other New Deal liberals. The liberal branch of the establishment found it difficult to believe that Russia was interfering in Balkan affairs to the detriment of free elections. While still in Washington, Ethridge was invited by Eugene Meyer to meet with a group of liberals, including Walter Lippmann, Lyndon Johnson, and Estes Kefauver. They found his account of his findings quite contrary to their expectations, and seemed to wonder if the liberal editor had not turned into a red-baiter.[42]

The policy of firmness—of resisting Soviet pressure on specific issues of principle—was favored by President Truman and had as its strongest supporter Admiral Leahy, who had continued in his role as chief of staff to the commander in chief. This view was also held by Dean Acheson, undersecretary of state, by career Foreign Service officers with Soviet experience, by a substantial majority of leaders in the Congress, and by most of the press.[43]

In preparing for the December meeting of the Council of Foreign Ministers, the department's Office of European Affairs proposed terms for Bulgaria essentially along the lines of Ethridge's telegram from Moscow of November 14. This proposal was watered down by the secretary, however, before presentation to the conference. He proposed that a reorganization of the Bulgarian government be "suggested" by the three powers; that the reorganized government be pledged to hold free elections within six months; and that the national assembly elected in November should adopt a restricted legislative program pending the new elections. If these conditions were met, the United States would agree to recognize the reorganized government before the elections were held. There was no mention of neutralizing the Ministries of Interior and Justice and, more striking, no reference to the Yalta declaration.[44]

This proposal was further diluted in the course of Byrnes's direct negotiations in Moscow with Molotov and Stalin, to whom he showed the Ethridge report as a means of conveying American objections to recognition. The final compromise reached on December 27, at the very end of the conference, provided that the Soviet government alone would give "friendly advice" to the Bulgarian government regarding the desirability of including in the Fatherland Front cabinet "two

42. Letter from Ethridge to author, February 13, 1951.
43. Martin, *United States Diplomacy*, pp. 489-504.
44. *FRUS, 1945*, 2:700-701.

representatives of other democratic groups, who (a) are truly representative of the groups of the parties that are not participating in the government, and (b) are really suitable and will work loyally with the Government." When the United States and the United Kingdom were convinced that this had been accomplished, they would recognize the reorganized government.[45] At the same time, among many other issues decided at the conference, the USSR agreed to accept no more than a nominal role in the occupation arrangements for Japan.

Most of Byrnes's advisers at Moscow were opposed to the extent of the concessions involved, and in Washington it was widely regarded as a sellout. President Truman himself was deeply disturbed by this outcome. While this negotiation was only one of many issues that divided the president and his secretary of state, it played its role in the replacement of Byrnes by George C. Marshall a year later. Among Byrnes's few supporters, interestingly enough, was Ethridge, who wrote in the *Louisville Courier Journal* on January 2 that if the Bulgarian government followed through on the Soviet advice in good faith it would lead to a more representative government.[46]

As it turned out, the Moscow compromise proved to be impossible to implement. Petkov and his colleagues in opposition refused to accept positions in the government unless the Ministries of Interior and Justice were removed from Communist control, new elections were held with separate party lists, and other steps were taken to relieve the political repression. Byrnes flirted for a while with a proposal to recognize the Bulgarian government if it simply pledged to hold new elections, with no other conditions attached. He was dissuaded from this by his advisers, however, and U.S. policy now reverted to its pre-Moscow position of simply withholding recognition.[47]

A reorganization of the Fatherland Front government in March 1946 strengthened the influence of the Communists, and in September a republic was proclaimed after a referendum. New elections were held in October, and this time the combined opposition ran on a separate ticket and won 101 of the 465 seats in the new assembly. Considering the control exercised by the Communists over all aspects of electoral procedure, and Georgi Dimitrov's announcement on the eve of the elections that all those who voted for the opposition would be regarded as traitors, this was a remarkable achievement. Petkov and his colleagues now continued their attacks on the government as members

45. Ibid., p. 822; a full account of the Moscow negotiations is available in Martin, *United States Diplomacy*, pp. 539-65.
46. Martin, *United States Diplomacy*, pp. 567-72.
47. Ibid., pp. 591-609.

of the assembly under the protection of their parliamentary immunity, but with a government now headed by Dimitrov himself the Communists were prepared to make no further concessions to improve their chances for recognition.

Byrnes now became reconciled to recognition of the existing government, and went ahead with the negotiation of the peace treaties with Italy, Romania, Bulgaria, Hungary, and Finland. He resigned as secretary of state on January 7, and was succeeded by George C. Marshall. The peace treaties were signed in February 1947, and on June 5 they were ratified by the U.S. Senate. On the following day Petkov was arrested, following removal of his parliamentary immunity, and charged with plotting to overthrow the government.

Meanwhile Barnes had returned to Washington in April. Upon learning on June 9 of the final decision of Secretary Marshall to recognize the Bulgarian government following the coming into force of the peace treaty and to deny Barnes's request that he return to Bulgaria to work for the release of Petkov, Barnes decided to resign from the Foreign Service.[48] Petkov's trial lasted from August 5 to 15, and he received a death sentence, which he appealed. The Bulgarian peace treaty came into force on September 15. On September 19 the United States informed Bulgaria of its intention to establish diplomatic relations. On September 23 Petkov was executed after his appeal had been denied. On October 1 the United States granted formal recognition.[49]

RETROSPECTIVE REAPPRAISAL

The foregoing has been written essentially as the events appeared at the time, on the basis of personal recollections enriched by the subsequent publication of contemporary documents. There has been no mention of the Cold War because the term was not used by us at the time, and no one suspected that we were involved in "the origins of the Cold War."

With the benefit of hindsight, some of the controversial issues relating to these events now deserve our attention: (1) Did the United

48. *FRUS, 1947,* 4:163-64.

49. *The Trial of Nikola D. Petkov* (Sofia: Ministry of Information and Arts, 1947), is an official record of the proceedings. Dr. G. M. Dimitrov published an appraisal of his Agrarian colleague in "Bravest Democrat of All," *Saturday Evening Post* 220 (December 6, 1947):28-29, 208-10. See also the account of these events by the acting American representative in Sofia during Barnes's absence, John E. Horner, "The Ordeal of Nikola Petkov and the Consolidation of Communist Rule in Bulgaria," *Survey* 20 (Winter 1947): 75-83; and Michael Padev, *Dimitrov Wastes No Bullets. Nikola Petkov: The Test Case* (London: Eyre and Spottiswoode, 1948).

States use "atomic diplomacy" in Bulgaria? (2) Did the American representatives in Bulgaria misrepresent the local political situation in their reports to Washington? (3) Did American officials, especially Barnes, conspire with Nikola Petkov in a counterrevolutionary policy against the Fatherland Front? (4) What was the United States seeking to accomplish in Bulgaria, and why did it fail? (5) How did the Cold War originate, as seen from the Bulgarian experience?

(1) It has been alleged that the United States resorted to "atomic diplomacy" in 1945 and that, more specifically, the successful use of atomic bombs against Japan in early August gave Truman and Byrnes new confidence and encouraged them to demand the postponement of the Bulgarian elections. This view has been presented in its most direct form by Gar Alperovitz, who notes that Byrnes's communication of August 13 to Bulgarian political leaders criticizing the electoral procedures (but not demanding postponement of the elections, as Alperovitz asserts) occurred four days after the bombing of Nagasaki.[50] Alperovitz concludes his account of the events leading to the postponement of the elections scheduled for August 26 with the comment that the atomic bomb represented "a threat." The American success in getting the elections postponed, he says, "could only be attributed to the atomic bomb." He argues further that the atomic bomb "determined much of Truman's shift to a tough policy aimed at forcing Soviet acquiescence to American plans for Eastern and Central Europe."[51]

The only evidence that Alperovitz cites to support his allegation that the atomic bomb brought the postponement of the elections is the timing of the note of August 13. To the best of my recollection, the atom bomb played no role in United States policy toward Bulgaria, and the timing of this and other communications in the course of the election crisis was not related to the deployment of the nuclear weapons against Japan.

A more balanced view of the role of nuclear weapons in American policy at this time is represented by the work of Martin J. Sherwin, based on recently declassified documents. It is his conclusion that news of the successful test on July 16 made President Truman more self-confident and assertive at the Potsdam Conference. The president and his colleagues anticipated the U.S. possession of the bomb would influence Soviet policy, and were surprised when it had no perceptible effect. At no time, however, was there any intention of using the bomb

50. Gar Alperovitz, *Atomic Diplomacy: Hiroshima and Potsdam* (New York: Random House, 1965), pp. 211-12.
51. Ibid., pp. 216, 13.

as a "threat."[52]

Barnes reported on August 24 that "we are not afraid of atomic bomb" was one of the electoral slogans employed by the Fatherland Front,[53] but I have seen no evidence that U.S. possession of the bomb had any influence on Bulgarian or Soviet thinking. Subsequent accounts of these events published in Bulgaria and the USSR make no mention of a nuclear "threat." As already noted, U.S. bargaining power at this time was based not on the bomb but on the withholding of diplomatic recognition.

(2) It has also been alleged, as part of a general criticism of American postwar diplomatic reporting, that Barnes misrepresented the political situation by portraying the "Agrarian party" as devoted to civil liberties and the Communist party as the enemy of democracy.[54] Apart from the fact that there was no "Agrarian party," but numerous Agrarian factions, only the most radical of which was included in the Fatherland Front, readers of the foregoing account will recognize that this allegation greatly distorts the situation.

What is significant in this context is that Barnes and the rest of the U.S. government did accept the political groups included in the Fatherland Front when it seized power in September 1944 as "broadly representative of all democratic elements of the population." Indeed, U.S. policy might well have been criticized for not including in its definition of "all democratic elements" the members of the pro-Western Muraviev government of September 2-9, 1944, who were more traditionally "bourgeois" (if one wishes to use that term) than the more populist followers of Petkov. The issue to which Barnes's dispatches and Ethridge's report were addressed was not whether the Fatherland Front as originally constituted was representative, but whether the prevailing electoral procedures would permit a free choice among its constituent parties.

Barnes was certainly more of an activist than most American diplomats. He had been appointed as vice-consul in Patras a few months after graduating from Grinnell College in 1919, and he had served in Smyrna during the Greek-Turkish war, and at the Lausanne Conference, as well as in Sofia in 1930-34. Strongly anti-German and pro-French, it had been his sad duty to close the American embassy in Paris in

52. Martin J. Sherwin, *A World Destroyed: The Atomic Bomb and the Grand Alliance* (New York: Knopf, 1975), chaps. 8 and 9.

53. *FRUS, 1945,* 4:308.

54. Ernest R. May, *"Lessons" of the Past: The Use and Misuse of History in American Foreign Policy* (New York: Oxford, 1973), pp. 27-29; and more recently Martin Weil, *A Pretty Good Club: The Founding Fathers and the U.S. Foreign Service* (New York: Norton, 1978), pp. 195-97.

May 1941, and he was critical of his government's support of the
Vichy government. He believed that the Yalta declaration meant what
it said, and pressed for nothing more than a government representing
the political forces that had joined together to form the Fatherland
Front coalition in 1944. He was in agreement with Washington when
the decision was finally made in the winter of 1946-47 to recognize
Bulgaria upon the negotiation of the peace treaty. He saw this not as
a surrender, but as an opportunity under changed conditions to continue to press for a more liberal political regime in Bulgaria. He also
hoped that Bulgaria's need for economic aid might be used as bargaining power.[55] Only in the summer of 1947, when the State Department
decided not to alter its timetable of recognition despite the arrest of
Petkov, did Barnes come to feel that pragmatism had been carried
too far.

Barnes set forth his views in a lecture at the National War College
in June 1947, in which he emphasized that under existing conditions
Bulgarian foreign policy should be "closely integrated" with that of the
USSR. "It is also clear," he added, ". . . that any government in which
the Communists did not play an important part could not possibly
last." At the same time, he argued, since most Bulgarians did not
support the Communists, the United States should seek to bring about
a state of affairs in which the Communists and other Fatherland Front
parties could coexist in what would in effect be a coalition government.[56] It was toward this end that he urged American support for
Petkov and his colleagues.

There is evidence that Secretary of State Byrnes was distrustful
of professional diplomats generally and that both he and Benjamin V.
Cohen, his principal personal assistant in these matters, thought that
Barnes was too sympathetic to the dissident members of the Fatherland Front.[57] Indeed, one of the reasons for sending Ethridge to the
Balkans was to make an independent evaluation of the situation there.
Byrnes accepted Ethridge's findings, however, and the compromises
he finally agreed to were based not on doubts about the facts, but on
the pressures he felt to conclude the peace treaties and to reach an
accommodation with the USSR on the larger issues of postwar policy.

(3) Did American officials, especially Barnes, conspire with Nikola
Petkov in a counterrevolutionary policy against the Fatherland Front?

When Petkov was brought to trial in 1947, he was accused of organizing a conspiracy that aimed at overthrowing the Fatherland Front

55. *FRUS, 1947*, 4:145-48.
56. Barnes, "Current Situation in Bulgaria," pp. 8-9.
57. Martin, *United States Diplomacy*, pp. 225, 230.

government and handing over power to a Petkov government.[58] The accounts of these events published in Bulgaria in recent years continue to describe Petkov and other defectors from the Fatherland Front with such epithets as "anti-democratic," "anti-revolutionary," "fascist remnants," and "traitors" working in collaboration with the United States and the United Kingdom.[59]

Certainly Petkov and his colleagues expected support from the American and British members of the ACC in their efforts to get free elections—that is, elections free from police terror and permitting parties to run on separate lists. They counted on this support in 1945, however, not as the result of personal commitments from the American representatives in Sofia but because of the goals set forth in the Yalta declaration and such indications of U.S. determination to achieve these goals as were reflected in its refusal to accept the Fatherland Front's electoral procedures and the protection it afforded to Dr. Dimitrov.

Petkov broke with the Fatherland Front in July 1945 because he came to realize that the Communists were intent on preventing him and his colleagues from exerting any influence on government policy. During the Second World War, Petkov had been one of the principal Agrarian advocates of cooperation with the Communists, and he was closely associated with them and Zveno leaders in the seizure of power in September 1944. Throughout 1945 he believed that Western pressure on the USSR, and popular support within the country, would make it possible for him to seek an independent position for the Agrarians within the Fatherland Front coalition. The Zveno members of the Fatherland Front, as noted earlier, thought that Petkov had made a mistake in resigning and that Communist influence could best be limited by pressure from within the government.

In reflecting on these developments it is important to recall how the balance of influence between the U.S. and the USSR appeared in 1945. From the perspective of Soviet policy, the postponement of the

58. *Trial of Nikola D. Petkov*, p. 40.

59. Voin Bozhinov, *Zashtitata na natsionalnata nezavisimost na Bulgaria, 1944-1947* [The defense of the national independence of Bulgaria, 1944-1947] (Sofia: Bulgarian Academy of Sciences, 1962); K. Kukov, *Razgrom na burzhuaznata opozitsiia, 1944-1947* [The rout of the bourgeois opposition, 1944-1947] (Sofia: Bulgarian Communist party, 1966); Ilcho Dimitrov, *Godini na prelom: Tri ocherka iz nai-novata bulgarska istoriia* [Years of crisis: Three sketches from contemporary Bulgarian history] (Sofia: Dimitrov Communist Youth League, 1969); and Mito Isusov, "Otechestveniiat Front i opitite za deformirane na novata parlamentarna sistema v Bulgariia, 1945-1946" [The Fatherland Front and the efforts to undermine the new parliamentary system in Bulgaria, 1945-1946], *Istoricheski Pregled* 30 (July-August 1974):160-88.

elections in August reflected their interest in gaining American and British recognition of the Bulgarian government. The essential American bargaining power at this point was the threat of withholding recognition. The USSR was willing to compromise in some measure to achieve recognition.

This was not the first time, from the information then available to us, that the Soviet authorities had shown themselves sensitive to British and American pressure in regard to Bulgaria. When the Soviet troops first entered Bulgaria in September 1944, General Biriuzov had advised the Bulgarian army to remain in the occupied Greek territory of Thrace, but Moscow later ordered withdrawal at British and American insistence. Bulgaria and Yugoslavia had made plans in January 1945 for federation, and later for alliance, but the Soviet government vetoed these plans as unacceptable to the United States and the United Kingdom.[60] When Dr. Dimitrov sought asylum, the Soviet authorities were unwilling to take him by force from Barnes's villa. Biriuzov did suggest to the Bulgarian government that it request such action, but the latter declined to take the initiative, likewise for fear of antagonizing the United States.

After the announcement of the Moscow compromise in December 1945 it was clear that American and British policy was seeking to retreat from the objectives set forth at Yalta, but Petkov's refusal to enter the Fatherland Front government on its terms led to the failure of this effort. In the course of a meeting with Byrnes in January 1946, Vyshinsky charged specifically that Barnes was advising the opposition in Bulgaria not to accept the Moscow compromise. He added that his government "found it difficult to understand why a U.S. representative should endeavor to sabotage an agreement that had been reached by the Secretary of State in Moscow. . . ."[61] Byrnes replied that he would look into the matter, but in fact he supported Barnes in not seeking to bring pressure on Petkov and his colleagues. In a personal message to Barnes shortly thereafter, the secretary said that "we do not regard the decision at Moscow as requiring us to urge the abandonment of the opposition's principles."[62] At this point not only Byrnes but also President Truman and most of those concerned with foreign policy in Washington were firmly opposed to recognition.

(4) This brings us to the fourth question: what was the United States seeking to accomplish in Bulgaria, and why did it fail?

The remarks of Barnes in 1947 are as clear a statement as one is

60. *FRUS, 1945*, 4:250-51.
61. *FRUS, 1946*, 6:60-61.
62. Ibid., p. 66.

likely to find in the contemporary record of American aims in Bulgaria: a government that took into account the priority of Soviet security interests and the related role of the Communist party, but that also provided for the freely elected representation of other parties. Of the countries bordering on the USSR, Finland is the only one in which such a state of affairs was brought about. The compromise reached in Finland was not an achievement of American policy, but it provides evidence that the type of solution sought by the United States in Bulgaria was at least theoretically within the realm of possibility.

There was a dramatic reduction in American objectives in Bulgaria during the period under consideration—from the goal of "the earliest possible establishment through free elections of governments responsive to the will of the people," as enunciated in the Yalta declaration in February 1945, to the granting of diplomatic recognition in October 1947 to a government fully dominated by the Communist party.

In the case of the Yalta declaration, one need not assume either that Roosevelt did not intend it to have any practical effect or that he expected it to be literally implemented. Like other declarations of this kind, it was intended not as a formal commitment but as a statement of goals that policy makers should seek to achieve. It is quite clear that at no time did Roosevelt believe that the United States should take direct responsibility for its implementation. He left the main burden of the final negotiation of the Bulgarian armistice to the United Kingdom and the USSR, and he let a British officer sign it on behalf of the United States.

In the course of preparing for the Yalta conference Roosevelt, as noted above, explicitly rejected the proposal that a four-power High Commission for Liberated Europe be established to implement the Yalta declaration. After his death in March 1945, changing American official attitudes toward the Yalta declaration reflected the prevailing political confusion and uncertainty. In the first three months of his administration, Truman was inclined to view the Yalta declaration as a contract that should be fulfilled to the letter. Byrnes, following his appointment as secretary of state in June, sought to implement what he and his New Deal associates believed to be Roosevelt's policy of accommodation with the USSR. A further turning point came in the spring of 1946, when a series of confrontations with the USSR led to a general consensus in the American foreign policy establishment that accommodation was not feasible. The issue now was no longer one of implementing the Yalta declaration but of building a barrier to what was perceived as an aggressive Soviet threat to Greece, Turkey, and Iran.

By this time, U.S. policy was in effect prepared to trade what remained of its influence in Bulgaria, and also in Romania and Hungary, for a predominant role in Italy and Japan. When the question of Japan was raised at Potsdam and at the meeting of the Council of Foreign Ministers in Moscow in December 1945, Byrnes had found it difficult to insist on a strong position in Bulgaria while seeking to limit severely the Soviet role in Japan.

The main goal of U.S. policy in southeastern Europe by 1946 was to contain what was perceived as an expansionist Soviet policy, and it was generally agreed that the best place to take a stand was at the line separating Anglo-American and Soviet occupation forces at the end of the war. The main reason advanced for Senate ratification of the Bulgarian peace treaty in June 1947 was the security of the eastern Mediterranean. The treaty required the withdrawal of Soviet troops from Bulgaria within ninety days, and to this extent the pressure on Greece would be relieved.[63] The United States had by now assumed the role in Greece originally allotted to the United Kingdom, and the spheres of influence that Roosevelt had rejected when negotiated by Churchill and Stalin in October 1944 as a short-term accommodation were now accepted by American policy, in practice if not in theory, for an indefinite term.

(5) Finally, what light do these Bulgarian events shed on the origins of the Cold War? The foregoing suggests the conclusion that the Cold War arose from the long-term differences in the ideology and national interest of the United States and its Western Allies, and of the USSR.

The view that the USSR started the Cold War rests on the assumption that at Yalta the Western Allies and the USSR negotiated a binding agreement, in effect a treaty, the terms of which were clearly understood by both parties; and that the USSR subsequently violated the agreement. But this is not what happened. In the case of Bulgaria, the USSR certainly violated the Yalta declaration if one regards it as a binding agreement and interprets "democratic elections" from a Western point of view. There is no reason to believe, however, that Stalin any more than Roosevelt or Churchill regarded it as a formal contract, or that he accepted the Western view of democracy. The Yalta declaration was in fact quite casually adopted and no effort was made to negotiate a clear understanding as to its meaning.

The view that the United States started the Cold War rests on the assumption that it wished for political and economic reasons to exert a

---

63. *Executive Sessions of the Senate Foreign Relations Committee*, vol. 1, *Eightieth Congress, First and Second Sessions, 1947-1948* (Washington, D.C., 1976), p. 45.

predominant influence in the countries of Eastern Europe, and pressed for the adoption of the Yalta declaration in the expectation that free elections would bring pro-Western governments to power. In fact, a lack of carefully considered long-term policies in regard to Eastern Europe was the dominant feature of the American posture in 1945. The available evidence supports the view that neither Roosevelt nor Truman wished to become involved in any significant way in political and economic developments in these countries. At best, U.S. policy in Eastern Europe was one of moderating exclusive Soviet influence to the extent possible with limited means, mainly by withholding recognition. At worst, it was simply a "nonpolicy," an exercise in *"word* politics."

There remains the third alternative: the Cold War arose as a result of long-term differences in ideology and national interest, rather than being "started" by either side. It is true that in Finland, and eventually in Austria, solutions were found that satisfied both Soviet security concerns and Western political values. In both of these cases, however, the solutions were primarily an achievement of the two countries concerned. One can imagine conditions under which similar conditions might have been achieved in Czechoslovakia, and possibly also Hungary. It is very difficult to imagine compromises of this type being reached in Poland, Romania, or Bulgaria. Britain had harbored no illusions about sharing political influence in this region with the USSR, and from the start had favored a division into separate spheres. It did not take the United States more than a couple of years to accept this as the only workable solution. In particular, exclusive American influence in Japan soon came to be regarded as adequate compensation for exclusion from Bulgaria and Romania.

The differences in values and interests reflected in the Cold War go far beyond the early postwar problems of Bulgaria and the other countries of Eastern Europe. These differences can be overcome only as the contending parties come to recognize that their common interest in a stable world order is a matter of higher national priority than exclusive spheres of influence. In the perspective of thirty-five years since the Yalta declaration, only modest progress has been made in the reorientation of values and interests from Cold War to world order.

WILLIAM HARDY MCNEILL

The View from Greece

The sun shone bright on the morning of November 10, 1944, when I approached Greece for the first time on board an almost empty Liberty ship that had sailed from Alexandria on the preceding day. It was bringing Allied personnel and their equipment to a country that had been liberated from the Germans only two weeks before. As a young assistant U.S. military attaché to the Greek government since April 1944—a graduate student of history in uniform—I was among those on board, and I watched the wine-dark seas and emerging shoreline of the Saronic Gulf with eyes made eager by my exposure when in college to the magic of Herodotus, Thucydides, Plato, and the other ancients. To find the Byzantine past more prominent in the minds of contemporary Athenians than anything from the classical age was only one of the surprises awaiting me.

The ship approached Piraeus, the harbor of Athens, slowly, follow-

William Hardy McNeill was Assistant Military Attaché to Greece from 1 April 1944 until 30 June 1946. In this capacity he was stationed first in Cairo and then, from November 1944, in Athens, charged with the duty of reporting matters of general concern to the U.S. Army. Access to a jeep allowed him to travel widely in Greece during 1945 and 1946 when few others could do so.

After the war he became a Professor of History at the University of Chicago. Among his works are: *The Greek Dilemma: War and Aftermath* (1947); *Greece: American Aid in Action, 1947-1956* (1957); *The Metamorphosis of Greece Since World War II* (1978); *America, Britain and Russia: Their Cooperation and Conflict, 1941-1946* (1953); and *The Rise of the West: A History of the Human Community* (1963).

ing a path prepared by mine sweepers. It anchored several hundred yards offshore, for the port itself was a shambles. The departing Germans had systematically wrecked the country's entire transport system to hinder pursuit. I therefore came ashore in a small lighter, and watched a jeep, which was to be my main method of travel in the months ahead, follow me precariously ashore. Allied vehicles were then still sufficiently unusual in Athens that during the trip into the city occasional clusters of bystanders waved enthusiastically.

My jeep made little show, coming as it did, just a day after a brigade of Greek troops, transferred from the battlefront in Italy, had marched through Athens, accepting the plaudits of those Athenians fearful of social revolution. Other Athenians, supporters of a future reordering of Greek society, either stayed away or, for the time being, subordinated their revolutionary sentiments to their nationalistic ones. Consequently, the city when first I saw it was quiet in the sense that political strife was in abeyance. Everyone was still too glad to see the end of the dread occupation, inaugurated, as it had been, by national defeat, and by a famine so severe that people had literally died in the streets from lack of food in the winter of 1941-42. Things had subsequently improved, thanks, largely, to wheat imported from abroad by the Swedish Red Cross, but no one in Athens or in Greece could look upon the years of German occupation as anything but disastrous. Liberation, so long hoped for, had come. Life was bound to become easier, or so, I suppose, everyone hoped and believed. The only question was, how soon?

Athens was definitely shabby, but, except for the port installations, physically it remained almost intact. The Germans had refrained from damaging such vulnerable systems as the water supply. But the social-economic structures that constitute a modern city had broken down far more completely than the outward appearance of the city suggested. Economic and administrative activity was at a near standstill. Hundred billion drachma notes, left over from the occupation regime, were the only currency in circulation. A wad of such bills about half an inch thick sufficed to buy a newspaper. There was remarkably little else for sale. Bushel baskets had long since replaced purses for carrying the all but worthless currency around, and individual bills drifted in the wind across the streets—too valueless for anyone to bother picking them up.

Yet for all the poverty and genuine human suffering such circumstances entailed, the people of Athens and of Greece generally still had their pride. The country's war record was heroic. In Britain's darkest hour, Greece alone among the nations of the world had fought on the British side—vainly to be sure; and only in Greece and Yugoslavia, among all the occupied countries of Europe, had an active guerrilla movement arisen to harass the occupiers, even in their days of greatest strength. Tangible evidence of Greek pride was the very surprising absence, for someone recently come from Cairo, of beggars in the streets of Athens, despite the many ragged coats and ill-fitting costumes patched together from miscellaneous leftovers and hand-me-downs. But for the moment, cold and hunger only intensified hope for the future and pride in the past—a combination that made current hardship bearable, on the condition that unmistakable improvements would take place in time to come. Given the urgencies of the situation facing everyone in the city, that future could not be long delayed.

The euphoric mood I met on my first arrival wore itself out in the course of November. Even with the best will in the world, the Allies could not deliver enough supplies to Greece to meet pressing needs adequately. The destruction of the port of Piraeus and of almost all other means of transport within the country had been so thorough that appropriately massive deliveries could not be arranged. Hence liberation did not bring better times. Instead, adminstration was more chaotic and food supplies shorter than in the days of the occupation. Accordingly, disappointment and anger began to replace the earlier euphoria. Someone, surely, must be at fault when nothing got done! Renewal of political quarrel was therefore inevitable, and by the end of November it had become critically acute.

Lines had been drawn long before, during the years of occupation. Armed factions, bitterly at odds with each other, had formed within the Greek body politic in 1942, and active civil war in Greece dated back to 1943. In that year, after the surrender of Italy, Italian occupation forces stationed in Greece allowed substantial quantities of weapons and ammunition to fall into the hands of a guerrilla force called ELAS, an acronym for Greek People's Liberation Army.

ELAS and its leaders thereupon tried to monopolize armed resistance to the Germans by attacking and dispersing all rival armed bands. ELAS was an armed extension of a Communist-led political organization known as EAM, the acronym for National Liberation Front. In addition to guerrilla bands in the hills, numbering about fifty thousand men by 1944, EAM had organized secret cells in the towns and cities, and had also created an ELAS reserve ready to be called into action if and when circumstances called for armed intervention in urban areas. But no one knew just how strong such secret organizations were, not even their leaders. Until tested in action it was impossible to tell how many men would respond to a summons to battle. Everything obviously depended on circumstances, which were in rapid flux in the late autumn of 1944.

Supporters of EAM/ELAS were sustained by a lively sense of their own righteousness in leading the nation in resistance to the Germans. Vague but heartfelt hope for a better world, once the occupation ended, was more important among the rank and file than any detailed political program. The Greek Communist party had systematically played down social revolution during the war. Instead it had sought to appeal to a broad spectrum of Greek opinion by emphasizing patriotism and populist reform. On one point EAM was firm: King George II must not come back to power. He was responsible, they held, for establishing the Fascist dictatorship exercised by General Metaxas from 1936 to 1940, and had thereby sacrificed any legitimacy the house of Glücksburg had ever had. Rejection of the king symbolized rejection of prewar injustices and inequities generally; but except for denunciation of collaborators, the Greek leftists never spelled out what changes they wished to bring to government and society. The slogan, "Power to the people, and no King," left much unclear, but like all good slogans carried an enormous emotional freight in 1944.

In spite of EAM's programmatic vagueness, the Greek Right believed that their lives and property would be endangered if EAM/ELAS came to power. Yet the opponents of EAM were by no means united among themselves. Some of the most fanatic were out and out collaborators. Far more numerous were those who had survived the occupation by dint of various compromises with constituted authority, and who feared being charged with the crime of collaboration as a result. Almost every property owner was vulnerable: how else could he have kept hold of what he owned under the occupation? A rigorous interpretation of the crime of collaboration, in short, could result in wholesale property transfers; a lenient interpretation of the term would mean essential continuity between the occupation and the liberation regimes. Which was it to be?

This critical issue was complicated and confused by older lines of fissure within Greek society, dating back to World War I. Two rival elites had emerged from the upheavals of 1917-23, one "Royalist," one "Republican," and heirs of those quarrels continued to occupy prominent positions within what Greeks called the political *kosmos,* that is, that small circle of public figures who aspired to political leadership. Among these men, personal rivalries flourished freely, unrestrained by any responsibility to larger party structures, for, with the exception of EAM (which did have a well-developed system of local committees in nearly every part of the country), no organized political parties worth the name existed during or immediately after the occupation.

The Right did, however, have its armed supporters. In Epirus, Colonel Napoleon Zervas commanded a guerrilla organization, some ten thousand strong, known as EDES (Greek Democratic National Union). Zervas's followers had survived a series of battles with ELAS in 1943 by withdrawing to Epirus in the remote, backward, northwest corner of Greece. There British deliveries of arms and funds, from nearby bases in Italy, kept the EDES bands going. Indeed, the survival of EDES was directly due to active British patronage, and especially to energetic diplomatic intervention at ELAS headquarters, demanding an end of civil strife. An agreement, concluded in February 1944, had defined the boundary between ELAS and EDES territory, and this agreement held, with minor infractions, until December 1944.

EDES had no very pronounced ideological color, save opposition to EAM. Zervas had once been republican but in 1944 he was so tied to British paymasters and suppliers that his forces could be counted on to do more or less anything the British wanted. The same was not true of two other rightist armed organizations. One, known as "X," commanded by Colonel George Grivas, was professedly royalist, and numbered perhaps one thousand men, located in the Athens area. It was, like the ELAS reserve of Athens, a secret organization and had never been tested in battle. Another rightist armed force was constituted by the Athens police and Greek gendarmerie. These official instruments were badly demoralized in October 1944 by prolonged and public association with the occupation regime, but their numbers (about 4,000), visibility, and discipline made them significant elements in the general balance of forces in postliberation Greece. The political loyalties of the police and gendarmerie were vague in the extreme. Protection from a vengeful Left, and the chance to hold onto their accustomed position and salary was what most of the rank and file probably wanted.

Yet these armed organizations of the Right were little more than ragtag and bobtail when compared to the strength of ELAS, buoyed as that guerrilla force was by a sense of having outlasted the Germans and of having embodied the noblest heroic traditions of the Greek people in a time of national disaster. EAM/ELAS was by no means a completely Communist movement. Most of the soldiers of ELAS were peasant boys, patriotic Greeks, eager to escape from poverty-stricken lives. In hill villages where local food resources did not suffice to feed the inhabitants throughout the year, it was impossible to survive if opportunities for work in the cities and plains disappeared; but this is what had happened from the beginning of the occupation, when severe economic dislocation descended upon the country. When the hillsmen would no longer hope to earn enough to buy the food needed to keep body and soul together in their remote, rock-bound villages, long-standing tradition defined what young and vigorous men should do. Heroism beckoned along the path that privation dictated. Their ancestors had taken to arms to seek by force the food they needed, whenever peaceable means of making good the local food deficiencies broke down. These *kleftic* traditions were living reality in Greek hill communities in 1942-44; young men's response to the call to resist the occupation was correspondingly strong.

In this circumstance, therefore, it was easy for Communist agents from the towns to organize guerrilla bands whose members came mostly from poverty-stricken hill villages. The political ideas and ideals EAM proclaimed fitted in well with the circumstances facing such young men. They sensed the basic injustice of a system that condemned them to precarious poverty, and readily believed that new leaders, supported by their arms, could shape a better postwar world, if only by substituting themselves and their kind for the corrupt urban leadership that was disgracing itself by submitting to all sorts of craven compromises and collaboration with the enemy.

Material support for the guerrilla bands came mainly from villages of the plains, where extra food could ordinarily be found. In such villages an extensive system of secret EAM committees assessed contributions, payable in kind. These secret committees often operated right under the noses of occupation authorities. Hence as German power diminished and drew in toward the urban centers of Athens and Salonika during 1944, the power of EAM/ELAS surged forward automatically. EAM committees, previously functioning secretly, simply came out into the open in one community after another and organized more systematically (and sometimes vengefully) the collection of supplies for the support of ELAS and a growing body of EAM activists and administrators.

What villagers of the plains thought about EAM/ELAS was far from clear. Heroic and patriotic sentiments were just as lively among them as among hillsmen, and there was much sympathy for the resistance on that account. Still, it is hard not to believe that most villagers would have preferred to keep possession of whatever extra grain (or other food) their efforts in the fields had produced, even if it meant selling such surpluses to townsmen working and living under German administration. Sales to such persons might be expected to bring valuables in exchange. All that EAM/ELAS could offer was patriotic rhetoric and freedom from molestation.

In most plains villages, a few (in some even a majority) of the inhabitants tried to resist EAM assessments. Such individuals became obvious targets for retribution once EAM authority came out into the open, though many of them, seeing the way things were going, fled into Athens or some other town, where they powerfully reinforced rightist sentiment. As a matter of fact, in their last months of power, the Germans had recruited so-called Security Battalions from this floating urban population, and used them for policing main roads. These battalions disintegrated as the Germans departed, but their members survived and constituted a volatile, endangered element in Greek society immediately after the liberation. Some kept their guns, and drifted into Colonel Grivas's "X."

Yet the great majority of Greek plains dwellers went along with EAM assessments much as they had traditionally submitted to a more formal taxation. Hence order prevailed in the Greek countryside as German power retreated. Vigorous local government, claiming legitimacy on the basis of swiftly organized local elections, sprang up in most EAM-controlled communities. Energetic self-help, political awareness, and naïvely optimistic planning for the future were all part of the EAM movement. Whatever reservations plainsmen may have felt at having to give part of their hard-earned harvest to EAM agents were well hidden, for any public gesture of protest provoked swift and severe retaliation.

As EAM power advanced in this fashion, village by village, across the plains of Greece, the effect was to cut the cities and towns off from the countryside more and more effectually. In the course of 1944, Greek villages ceased to feed the country's urban populations, which depended instead on food imported from abroad under the aegis of the Swedish Red Cross.[1]

The result was a curious dual economy: in the countryside an exchange occurred between plainsmen and hillsmen, whereby the former helped to feed the latter, who had armed themselves and organized a quite effective guerrilla army. Isolated in the midst of this political-economic system were two important urban enclaves—greater Athens and Salonika—where unemployed or underemployed populations depended on rations of imported food, whose equitable (i.e., egalitarian) distribution was supervised by foreigners presumed to be politically neutral as far as Greek domestic quarrels were concerned.

The obvious dénouement of this sociopolitical situation would have been a clean sweep for EAM/ELAS. Moving from control of villages to control of provincial towns, and from control of provincial

1. This arrangement had been inaugurated after the famine months of 1941-42. The grain in question came from Allied lands, and was imported into Greece by agreement of both Axis and Allied authorities. Distribution was supervised by Swedes, but in practice by 1944 only townsmen got rations since internal transport systems had generally broken down or been usurped for military use only.

towns to control of the cities seemed fully within the capacities of the movement; even if local armed organizations, especially in Athens, might have offered resistance, no one can doubt that ELAS would have prevailed if appropriate orders had been issued in the days just before and during the German withdrawal. But no such orders were issued. In the critical month of October 1944, ELAS extended its jurisdiction modestly, taking over all the provincial towns and the highways connecting them with Athens and Salonika. By the end of October, when the last German units had finally left mainland Greece, Athens and Salonika were therefore ringed round with ELAS check points set up on the highways leading into and out of the two cities. No one could move across such lines without permission of EAM/ELAS authorities.

Yet no move was made against EDES in Epirus, and no effort was made to extend EAM authority into the two principal urban centers of the land. Why? The answer is to be found in Great Power politics rather than in anything happening within Greece. In May 1944, Winston Churchill concluded an agreement with Stalin that Greece would become a British "sphere of operations" while Romania would fall to the Russians.[2] Churchill was able to win grudging American acquiescence in the deal, though President Roosevelt and many of his associates distrusted such arrangements as smacking of imperialism and the Old Adam of power politics. In their eyes, a new dispensation characterized by international law and cooperation was scheduled to supplant the faulty regime of the past, if, that is, American evangelists could fully convert Britain and the USSR to the new gospel as to how international affairs should be managed in the future.

But in 1944 American concern with Greece was marginal. No one thought that high principle was worth a quarrel with Britain and Russia, and FDR had in him a streak of naughtiness that took sporadic delight in playing the game of power politics with his allies. As a skilled fisherman plays a great fish, paying out line when it rushes away only to reel it is again when resistance weakens, so President Roosevelt imagined himself playing with his British and Russian colleagues, yielding to them at the proper times to lead them eventually, even against their will, toward the new American vision of a better postwar world. As for Greece, he concluded that by carefully underlining American disinterestedness and neutrality at every suitable opportunity, it was safe enough to entrust management of affairs to the British. American involvement would be strictly limited to the delivery of relief and re-

2. William H. McNeill, *America, Britain, and Russia: Their Cooperation and Conflict, 1941-1946* (London: Oxford University Press, 1954), pp. 422-23.

habilitation supplies. Residual American distrust of British imperialist proclivities could be expressed by cutthroat competition for postwar air-landing rights.

No doubt the role of the Great Powers was magnified by a deeply ingrained Greek political habit of seeking foreign patrons in the struggles for power at home. But the terrible impoverishment that the occupation had brought to the land reinforced dependency and made the early postliberation governments all but helpless. Hence one might almost sum up the two years that followed the liberation as turning upon the question of when and whether the USSR on the one hand, or the United States on the other, would and could shift from their hands-off policy of 1944 and intervene actively in support of one or another of the struggling factions within Greece. As is well known, the United States did eventually decide in the spring of 1947 to come to the support of the duly elected Greek government, which happened to be emphatically anti-Communist. The USSR always held back. Power struggles within the Communist movements of Eastern Europe— in particular Stalin's mounting distrust of Tito—played a role in defining this result. Unwillingness to confront Great Britain and the United States directly was probably no less important, but the actual calculations and fears that may have guided Soviet policy during and after World War II remain matters for speculation.

All the same, a good deal is now known about how Russian agents implemented Stalin's 1944 deal with Churchill over Greece, but to understand Russian actions in 1944-45, I must first sketch the Greek political scene more fully. In March 1944, EAM had established a Political Committee of National Liberation that proceeded to act like a provisional government, holding elections for a National Assembly in May and setting up a prime minister and cabinet with ministers for agriculture, justice, foreign affairs, and so forth. The German puppet government in Athens as well as the royal government in exile, based in Cairo, thus confronted a new rival. The power EAM could exercise was demonstrated in April 1944, when mutinies broke out in Greek army and naval units that the exiled government had scraped together in Egypt. Soldiers and sailors defied military discipline to demand that the exiled government negotiate a merger with the new shadow government in the mountains. Mixed up in this affair was a scheme hatched among republican politicians and officers to bring themselves to power as the only suitable mediators between conservative royalists and leftist revolutionaries. The plan backfired, however, for the mutiny was eventually put down and King George remained formally sovereign of the government in exile. By far the most important upshot was a political purge of Greek forces in the

Middle East. Only officers and men who had refrained from mutiny remained under arms, while the rest were put into detention camps. A "Third Brigade" was formed from the remnants of the former First and Second Greek brigades. It fought briefly on the Italian front before being transferred to Athens in November 1944. Because it was aggressively anti-Communist, the arrival of the Third Brigade in Greece on the day before I got there emphatically changed the political balance of the country's armed forces—which helped to trigger the eventual decision by the Left to resort to force in December.

In spite of many rumors to the contrary, Russian agents seem to have played no role whatever in the mutiny of the Greek troops in the Middle East. It was only in July 1944 that Russian policy became apparent. In that month Colonel Grigorii Popov parachuted into ELAS headquarters with a team of radio technicians, opening up communication between ELAS and Russian higher authority for the first time. Colonel Popov's arrival disconcerted the local British liaison officers, who had long been accustomed to advising the Greek guerrillas in the name of all the Allies. But as it turned out, they should have welcomed him, for the message he brought to the EAM/ELAS leadership was not at all what the Greek Communists expected or wanted to hear. Instead of encouraging their drive to set up a new Communist-colored government for Greece, Colonel Popov told them they had to come to terms with the British-sponsored exile government in Cairo. This government, tattered and torn though it might be, and compromised by its legal connection with the king, was to be the frame within which the post-occupation regime of Greece would be formed. There is no question that it was Russian advice that persuaded EAM leaders to submit to this procedure.

The negotiation was somewhat sweetened for EAM by the placement, in the wake of the suppression of the mutiny, of a new prime minister, George Papandreou, in charge of trying to create a new Government of National Unity. Papandreou was a man of eloquence and stood somewhere in the middle of the Greek political spectrum— which meant that he had no real personal basis of support within the country, since the events of the war had acted to polarize opinion sharply between EAM and its opponents. But Papandreou did have the support of the British ambassador and government, and in view of the deal Churchill had made with Stalin, this proved all-important. Colonel Popov's advice, supplemented by urgent admonitions from British agents at ELAS headquarters, persuaded the leaders of the movement to send negotiators to Cairo to see what terms might be arranged. A long secret conference spelled out the deal Papandreou was prepared to make, allocating five seats in his cabinet to representatives of EAM. The other fifteen seats were reserved for politicians whose authority within Greece was as tenuous as Premier Papandreou's.

The EAM delegation returned to the Greek mountains to report. Long weeks went by while what must have been heated and perhaps agonizing debates took place among the top brass of EAM/ELAS. To join Papandreou's government with only a quarter of the seats would forfeit real power; to join the government without securing some definite promise that the king would not come back meant a renunciation of one of the key propaganda points of the EAM program. Yet eventually, and no doubt reluctantly, the EAM/ELAS leadership decided to go ahead and designate five men for membership in Papandreou's Government of National Unity. When the EAM ministers arrived in Cairo at the end of August 1944, two of them, representing the Communist party, called on the Russian minister in Egypt, perhaps to check up on the authenticity and authority of the advice Colonel Popov had been giving them. The Russian minister told them to take their assigned portfolios in Papandreou's cabinet without further ado and they were accordingly sworn in on September 2, a mere five weeks before the German withdrawal from Greece became definite.[3] The shadow government in the mountains faded away without being formally disbanded. EAM/ELAS prepared to welcome the liberation on terms imposed on them by the common front of British and Russian diplomats.

What happened next was even more remarkable. Papandreou and his cabinet hurried off to Italy, where Papandreou met Churchill and lesser British authorities to settle last-minute details about the way his government would take over power in Greece in the wake of the retreating Germans. The most important matter agreed upon on this occasion was how military command would be arranged. Papandreou agreed that all Greek forces would become subordinate to the Allied Force Headquarters (AFHQ) in Caserta, and that a British general, Ronald Scobie, would exercise command in Greece in the name of AFHQ. General Sarafis, commander-in-chief of ELAS, was present at AFHQ in Caserta, along with Colonel Zervas, commander of EDES, and both guerrilla chieftains accepted the arrangement. ELAS specif-

---

3. In 1946, Alexander Svolos, a Socialist member of the EAM ministerial delegation, told me that the decision to join Papandreou's government without further negotiation was due to the instructions his Communist colleagues received from the Russian minister. Svolos was a man of unusual probity and I am sure he was telling the truth. The result, incidentally, disappointed a group of republican politicians who had resigned from the cabinet in anticipation of the arrival of the EAM delegation, expecting to make common cause with the newcomers to overthrow George Papandreou.

ically agreed not to move into the Athens area when the Germans withdrew.

When the long-expected day of liberation finally arrived, early in October, a few detachments of British paratroops landed in Patras and followed hot on the heels of the withdrawing Germans. No one tried to harass the retreat. There had been more than enough violence and bloodshed in Greece since 1940, and everyone was wondering about who would rule in the future. The arrival of Papandreou's Government of National Unity in Athens on October 18, 1944, provoked rapturous outpourings from all segments of the population, but did not really do much to settle the question of how power would be distributed in postwar Greece. The British were, of course, acutely aware of ELAS's preponderance in arms, men, and morale. To keep that preponderance in check, it seemed vital to back up diplomatic arrangements with at least a show of force. But Great Britain had no troops to spare from the Italian front or from other commitments around the world. To make the most of limited resources, British planners therefore decided to use Greece as a place for rest and recuperation for units exhausted by front-line duty in Italy. About thirteen thousand battle-weary troops were accordingly assigned to Greece, and took up billets in and around Athens and Salonika during the month of October.

In addition, a joint American-British military liaison team was sent to the country to superintend the delivery of emergency relief supplies. In spite of such efforts, transport was so disorganized that the flow of food into Greece from the Allied world actually decreased during the first weeks of liberation from what the Swedish Red Cross had previously administered.

This was the situation into which I came in November 1944, assigned to observe events and report what I could find out to the U.S. War Department. Information was easy to come by: Greeks in official positions and others hoping to gain a place in some future government were eager to talk to Americans. The only problem was deciding what to believe, or disbelieve, for rumors and grossly partisan accounts of past events and present intentions were the staple of Greek public discourse. Greeks who wished to reach the attention of people like myself had to be able to speak French or English, for almost none of the official representatives of either the British or the American government spoke Greek, and most of those who did, being of Greek-American extraction, were little respected, since they bore too many marks of their parents' peasant origins to rank as "real" Americans.

Within the small circle of embassy personnel, informal exchanges of view took place constantly. A vaguely pro-British tone predominated.

Yet general sympathy did not inhibit criticism. The United States'
preferred role was that of interested and sympathetic bystander, supporting peaceful and humane solutions to all problems that might
arise in accordance with democratic and liberal tradition. As far as
Greek affairs were concerned, sympathy with the urban elite of Athens,
whose leadership in Greece was endangered by the ambitions of EAM/
ELAS, was stronger than sympathy for the aspiration to make all
things new that prevailed in the ranks of EAM/ELAS. Input to American officials was lopsided, if only because Greeks able to speak English
or French, and capable of holding their own in informal encounters
with members of the diplomatic corps were, by definition, members of
the established urban elite. But American officials disapproved of
violence and extremism of the Right as much as of the Left. However,
leftist violence had far greater scope in Greece immediately after the
liberation because of ELAS preponderance in most of the country,
which meant that American moral principles and a stance critical of
the Left tended to coincide.

How such attitudes were generated and propagated among the
embassy personnel is hard to say. There was a close conformity of
view among all concerned, from Ambassador Lincoln MacVeagh on
down. Several key figures in the embassy circle had lived in Greece
before the war and swiftly reestablished prewar ties and connections
within the Athenian elite. Some Americans were influenced by memories of the war years, when repeated leftist and republican assaults on
the legitimacy of the royal government in exile had sometimes seemed
disruptive of the war effort. (The mutiny of April 1944, after all,
reduced Greek armed forces from two brigades to one.) Travel outside
of Athens was impossible in the first weeks. ELAS check points on
the roads stopped foreigners as well as unauthorized Greeks only a few
miles outside Athens, and not without reason, for roads were impassable
to wheeled vehicles for more than a few miles at a stretch, and in some
places were still mined. Nevertheless, the effect was to confine the
information reaching the U.S. Embassy to what a small circle of west-
ern-educated Greeks in Athens had to tell.

The most important thing about American official views, however,
was that for all the democratic idealism and humane intention that
dominated them, no American felt in the least responsible for what
happened. Impasses and difficulties could always be blamed on Greek
or British shortcomings, and were. British officials, both in the British
embassy and on General Scobie's staff, were correspondingly curt
and condescending in their dealings with Americans, at least those
beneath the ambassadorial level. They kept their own counsel for
the most part, and tended, perhaps, to regard American officials as a

weight to be carried if not an obstacle to be overcome. As for Russia, Colonel Popov remained Stalin's sole official representative, linked to the outside world by the radio operators who accompanied him almost everywhere. He, too, kept his own counsel, though once, when I had occasion to compliment him on his excellent command of spoken English, he remarked that his first language was Chinese! He claimed, also, to have been a member of the first parachute class trained by Red Army some time in the early 1930s, and was, altogether, an impressive representative of the USSR: athletic, bold, secretive and self-controlled, as well as being extremely well educated.

During the latter part of November 1944, as the initial euphoria of liberation waned, it became increasingly clear that Papandreou's government was incapable of dealing with the situation. The ministers were unable to agree on anything important, and lacked any sort of administrative instrument with which to implement decisions they did make. Financial and administrative chaos, and policy disagreements, all ran up against the divided sovereignty within Greece, inherited from the last days of the occupation. The countryside belonged to EAM/ELAS (in Epirus to EDES), while the cities had become a spooky no-man's-land. EAM's urban supporters more or less counterbalanced all the miscellaneous groups in Athens and Salonika that feared and hated EAM, but no one knew for sure which side was stronger, since the arbitrament of force had been forestalled by the way Papandreou's government returned to Greece under British protection.

From the start, British experts believed that Papandreou's first essential task was to establish a monopoly of military force. How to achieve this end was hard to say. Only if the EAM ministers were to agree to the demobilization of ELAS, tied perhaps to the incorporation of suitable ELAS personnel into a new national Greek army, could such a change occur peacefully. But to disband ELAS would surrender the principal instrument through which EAM exercised the hard-won power it had built for itself during the occupation years. Before agreeing to such a policy, EAM leaders might be expected to demand far-reaching guarantees to insure that their preponderance in Greece would not be undermined as a by-product of ELAS demobilization.

What the ELAS rank and file may have felt and thought about disbandment is unclear. The ostensible purpose of the resistance had been accomplished. Greece at last was free of German control, and ELAS soldiers may have felt that disbandment was the logical response to the end of the occupation. Had it meant a chance to live off food imported from abroad until jobs for deserving veterans of the resistance opened up in government, in the army, or in private business, probably most of the ELAS soldiers would have been glad to slough off military discipline and start life anew. On the other hand, disbandment followed by idleness and incipient starvation in their home villages lacked all charm; and unless large-scale delivery of relief supplies could be organized very swiftly, that was, in fact, what would confront most ELAS veterans. How they assessed their situation no one can say, but uncertainty about morale of the ELAS rank and file in a fight against Great Britain may have been a factor limiting EAM leaders' policy decisions.

Assuredly the government of Greece could not function as more than a shadow play as long as ELAS check points stopped traffic a few miles outside of the city and permitted only those approved by EAM authorities to proceed. The stark alternatives that had seemed so clear in the spring of 1944 had been staved off but not really exorcised by Russian and British diplomatic action between May and October. If Greece were to be governed as an entity, either EAM/ELAS had to prevail throughout the land, or its power would have to be dissolved and some new military and administrative structure pieced together to govern the country. All the ingenuity and effort at compromise that Greek politicians and British diplomats were capable of could not alter this fundamental reality. Very quickly, therefore, controversy focused on how to go about creating a new national army.

The Greek Third Brigade had arrived from Italy the day before I did on November 9, and its royalist political coloration inspired ELAS to bring some of its troops closer to Athens to counterbalance this increment to the rightists' armed strength in the capital. Such surreptitious movements showed how limited General Scobie's real control over ELAS was, for he had not authorized such a shift. This reminder of military realities hardened British will to get EAM's "private army" out of the way. When efforts to find a formula that would be acceptable to all members of Papandreou's government broke down, General Scobie took the initiative, and on December 1 issued a proclamation setting December 10 as the date upon which ELAS and EDES would disband. Nothing was said about the Third Brigade, but it was clearly Scobie's intention to allow that unit to remain in being and use it as a cadre for the Greek national army. If so, the new army would, at least to begin with, be officered by men of the Right. Such an arrangement was completely unacceptable to the Left. The EAM ministers therefore resigned from Papandreou's government in protest against Scobie's high-handed intervention in Greek affairs.

EAM organized a huge demonstration in Athen's central square on December 3 to demand reorganization of the government. Popular patience had already worn thin, and the provocation was real: hence response to EAM's summons was massive and intense from the start. In the course of the demonstration, gunfire from the ranks of the Athens police killed and wounded a few of the advancing crowd. This violence in the capital's principal public square occurred before the eyes of the newspaper correspondents (who were shocked) and very effectively added fresh fuel to the fires of EAM anger.

Neither EAM leaders nor the British expected or were really prepared for armed combat against one another. But as neither side would back down, that was what eventuated. EAM called out the ELAS reserve of Athens, and this was the force that did most of the fighting. Its superiority over the various armed rightist groups within the city was demonstrated early; but against British forces, in the center of Athens, and the Third Greek Brigade, stationed on the outskirts of the city, the ELAS reserve could not prevail.

Nevertheless, for a few days the isolated enclave in central Athens held by British troops was in real danger of collapse, since food and other supplies were very short. The area held by the British was quite small so that ELAS mortar shells could easily reach into every corner of the defended zone, including the Grande Bretagne Hotel where the army mess for British headquarters had been established. Colonel Popov and his radio technicians appeared there each day for meals throughout the siege; so, for that matter, did I and one or two other American military personnel who had also been admitted to the mess. A group of war correspondents completed the motley group that lived and ate in the hotel. The arrival of an occasional mortar shell (three or four hit the building in the course of the critical three weeks) added excitement and a sense of risk to the situation without really disrupting regular routines of life for any of the hotel's denizens.

After the middle of December, the balance of forces turned decisively in the British favor, thanks to the arrival of reinforcements from Italy. ELAS never brought its main field armies into Athens at all.[4] Travel was difficult, and British airplanes strafed all that moved on the roads. Moreover, head to head military collision with British forces was never part of the EAM/ELAS intention.

Each escalation of force aimed at a political result, and the British proved to have the last word in that game, both on the military and on the political side. The arrival in Athens of battle-hardened British troops from Italy in mid-December was soon followed by important political concessions that took much of the steam out of EAM's pro-

4. A swiftly organized assault on EDES drove that force from Epirus in the first two weeks of December 1944, thus consolidating ELAS control of all the Greek mainland except for enclaves in Athens and Salonika.

test. Churchill had been seriously embarrassed by the flare-up of fighting in Athens, especially since the general tenor of newspaper reporting, both in the United States and in Great Britain (but not in Russia), was critical of British actions. How could use of British troops to attack heroes of the Greek resistance be explained at a time when Hitler had yet to be defeated, and when the reinforcements for Greece had to be withdrawn from the battlefront in Italy? How indeed? Recognizing the seriousness of his dilemma, Churchill visited Athens at Christmastime and arranged for a conference attended by all the principal political figures, including representatives of EAM and of the Greek Communist party. No agreed solution resulted, but Churchill did convince himself that he would have to persuade King George II to transfer his royal powers to a regent and promise to return to his throne only after a plebiscite had been held to determine whether or not the Greek people wanted him back. Churchill was able to browbeat the Greek king into acquiescence with this plan after his return to London, where King George was still living. (Incidentally, the way in which King George II had come to the throne in 1935, after a blatantly falsified election conducted by a government that owed a good deal to British support, explained much of the distrust Greeks felt in 1944 for British intentions with respect to King George.)

In addition, Churchill decided that Papandreou had outlived his usefulness as prime minister, and instead fixed upon Nicholas Plastiras as a suitable figure to head the Greek government. Plastiras was an old-fashioned republican who had lived in exile in France since 1933 when he led an abortive coup intended to head off the king's return to office. By placing Plastiras at the head of a government that would function under the regency of archbishop Damaskinos (a man of no pronounced political affiliation), EAM's charge that the British were planning to return King George to his throne by force and fraud lost plausibility; and many Greeks who disliked the prewar dictatorial government, and who had suspected that British machinations were aimed at restoring a dictatorship to the country, swung round to a warmer acceptance of the legitimacy of the Athens government.

These political concessions, following swiftly upon the demonstration of British determination to use superior force against ELAS in Athens, persuaded EAM's leaders to agree to armistice terms dictated by General Scobie. Accordingly, by mid-January, 1945, the fighting ended. The armistice was succeeded by the Varkiza agreement, concluded in February, by which ELAS agreed to disband and disarm. The Greek government agreed in return to purge the police and gendarmerie of collaborators and to set up a national army based on conscription. Nothing was said about the Third Brigade, which in fact became the kernel out of which the new Greek army developed.

Thus by February 1945, EAM had been defeated by British force and determination. In the following weeks, ELAS disbanded punctually and according to the Varkiza agreement. But with the disappearance of leftist armed force from one community after another, political reaction spread throughout Greece. It proved far stronger than anyone had expected. The impetus came from Athens, where, toward the end of the fighting, ELAS had taken several thousand hostages. When the defeated army withdrew, it dragged its hostages along. Some died, and survivors suffered severe mistreatment. This, together with the discovery of a mass graveyard in the outskirts of the city where several hundred persons had been executed during the fighting, provided a quite tangible basis for the accusations extreme rightists had made against EAM before December 1944. Many Athenians now came to feel the same way, and as ELAS power melted away from the villages, similar reactions also occurred within most rural communities of the plains. Individuals who had been especially active in support of EAM began to suffer persecution like what had been visited upon those who dared to resist the power of ELAS.

Feeling that their time had come, rightists formed armed bands in many parts of the country and engaged in extra-legal acts of terrorism against known or suspected leftists. Purely private vengeance for acts committed when EAM was in power added to the violence. Continued economic hardship sharpened political polarity everywhere, and the efforts of the United Nations Relief Rehabilitation Administration personnel (who took over responsibility for delivery of relief supplies from the military liaison staff early in 1945) to relieve the situation proved grossly inadequate to coax Greek society and economy back to normality.

British authorities, from Churchill on down, had regularly sought to identify their policies with those of the Allies as a whole, and throughout the crisis period in Athens it was the Americans more than the Russians who sought escape from this designation. Colonel Popov remained taciturn throughout the fighting. As an official representative of the Russian government, he attended the conference of Greek political figures that Churchill convened just after Christmas, and it seems certain that he gave EAM and the Greek Communist party no encouragement whatever, either before or after the outbreak of hostilities.

The Russian press said next to nothing about events in Greece. Stalin was honoring his agreement with Churchill to the letter, as Churchill himself later acknowledged. The United States, however, showed its disapproval.. Official statements issued by Secretary of State Edward Stettinius on December 3 and 5, 1944, underlined the unwillingness of the United States to interfere in the affairs of other countries. His statements were a thinly veiled criticism of British action in Greece. On the spot, the personnel of the American embassy remained ostentatiously neutral, although because the United States Embassy was located within the British perimeter in Athens, contact with the Left was pretty well cut off. The experience of living within a zone exposed to sporadic mortar and artillery fire from ELAS forces tended to put official American representatives willy-nilly into the same boat as the British. Some counterweight came from reports of a few Office of Strategic Services agents scattered through the provinces, who tended to sympathize with EAM/ELAS; and the U.S. members of an UNRRA advance party, who occupied a hotel that came under EAM control during the Athens fighting, were also inclined to believe EAM rather than British versions of what was happening and why.

Such divergences of view within the American official community mattered little at the time, and were not very sharp since everyone blamed both sides and differed only in the vigor with which one or the other combatant was held responsible for what had happened. The way Anglo-American newspaper opinion was defined played a conspicuous role at the time, and in the short run probably had a good deal to do with how the American and British people and governments reacted to the conflict in Greece.

As soon as violence flared in Athens, some two-score accredited war correspondents converged on the scene. Most of them made the bar of the Grande Bretagne Hotel their informal headquarters. Daily briefings by British and Greek government spokesmen were supplemented by an informal but very powerful communications network that arose spontaneously among the correspondents themselves. Any bit of news or opinion was discussed and shared among the frequenters of the GB bar. In this way a rather close consensus arose about how to interpret the day's events. A few Greeks took active part in this process, contributing background information and spelling out Greek proper names and the like for the benefit of correspondents to whom such matters were a mystery. One such, an Athenian lady of upper-class origin, was reputed to be the spokeswoman for EAM. Whether or not she played this role officially, secret communications from EAM headquarters did reach the correspondents from time to time. When a document arrived from the "underground," it had an aura of the forbidden about it. For some correspondents this reinforced its credibility. A few newspapermen played a lone hand and refused to share their information with their fellows, but such persons were exceptional. During the crisis period, the informal discussion of each day's events in the GB bar set the tone for the news dispatches sent from Athens to English-language newspapers around the world.

It is very difficult to say just how consensus among the correspondents was arrived at. Newcomers, burdened with the duty of filing a dispatch on the day of their arrival, took their cues and background information from correspondents who had arrived a few days or even hours before they did. A tiny number of "old Balkan hands" with prewar experience of Greek affairs acted as doyens and wise men, though some of them refused to join the rituals of the bar and nursed their expertise in private, hoping perhaps to achieve a scoop or to preserve a personal, idiosyncratic tone in their stories. In general, preconceptions played a larger role than on-the-spot observation in determining the political thrust of the correspondents' stories. They had no chance to see the other side. Escape from the narrow perimeter of the British defense lines was impossible and, within that circuit, official information, set forth in the daily briefings, had to compete with a rash of rumors and counterrumors about what was really going on. The conviction that it was morally wrong for British troops to fight against the Germans' enemies in Greece dominated the minds of most correspondents. Information doled out to them through official channels did little to alter their ingrained suspicions of British policies, which, they thought, had provoked the fighting.

With the end of hostilities, the war correspondents dispersed to more active battlefronts, and the world's interest in Greek affairs flagged. A very small corps of newpapermen—persons who had resided in Greece before the war and were able to speak the language—took over. Some of them, for instance the *New York Times* correspondent, not only knew Greece well but shared the political passions that swept the country, so that his dispatches bent with the wind of reaction that blew so strongly across the country in 1945 and 1946. Then, when Greece threatened to become a battleground once again in the course of 1946, roving correspondents arrived in Athens from time to time and interpreted events in accordance with their diverse political predilections. But the intense collegial interaction of December 1944—and the consequent near unanimity of viewpoint—never again arose.

As for the views of American officials on the spot, after January 1945, they became more and more sympathetic to the line taken by British diplomats in Greece. Two things conduced to this result. On the one hand, British policy became more moderate in the sense that instead of encouraging rightists against EAM, as in the crisis period of 1944, British diplomats set out to restrain the more flamboyant expressions of rightist sentiment, seeking a middle way that the dynamic of Greek society could not, of its own accord, establish. This conformed to what Americans thought wise and right. Accordingly, occasions for friction between British and American officials diminished and all but disappeared.

A second factor that led to the same result was that American policy in southeastern Europe became more active during 1945 and 1946. Instead of sitting back and criticizing the mismanagement of affairs by all concerned, which had been the American line through 1944, Americans began to try to do something to put the governments of Eastern Europe on a sound, democratic basis. In particular, this meant advocating and, in Greece, attempting to organize, free and honest elections. The Americans hoped, indeed, to manage elections in Greece so well that what happened there could become a model for similar elections to be organized in other East European countries— Poland, Romania, Bulgaria, and so forth.

Ironically, however, the shift of power from Left to Right that took place in 1945 meant that moderate and republican as well as leftist politicians began to evince a lively distrust of the democratic process as applied to a country still in a state of economic collapse. Following the victory of the Labour party in July 1945, British diplomats sought to counter the swing to the Right in Greece by putting a middle-of-the-road, republican government in charge in Athens. But the new government was as ineffective in meeting the administrative and economic problems of the country as its predecessors had been. Indeed, the new cabinet's chief idea was to keep itself in power by postponing elections until conditions became more normal, that is, until a moderate middle-of-the-road politician had a good chance of winning. Official American opinion was unsympathetic. If democratic theory meant anything, it meant that elections had to take place whether or not the party in power expected to win. If the only time to hold elections was when the existing government expected to prevail, then the reality of democracy would be gone, and with it the chance of moderating Communist control in other East European states. Hence the logic of the American democratic creed had the effect of aligning official U.S. sympathies with the Greek Right, which, sensing victory, clamored for speedy elections.

One concession to the republican point of view was made: instead of holding a plebiscite on the king's return before electing a new government (as had been specified by the Varkiza agreement of February 1945), British and American officials agreed to reverse the procedure, and hold elections first, then the plebiscite. But this was as far as the Anglo-Americans would go to accommodate leftist and republican fear of defeat at the polls. American and British advisers sternly rebuffed all subsequent efforts to postpone the election. Instead, an elaborate Allied mission for observing the Greek elections (AMFOGE) was dispatched to the country, in the hope of inhibiting coercion and fraud. The result was to prevent the government from

using its administrative machine to influence the election in a republican direction—something that might have been impossible anyway,
given the still demoralized character of Greek bureaucracy and the
prevalence of anticommunism in its ranks.

The election, held in March 1946, thus turned out to be a smashing
victory for royalist and conservative politicians. A new government,
organized on the basis of a freely elected parliament, set out as speedily
as possible to organize a plebiscite for the return of the king. In September 1946, the king was duly recalled by another overwhelming
vote, observed as before, though less intensively, by an Allied election
mission.

By the last months of 1946, therefore, American ideas about how
to reestablish sound, democratic government in Greece had been
acted on, and with all possible external guarantees of the legitimacy
of the procedure. This meant that in the eyes of the United States,
the conservative nationalist regime that emerged from the elections at
least deserved a chance to govern the country, until such time as the
Greek public might tire of its policies and a new election bring some
other government to office.

The unsatisfactory character of elections held under conditions
of socioeconomic disorganization and among a still predominantly
peasant people were familiar enough to the members of the U.S. Embassy in Athens. After March 1945, travel in Greece became possible
for anyone who had a jeep and the hardihood to withstand the pot-
holes that had become ubiquitous after five years without road main-
tenance. I was able, for instance, to travel in advance of the new Greek
armed forces, as they expanded their jurisdiction from one provincial
town to another, and on two occasions observed the sort of local
counterrevolution the arrival of army units obedient to Athens meant.
EAM regimes lasted to the end, and efforts to convince a visiting
American of their legitimacy were fierce and frantic. Rightists were
not happy at my presence, which may, in fact, have inhibited direct
resort to beatings and other overt forms of violence, as power shifted
before my eyes. But the process whereby the EAM ruling committee
was evicted from town offices was plain enough, for they left only
under duress. And the hatred, fear, and irreconcilable distrust that
divided the erstwhile local rulers from their successors was plain for
anyone to see.

It took no imagination at all to recognize that free elections were
not an adequate cure for situations in which the loss of political power
meant the loss of personal security and, not infrequently, of life itself.
But no American had anything else to suggest as a way to legitimize
government and get the country back on its feet.

In Washington, further from the reality, the missionary urge to show the British and Russians how to be really democratic prevailed. The result was the extravagance of AMFOGE. This mission sent several hundred men in Allied uniforms to carefully selected sample voters to ask how the individual in question intended to vote in the upcoming election. Greeks reacted by telling each such formidable interlocutor whatever they figured he wanted to hear, thereby destroying the value of the scientific sampling of opinion that naïvely ethnocentric American political scientists had carefully contrived as a check upon the fairness of the actual elections. On the spot, such antics seemed as ridiculous as they turned out to be, since Greek voters, characteristically, looked upon politics as an affair of the mighty, their personal pursuit of the good life. In most situations a wise man dissembled and voted for whomever had the power already and was thus destined to win. EAM elections, so unanimous, had registered this Greek penchant in the early 1940s; royalist victories in 1945 and 1946 did the same.

But few Americans recognized the pitfalls of democratic practice in a peasant land such as Greece, and high policy in Washington most certainly did not take such quibbles into account. However imperfect the performance, Greeks had gone to the polls and elected a government that thereby became legitimate. This simple-minded view soon collided with a new, awkward reality, as it became evident that the duly elected authorities might not be allowed to govern Greece peaceably.

For in the summer of 1946, Communist-led armed bands again appeared in northern Greece, and a vigorous propaganda campaign, orchestrated from Belgrade and Moscow, began to denounce the "monarcho-Fascist" regime in Greece as a threat to Balkan peace. Postponed elections in Poland and Romania—postponed until such time as the existing governments could be sure of victory at the polls— matched this new Soviet line against the properly elected Greek government. Whatever its shortcomings, Americans found themselves compelled to support a government whose establishment they had done so much to bring about.

By August 1946, therefore, when the Greek situation came up in the United Nations on the complaint of the Ukrainian representative, Americans were entirely ready to back the British and Greek royalists against the charge that the Greek government was a threat to peace. This, of course, was only part of the more general realignment between East and West of these months, and even though individual Americans still had reservations about the nature and policies of the government that elections had brought to power in Greece, the view prevailed that Greece was becoming one of the testing grounds in a global struggle between Communist revolution and democratic self-determination.

When, therefore, early in 1947, financial difficulties compelled the British government to terminate most of its expenditures in Greece, the United States government was ready to accept the vacated British role, and this despite (or rather because) the scale and formidability of the renewed guerrilla movement had grown very rapidly. Help from Yugoslavia and other Communist regimes to the north accelerated the guerrilla resurgence; but it was continued economic dislocation within Greece that made it so easy to recruit manpower for the new bands—as well as for the royal army that opposed them. And, of course, the spread of armed violence intensified economic dislocation, so that the country found itself once again, as during the occupation, caught in a vicious circle.

When the American Congress approved President Truman's request (March 1947) for funds to shore up the faltering Greek government, no one imagined how long and difficult the task of checking Communist aggression in Greece would turn out to be. Victory did not come until 1949, and before it had been won, American intervention in the Greek political process became almost as high-handed as British intervention had been in 1944. The exigencies of civil war everywhere hardened opinions. Harsh and radical anticommunism flourished exuberantly, both among American advisers and among the Greek officials and army personnel with whom they had dealings. And as had been true of the Germans in 1941-44, and of the British in 1943-46, so also the Americans, once involved in trying to manage Greek affairs in 1947-50, had to send inexperienced personnel to the scene. These newcomers, unacquainted with the peculiarities of Greek society, came suddenly into positions of key importance, and characteristically plunged ahead, often unaware of and indifferent to the larger consequences of their actions and advice.

It is tempting to be wise after the event by criticizing unfairly men responsible for making day-to-day decisions on the basis of inadequate information provided by Greek collaborators whose goals were different from their own. But we are today far enough removed from these events to be able to recognize that German, British, and American officials successively played similar roles in Greece. Each dealt with and depended upon collaborators stemming from the established urban elites of the country. Moreover, German, British, and American policy was fundamentally the same in the sense that each strove to extend control from the urban centers of the country to remoter provinces and hill villages, and each had to face armed opposition that drew its strength from the food-deficient villages of the hills organized and given political direction by Communists drawn from various walks of urban life.

In these prolonged and painful struggles, a decisive factor was always the level of outside support the rival Greek elites could mobilize. Urban control over the Greek hinterland faded under the Germans because the hill-based guerrillas had significant Allied (actually only British) support from outside the country. In the next phase, British intervention allowed the urban elite to re-establish control because outside support was temporarily withdrawn from the guerrilla forces based in the hills. When Yugoslavia, Bulgaria, and Albania renewed such exterior support in 1946, the ground was laid for a new encounter between an American-supported, urban-based regime and the hill villages of Greece.

At no time did the USSR lend direct or unambiguous support to the Greek Communist cause, though exactly how Stalin threaded his way among the competing demands of Greek, Bulgar, Yugoslav, and other Balkan Communist parties, while keeping a wary eye on his relations with the United States and other great powers, cannot be known until such time as secret Soviet records are made public. The American record of involvement in Greek affairs, is, by contrast, almost entirely in the public domain. High principles, good intentions, and inattention to local realities that deprived democratic, made-in-America panaceas of their power were the factors that mobilized American resources for the struggle in Greece. Economic interests, military cameraderie, and anti-Communist crusading came later, but they were not, to begin with, significantly present in American official or unofficial circles.

CORTLANDT V. R. SCHUYLER

The View from Romania

One morning in early October 1944, I was sitting in my office at Camp Maxey, Texas, gloomily pondering my future prospects. I was a brigadier general with some twenty years of experience in the antiaircraft artillery. Thus far during the war, I had been deeply involved in the training of antiaircraft battalions and preparing them as quickly as possible for shipment to combat zones overseas. But now that our Allied air forces had achieved virtual mastery of the skies over Western Europe, more antiaircraft units were no longer needed. Indeed, those already in place were fast being retrained for other missions. Therefore, it was evident that I could anticipate a new assignment shortly. I had applied on several occasions for service in a combat theater, but to no avail. My performance record to date had been reasonably good, but I had not the foggiest idea of what my next job might be.

Cortlandt Van Rensselaer Schuyler, General, U.S. Army (Retired), was graduated from the United States Military Academy in 1922, and spent his first twenty years of military service primarily as an antiaircraft officer. In 1943, he became Chief of Staff of the U.S. Antiaircraft Command with the rank of Brigadier General. In the fall of 1944, he was assigned to Bucharest, Romania, as United States Military Representative on the Allied Control Commission for Romania.

He returned to U.S. Army Headquarters in Washington in 1947 where, as Chief of Plans, he participated in preparations for the establishment of the North Atlantic Treaty Organization. In 1951, promoted to Major General, he joined General Eisenhower in Paris and assisted in the establishment of Supreme Headquarters Allied Powers Europe (SHAPE). In January 1953, he became Commanding General, 28th Infantry Division in Germany. In July of that year, he was promoted

Just as I had reached the conclusion that it was best to let the future take care of itself, my secretary entered to say that the Pentagon was calling. It was the assistant chief for personnel. He directed me to proceed as soon as possible to Washington, where I was to receive orders to Bucharest, Romania. Delighted that at long last an overseas assignment was at hand, I packed quickly, and twenty-four hours later was on my way. En route, I busied myself trying to piece together what little I knew about Romania. It wasn't much. I had naturally followed with interest the newspaper accounts and occasional official reports of military operations in that area. I knew of the initial advance by German and Romanian armies into Russia and of their later disastrous defeat following a powerful Russian counteroffensive. I had been elated by the news of Romania's surrender the preceding August and of the precipitate withdrawal of the Germans from the entire country in the face of relentless Soviet pursuit. Beyond these few facts, I knew very little. I was particularly in the dark as to what American military interests might require the presence of an American general in Bucharest.

Arriving at the Pentagon, I was handed orders that explained the mystery. I had been appointed chief U.S. military representative on the Allied Control Commission for Romania, and I was to proceed

---

to Lieutenant General and was recalled to SHAPE as Chief of Staff to General Gruenther, who had become NATO Supreme Commander, Europe. Promoted to full General in May 1956, he continued on as Chief of Staff at SHAPE under General Lauris Norstad, retiring at his own request on November 1, 1959. He has been awarded the U.S. Legion of Merit and the Distinguished Service Medal (with Oak Leaf Cluster), and has been decorated also by the governments of Netherlands, France, Belgium, Germany, Italy, and Luxembourg.

In November 1959, General Schuyler joined the staff of New York Governor Nelson Rockefeller. In October 1960, he was appointed State Commissioner of General Services, remaining in that position until his retirement in January 1971. From 1963 to 1969, he served also as Chairman of the State Civil Defense Commission.

NOTE: This chapter is a personalized account of what I saw, heard, and experienced during my tour as U.S. Representative on the Allied Control Commission for Romania. It is based entirely on my personal recollections, substantiated in large part by information from the diary that I kept in my office from January 1945 through September 1946. During this period I dictated entries every day or two, covering events that occurred and activities in which I participated. It includes my own reactions to major developments as they came to my attention.

The diary has not been published. However, it was made available to Dr. Paul D. Quinlan in connection with his excellent book, *Clash over Romania: British and American Policies towards Romania: 1938-1947*. In certain instances I have used his study to refresh my memory concerning dates and occurrences not fully covered in my diary.

to Bucharest as soon as arrangements could be completed. The British representative, Air Vice-Marshal Donald Stevenson, was already en route; the Russian chairman of the commission, with a full staff of officers, had been functioning in Bucharest for several weeks.

My next few days were crammed with briefings by a variety of officials of the War, Navy, and State departments. I also acquired much useful background on developments in Romania leading up to the expulsion of the Germans and the realignment of the Romanian army on the Allied side. It might be useful to the reader to record here a few of the more important events of this period.[1]

Prior to the war, Romania, under King Carol, had been allied with France and Britain under a treaty of mutual assistance. However, as Hitler's forces began to sweep across Eastern Europe, it became apparent to Carol that his Western allies could offer no help in stemming the German tide and that opposition by Romania alone would be foolhardy. Accordingly, as a matter of self-preservation, Carol began developing close ties with Germany, and in 1940 he renounced entirely the Anglo-French guarantee. During that summer, however, Soviet Russia proclaimed the annexation of Romania's eastern provinces of Bessarabia and Northern Bucovina, and Hitler forced the king to cede much of Transylvania to Hungary and southern Dobruja to Bulgaria. Carol, having thus lost a third of the nation's territory without firing a shot in defense, became highly unpopular and in September 1940 was forced to abdicate in favor of his youthful son, Michael.

Power was quickly seized by the pro-German Gen. Ion Antonescu, who ruled as a dictator, retaining nineteen-year-old Michael as a symbol of legitimacy for the regime, his duties being largely restricted to awarding decorations and appearing occasionally at ceremonies. Antonescu cemented the nation's ties with Germany, allowed Hitler's troops to enter the country in force and in June 1941 at Hitler's behest, declared war on Russia. Romanian troops thereupon joined with the Germans in an offensive that regained the lost provinces of Bessarabia and Northern Bucovina, and then pushed on for a considerable distance into southern Russia.

By the spring of 1944 however, it became clear that the tide had turned in favor of the Soviets, and Romania began to seek a way out of the war. Informal discussions were held with Soviet representatives in Stockholm and with the British in Cairo, but nothing definite had

---

1. The next few paragraphs describing major events in Romania prior to my arrival in November 1944, constitute a very brief summary, derived primarily from Paul Quinlan's *Clash over Romania* (Los Angeles: American Romanian Academy of Arts and Sciences, 1977). For a detailed account of developments during this critical period see chaps. 3 and 4 of Dr. Quinlan's study (pp. 49-104).

been arrived at when in August the Russians launched a major counter-offensive in the south. The Red Army advanced quickly and by August 22 all of southern Russia, Bessarabia, and Northern Bucovina had been cleared of German and Romanian forces. Soviet troops then massed at the Prut River for a giant sweep across all of Romania.

At this point Michael decided it was time to act. He had been secretly assured of the backing of all four of the nation's principal political parties—the National Peasants, by far the most numerous, under Juliu Maniu, a former prime minister, greatly revered as a wise and sagacious leader; the Conservatives under Constantin "Dinu" Bratianu; the Social Democrats under Titel Petrescu; and the Communists led by Lucretiu Patrascanu. Accordingly, on August 23 Michael invited Antonescu to the palace, had him arrested by the palace guards, and broadcast the welcome news that Romania had ceased hostilities, had withdrawn from her German alliance, and was forming a new government in preparation for entering the war on the side of the Allies.

Michael's popularity with the Romanian people was thus assured. He had demonstrated courage and leadership at a critical moment in Romanian history, and the people loved him for it. His mother, Queen Helen, was almost equally revered. She had stayed close to Michael through the troubled years of his boyhood and had thus become his close confidante and counselor. During the months following Michael's coup, Soviet forces swarmed into Romania, overrunning the entire country. The new government sent delegates to Moscow, where the armistice terms were signed on September 13.

I learned about the discussions preceding the armistice only in October, after I arrived in Washington and was given access to the official reports. The Soviet minister of foreign affairs, V. M. Molotov, had insisted that the Soviet chairman of the Allied Control Commission in Romania be given full authority to run things in that country. When the American and British ambassadors objected strenuously, he pointed out that in Italy final authority on the commission rested with the American and British authorities; correspondingly, in Romania, a nation entirely within the zone of operations of the Soviet armies, the Soviet chairman of the commission must have complete control. He had added that United States and United Kingdom members would be furnished all information necessary for their governments and that they would be given full opportunity to express their views. The United States and the United Kingdom were far from happy with such an arrangement, but yielded eventually. Accordingly, the armistice agreement provided that the control commission would function under the "Allied (Soviet) High Command."

Most of the other articles of the agreement also had a distinct

Soviet flavor. For example, it was provided that all German war material would be handed over to the Soviets; that Romania must make
regular payments in currency to the high command "for the fulfillment
of its functions" and must provide fuel, food, and other materials and
services as directed; that Romania must pay to Russia, as reparations,
commodities to the value of 300 million U.S. dollars over six years;
that she must return to Russia all valuables, materials, and other property taken from Russian territory during the war; and that the high
command would supervise operation of the Romanian radio, postal,
telegraph and telephone facilities, the press and other printing activities,
film producing, and theatrical productions.

All these facts became quite clear during the course of my briefings. Not so clear, however, in light of the dominant role of the Soviets
on the commission, was the question of my own duties and responsibilities. I received many suggestions but few explicit instructions. Evidently, I was expected to "feel my way," doing whatever I could to
protect and advance the interests of the United States. I gathered that
I was to "work with" my British and Soviet counterparts, reporting
frequently and extensively on ACC operations, on developments
within the country and on Soviet military actions in my area. I was
also to insure that U.S. views on pertinent matters were presented to
our Soviet chairman. A challenging, but somewhat nebulous, bit of
guidance.

On all sides, and particularly within the War Department, I found
universal admiration for the wartime achievements of the Red Army.
Moreover, our military leaders were eagerly anticipating ever closer
cooperation with the Soviet forces in our next and, it was hoped, final
drive against Germany. State Department officials were looking even
further ahead. They spoke in terms of the urgent need for Soviet-
American cooperation in the development of a united nations organization for a postwar world. No one mentioned even the possibility that
serious disagreements might develop over problems in Romania.

With background briefings completed and other matters arranged,
it was time to get going. I was full of enthusiasm for this new and
somewhat unclear assignment, convinced that in the light of top-level
agreements already reached, I could anticipate a frank and cordial
working relationship with my British and Soviet counterparts.

My first stop was Caserta, where I touched base with Gen. Joseph
McNarney, who commanded our Italian theater. Our meeting was short
but memorable. At its conclusion, he remarked: "Well, Schuyler,
you will be on your own, so don't get into trouble. If you do, don't
expect me to come and bail you out. I have no surplus troops available,
and if I did, I certainly wouldn't commit them to Romania!"

At McNarney's suggestion, I made a quick visit to the offices of the Italian Armistice Control Commission in northern Italy. The chairman was a U.S. naval officer. He told me that his staff, a fairly large one, consisted entirely of U.S. and U.K. nationals. When I asked about Soviet participation, he said there was virtually none. The Russian chief representative was advised of formal meetings, but seldom appeared. Russian delegates occasionally came to ask questions, which were fully answered. Otherwise, there was little indication of Soviet interest. I drew no comfort from this information.

Back at Caserta, I found my C-47 plane awaiting, so I flew on to Athens. There, after an overnight stop, I was notified that my long-awaited Moscow clearance for the flight through the Soviet zone had at last arrived. We took off at once, finally reaching Bucharest about noon one day in early November, 1944.

Not knowing what we might encounter on arrival, we were all in field uniform with helmets and sidearms. As soon as our plane stopped, my little three-man security detachment jumped out smartly and took positions on both sides and rear of the plane. The rest of us then disembarked with some show of dignity. As we stood around wondering what to do next, we observed a cavalcade of shiny automobiles approaching across the field. They stopped in front of us and out stepped eight or ten officers in blue full-dress uniforms, complete with gold epaulets, medals, and glittering sabers. They presented themselves as senior officials of the king's household and informed me that His Majesty welcomed me to Romania and hoped I would call at my convenience. At that moment a shabbily dressed Russian captain, cradling his tommy-gun, stepped forward and advised that he represented General Vinogradov, who would be glad to see me when I was settled. He then ambled off by himself across the field.

Finally, a young American in naval uniform stepped up. He presented himself as Comdr. Frank Wisner, chief of our Office of Strategic Services detachment in Bucharest. He had been in the city for some weeks arranging to send to Italy the U.S. airmen who had been shot down and captured during our air strikes at the Ploesti oil refineries. He had also made a number of preparations for our arrival, including commandeering living space at a hotel, taking over a building for our temporary offices, and requisitioning a number of automobiles for myself and my staff. Wisner proved to be an outstanding officer, ideally suited for his task in Bucharest. Later he returned to Washington, where he took over the Special Operations Division of the newly created Central Intelligence Agency.

During my first few days in Romania, I was very busy organizing my little mission staff, seeing to the establishment of my radio communication link with Caserta, and holding initial meetings with Mr.

Burton Berry, the State Department representative, Air Vice-Marshal Stevenson, my British counterpart on the control commission, and young King Michael and Queen Mother Helen, both of whom were extremely cordial.

Of course, one of my earliest calls was on Gen. Sergei Vinogradov, deputy chairman of our commission. (Officially, our chairman was Marshal F. I. Tolbukhin, commanding Russia's southern group of armies. He never appeared at our meetings and apparently left all ACC operations to his deputy chairman.) But, some hours prior to our meeting, I found myself confronted with my first ACC problem. Early that morning I received a request from Mr. Rica Georgescu, director of operations for the American-owned Romana-Americana Oil Company, for an immediate meeting. Upon receiving him, I was told that the Soviet ACC representative at Ploesti had presented the company written instructions for the loading of large quantities of casings and other oil drilling equipment on flatcars for shipment to Russia. The order stated that such equipment, which had come from Germany, was war booty, and that under the terms of the armistice, it should be turned over to the Soviet Union. The loading had been taking place for several days. Georgescu asked my immediate intervention to stop these Soviet seizures. After discussing this matter briefly with Mr. Berry, we both agreed that I should intervene as soon as possible.

Accordingly, during my first call on General Vinogradov, and after a short exchange of pleasantries, I said that I must raise a substantive problem that required our immediate attention. I pointed out that much of the oil equipment was stamped to show that it had been produced in the United States and that even though it may have been shipped through Germany, it had been paid for with the American funds of Romana-Americana and was therefore clearly American owned. I requested that the loading operation be halted until we could fully explore the matter together and either reach a common understanding or refer our differences to our respective governments. Vinogradov refused, saying his orders required that the material be loaded and shipped as soon as possible, and he had no authority to deviate from these instructions. He said he would report my objections to Moscow and would advise me if and when he received further guidance. As time went on I was to find that this was to be the standard Russian reply to the vast majority of protests presented by either the British or ourselves. On occasion, we would be told, in due time, that Moscow had rejected our protests. More often, our further inquiries would elicit a reply, in effect, that "Moscow has not yet replied; if any further action is desired, I will be so informed, and will advise you." That seldom, if ever, happened.

Of course, I at once radioed Washington the details of my futile protest to Vinogradov. I learned later that the question was raised by Averell Harriman, our ambassador in Moscow, on several occasions over the next few months, but Molotov stuck tenaciously to his original position that the equipment in question was war booty and hence subject to recapture by the Russians under Article XII of the armistice agreement.

Our first formal ACC meeting, with both Air Vice-Marshal Stevenson and myself present, took place a day or two later. Vinogradov outlined the operational arrangements he had been instructed to establish. Formal ACC meetings would be called every week or ten days. British and American airplane flights to and from Bucharest had to be cleared beforehand by the commission (ostensibly so that Russian antiaircraft batteries could be advised and thus would not open fire). Our planes would be subject to inspection by commission personnel on arrival and take-off. Our personnel would notify the commission of any trips outside the city and would be expected to take along a commission liaison officer. Between formal meetings, Vinogradov or his assistants would be available to discuss any matter either Stevenson or I felt to be urgent. We would also be kept fully informed of commission actions of interest to our governments.

Stevenson and I objected to a number of these restrictions, but Vinogradov replied that he was simply carrying out orders. He urged us to try out the procedures for a short time before lodging any formal protests, saying that he was sure we would not find them onerous.

Actually, in these early weeks, Vinogradov turned out to be right. Our plane clearances came through with welcome regularity. Our pilots established friendly relations with Russian officers at the airport so that arrival and departure inspections became more and more perfunctory, often amounting to nothing more than a casual wave of the hand. On trips into the surrounding country (I or one of my staff was making such a trip virtually every day), we were more often than not asked to go ahead on our own, since no liaison officer was available.

My chief concern during this early period was that we were receiving very little information as to actual work being done by the commission. At our formal meetings and in our occasional informal discussions, Vinogradov always spoke in general terms, but seemed unwilling to get down to specifics. My staff encountered the same difficulty in dealing with the Russian staff. For example, Vinogradov often mentioned his dissatisfaction over the slow progress by Romania in making reparations deliveries, in turning over German property, and in purging the government of former Fascists. But, despite our questions, he was unwilling to cite specific instances. I sought to learn of a few actual cases of nonperformance by the Romanians so that my staff could go into them, find out how such matters were handled by the commission staff and how the Romanians responded. No doubt Vinogradov sensed my purpose and very evidently did not want to see us involved to any such extent. Thus the details were simply not given us. Nor, except in a few very rare and unimportant instances, were any copies of commission directives or instructions to the Romanian government furnished us. This same pattern was followed both by Vinogradov, and later by his successor, throughout the entire life of the commission.

The result of all this was predictable; we turned to officials of the Romanian government for our information, and they, of course, were only too happy to oblige. Through them we obtained reports on all significant meetings on armistice matters, copies of Soviet communications to the government, and much other very useful material. Even in the last few months of the commission, when the Communists were fully in control of the government, there were still a number of officials, some of them ostensibly Communists themselves, who continued, often at great personal risk, to come to us with this same type of information.

I soon discovered that Burton Berry was an indispensable source of encouragement and support. He was not accredited to the Allied Control Commission. Rather, he was the State Department's representative, working out of the former U.S. Legation in Bucharest. His primary task was to establish and maintain informal channels with the king and the Romanian government, thus facilitating a post-peace treaty transition to full diplomatic recognition. An experienced diplomat, he was friendly, congenial, highly intelligent, and extremely articulate. His messages were a joy to read. During our early meetings, we both came to realize that the question of precedence between us required prompt resolution. His channel was, of course, direct to the State Department, mine to the Pentagon. Assuming reasonable coordination at the Washington end, we needed a corresponding allocation of responsibilities at our level in Romania. Accordingly, we agreed that all official approaches to the king and the Romanian government should be Berry's primary responsibility, while all dealings with the control commission and with the Russian delegation would be chiefly my concern. We would each be free to discuss matters of any nature with any individual we might wish to see, keeping each other fully informed of such discussions. We would meet frequently and would have free access to each others' incoming and outgoing cables and directives. Our staffs, of course, followed the same procedure. The arrangement worked well throughout our tour in Romania. We never found ourselves at cross-purposes, and our reports to Washington reflected the full understanding and collaboration established between us.

It did not take us long after our arrival and settling-in period to sense that things were not going well either for the Romanian government or for the country generally. The loose association of the four major parties—National Peasants, Liberals, Socialists, and Communists— that had supported King Michael in his successful coup against the Germans in August had begun to fall apart in September. Gen. Constantin Sanatescu, Michael's early choice as prime minister, proved incapable of strong leadership, and by the time of our arrival in November the government seemed to be simply drifting along, with almost all factions equally discontented. There had been no real program established for the timely discharge of armistice obligations or for reorganization of government offices, which had been thoroughly infiltrated by German sympathizers during the Antonescu regime. Land-reform legislation, corrective economic measures, and other needed governmental actions were all blocked by one or another of the political parties and got nowhere.

In early December, Michael, sensing the general disenchantment, called for Sanatescu's resignation. He appointed in his stead Gen. Nicolae Radescu, a strong-willed, outspoken officer with no ties to any party, who had spent a year or more in concentration camps for speaking out against Antonescu's pro-German policies. Several other changes in cabinet assignments were made, but the general balance between parties was left undisturbed. The king told us that Andrei Vyshinsky, the Soviet Deputy Minister of Foreign Affairs, who was visiting Bucharest at the time, seemed well pleased with the new appointments.

But Soviet approbation for the Radescu government did not last long. Soon a new political force appeared on the scene, known as the National Democratic Front (FND). It was an alliance of all Romanian leftist parties, including the Communists, Social Democrats, and the Ploughmen's Front, as well as several small and unimportant groupings. The Ploughmen's Front, under Dr. Petru Groza, consisted largely of dissident peasants in the Transylvanian region who were unhappy with Maniu's leadership of the National Peasant party. They demanded immediate land reform and more government attention to local peasant needs.

The FND had reluctantly supported Radescu's appointment, perhaps largely because Dr. Groza had been added to the government as deputy premier. But they openly criticized and sabotaged many of Radescu's efforts to control disorder in the country, and they encouraged workers in industry to demand higher wages, improved working conditions, and a larger voice in management decisions.

By mid-January it had become clear to Burton Berry and me that the Soviets were secretly, though perhaps only indirectly, supporting the Romanian Communists. At leftist political rallies, more and more Soviet-type firearms were turning up in the hands of party members. With greater and greater frequency National Peasant and Liberal newspapers were being suspended or closed down by orders from the ACC, for seemingly trifling violations of censorship provisions. Greater pressure was exerted on the Romanian government for the disarming or disbandment of army units, particularly Romania's only tank regiment, charged with maintaining order in and around Bucharest.

Stevenson and I both raised these questions at ACC meetings, but Vinogradov denied any Soviet aid to political parties. He assured us that newspapers were disciplined only when they printed attacks on one of the Allied governments, and he claimed that Romanian forces in Bucharest were far stronger than necessary to maintain order. He proclaimed the oft-repeated Soviet line that Romania needed the continuance of a coalition government and that Russia did not wish to see a Communist-controlled regime in power since the nation was simply not ready for communism.

By mid-February 1945 the political situation in all of Romania had become critical. In many cities and towns Communists took over control of local governments by force. Riots and bloodshed were daily occurrences. Radescu used what forces he had to stem the tide, but these were insufficient. In one instance, Radescu made plans to fly to Craiova to direct his troops in stemming a riot, but was told by the ACC that he must give at least two days' notice before his plane could be cleared for such a trip. Soviet troops and police appeared with greater frequency on city streets and rumors were rife of an impending Communist coup.

Within the ACC, Stevenson and I noted that our frequent protests and constant probing of sensitive issues were producing their own strains on our Soviet relationships. Our plane clearances became increasingly difficult to arrange—sometimes with no arrivals or departures allowed for several weeks at a time. On one occasion, a trip by Berry in my plane to Istanbul was delayed on various pretexts for upwards of four weeks. Clearances for trips outside the city, particularly visits to politically disturbed areas, began to meet with frustrating delays. We frequently went ahead with these local trips on our own and were often stopped by Soviet patrols, but were never turned back.

On February 20, following an ACC meeting, I remained for a discussion of the Romanian political situation with Mr. Pavlov, newly appointed political representative on the commission. Mr. Berry had told me that Pavlov was regarded as Vyshinsky's right-hand man. He was very forthright in expressing to me his views as to the unwillingness,

and perhaps the inability of the present government to meet its obligations. He ended our discussion by indicating that Russia regarded Radescu, the Romanian army, and both the National Peasant and Liberal
parties as "Fascist," and that the only political group truly representative of the Romanian people was the National Democratic Front.
Later, after discussing with Berry the details of my meeting, we both
concluded sorrowfully that the days of any all-party government in
Romania were numbered and that the nation would shortly find itself
in the grip of a leftist, minority regime, probably imposed by Soviet
Russia.

February 24 turned out to be a crucial day for General Radescu.
On that afternoon a huge demonstration by FND adherents (some of
them armed) took place in the square adjacent to the Ministry of the
Interior. Orderly at first, the crowd was later roused to action by in-
flammatory speakers. Many rushed the fence surrounding the building
and began to tear away the pickets. At this point a few shots were fired,
but my officers who were on hand as observers could not determine
whether the first rounds came from troops inside the fence or from
individuals in the crowd. As the excitement intensified, the troops
fired into the air to discourage the attackers, but with little effect.
When the troops themselves were fired upon, they returned the fire,
directly at the advancing mob. One bullet, fired from somewhere in
the square, crashed into the office where Radescu was sitting and
lodged in his desk. The crowd was finally dispersed, leaving ten to
twenty people lying dead or wounded in the square.

That evening Radescu made a nation-wide radio broadcast in
which he denounced the Communists for causing the riot and urged
continued support for his coalition government. He told us that an
hour or so later he was called to the control commission, where he was
upbraided for speaking on the radio without commission authority and
was personally blamed for the death of "innocent citizens."

Had there been any residual doubts left in our minds as to Soviet
interference in Romanian internal affairs, they would have been dis-
sipated by the events of February 27 and the days following. On the
twenty-seventh Vyshinsky arrived, unheralded, direct from Moscow. He
went straight to the palace for an interview with the king. What transpired at that meeting and at several succeeding encounters was related
to me and to Mr. Berry a few days later by Michael himself.

At their first meeting Vyshinsky began by stating abruptly that
Radescu must resign. He said the government had lost the support of
the Romanian people, it could no longer maintain order, and it must
be replaced by a "homogeneous" government that could look after
the peoples' interests and get on with the war effort. The king, taken

aback by Vyshinsky's bluntness, referred to the just published Yalta declaration calling for broadly representative governments in all liberated countries. Vyshinsky cut him short by saying that the Yalta declaration mentioned nothing about General Radescu. He then departed abruptly, announcing that he would remain in Bucharest for several days.

That night, for the first time since my arrival, a considerable number of Russian patrols, with bayonets fixed, moved through the streets—an obvious reminder of Russian power.

Next morning the king began a round of conversations with party leaders, as required by Romania's constitution. However, that afternoon, Vyshinsky appeared once more. Annoyed to learn that no definitive action had yet been taken, he pulled out his watch and said to the king: "All right, you have two and one half hours to make up your mind. I shall expect to hear of Radescu's resignation by six o'clock tonight." He then turned on his heel and stalked out, slamming the door behind him so hard that pieces of plaster broke from around the doorjamb and dropped to the floor.

Michael felt that he had no choice but to conform to Vyshinsky's demand. Accordingly, at six o'clock the Bucharest radio announced the resignation of General Radescu and his entire cabinet. The king also wished to announce that Prince Barbu Stirbey, an elderly but venerated diplomat, had been asked to form a new government. However, the Russian censor refused to permit it, apparently anticipating Stirbey's failure. This, in fact, proved to be the case, for next morning the FND refused flatly to join any Stirbey-led regime. At this juncture Vyshinsky advised the king that Dr. Petru Groza was the Soviet's choice for prime minister. Thereupon, Michael, with considerable reluctance, called in Groza and handed him the mandate to form a broadly representative government.

Groza proceeded on a round of consultations with various party leaders. He found the National Peasants and Liberals steadfastly unwilling to participate, perhaps because he insisted that all important cabinet posts must be filled by FND members. Abandoning his efforts to establish a broad coalition, Groza at last presented the king a cabinet list composed largely of FND leaders, but also including several dissident Peasants and Liberals who had broken with their parties and had announced their support of the FND. One of this group was the Soviet choice for vice-premier, George Tatarescu, a brilliant but unscrupulous politician, who had risen to some eminence under King Carol and the Iron Guard, through his seemingly implacable hatred of communism. Now, however, he had gained favor in Russian eyes by vociferously backing the FND.

Michael initially rejected Groza's cabinet as being insufficiently representative and considered withdrawing Groza's mandate. He was warned, however, that the Soviets would regard such a step as being hostile to their interests. Groza told the king he must either abdicate or approve the proposed cabinet. He warned that the FND, with full Soviet backing, was planning a huge demonstration on March 6. At that time, if necessary, the people would "elect" the new government and force the king's abdication. Michael told us later that he pondered deeply these two options. The queen favored abdication, but Michael at last decided that if he stayed, he might still be of some help to his people. Therefore he yielded, and at the demonstration on March 6, the new Groza government was announced, amid great jubilation among the assembled crowd.

For several days following Vyshinsky's arrival, Stevenson and I bombarded Vinogradov with urgent requests for an ACC meeting, but received no reply. Finally, after a delay of four days, he did call a meeting, but announced when we assembled that his purpose was only to introduce his successor, Col. Gen. Susaikov. Vinogradov was to stay on as chief of staff. I at once raised the question of the Vyshinsky visit, but Susaikov interrupted to say that he had only just arrived, was unfamiliar with the situation, and would have to postpone substantive discussions to a later date.

Two days later I managed to arrange a meeting with Susaikov. I protested vehemently against Vyshinsky's pressures on the king and his consequent interference in Romanian affairs. Furthermore, I said I could not understand why I had received no information from the ACC concerning this grave matter and had not been consulted in any way. Susaikov said very little in direct reply. He launched into a tirade against what he termed the sorry record of the Radescu government, and ended by stating simply that he would forward my views to Moscow. I left the meeting feeling that once again my protests had accomplished little, except perhaps to indicate that my government was fully aware of what was going on, was strongly opposed to Vyshinsky's actions, and would no doubt make its position clear at top government level.

From the very beginning, Susaikov proved to be a difficult man to deal with. Unlike the usually courteous Vinogradov, he was rough, tough, and sometimes actually surly. A Russian source told me later that he had been a village blacksmith before the war. Following his induction into the army, he rose rapidly through all grades to the rank of colonel general, commanding one of Russia's tank armies. He had fought in numerous battles and was wounded seriously several times. Though cooperative when it suited his purpose, his usual attitude was one of antagonism toward any Western official.

Throughout the tumultuous period of the preceding two weeks, both Berry and I kept Washington fully informed. We had received messages in reply with a good deal of useful guidance, but very few words of advice or encouragement that we could pass on to King Michael. We did learn, however, that both the U.S. and British governments had instructed their ambassadors to Moscow to protest in the strongest terms against Vyshinsky's activities, particularly the pressures he had placed on the king to remove Radescu and accept Groza. We were told that such protests had been duly delivered, but that Molotov had stubbornly refused to give an inch. He proclaimed that the Soviet government could not tolerate disorders in the rear of advancing Soviet armies, and that Groza's regime was the only one that could insure order and tranquility. Harriman was instructed to reply that the U.S. government could not recognize the Groza regime as being truly representative within the standards agreed upon at Yalta and, accordingly, could not participate in peace negotiations with that government. Unhappily, we learned also that just at this time, the Polish political situation was hitting the front pages of the newspapers, and that certain other very serious matters of disagreement with the Soviets were beginning to surface. Berry and I surmised that in the light of these developments, the United States would be most reluctant to force an open break with Russia over Romania.

During the next few months the situation remained outwardly calm. The FND used the period to reorganize and consolidate its position. The police was reoriented along Communist lines and new left-leaning judges were appointed to virtually all the local courts. The army was reduced in strength, recruits were deprived of their weapons and sent home. Many new Communist officers were appointed to key posts, while former commanders, including many with excellent war records, were relieved and some dismissed. During this period, the Tudor Vladimirescu Division was returned from Russia and stationed in Bucharest. This division consisted entirely of Romanian prisoners of war, captured during the German retreat. They had embraced communism and volunteered, which was obviously an attractive alternative to the arduous life of Russian P.O.W. camps. The division was thoroughly trained in Russian tactics and by the time of its return was regarded by the Soviets as the most trustworthy unit in the Romanian army. Its arrival in Bucharest was celebrated by an elaborate parade through the streets. The men rode in newly painted trucks and combat vehicles, all of American origin, no doubt obtained under the Lend-Lease program. Units of this division were later used by the government for street patrols. They were also much in evidence at public gatherings and demonstrations.

The new government quickly passed a land distribution law, confiscating all private landholdings greater than fifty hectares. The king felt obliged to sign the act since it had been legally enacted by the government he had accepted. He noted to Groza, however, that the courts might find the law unconstitutional due to its confiscatory provisions. Thereupon, a few days later, Groza presented for Michael's signature an edict modifying the constitution to validate the law. This Michael refused to sign on the grounds that the constitution did not authorize modification by governmental edict.

The Groza government exerted every effort to meet Russian demands under the armistice agreement. By mid-spring 1945, these demands were running around fifty billion lei (about twelve million dollars) per month. Of this amount, only about fifteen billion lei represented reparations under Article XI. Over twice that amount, more than thirty billion, was being demanded under the Soviet interpretation of Article X for upkeep of the one-million-strong Red Army on Romanian soil. The remainder represented demands under Article XII. All of these costs were naturally to escalate drastically in the months ahead, as the purchasing power of the lei continued to drop.

The Groza regime also moved to consolidate its power. Workers' committees, set up in the oilfields and in many other industries, were encouraged to demand higher wages, shorter hours, and special benefits, in the form of food, clothing, and family allowances. These committees also played an ever more important role in management decisions. In rural areas, local leaders of the National Peasant and Liberal parties were arrested and either deported or imprisoned. Most of the few remaining Peasant and Liberal newspapers were closed down by ACC orders, on one pretext or another.

In April 1945, at my request, I was ordered to return to Washington for consultations. I wanted the opportunity to explain in detail the situation within the country and to point out that the Groza government, with strong Russian support, was strengthening its hold on the nation almost daily. On arriving, I found that Gen. John A. Crane, our representative on the ACC in Bulgaria, had been called back also. I passed a week or more in meetings in the War, Navy, and State departments, and found that my cables, and those from Mr. Berry, had been given wide circulation so that everyone seemed well informed on the Romanian situation. General Crane and I had a meeting lasting several hours with Acting Secretary of State Joseph Grew, at the conclusion of which he took us to see President Truman, who had just taken office and who was trying to decide what policies he should follow with the Russians. At Grew's request I outlined to the president the problems we were facing, stressing particularly Vyshinsky's pressure on the king to accept an unrepresentative government. I described the restrictions that inhibited our participation in ACC decisions and that prevented American newspaper reporters, businessmen, and even new members of our own staffs from circulating freely. The president's immediate reaction was: "Why don't we just pull out, instead of staying there to be kicked around ignominiously?" Secretary Grew replied that such an action would be playing directly into Soviet hands. They would be delighted to be able to pursue their course in Romania unobstructed by American objections. The Soviets were oblivious to world-wide opinion. The State Department, he said, was preparing a study on the basic policy differences that were developing in a number of areas between ourselves and the Russians. He said that he hoped the study would propose a set of policies covering the entire spectrum, together with implementing action. The president seemed content to let it go at that. He asked me to prepare a memorandum for his study, covering the points I had made to him orally. This I did, a few hours later.

I also had several interesting talks with Ambassador Harriman, who was visiting Washington at that time. He told me how he had presented to the Russian government the numerous U.S. objections to Soviet actions in Romania, but to no avail. Molotov had stood absolutely firm, even refusing to discuss possible compromises that might conceivably have resolved the differences between us. Harriman felt that a final solution must await the next meeting of heads of government, now planned to be held at Potsdam. In the meantime, he would continue pressure for broadening our ACC responsibilities so that we might participate in all decisions taken at our level.

I returned to Bucharest early in May, with little encouraging news for Mr. Berry. I had, however, a far better understanding of the major differences between ourselves and the Russians with respect to almost every country in Central and Eastern Europe, including Italy and Germany. I realized that any agreement on Romania had to be achieved within the context of an over-all understanding covering the entire area, and this would require action primarily at the highest level. We, in Bucharest, could do little to alter the situation. I resolved to renew my efforts to improve relations with my Russian counterparts, but to continue to object to ACC actions or procedures that I considered improper. Finally, I would endeavor to handle at my level all disagreements on local problems, avoiding further involvement of the U.S. government, pending receipt of additional guidance from Washington.

Back in Bucharest, I learned that the Romanian government had encountered many difficulties in the implementation of the Agrarian Reform Law. It was found that while there were some 1,500,000 hectares of land confiscated, there were at least 4,000,000 peasants entitled to participate in the redistribution. Therefore, reallocation had to be made on a highly selective basis, with widespread dissatisfaction among those who received little or no land.

The government also seemed to be deep in financial trouble. It had begun debate on an 800 billion lei annual budget, a sum that obviously could be provided only through the printing of more and more paper money, thus bringing ever increasing inflation. However, at this time, the Russians took an important step that altered significantly the financial picture. In late May, Moscow announced the conclusion of a five-year trade agreement with Romania, under which virtually the entire exportable production of the nation in oil, agricultural products, and industrial items was committed to Russia. In return, the Soviets promised to supply badly needed war materials, machinery, and technical assistance. The agreement provided for the creation of joint Soviet-Romanian (SOVROM) companies controlling much of the oil, agricultural, and water navigation operations in Romania. The door was left open for the formation of similar companies in other fields as the need might arise. Stock in the companies would be owned fifty-fifty by each nation, but most of the key operational posts would go to the Russians. The agreements offered considerable promise for stabilizing the sagging Romanian economy in the years ahead, but at the same time, they linked the nation's economic life to that of Russia. Moreover, the provisons for controlling prices, wages, and the allocation of fuel and raw materials presaged the gradual throttling of private enterprise.

The U.S. government strongly protested the establishment of these SOVROM companies on the grounds that they not only prevented American business interests from playing a part in Romanian economic life, but also, through the transfer of formerly German-owned property and stock shares to the new companies, they were denying the United States its fair share of such German assets. The Russians, however, rejected all protests.

My diary covering this period notes an interesting meeting I had with Mr. Vladescu, secretary of the newly appointed chairman of the Romanian Commission for Execution of the Armistice. Information he provided is illustrative of the toughness of the Soviets concerning the full execution of the armistice obligations, even though they were by this time dealing with the friendly Groza regime. It seems that quite by accident the Russians came upon a report by the Romanian administrator of Transnistria during the German-Romanian occupation. He was a man who took pride in demonstrating his superior administrative ability. According to Vladescu, the report, which listed all items taken by the invaders from the Russian population, was highly exaggerated. The totals listed were more than double the amounts previously reported by Romania and accepted by the ACC as the quantities returnable under Armistice Article XII. Moreover, much of the booty carried off remained under German control, and was apparently retained by the German armies in their retreat from Romania following the coup of August 24, 1944. Nevertheless, Vladescu said, the Soviets were now insisting on full repayment or replacement for the total quantities shown in the administrator's report—a large and unanticipated new claim against Romania's dwindling resources.

Through the spring and early summer the king endeavored to discharge his responsibilities strictly as prescribed by the constitution. Even though he did not approve of them, he signed a number of legislative acts and decrees that appeared to have been enacted legally. He held scrupulously to the policy of seeing U.S. and U.K. representatives only as frequently as he met with Russian officials. This did not prevent Berry and me from occasionally visiting the palace, since the Russians had begun to heap more honors and attentions upon the king. They even, with great pomp and ceremony, awarded him Russia's Order of Victory, the most honored Soviet decoration that could be bestowed upon a foreign official. During one of our visits, Michael informed us that he was under continuing pressure from Maniu and Bratianu to withdraw Groza's mandate before it was too late. Actually, we had been visited by both party leaders, seeking our advice concerning a similar course. They went so far as to suggest that action by the king might precipitate civil war in the country, which in turn could lead to a definite break, perhaps even open conflict, between the United States and Russia. Though not wishing to discourage them from any nonviolent action they might be planning, we reminded them that Romania remained under ACC control, and that with the country still under occupation by one million Soviet troops, a resort to arms would surely be met with stern repressive measures. We advised them to abandon, as dangerous fantasy, any thought that disagreement over Romania's internal affairs could precipitate armed conflict between Russia and the West. We answered inquiries from the king in a similar vein. He told us that he would refrain from definitive action unless and until he received official support by the British and Americans.

My efforts toward improving relations within the ACC met with sporadic results. I had a number of pleasant meetings with Susaikov, Vinogradov, and Pavlov. We engaged in a good deal of cordial conversation and we had several frank exchanges of view covering the attitudes of our respective governments concerning the situation in Romania. The problem of plane clearances eased considerably once more. Supply flights for my mission began arriving with fair regularity, but clearance for visits by correspondents and businessmen remained very sticky. I got nowhere in my efforts to play a role in ACC decision making, or to be better informed on the commission's daily activities. In particular, Susaikov was very firm in his view that deliveries and payments to Russia under the armistice were matters strictly between Romania and Russia. He felt that neither the United States nor the United Kingdom should have any interest in them whatever.

Thus matters rested within the ACC until July 17, when General Susaikov called me to a conference and presented a copy of a directive, emanating from Moscow, that he said established a new and far more responsible role for British and American ACC representatives. As stated in my diary, the directive provided for:

1. A formal meeting of chief representatives every ten days.
2. Consultation with British and Americans prior to issuance of directives.
3. General conferences at all ACC levels with British and Americans present in appropriate cases.
4. Complete freedom to travel throughout Romania.
5. Specific clearance procedures governing air travel and supply shipments.
6. Full authority for British and Americans to determine the size and composition of their own staffs.

Susaikov asked for my agreement to these new procedures. However, I already knew that Washington was preparing a proposal, for discussion at the Potsdam Conference, providing for a truly tripartite control commission. Therefore, I replied to Susaikov that since his paper did not indicate any coordination with the U.S. and U.K. governments, I must await a response from Washington before providing my official comments. At his request, I agreed to work temporarily under the new arrangements, pending later instructions from my government.

After studying Susaikov's paper in detail, I concluded that many of the provisions were still so vague as to afford Susaikov a great deal of leeway in their implementation. Should he wish to do so, his new authority would allow him to afford us a far greater participation in ACC operations than had hitherto been the case. But, if he still wished to keep us at arm's length, he could do that instead. As matters developed, Susaikov frequently chose to follow this latter course.

Our first meeting under the new procedures was a three-hour affair. It began with a long presentation by the Romanian Minister of Education, pointing out the many changes underway in Romanian education, including the rewriting of numerous textbooks to eliminate all criticisms of Allied governments. Mr. Pavlov followed with a lengthy summary of actions taken by the Groza government to get rid of "Fascists" and "Fascist tendencies" in Romanian life. He compared this with what he termed the complete lack of progress under the Radescu regime. The meeting produced very little we had not known before. Near the close, I raised the question of my several recent letters of protest on the transfers of German-owned property to the new SOVROM companies, asking that they be suspended until the matter could be discussed at government levels. Susaikov replied that his orders required him to expedite the transfers; he had no authority to delay or suspend them. All he could do was to forward my protests to Moscow, and this he had done. He reminded me that under the armistice terms the executive power in the ACC rested with the Russians, with the British and Americans as observers, and that nothing that had occurred since could change that fundamental concept. This, to me, was a clear indication of the "window dressing" nature of the so-called new procedures.

On August 3, we received our first reports on the outcome of the Big Three meetings at Potsdam. The news, in so far as problems in the Balkans were concerned, was a severe disappointment to Roy Melbourne and me. (Berry had taken leave in the United States, and his deputy, Melbourne, was taking his place.) Apparently the United States had got nowhere in its efforts to create truly tripartite control commissions, and no agreement had been reached on the broadening, or the replacement, of the Groza government. We felt badly let down. And we took no cheer from the press reports, just then received, that Russia had extended official recognition to Groza's regime.

Finally, on August 12, Melbourne received from Washington the policy guidance we had so long awaited. He was advised that, without commenting on any specific course of action, he might tell the king that the U.S. government would not discourage attempts by Romanian leaders to achieve full freedom of expression for all democratic groups, that we looked forward to the opportunity to establish diplomatic relations with a government in Romania more representative of the people, and that, if necessary, the king might call upon the three Allied governments for assistance as provided for in the Yalta declaration. Melbourne proceeded at once to present these views to the king, who was obviously very pleased.

Michael spent the next few days in consultations with his various party leaders and advisers: Maniu, Bratianu, Petrescu, Groza, and Patrascanu. All except the latter two were in favor of demanding Groza's immediate resignation. Accordingly, on August 20, the king summoned Groza once more and called on him to resign, on the grounds that his government was not broadly representative and thus could not, under

the Yalta declaration, represent Romania in forthcoming peace negotiations. Groza categorically refused the king's order, saying that he had
the full backing of the Russians, and that his continuance in power
was in Romania's best interest.

From that moment, Michael considered the Groza regime to be
illegally in office, and he at once prepared separate notes to each of
the three chief ACC representatives, asking for assistance from their
governments.[2] He delivered the notes at meetings with each of us in
turn. My meeting, to which I asked Melbourne to accompany me,
occurred immediately after the king had met with Susaikov and Pavlov,
and we were told the gist of their conversation. When the king handed
Susaikov his note, he explained that his dismissal of Groza had the
support of the majority of party leaders. Susaikov was greatly perturbed, protesting that had he been consulted earlier, the matter could
have been resolved to everyone's satisfaction. He urged the king to
withdraw his decision for Groza's resignation, adding that Maniu and
Bratianu were both Fascist and anti-Russian, as were their parties,
which could be disbanded under the terms of the armistice calling for
elimination of Fascist groups. The king stood fast, and Susaikov departed in a huff.

At our interview, the king seemed quite nervous. He said he had not
decided on his future course, and he wondered particularly what he
should do if he received any specific orders from the Russians. We
could not advise him directly, but we reminded him that since Russia
was still exercising military jurisdiction, any hasty or injudicious action
on his part might have very serious consequences. We asked that, if he
received any such orders, he inform us immediately.

It is of some interest at this point to note the U.K. reaction upon
learning of Washington's instructions of August 12 to Melbourne.
London's first messages to Stevenson on the subject expressed concern
that the United States had gone so far in encouraging the king as to
trigger actions that neither the United States nor the United Kingdom

---

2. Dr. Quinlan in *Clash over Romania* (pp. 142-43) refers to a message to
State from Melbourne describing the king's tentative plan, if Groza refused to
resign, to proclaim publicly the government's illegality and to call on the Court
of Cassation and the army to remove it. Quinlan also adds that, in view of the
weakness of the British position, the king finally decided to forego both public
announcement and appeal to the army, and instead to move directly to an appeal
to the Allies under the Yalta agreement. I do not now recall this aspect of the
king's plan and my diary does not mention it. However, with Romania's two
Russian-trained divisions controlling Bucharest, and with the high probability of
Soviet intervention if fighting should erupt, any appeal to the army for support
against the government might well have been disastrous, regardless of the strength
or weakness of the British position.

could effectively support. I learned that, unfortunately, a message setting forth this view had been shown to several of Michael's advisers. This caused a good deal of worry among those close to the king and, in fact, delayed for twenty-four hours or more the demand for Groza's resignation. In the end, however, all concerned, relying mainly on the strong U.S. position, agreed to advise the king to proceed with his demand that Groza resign.

A. V. M. Stevenson told me privately that, a day or so after receipt of the first U.K. message, he had received a new set of instructions advising him to support fully the U.S. position before the ACC, in whatever representations we might make with respect to the Groza government. This he did very effectively at our later meetings.

During the first several days following the effort to dismiss Groza, Michael found himself under a great deal of pressure, both from the Soviets and from FND leaders, to alter his position. The special celebration planned for August 23, the first anniversary of Michael's successful coup against the Germans, was a particular complication. An elaborate military parade, to be reviewed by the king and by representatives of the ACC, had been planned, with all the cabinet and various foreign dignitaries present, and a national holiday had been proclaimed. Michael however stood firm. Maintaining that Groza's government was now illegal, he declared he would not attend the parade or take part in any other government-planned festivities.

Early on the morning of August 23, Susaikov presented a letter to the king that stated that the Soviet government had considered carefully the Romanian request for assistance and desired to state that it was definitely opposed to the resignation of the Groza government. Susaikov then departed, pausing on his way out to glare at a small group of the king's advisers and to announce: "You are the men responsible for this trouble. Many of you will be in tears shortly." The parade took place as scheduled, with only Groza, Susaikov and a few ministers in the reviewing stand. The royal box, beautifully decorated with red and gold canopies and carpets, remained empty.

That afternoon, Susaikov called a meeting of the ACC. He began by reading the Soviet reply to the king's note. I interposed that Washington had advised me that an early meeting of the three Allied governments had been requested to consider the matter, as contemplated in the Yalta declaration, and that in the interim I was to oppose any ACC action that might complicate the situation. With Stevenson supporting me, I urged that the ACC insure preservation of order, and prohibit any local demonstration that might give rise to trouble. Susaikov replied that he had full confidence that the Groza regime would maintain order. He added that the political crisis had been brought about solely through actions of the British and American representatives, about which he, as deputy chairman, had not been informed. Stevenson and I took exception to his remark and defended the positions of our governments, but the argument of course got us nowhere.

Following receipt of the Soviet note, the king informed Melbourne and me that he had decided on the course of action. He and his mother would retire to their palace at Sinaia, staying completely aloof from the Groza regime until he had received, from each of the three Allies, definitive replies to his note calling for assistance. Before departing, the queen mother asked me privately whether, in case of threats against the lives of the king or herself, they might seek sanctuary under my protection. Having anticipated this request, I had already received instructions. Therefore, I replied that in the event of direct evidentiary threat to their lives or persons, I would give them sanctuary at my villa, reporting my action at once to the ACC. Thereafter, I would be bound by any decisions reached by the ACC, with tripartite agreement. The queen mother appeared greatly relieved.

Thus began a sort of suspended crisis between king and government, which was destined to last more than four months. The Russians seemed in no hurry to undertake the government-level consultations. While not actually refusing to consult, they did insist that the matter be held in abeyance pending the outcome of the foreign ministers' meeting scheduled for September. But that meeting produced no change in the situation. We learned that Molotov remained as obdurate as ever, refusing even to consider any change in the Groza government. In Bucharest, Susaikov was equally stubborn in refusing to discuss any meaningful change in the roles of the U.S. and British representatives on the control commission.

For Groza, these continuing delays seemed to be working out greatly to his advantage, and he appeared to feel more secure in his position than before the crisis began. The government stepped up its campaign against the opposition. Arrest and imprisonment of known National Peasant and Liberal party members occurred on an almost daily basis. Their attempted meetings were broken up by strong-arm squads, many participants being abused and beaten. The last remaining few of the non-FND newspapers were closed down.

In October we learned of Mr. Mark Ethridge's impending visit. Mr. Ethridge, the highly respected publisher of the *Louisville Courier Journal,* had been selected by Secretary of State James Byrnes to visit Bulgaria and Romania and to make a frank and independent appraisal of the situation as he found it. The Communists soon spread the rumor that the secretary, fed up with the one-sided reports he had been receiving from the ACC mission and legation, was at last moving to have an objective view presented to him. They expressed confidence that at last the American people would see things in their proper light.

Mr. Ethridge arrived about November 20, having already spent several weeks in Bulgaria. He had also paid a short visit to Moscow, where he had a brief meeting with Vyshinsky, as well as with other officials. In Romania, he had several long talks with Berry and me, an hour or more with Susaikov, and extended conferences with Groza, Radescu, and other party leaders. He paid several visits to the king, and saw a number of businessmen, diplomats, prominent government officials, and many others. After some ten days of extensive consultations, he prepared a message to the secretary summarizing his findings. He showed it to Berry and me prior to dispatch. My diary summarizes his conclusions, which pleased but hardly surprised us:

1. The Groza government was not broadly representative of the Romanian people.
2. Elections conducted by that government would be a farce.
3. The situation has progressed too far to be rectified solely by the Romanian authorities.
4. The only acceptable solution would require the agreement of the three Allied Powers, at top level, to the installation of a truly representative government, which would then be called upon to hold elections under the watchful eye of a fully tripartite ACC.

Ethridge delivered a copy of his message to Susaikov. We learned later that Byrnes furnished Stalin a copy also.

Thursday, November 8, was the king's name day. In the morning, in observance of long established Romanian custom, thousands of people began to assemble in the square in front of the palace to do homage to their sovereign. Many carried placards displaying the king's picture or banners with patriotic messages. My observers estimated that by 11:00 A.M. almost 15,000 people had gathered. Most of these, of course, were members of the National Peasant or Liberal parties. They appeared to be unarmed. Troops of the Tudor Vladimirescu Division were lined up on all sides of the square. The crowd remained orderly, shouting for "King and Country!" and waving their placards, until about noon. At that time, a number of trucks filled with police and plainclothesmen, wearing sidearms and carrying clubs, entered the square and began circling among the people. The attitude of the crowd changed at once. Fists were raised and insults exchanged. At that point, the police and plainclothesmen descended from the trucks and began making arrests. Fights broke out, shots were fired, and the police were quickly overwhelmed. Several trucks were overturned and caught fire. The troops around the square opened fire, aiming first into the air, then directly into the crowd. The people began quickly to disperse, running in all directions to dodge police and soldiers. They left thirty or forty dead or wounded on the ground. Romanians reported to us later that some four hundred arrests had been made. Those in custody were taken to the soldier's barracks, where they were beaten or tortured and forced to sign "confessions" implicating Maniu and Bratianu.

That evening, Stevenson and I each urged Susaikov to call an immediate ACC meeting to discuss the disorders. Susaikov began by stating that he was still studying reports and was not ready to form a conclusion. With backing from A. V. M. Stevenson, I urged Susaikov to establish a joint committee of U.S., U.K., and Russian members to investigate thoroughly the situation causing the riots, as well as the disorders themselves, and to make a full report to us, with recommendations as to what action the ACC should now take to prevent any recurrence. Susaikov said he would take my proposal under advisement and report to us later. Several days thereafter he informed us that he was rejecting my suggestion on the ground that it would constitute undue interference in Romanian affairs. He said the Groza government was conducting its own investigation and would report the results to us. He added that he had full confidence that the government would handle the matter promptly and properly.

In the meantime, the government staged a mass public funeral for the police and government supporters who had been killed. Shops and factories were ordered closed, and all workers were forced to attend the ceremonies. National Peasant and Liberal party members who lost their lives were permitted no public funeral of any kind. They had to be buried late at night, in simple, private ceremonies.

By early December, the situation in Romania had become relatively quiet. The brutal actions of the government in quelling the disorders of November 8 apparently ended for good the last hopes of the Liberals and National Peasants for mounting any effective opposition. The army had been completely reorganized, with Communists or sympathizers in all key posts. The police and the local judiciary were filled with FND supporters. The peasants who now owned land found they could obtain allocations of seed and help with their plowing only if they demonstrated support for the government. Those still landless were entirely dependent on local peasant committees for such small jobs as became available. Workers in shops and factories saw advancement going only to their FND comrades, through recommendations by their workers' committees. Others, considered less reliable, were assigned the more menial tasks, and many simply lost their jobs. SOVROM companies were now predominant in many fields, including oil production, banking, lumber, navigation, land transportation, and aviation.

Berry and I still continued to receive a large number of visitors, including businessmen, bankers, politicians, and even an occasional government official, who wanted to tell us about what they saw taking place all around them. But now these people preferred to come only after dark, and they made certain that they were not observed entering or leaving our offices.

At last, about December 10, we received the welcome news that the foreign ministers conference that Byrnes had so long sought would take place in Moscow on December 15. We felt that this meeting would prove to be of vital importance to the future of Romania, and we followed with avid interest the progress as reported to us by Harriman. Molotov stood firm in his unconditional support of the Groza regime, even though Byrnes and Bevin insisted that they could not accept that government as a representative one. At last, just when the participants seemed to be losing all hope for an acceptable solution, Stalin put forward a "compromise," which was accepted.

In my diary I recorded my reaction to Stalin's proposal and the decision by Byrnes and Bevin to accept it:

It appears to Mr. Berry and myself that the United States and Britain have given way almost completely to Russia's demands . . . . Vyshinski, Harriman and Clark-Kerr (British Ambassador to Moscow) are to come to Bucharest at once and to recommend to the King that he take into the Groza government one representative each from the National Peasant and National Liberal Parties. With these two additions, the Groza government is to continue in office exactly as it is formed at present, and upon receipt of assurances that it will permit freedom of speech, freedom of assembly and freedom of press to all political parties, the United States and Great Britain undertake formally to recognize the government. Thus the same government which for the last nine months has been completely selling out Rumania, has with cruelty and tyranny suppressed all efforts of Rumanian patriots to alter the situation, and has been decidedly hostile toward British or American suggestions, that same government with only two additional members is now to receive full recognition. Last March when Groza was forming his government, he offered to Maniu and Bratianu two places each in the Cabinet, but was flatly turned down because such minority representation was considered totally inadequate for parties which together represented over 75% of the Rumanian electorate. Now, with only half as many representatives in the Cabinet, the Groza regime is being recognized by the Anglo-Americans as truly representative. Both Mr. Berry and I are very much discouraged over this outcome, and we feel that the agreement can only be regarded as a complete sell-out to Russian demands.[3]

On January 1, 1946, Ambassadors Harriman and Clark-Kerr and Mr. Vyshinsky arrived in Bucharest to arrange for the carrying out of the Moscow agreement. That afternoon they met with the king and formally advised him of the details of the new agreement. Meetings were

3. Diary, December 27, 1945, pp. 430-32.

then held with Groza, and with Maniu and Bratianu. Names initially put forward by party leaders to fill the two ministerial posts were declared unacceptable by Vyshinsky and Groza, but, finally, agreement was reached all around on Emil Hatieganu for the National Peasants and Mihai Romniceanu for the Liberals. Both men were highly respected by the rank and file of their parties.

Several days later, the two candidates were formally sworn into the government, and Groza made his government's pledge to observe scrupulously the principles of freedom of the press, speech, and assembly.

Before departing, Harriman met privately with Berry and me. He told us, as we had surmised, that both he and Byrnes were unhappy over the solution for Romania, but that Stalin had insisted that the Groza regime remain in office and had refused to discuss any other world problem until the Romanian matter was settled. However, once the Stalin compromise was accepted, real progress was achieved quickly on virtually all other outstanding problems.

In late January I was again summoned to Washington for consultations. Officials in both the War and State Departments were once more greatly interested in my firsthand accounts of what had transpired in Romania, but I detected a distinct feeling of relief that the impasse had been resolved so that attention could now be devoted to U.S.-Soviet problems in other areas.

I did not see the president during this visit, but I did have a long meeting with Secretary Byrnes. He told me that while the Moscow agreements fell short of what he had hoped to accomplish, he was encouraged by Berry's recent messages that reported the government's actions in allowing greater freedom of the press and freedom for all parties to hold meetings and express their views. I replied that although the signs might be encouraging at the moment, there was no assurance that such attitudes would continue once the general interest in the Moscow arrangements had died down. I said both Berry and I felt that, in the absence of strong pressure from the United States and the United Kingdom, the government would not hold elections before the conclusion of peace negotiations. The regime was still unpopular with the great majority of the electorate, both because of their repressive measures and also because, in the Romanian view, they had given in so completely to the excessive Russian demands for payment of armistice obligations. I added that we both felt that the government wanted very much to remain in power until the treaty was ready so that theirs might be the regime to sign the treaty. Mr. Byrnes concluded our meeting by expressing a very high opinion of Mr. Berry, saying that both his messages and mine had enabled State to keep fully abreast of Romanian developments. I left with my previous impression confirmed that the secretary was relieved that, with the Romanian problem no longer pressing, he could now devote his efforts to other tasks.

Before leaving Washington I arranged for Mrs. Schuyler and my teen-age daughter and son to join me in Bucharest. They arrived in due course and this naturally made the remainder of my stay in Romania much more pleasant than it would otherwise have been.

On my return to Bucharest I found that conditions in Romania had improved considerably after the United States and the United Kingdom recognized the Groza regime. National Peasant and Liberal party newspapers had been allowed to resume printing and opposition party meetings were being held with a minimum of government interference. At a chance meeting with Romniceanu over cocktails, he told me that he and Hatieganu had been cordially welcomed at cabinet meetings. They were extended full access to all departments and had ample opportunity to express their views at meetings. While their presence in the government had not yet produced any change in policy, he had hopes that if current attitudes continued, even this might come about.

Relations on the ACC level had now become much more cordial. Though still not told of the many meetings between the Russian staff and government officials, Susaikov did make an effort to introduce and discuss one or two subjects of mutual interest at each of our weekly ACC meetings. Plane clearances were now causing no problems and my officers were able to move freely about the country without escort.

However, this improved situation did not last long. By mid-April all parties began organizing for political campaigns in anticipation of late summer or early fall elections. Romniceanu and Hatieganu began to encounter difficulty in learning what the government was doing. They no longer had easy access to the various departments, and they began to feel that they were excluded from most discussions. Moreover, National Peasants and Liberals found their meetings once again disrupted by strong-arm squads, and they were unable to obtain police protection. Arrests of opposition party members grew in frequency, and several newspapers were closed down. On one occasion, both Hatieganu and Romniceanu, on their way to attend political meetings in different parts of the country, were molested and ill-treated. Hatieganu's car was stopped, his tires blown out, and he and wife insulted. Romniceanu's experience was similar. When he was stopped, two of his friends were pulled from the car and beaten up. Both ministers presented strenuous complaints to Groza, but no effort was made to apprehend and punish the perpetrators.

In May, Berry addressed a strong note of protest to the Romanian government citing a number of instances in which rights of free speech, freedom of assembly, and freedom of the press had been violated. The British followed with a similar note. The Romanian reply was indefinite and unsatisfactory. I addressed a similar protest to Susaikov, with the anticipated result. He simply replied that this was a matter to be handled by the United States with the now fully recognized government of Romania.

Also in May, Reuben Markham, correspondent for the *Christian Science Monitor,* who had been sending out accounts of incidents he had witnessed, was called to ACC headquarters by General Vinogradov. He was told that his articles showed a strong anti-Russian attitude, included insults to the Red Army, and that he had participated in Romanian party politics. Accordingly, Vinogradov told him his visa was thereby withdrawn and he must leave the country within five days. Markham objected, but to no avail. When I learned of the incient, I interviewed Markham, read his dispatches carefully, then went to see Susaikov with a letter of protest. I objected not only to the Soviet action on the basis of charges that I felt could be easily refuted, but more importantly, because I had been neither consulted nor informed beforehand. Susaikov refused to consider my arguments and simply stood firm on his decision. Of course, I reported at once to Washington and was advised that Harriman would raise the question on the Moscow level. I later learned that the Soviet government had fully supported Susaikov and had refused to make any modification in his decision expelling Markham.

At this time we began to detect a distinct hardening of the attitude of the Romanian government toward Americans. Both Berry and I were only rarely receiving visits from Romanian officials, and Berry's request for meetings with government ministers began to take a week or more to arrange. Even when ministers did see him, they received him coldly, and they seldom made helpful responses to his questions.

About June 1, one of my Romanian employees, Mr. Manicatidi, a young engineer who had worked previously for the Romanian War Ministry, was arrested outside our mission offices. One of my officers who had observed the arrest went at once to the police station where Manicatidi was being booked prior to incarceration. The officer demanded to know the charge and was told it was treason, transmitting military information to a foreign power. My officer became furious, said that such action was an insult to the United States, a member of the control commission, and insisted that Manicatidi be released at once to his custody. Manicatidi was then taken to my office, where I placed him under my protection. I informed the government, through Mr. Berry, that I could not recognize any such charge and would hold Manicatidi under my protection until the case was dropped. The government protested my action to Susaikov, who merely passed on the protest, as a matter for me to handle with the government. I reported the case to Washington and received full support for my actions. A month or so later when the furor had died down, but the charge had not been dropped, I put Manicatidi with his wife and small son on one of my planes to Italy. He was later tried in absentia and given a stiff sentence.

One of Mr. Berry's most trusted secretaries, Miss Olteanu, was also arrested and jailed on a similar, trumped-up charge. Despite his vigorous protest, Berry was unable to secure her release. He urged the State Department to withhold final acceptance of Romania's first ministers to Washington pending resolution of the Olteanu affair. State, however, apparently eager to avoid any further trouble with Romania, failed to support him.

The Allied conference for preparation of the peace treaties with Germany and her former allies, which met in July 1946, dragged on through the summer and early fall. In fact, the conference was still in session when the date selected for the Romanian elections, November 19, finally arrived. The electoral campaign had been a farce in every sense of the word. The National Peasants and Liberals were prevented from holding a single public meeting, each attempt being broken up by thugs armed with clubs or sidearms. The police interfered only at the last minute, and then simply to arrest party members as perpetrators of the disorders. All individuals who had served in the army during the campaign against Russia were denied the right to vote. Pursuant to Romanian law, voting lists were prepared and posted, carrying the names of all qualified voters who had registered. Yet, thousands of opposition party members who had duly registered found that their names had been omitted from the lists. All opposition newspapers were closed down, while every day the Communist press was filled with harsh criticism and unsupported charges aimed at the opposition. On election day hundreds of government trucks and buses circled through outlying villages, picking up their supporters and taking them to the polling places, while opposition members were forced to get to the polls as best they could. When they did arrive they found every polling place guarded by police and other government agents who jostled them, pushed them around, and actually prevented some from voting at all.

A few days before the elections, the United States and the United Kingdom addressed notes to the Romanian government protesting against these and other violations of the rights that that government had pledged to observe. They received the bland reply that since one of the three Allied governments had not seen fit to raise any objections, the two notes received could not be considered an agreed view of the three Allies, and therefore would be disregarded.

Under these conditions, Berry and I were not at all surprised when, two days after the elections had taken place, the government announced that all FND candidates had been elected with huge majorities. Berry's message to the State Department reported that the government, in its actions during the campaign and on election day itself, had "established a new low level for Balkan elections."[4]

The months following the elections were relatively quiet ones. Maniu and Bratianu told me they had virtually abandoned hope for any improvement in the situation. Michael sent us word that there was little more he could do to alter or even to delay the trend toward full Communist domination. He felt in fact that his days as king of Romania were numbered. The peace treaty was signed in February 1947, and thereafter, the role of the Allied Control Commission virtually ended. The Russians appeared to keep busy monitoring the continuation of their reparations programs, but there was little of interest to warrant my attention.

In early February, I received news that Moldavia and adjacent areas of northeastern Romania were in the grip of a severe famine. The harvest of the preceding fall had been disappointingly small and during the winter Red Army troops had swept the area clean of the small reserves of food that the peasants normally kept for just such an emergency. I made a tour of the stricken district in my jeep and found conditons even worse than had been reported. In village after village I visited peasant huts where whole families appeared on the brink of starvation. Local agencies had exhausted their resources, and the government seemed unable to help.

Returning to Bucharest, I went at once to see Susaikov, told him of the deplorable conditions I had found, and urged him to join me in an appeal to our governments to send food and medical supplies to the area. He looked at me for a moment, laughed and replied, "Of course I won't join you. We have famines in parts of Russia almost every year. The weak die and the strong survive. That is Nature's way. Besides," he added, "these people were our enemies two years ago. They brought this on themselves. Let them now get themselves out of it."

I returned to my office and sent off an immediate message to Washington, urging that it be brought to the attention of the president. I painted, as vividly as I could, a picture of the deplorable conditions I had found, told of Susaikov's negative attitude, of the Romanian gov-

4. U.S. Department of State, *Foreign Relations of the United States, 1946*, 6 *Europe:* 655, as cited in Quinlan, *Clash over Romania*, p. 156.

ernment's impotence, and urged, in the name of humanity, that we
provide food.

Two days later I had my reply. A ship, on its way with several
million army emergency rations, intended as reserves for our troops in
Germany, had been directed to change course and discharge its cargo
at Constanţa, Romania's seaport on the Black Sea. A considerable
shipment of grain was to follow shortly. It would be our task to effect
proper disposition of all supplies furnished. We were ready at Constanţa when our first ship arrived and, with the help of the Romanian
Red Cross, which had not yet been communized, we got our cargo
loaded onto flatcars and delivered to the stricken area, where other
Red Cross workers completed the distribution. While visiting the area
to observe the progress of the operation, I arrived at one small village
where the rations had been handed out just a few hours before. Word of
my coming had preceded me, for upon arriving I found the local priest
with his entire flock assembled in the village square, offering a prayer of
thanksgiving to our great president and to the wonderful American
people for their generosity. It was indeed a moving sight. I am sure
that we saved many lives that spring and that we earned the gratitude
of thousands of Moldavian peasants.

Following that incident, my tour in Romania drew uneventfully to
a close. In mid-spring I received orders assigning me to the Pentagon as
head of the army's Strategic Plans Branch. I left Romania with my
family in June 1947.

It was in Washington that I learned of the arrest in July of Maniu
and Bratianu, of their trial and imprisonment, of the outlawing of
their parties and, finally, in December, of the forced abdication of
King Michael. On December 30, 1947, the Kingdom of Romania became The People's Republic of Romania.

IN RETROSPECT

In looking back on the turbulent and often confusing events that I
have described, a number of very basic questions arise. Were the Anglo-
Americans or the Russians mainly responsible for the development of
the Cold War in Romania? Could it have been avoided? Did the United
States use "atomic diplomacy" in Romania? Was U.S. policy toward
Romania generally consistent throughout the period? Were we justified
in continuing to oppose Soviet objectives in Romania? And, more
specifically, did we go too far in encouraging Michael to break with
Groza, thus creating a difficult and dangerous, yet unproductive,
confrontation between the king and the Soviets?

As for the Cold War, in my view it developed from an inherent
conflict in objectives for the postwar world. We Americans believed

ardently, even passionately, that lasting peace in Europe could be realized only through the abolition of dictatorships and their replacement by freely elected governments responsive to the will of their peoples. Russian objectives, however, appeared to be quite different. First, there was their oft-proclaimed sympathy and support for the "struggle of peoples" against "the yoke of capitalist imperialism." War-ravaged Europe, with its industry in ruins, its economy in chaos, its people demoralized, seemed to afford an uprecedented opportunity for progress toward this objective. Secondly, the Soviets were convinced that their peace and security required the establishment, in states along their frontiers, of governments friendly to Russia and linked closely to her by economic and military ties.

Both Burton Berry and I felt some sympathy for this second Soviet objective. Only a few years before, Romanian and German armies had overrun a considerable slice of Russian territory. Russian farms and villages had been pillaged, many Russian families left destitute. Now that the tide had turned so dramatically, it was understandable that the Soviets would take steps to insure that never again would Romania become a hostile neighbor.

The trouble was that it was very difficult—perhaps impossible—to create a representative government in Romania that was at the same time friendly to Russia. At all levels of Romanian society there existed a deep distrust of the Soviets. Maniu once told me that on seven different occasions over the past four hundred years the country had been invaded by "barbarians" from the east, and each time the invaders had departed only when forced out at the point of the sword. Moreover, Russian annexation of Bessarabia and Northern Bucovina, areas long regarded by Romanians as part of their homeland, heightened the fears of still further Soviet incursions. Thus when Russian armies swept over the nation in late 1944, they found a population imbued with hostility and distrust. It must have been clear to the Soviets from the outset that in Romania no government but a Communist one could ever be a trustworthy ally. (Even a Communist one later proved to be untrustworthy.)

Of the four parties that supported the king in his coup of August 24, 1944, the Communists were much the smallest. Moreover, they were split between the militant, or "Muscovite" wing under Moscow-trained Ana Pauker and Vasile Luca, and the main body under Lucretiu Patrascanu. He, it seemed to us, shared his countrymen's concern over the growing Soviet influence in the party.

In point of fact, Vinogradov was no doubt speaking the truth when he told me in January 1945 that the nation was not ready for communism. He might have added that it was to be the job of the Soviet-dominated ACC to change all this—to generate, promote, and support a program of rioting, bloodshed, arrest, imprisonment, suppression, economic disruption, and political blackmail, all designed to destroy completely the basic fabric of Romania's capitalist society and to prepare the nation for a Communist takeover.

Thus the Cold War in Romania, as elsewhere, began as the manifestation of the utter incompatibility of two competing political philosophies. On our side, in the Atlantic Charter, the Yalta declaration, and in countless speeches by political leaders we had fervently proclaimed our postwar goals. Where they were not being achieved, we wanted the world to know why. The Soviets on the other hand, just as fervently committed to their objectives, and in Romania possessing the power to achieve them, moved ruthlessly toward that end. In so doing, they concealed, disguised, or misrepresented their actions to minimize criticism and avoid open opposition by the West. Hence the Cold War. It was inevitable.

Theoretically, of course, the Cold War could have been avoided by either side—we, by refraining from objecting, both diplomatically and publicly to all the bad things the Soviets and their cohorts were doing, and they, by refraining from doing those things and, instead, conforming to the letter and spirit of Yalta. Since neither of these courses of action was possible in the existing circumstances, the Cold War was, in fact, predestined.

With the Romanian example in mind, it is no great surprise to see that only in cases like Italy, Greece, and Japan, where Anglo-American forces were in control, were our postwar objectives realized, and that in regions where Soviet military strength predominated governments on the Soviet pattern emerged.

As for the atom bomb, it does not appear to me to have had any effect whatever on either American or Soviet attitudes in Romania. I never discussed the question with my Soviet associates. Atom bomb or not, Berry and I were in agreement that, for the United States, what happened in Romania was of little strategic significance. And though certain American-controlled firms, like Romana-Americana, were eager to recoup as much of their prewar investment as possible, we were never under pressure from Washington to risk an open break with the Soviets on their behalf. In fact, armed conflict with the Soviets because of disagreements over Romania was inconceivable to us. My several trips to Washington provided full support for this view.

U.S. policy toward Romania cannot be said to have been consistent. Indeed, it should not have been. In September 1944, when we signed the Romanian Armistice agreement, we had very little knowledge of Russia's plans for the future of the Balkan area. The agreement was a document that set forth clearly and concisely the extent of Romania's obligations to Russia, but made only brief mention of U.S. and U.K. interest. More importantly, it established a control commission with a Soviet chairman having the power of decision on all matters within its purview.

Whatever the reasons for accepting the document—and a number have been suggested—we must have understood that in so doing, we would be relying on Russia to deal as fairly and as equitably with our interests as with her own. It did not take long after Berry and I arrived in Bucharest for us to discover that, in fact, the Soviets were acting entirely to further their own ends, and were giving no attention whatever to our interests or our principles. By the beginning of 1945, the true situation was clear also to the people in the State and War departments. U.S. actions and attitudes toward the Soviets began to change accordingly. Thus, from that time onward, Soviet and U.S. policy toward Romania drifted ever further apart.

For the Romanian nation, the critical turning point was not the U.S.-U.K. acceptance of the Stalin "compromise" of December 1945; nor was it Groza's refusal in August of that year to bow to the king's request that he resign. Rather, it was the moment in March when Michael, acceding to Vyshinsky's unyielding demand, agreed to accept Groza's minority government. That event constituted also an important milestone in the changing U.S. attitude. Up to that point, State seemed largely to be following Britain's lead—backing up protests initiated by Berry or me, but not taking too seriously our warnings that the Soviet screws were beginning to tighten on Romania. But within a week after the Vyshinsky episode we detected a new sense of urgency in the telegrams from Washington—a genuine concern not only that free government in Romania had received a near-mortal wound, but also that, in the absence of effective counterpressures, Vyshinsky-type actions could be anticipated in other areas under Soviet control.

This was the mood I encountered at State when I visited Washington in April 1945 and that no doubt prompted Secretary Grew to set up my meeting with President Truman. The president's expression of deep concern following my briefing must have been exactly the reaction Grew was hoping for. But major U.S. policy initiatives can seldom be developed quickly, and it was not until we read the telegram from the State Department on August 12, 1945, that the tougher U.S. stance became apparent to us in Bucharest.

Thus, although U.S. policy concerning Romania did indeed change markedly during the period from August 1944 to September 1945, it was my feeling at the time, and so remains today, that given the circumstances, U.S. attitudes and actions had to change.

There remains the question as to the wisdom of our decision to encourage Michael to demand Groza's resignation. It appears to me that there were several important factors that influenced the United States in this decision:

1. In the summer of 1945, the State Department was still deeply concerned over Vyshinsky's action in March in forcing upon Romania a minority government. This, in the U.S. view, flagrantly violated both the letter and the spirit of the Yalta agreement, only a few weeks after its promulgation.

2. All U.S. protest on this matter had been brushed off by Molotov as though he considered them to be of only minor importance.

3. The State Department was unable to persuade the Soviets to undertake serious top-level discussion of the issue. Even at Potsdam, in early August 1945, though the question was argued briefly by the heads of state, no progress toward an acceptable solution was achieved.

Hence State's encouragement of the king's proposed action appeared to us in Bucharest as perhaps a final U.S. effort to break the U.S.-Soviet deadlock that had existed since Vyshinsky's move in March. If Groza acceded to the king's demand (which we considered unlikely), the way would be open for the installation of a more broadly based government. If (as appeared more probable) Groza, with Soviet backing, refused to resign, then Michael could invoke Yalta by calling on the three Allied governments for assistance. Such an appeal would virtually assure a thorough tripartite discussion of the problem, with a reasonable prospect for some form of compromise solution. We did not share the British concern that widespread civil disorder might erupt. We felt that both the king and his party leaders had been duly impressed by our stern warning against provoking any situation that could invite Soviet military intervention. It seemed to us that State's move was a good one.

Nevertheless, when we learned in December, after four months of frustrating delay, of Secretary Byrnes's agreement to the Stalin compromise, Berry and I felt badly let down. Not only, we felt, did the agreement mark the final disappearance of representative government in Romania but, even worse, the United States had now become an official partner in its demise. To us, American prestige had reached an all-time low.

However, upon later reflection, Byrnes's face-saving cop-out at Moscow does not appear to have been all that bad since the alternatives open to us were more unpleasant. Had we refused Stalin's offer, the Soviets most probably would have decided to move ahead by themselves, concluding their own peace treaty with Romania and leaving us to follow suit or not, as we chose.

Dissolution of the ACC would have been inevitable, and the king would have been faced with the choice of abdicating at once, or else going, hat in hand, to Groza to apologize for having demanded his resignation. Almost certainly the king would have chosen abdication. Thus, our rejection of Stalin's offer could well have worsened the situation for Romania, while straining U.S.-Soviet relations to a point where profitable discussion on other postwar problems would have been more difficult. Realistically, we knew by that time that the facade of independence for Romania was crumbling fast. Stalin's offer provided a palatable way of giving recognition to that fact. We were well advised, I now think, to accept it.

A year or two after my retirement from the army, I lunched with Michael in New York City. We talked a little of his last years as king of Romania and I asked him particularly about his feelings concerning our Moscow compromise. He replied that he harbored no bitter feelings toward the United States on the outcome. He felt that he had received all the backing he could reasonably have hoped for, that by that time the final results were inevitable, and that there was little more the United States could have done to change the course of events.

In summary, it must be admitted that our efforts toward establishment of a freely elected government for Romania were doomed from the start. There was simply no way we could successfully challenge Soviet domination. Yet, given the mood of our nations, the statements of our leaders, and the earnestness of our commitment to a peaceful, freedom-loving, postwar world, we had no choice but to make the effort.

Romania was the first of a number of situations, mostly in Eastern Europe, where we found ourselves confronted by greatly superior Soviet power. We learned, I think, a number of lessons:

We learned, as others have said, that fruitful negotiations with the Soviets can be conducted only from positions of strength. Where Soviet power is dominant, they will pursue their predetermined course relentlessly, unmoved by arguments based on human suffering, public reactions, economic hardships, or justice for individuals, groups, or nations.

We learned also that, if it serves their purpose, Soviet interpretation of an agreement entered into can become very different from our own, so different in fact as to be incomprehensible to the Western mind.

And, most importantly, we learned that the Soviet belief in the continuing decay of capitalist society and the ultimate world-wide supremacy of communism is unchangeable.

MARTIN F. HERZ

The View from Austria

FIRST IMPRESSIONS OF VIENNA 1945

I was chosen to be in the lead jeep of the U.S. reconnaissance party that came to Vienna on July 22, 1945, to make arrangements for the setting up of Headquarters, U.S. Forces, Austria (USFA). I was a major at that time, and had been seconded to the headquarters company by the "political division" of USFA—then still located in Verona, Italy—which was the office of the political adviser to General Mark Clark and the precursor of the American legation in Vienna.

On the day after my arrival in Vienna, I had an interview with State Secretary without Portfolio Leopold Figl, who was the equivalent of vice-chancellor in the Soviet-appointed Renner government. That

Martin F. Herz, currently Director of Studies of the Institute for the Study of Diplomacy (Georgetown University, Washington, D.C.), is a former career Foreign Service officer who served in Vienna, Paris, Phnom Penh, Tokyo, Tehran, Saigon, and (as American Ambassador) in Sofia. Among his positions in the Department of State was that of Deputy Assistant Secretary of State for International Organization Affairs. Although born in New York, he was educated in Vienna and is thus bilingual in German and English (also in French). During World War II he specialized in psychological warfare, and as a major in General Clark's headquarters in Vienna was assigned to its Political Division, which later became the American legation. Upon entering the Foreign Service in 1946, he was again sent to Vienna as third secretary and political officer. Among his published works are *A Short History of Cambodia* (Praeger, 1958), *Beginnings of the Cold War* (Indiana University Press, 1966), *How the Cold War Is Taught* (Ethics and Public Policy Center, Georgetown University, 1978) and numerous articles for scholarly journals.

meeting arose by sheer accident, but to his dying day Mr. Figl, who later in 1945 became chancellor of Austria, attributed our encounter on July 23 to extraordinary sagacity on the part of "the American intelligence service which already then realized that I was destined to become the leader of my country."[1]

It was no accident, however, that I was a member of the political division and that I had been placed in the leading jeep entering Vienna. Although a native American, I had received most of my education in Vienna and could in fact pass for a native of that city. During the war in Europe my field of activity had been psychological warfare against German troops, facilitating their desertion, surrender, or capture. In that capacity it had been my special pleasure to write appeals to troop units made up predominantly of Austrians, such as the 5th Mountain Division and the 44th Infantry Division, calling their attention to the Moscow Declaration of 1943 in which America, Britain, and Russia had announced their decision that Austria "shall be liberated from German domination." In Italy in 1943-44 I had made a specialty of interviewing Austrian deserters and other prisoners, trying to gauge the extent to which the people of Austria still felt themselves part of the greater German Reich.

It is perhaps important to emphasize here, in view of my background and history, that I was not an emigrant and was not imbued with any particular political or emotional hangups with respect to Austria. I was interested in the country, felt well qualified to interpret some of its complexities to my superiors, and welcomed being among the first Americans in Vienna because I hoped to send reports to Verona about the Renner government, about which the Western Allies entertained the most serious reservations. So my first meeting with Figl, which had been a case of pure serendipity, was followed by another on July 24 in which I questioned him systematically about the Renner government and about his political beliefs. This in turn was followed by interviews with other members of the provisional govern-

---

1. The circumstances are really quite unimportant, but they are amusing. On the evening of our second day in Vienna, Colonel Smith, the headquarters commandant, asked me to locate "a place where we can buy a glass of beer." This proved a great deal more difficult than I had thought, and when we saw a number of cars in front of a house in the Schenkengasse, a small side street near the Federal Chancellery, I inquired whether the place was perhaps some kind of restaurant or (black market) bar. It turned out to be, instead, the headquarters of the *Bauernbund*, the Austrian peasant organization that was the backbone of the People's party. The director of the *Bauernbund*, Leopold Figl, received Colonel Smith and me as if we were a delegation dispatched to him by General Clark. The story has been recounted in greater detail in my article "A Glass of Beer with the Chancellor" in the *Foreign Service Journal*, vol. 30, no. 7 (July 1953).

ment, notably with Ernst Fischer, the Communist minister of education. Those interviews were sandwiched in between my other duties,
which had to do with finding quarters for the American headquarters
and its senior personnel.

The first impression we Americans got of Vienna was one of deep
shock. We had heard about the destruction from two teams of Allied
generals who had visited Vienna earlier (June 3 and July 16), but
since the Russians had been in occupation there since April we had
somehow expected that more would have been done in the way of
removing rubble and starting reconstruction.

Another thing that struck us was that the few people who were in
the streets would hurry along and look away from us as if trying not
to attract attention. Very few women were to be seen. Only when
people realized that we were Americans and not Russians did we become surrounded by persons eager to tell us about their experiences—
once they had been assured that the Americans were going to stay as
part of the occupation of the capital.

The stories we heard about the behavior of the Russian "liberating"
troops were so terrible that we at first refused to believe them. They
sounded too much like Nazi propaganda, and how could we know that
we weren't being misled?[2] Even the record of my conversations with
Figl, as transmitted from Verona to the State Department,[3] contained
the notation: "On several occasions he made embarrassing remarks
about the Russians, *which the American officers were careful to parry*.
One of his remarks was a prediction that considerable numbers of
Viennese would move from the Soviet zone of the city to other zones
not, it was stated, in order to obtain larger rations but 'particularly
because of personal feelings.' "[4] It must have taken extraordinary
sensitivity to interpret such a remark as "embarrassing," but the notation made in Verona shows that we were concerned that the Austrians
might try to drive a wedge between the American and Russian occupa-

---

2. A British survey of the period displays the same perplexity: ". . . when
they reached Vienna, all three of the Western Allies were besieged with stories of
the brutality of the Soviet troops, and it was some time before they realized that
many of these were true, and not, as they thought at first, the propaganda of Goebbels faithfully echoed by people who wished to drive a wedge between the victors."
Michael Balfour and John Mair, *Four-Power Control in Germany and Austria 1945-
1946: Survey of International Affairs, 1939-1946,* issued under the auspices of
the Royal Institute of International Affairs (London: Oxford University Press,
1956), p. 318.

3. Verona dispatch to secretary of state, no. 93 of August 3, 1945, in the
U.S. National Archives, file 863.01/8-345.

4. Wherever italics appear in this chapter, they have been supplied by the
author for emphasis, and are not in the original documents.

tion forces—and that we wanted Washington to know we would resist any such efforts.

The plain fact was that the Russian troops (which included a substantial proportion from Central Asia) had been allowed to go on a rampage of raping and looting when they occupied Vienna, behaving not in accordance with the Moscow Declaration that had referred to "liberation" but just as they behaved in Berlin. I was for a while skeptical about the tales of "tens of thousands" of raped women, but recall that a well-qualified doctor who had to do with the approval of abortions requested by rape victims, explained to me that he had arrived at an estimate, which he regarded as conservative, of 70,000 cases of rape by Red Army soldiers. As for the looting, it was of two kinds— by soldiers going from house to house to take any objects of value or alcoholic spirits they could find, and the systematic removal by the occupation forces of machinery and equipment, some of it vital to the running of the city. One thing that struck us was that buildings bore notations in white paint showing whether and by what Red Army unit they had been ransacked.

It is unpleasant to dwell on details of cruelty and bestiality, and my mention of them is only to explain the outrage and exasperation of the Viennese, which became of great political importance. So it must be recalled that among the raped women were some who were very old and very young; that many of the victims or intended victims committed suicide; that Soviet soldiers sometimes slaughtered animals in houses and apartments; that the occupation troops seemed to take delight in relieving themselves on the furniture and carpets of "capitalists"; and that many of their actions seemed to be calculated to humiliate rather than seek physical relief or financial gain.

Chancellor Karl Renner, in his report on the first three months of his administration, tried to deal with this phenomenon as delicately as he could by writing:

The superficial observer is inclined to overlook too easily the different circumstances under which the various provinces were occupied. In general it can be said that the eastern provinces, even with the deepest of grief, had to recognize that it was much more difficult for the Russian soldier to free himself from an urge for revenge after the complete devastation of an area of his own country which had been inhabited by perhaps 90 million people, than would be the case with armies of countries that have not seen a single enemy soldier on their own soil.[5]

A colleague of mine in the legation, Ware Adams, recalls that a Russian official used to remark that "the Austrians at Stalingrad were among

5. Dr. Karl Renner, *Drei Monate Aufbauarbeit der Provisorischen Staatsregierung der Republik Oesterreich* (Vienna: Oesterreichische Staatsdruckerei, 1945), pp. 8-9.

those who fought the hardest." Clearly, the Russians—and not only they—had difficulty forgetting that many Austrians had participated, willingly or not, in Hitler's invasion of Russia.

RUSSIAN AMBIVALENCE AND THE RENNER GOVERNMENT

It is my belief that the Russians came into Austria without any well-thought-out plan for the political management of the country. This belief is based on several considerations: Even while the city was subjected to terror and pillage by Red Army troops—a traumatic experience that can never be effaced and that hurt the Austrian Communist party terribly—the Red Army leadership laid wreaths at the monuments of Austrian cultural and other heroes and proclaimed its benevolence toward the population. While tens of thousands of Viennese women were being raped, Marshal F. I. Tolbukhin generously facilitated the early opening of the Vienna opera (not in its bombed-out building but in the Theater an der Wien). It was as if two mutually contradictory policies were being applied.

Even in his efforts to appeal to the Austrian population as a liberator, Marshal Tolbukhin made an initial gaffe that could be attributed only to lack of qualified advisers on his staff. In his first proclamation, as his troops were entering Austria, he wrote: "The Red Army stands on the basis of the Moscow Declaration of the Allied Powers of October 1943 about the Independence of Austria. The Red Army will contribute to the reestablishment of the conditions that prevailed in Austria *up to the year 1938.*"[6]

Now anyone even remotely familiar with the history of Austria in the 1930s would have known that in 1938, when the country was forcibly incorporated into the German Reich, it was not a democracy but a clerically oriented authoritarian state that had dissolved parliament and was ruling on the basis of a "corporate" constitution, patterned largely after that of Fascist Italy. So the declared intention to set the clock back to 1938 evoked exasperation and disbelief from the Austrian Socialists, whose party (then still called the Social Democratic party) had been outlawed in 1934. The matter never became a political issue because the Russians clearly had not meant what Tolbukhin had said in the proclamation.

One of the tragedies (from the Russian point of view) and ironies (from the Austrian point of view) was that the Red Army soldiers did not exclude the working-class districts of Vienna from their depredations. In fact, one of the stories going around Vienna was that when they entered apartments in the workers' housing projects constructed

6. *Oesterreichische Zeitung* (organ of the Red Army in Austria), April 15, 1945.

by the pre-1934 Socialist administration of Vienna, they would ex-
claim, "Ah, kapitalist!" because it was inconceivable to them that
anyone who wasn't a capitalist could live in the modest comfort—
extravagant by Russian standards—that the Austrian workers had attained under the Vienna Social Democratic municipal administration.

That the Communist party had been damaged by the behavior of
Russian troops, and that Moscow was concerned about this, was apparent from a number of indicators even before my arrival in Vienna.
In the State Department records is a letter written by John G. Erhardt,
the political adviser to General Clark, in which he called attention to
a report "obtained from 'a well-placed Austrian' recently in Vienna"
that the anticipated replacement of Marshal Tolbukhin by Marshal
Konev should not be attributed to the official reason, that Tolbukhin's
Third Ukrainian Army had by its fighting record earned early discharge,
but rather to the alleged fact that "Stalin was displeased with *the lack
of discipline among Tolbukhin's troops in their relations with the
Viennese.*"[7] The same letter also reported that a French agent named
Lambert, an Austrian who had been to Vienna recently, "reported
that [the Communist leaders] Koplenig and Fischer had lost a certain
amount of standing with the Soviets because of *their failure, so far, to
muster the expected popular support,* notably in factory elections in
which the Communists polled under ten percent."[8]

The very manner in which the Russians had come to appoint Dr.
Karl Renner as chancellor also indicates that they had no well-thought-
out plan for Austria. Renner had come to their attention when he went
to a local Soviet command in Gloggnitz, a village south of Vienna, to
complain against the outrages of the Russian soldiery. Identifying himself as the president of the last democratically elected parliament of
Austria and as chancellor of the first republican Austrian government
after World War I, he was escorted to a higher headquarters where he
was asked whether he would be willing to write an appeal to his countrymen to assist the Red Army in its fight against the retreating Germans.

Renner, as he recorded in a *Denkschrift* (memorial) published in
June 1945,[9] first thought of calling together the surviving members

7. Letter dated July 13, 1945, from John G. Erhardt to H. Freeman Mat-
thews, director of the Office of European Affairs, Department of State. U.S. Department of State, *Foreign Relations of the United States* (hereafter cited as
FRUS), 1945, 3 (Washington, D.C.: Government Printing Office, 1968): 568.

8. The "French agent" Lambert was actually an Austrian resistance fighter
by the name of Ernst Lemberger, who later became Austrian ambassador to Belgium, the European communities, and the United States.

9. *Denkschrift ueber die Geschichte der Unabhaengigkeitserklaerung Oesterreichs* (Zurich: Europa-Verlag, 1946; first published Vienna, June 1945). I am not

of the erstwhile Austrian parliament, and was surprised, when the Russians brought him to Vienna, to find that the old political parties— the People's party (successor of the prewar Christian Social party), the Socialists (erstwhile Social Democrats), and the Communists—were already fully organized and ready to discuss the formation of a coalition. It is clear from his *Denkschrift* and from other documentation that the Soviets only gradually came to think in terms of Renner heading a provisional government, that they gave him to understand that the formation of such a government would be coordinated with the Western Allies, and that their main concern was to have a functioning civil authority to which they could delegate the administration of the part of the country that was coming under their control.

Ernst Fischer, the Communist minister of education, whom I interviewed on August 2, immediately acknowledged that his party was at that time "a distinct minority." He added that

> had the Communists been able to come into Vienna all ready and organized to take over the city and assure order and discipline, they would now have a majority. As it is, with the entire system of government breaking down . . . the resulting anarchy [Fischer used that word on several occasions] harmed the Communists more than others. It is true that during this anarchy elements of the population plundered, raped and looted, and it is also only too true that *during this anarchy the Russian first-line troops were among the worst offenders.*

Even the emergency police, organized under Communist auspices, Fischer said, contained many of the lowest criminal elements of the population, and there were frequent cases where the very protectors of law and order used their position to do some looting of their own. "Gradually, order was brought into the city, and now such cases were the exception. Nevertheless, it must be said that the prestige of the Communists has suffered badly and they now have but a fraction of the popular support."[10]

---

unaware of a recent interpretation that considers that Renner's choice by the Russians "was no accident" (Wilfried Aichinger, *Sowjetische Oesterreichpolitik 1943- 1945* [Vienna: Oesterreichische Gesellschaft fuer Zeitgeschichte, 1977], p. 122). This is based on an article by S. M. Shtemenko in the Soviet publication *Neue Zeit* alleging that Stalin had given an order, "in the course of a conversation in the general headquarters," that it should be determined whether Renner was still alive, and if so, where he could be located. It is of course possible that the USSR thought in advance of Renner as the possible head of a provisional government, but on balance it seems more likely that, as often happens, Soviet historians feel uncomfortable that any important political action of their government could be attributed to chance.

10. Dispatch, "Memorandum on Conditions in Vienna," Verona no. 103 of August 7, 1945, signed by John G. Erhardt, political adviser. National Archives, file 863.00/8-745.

In a sense, of course, Fischer was trying to shift some of the blame away from the Red Army, but he was also by implication incriminating his colleague Franz Honner, the Communist minister of interior who had brought so many party members into leading positions in the police. I was impressed with Fischer's relative candor, and drew attention in my memorandum to his "extremely honest and idealistic manner of speaking and pleading." I noted that "he speaks very quietly but with insistence, giving the impression, however, that he is much more interested that you understand his point of view than that you share it. He often qualifies his statements, at times emphasizing that his is only one way of looking at a problem, and that policies may be proven wrong and may have to be changed." We know today that Fischer, who wrote his political autobiography[11] after breaking with the Communists over the invasion of Czechoslovakia in 1968, suffered on many occasions during his political career from what he saw as a need to close his eyes to some truths to serve what he saw as larger truths.

In the West, as mentioned earlier, the unilateral Russian creation of the Renner government had created the worst misgivings. It seemed hard to imagine that the seventy-five-year-old chancellor wasn't a puppet of the Russians. A high official of the British government remarked to the American ambassador that he believed "Renner . . . was selected merely to give the Government an air of respectability. A man of his age could not be expected to take an active part in the Government. The real work, he concluded, would be done by young, active Communists."[12] George Kennan, then our chargé d'affaires in Moscow, invited attention to

the significance of the Communist retention of the portfolio of Minister of the Interior. It is now established Russian practice to seek as a first and major objective, in all areas where they wish to exercise dominant influence, control of the internal administration and police apparatus, particularly the secret police. . . . If, therefore, Moscow has contented itself with only three members of the Austrian Provisional Government openly designated as Communists, this *should not be taken as an indication that the Russians would be prepared to accept willingly a permanent Austrian Government in which they would not have what they consider a controlling influence.*[13]

These were of course very reasonable suppositions, but they turned out to be wrong for several reasons. First, Karl Renner, despite his age,

11. Ernst Fischer, *Erinnerungen und Reflexionen* (Hamburg: Rowohlt, 1969).
12. Ambassador Winant to secretary of state, telegram 4376 of April 30, 1945. *FRUS, 1945*, 3:101.
13. Kennan to secretary of state, Moscow telegram 1424 of April 30, 1945, ibid., pp. 105-6.

proved to be not only vigorous but ingenious and courageous, and endowed with a surprising moral ascendancy over his cabinet colleagues, including the Communists. Second, the rapid restoration of the socialist and conservative parties not only kept pace with but quickly overshadowed the corresponding activities of the Communists. Third, and most important, the Russians did not insist that the Communists have their way in the government and, indeed, the Communists did not challenge the democratic majority even during the interim period when the Soviets were the only military force in Vienna.

The best example of this is what happened during cabinet discussion of the adoption of a provisional constitution that involved a return, essentially, to the last democratic constitution of Austria as amended in 1929, a proposal that the Communist ministers vigorously opposed (possibly because they wished to keep open the alternative of a "people's democracy"). Renner "declared that notwithstanding their opposition he regarded the measure as adopted if the minority did not indicate by their resignation that the proposals remained unacceptable to them."[14] Since the Communists refused to resign, and in spite of the unanimity rule of the provisional government, Renner simply declared that the cabinet had decided in favor of the old constitution. When one considers the many other ways in which this matter could have been handled, which would have led to a government crisis and perhaps intervention by the occupying power, one must marvel at the sangfroid with which Renner faced down such Communist opposition.

It deserves to be added, however, that Communist opposition during this interim period was the exception rather than the rule. Virtually all decisions of the Renner government were indeed taken unanimously, and even in the case of the Ministry of Interior a rule applied whereby undersecretaries of the other two parties had a right to hold up decisions of the Communist minister with which they did not agree. This system was later strengthened during the period between the convocation of a provincial conference in September and the national elections in November 1945, in which the Communists were shown to be such a small minority that they lost any plausible claim to a major portfolio in the government.

Nevertheless, during the period of May to November, the Communist minister of interior was able to appoint many of his party colleagues to leading positions in the police, notably Dr. Heinz Duermayer as head of the Vienna police. However, there were limits to what

14. Adolf Schaerf, *Zwischen Demokratie und Volksdemokratie* (Vienna: Verlag der Volksbuchhandlung, 1950), p. 18.

the Communists could do almost from the beginning. For instance, even before the Western Allies arrived in Vienna the Socialist under-secretary of interior, Oskar Helmer, managed to get the Russians to agree to recall the seventy-nine-year-old Dr. Ignaz Pamer, a former police president of Vienna, to replace Duermayer.[15] Although Pamer's authority was limited and the Communist Minister Honner then ap-pointed Duermayer to head the newly formed political police *(Staats-polizei)*, the presence of a seasoned professional at least nominally at the head of the Vienna police meant that by the time the Western Allies arrived during the latter half of August, the nucleus of a non-Communist police force was already in existence.

THE 1945 ELECTIONS

Among the first acts of the Allied commission when it was estab-lished in Vienna in August 1945—four months after the city had fallen to the Russians—was approval of a conference of provincial representa-tives *(Laenderkonferenz)* that was to give the Renner government an opportunity to secure a nationwide mandate, which in turn would allow it to hold national elections. As a result of that conference, some exponents of the Western-occupied provinces entered the government, notably Dr. Karl Gruber of Tyrol, who became undersecretary for foreign affairs. The *Laenderkonferenz,* however, did not bring the removal of Honner as minister of interior. As Renner explained to General Clark, "First, insistence on his removal would likely have em-bittered the Soviets and, second, it would have opened the way to agitation and trouble-breeding demonstrations on the part of the Austrian communists."[16] This illustrates the narrow margin on which the Renner government was operating even after the arrival of the Western Allies in Vienna.

National elections took place on November 25, 1945, and by all accounts they were completely free both in the Soviet zone of Austria and elsewhere. The question is sometimes asked why the Russians per-mitted free elections when the Communists were in such a precarious position, and the conventional answer is that they did not expect the Communists to lose so heavily. This implies, however, that they did realize that the Communists would poll less than either of the other two parties. Certainly even the Communists themselves did not pre-dict that they would win a plurality. When I saw Ernst Fischer in

15. Balfour and Mair, *Four-Power Control*, p. 362. William Lloyd Stearman, *The Soviet Union and the Occupation of Austria* (Bonn-Vienna-Zurich: Siegler & Co. KG Verlag fuer Zeitarchive, 1962), p. 57.

16. Memorandum of conversation transmitted as Vienna 257 of October 1, 1945. *FRUS, 1945*, 3:614.

October, he forecast that his party would win between 20 and 25 of the 165 seats in the Lower House, which would have corresponded to a maximum of 15 percent of the vote.[17] According to State Secretary Adolf Schaerf, the Communists told the Russians they expected 25 percent of the vote.[18]

I was at the Ministry of Interior during the night when the results were being posted, and it soon became apparent that the Communists would have trouble obtaining even the *Grundmandat,* the "basic" election of a deputy in one electoral district that would enable them to take a share of *Reststimmen,* the residual votes apportioned according to the Austrian electoral law only to parties that had obtained at least one directly elected deputy. It may be difficult to credit this in retrospect, since we know today how bad our relations with the Russians were to become, but that evening many of us (American as well as British observers) were hoping that the Communists would obtain their *Grundmandat* so that they would not be completely excluded from the political process in the National Assembly. In the event, they squeaked by and managed to obtain four seats with 5.4 percent of the vote. The People's party obtained eighty-five seats, an absolute majority, and the Socialists seventy-six seats.[19]

A few days after the elections I was entrusted with a "delicate mission" by C. W. Gray, the counselor of the Political Adviser's office. I was to seek out Figl, who as leader of the victorious People's party was the chancellor-designate, and tell him that I "had heard people in the Political Adviser's office express the opinion" that the interests of Austria would be best served by maintaining the coalition, including (reduced) Communist participation, even after the People's party victory. Figl didn't need convincing, nor did the others. But the Communists lost the Ministry of Interior and had to content themselves with a minor cabinet position.

I have always wondered why my instructions were cast in such tentative terms, and have come to the conclusion that it had more to do with the personality of the old-style diplomatic officer who gave them

17. Vienna dispatch no. 334 of October 18, 1945. National Archives, file 863.00/10-1845.

18. Adolf Schaerf, *Oesterreichs Erneuerung, 1945-1955* (Vienna: Verlag der Wiener Volksbuchhandlung, 1955), p. 18. Balfour and Mair, *Four-Power Control,* p. 323, report that the Soviets expected the Communists to poll 30 percent, which appears very high.

19. The American political adviser (Erhardt) in a telegram to Washington on November 27 (no. 498) reported: "Practically all Communists are stunned and disillusioned by shattering defeat which was expected by no one, and older leaders such as Fischer are trying to restore faith younger party workers." *FRUS, 1945,* 3: 665.

to me than with the State Department's instructions, which have meanwhile been published and were quite clear: ". . . suggest, in your dis-
cretion, to party leaders that coalition government should be maintained, at least until the end of military occupation, and Communist
representation should be retained in cabinet, in order to facilitate good
relations among four powers and to avoid impression that Volkspartei
victory automatically means anti-Soviet or anti-Communist policy."[20]
There was no American gloating over the Austrian conservatives gaining
an absolute majority. On the contrary, it was treated almost as a
problem—and it would have been a problem if the People's party had
not realized that it had more to gain from maintaining the coalition,
especially with the Socialists, than from attempting to govern alone,
which would have placed the Socialists together with the Communists
in an opposition role.

INTER-ALLIED RELATIONS—POLITICAL

I have not said much yet about the deterioration in relations between the Western Allies and the Soviet representatives in Vienna.
This is because in my opinion it was Soviet economic, rather than
political, policy in Austria that brought about that deterioration. It
is true that there were frictions in the relationship on the political level,
but during the first months of the occupation relations were basically
cordial—once the difficulties about establishing the various zones and
sectors had been ironed out. While it would be an exaggeration to say
that relations were friendly, there was informal discussion and even
some social entertaining, including informal lunches and dinners,
in which civilians of the Soviet element of the Allied commission
participated.

Sometimes small details that still stick in the mind can serve to
document a larger truth: That the atmosphere between the political
division of General Clark's headquarters and the political division of
Marshal Konev's headquarters cannot have been characterized by
"Cold War" attitudes appears also from my informal contacts with
E. D. Kiselev, the Soviet counterpart of Mr. Erhardt. Whenever I had
occasion to visit Kiselev's office, usually just to deliver messages or pick
up classified papers, I would take along some recent issues of the
New Yorker, for which Kiselev was very grateful. I confess that I
didn't feel exactly comfortable in the Soviet headquarters, which
seemed strange and vaguely threatening, but my relationship with
Kiselev, who was a high Soviet political officer, was an easy and in-

    20. Telegram no. 329 from secretary of state to U.S. political adviser for
Austrian affairs, December 4, ibid., p. 674.

formal one. My rank was too low, of course, for us to engage in substantive discussions, but the relaxed, chatty, bantering manner he
displayed toward me would probably have been unthinkable a year
later.

General Clark has expressed the opinion that the November 1945
elections marked the real end of anything other than pretended collaboration by the Russians and goes on to say that soon afterwards they
began both to restrict the freedom of the Austrian authorities in the
Soviet zone, and to give members of the Communist party greater
privileges.[21] There is no doubt that there was a cooling of relations
after the 1945 elections and especially as 1946 wore on, but I believe
this was a relatively slow trend that is better explained by Soviet
disappointment over the frustration of their economic, rather than
political, aims.

Political points of friction existed in connection with the precarious Western access to Vienna, across Russian-held territory. In
January 1946, General Clark ordered military police to prevent Soviet
personnel from boarding the American train (the Mozart Express)
that linked Vienna and Salzburg. When several Soviet officers and
and men nevertheless forced their way into the train at the demarcation
line, and when they refused to leave, an American MP killed one of the
officers and wounded another. Although Marshal Konev demanded that
the sergeant responsible be punished, he was acquitted by a military
court on the grounds that he was performing his duty.[22]

In Vienna one important point of friction was the abduction of
Austrians and exiles from Eastern Europe by Soviet security services.
Some were strong-armed into waiting cars, and one case that is vivid
in my memory involved an Eastern European refugee being rolled up
in a carpet and tossed into a truck. One day while I was in Vienna a
Russian was caught in the act of trying to abduct someone in the
American sector of the city. The four-power military police were
called and the man put aboard their jeep. The Russian member of the
patrol said the jeep was to proceed to his *Kommandatura*, but the
American driver said no, he would be taken to the international MP
headquarters. Thereupon the Russian pulled his pistol and put it to
the head of the American; whereupon the British member of the

21. Mark W. Clark, *Calculated Risk* (New York: Harper & Brothers, 1950),
p. 470: "The Soviets were both surprised and angered by the failure of the Communist party to show any strength. They obviously had been supporting the Austrian Government in the belief that it would lead to the establishment of a pro-
Communist state; when they found that the opposite was true, they began to
change their attitude toward the Austrian people."

22. Stearman, *Soviet Union* . . . , p. 37.

four-power patrol pulled *his* pistol and pointed it to the head of the Russian; and it was in this configuration that the vehicle rolled into the courtyard of the Auersperg Palais, the quadripartite police head-quarters, where the situation was disentangled. The remarkable thing about this episode is not, in retrospect, that it occurred, but that there existed a functioning four-power military police unit in Vienna.

By far the most important political development in the four-power occupation of Austria during the period immediately after the November 1945 elections was the negotiation of a new control agreement. It seemed reasonable that once a nationally elected Austrian government existed, it should no longer be required to subject its laws to the veto of any of the four occupying powers, as the original control agreement specified. An American proposal, worked out by First Secretary Ware Adams and first tried out very tentatively on an informal basis, envisaged that a new agreement should permit Austrian laws (except for fundamental laws of a constitutional nature) to go into effect unless they were disapproved by the council. This was a reasonable proposal, but would the Russians be willing to go along? Instead of having a veto over Austrian legislation, there would be a "reverse veto" under the new proposal by which any of the Western Allies could prevent the council from disapproving Austrian legislation, which would go into effect thirty-one days after submission unless unanimously disapproved.

This proposal for a revised control agreement was negotiated over five months, in the first half of 1946. Since the Russians did approve the reverse veto principle, there has been much speculation that somehow they did not know what they were approving.[23] However, the principal American negotiator (on the working level) insists that the Russians did not by any means go along by inadvertence. The draft, he wrote,

did not slide through unnoticed as many Westerners later thought must have happened, on the theory that the Soviet Government would never enter into an agreement which seemed so desirable from our point of view. Actually, every word of it came under close scrutiny. Article 6-A (the "negative veto") in particular was the special subject of repeated discussions in the Allied Council, the Exe-

23. Balfour and Mair, *Four-Power Control*, p. 328: "The Soviet authorities' attitude caused some surprise at the time, and indeed it was conjectured that they might have signed the new Agreement without fully realizing its implications. . . . It may be that the full implication was only tardily realized in Moscow, though that seems unlikely." Stearman *(Soviet Union . . . . , p.* 41) wrote: "It soon became obvious that the Soviets had unwittingly *[sic]* signed away their strongest hold over the Austrian government." He considered it a "plausible explanation" that Russian approval came from "a combination of poor coordination and an ignorance of Western legal terminology and norms" (p. 44).

cutive Committee, and the Political Directorate, as well as the four political divisions of military government, with a searching questioning of it on behalf of the Government in Moscow.[24]

In fact, when the agreement was sent to the governments for final approval, it was the Soviet high commissioner who first received the green light from Moscow. Then followed London and Paris in due course, but there was still no word from Washington. In June 1946 the State Department cabled that it was prepared to go along *"despite serious misgivings concerning Article 6-A"*[25] but thought the matter should await the outcome of the Council of Foreign Ministers. There is little doubt that in Washington the approval of the new agreement by the Russians made officials acutely uncomfortable. As Adams put it, "many Americans in those days, including bureaucrats, had a deep-seated, instinctive view (often explicitly stated with almost religious conviction) that anything good for the Communists must *ipso facto* be bad for us and vice versa."[26] Finally, American approval was telegraphed when it was pointed out by the political adviser in Vienna that a certain Austrian law having to do with restitution of property, which was a matter of some political sensitivity in the United States, might run afoul of a Russian veto if it were submitted to the Allied council while the old control agreement was still in force.[27]

I prefer not to speculate as to why the Russians deliberately weakened their hold on the Austrian government in this manner. It is certain that they came to regret their approval of the new control agreement, especially in connection with their disputes with the Austrians and the Western Allies over the matter of German assets in eastern Austria. Adams believes that, seeing America's role in Austria growing, the Soviets signed the more liberal agreement because they thought that although it would lessen their own influence on the Austrian government, the same would be true of American influence. ("We wanted to get the Russians out of Austria; the Russians equally wanted to get the Americans out of Austria.")[28] It is possible that the Russians had no political master plan for Austria—beyond keeping the country separate from Germany—but they knew precisely what they wanted out of Austria in the economic field.

24. "The Miracle of Austria—A Diplomatic Success Story" by Ware Adams, *Foreign Service Journal*, June 1971, p. 26.

25. Secretary of State telegram no. 543 to political adviser for Austria (Erhardt) dated June 11, 1946. *FRUS, 1946*, 5:349.

26. Adams, "Miracle of Austria," p. 26.

27. Ibid.

28. Ibid., p. 27.

INTER-ALLIED RELATIONS–ECONOMIC

We now return to the beginning of the story, early and mid-1945.
At the time when they entered Austria, the Soviets based themselves
publicly on the Moscow Declaration of 1943, which had identified
Austria as a country to be "liberated from German domination." However, it became known publicly only much later that at Moscow in 1943
the Soviet Union had pressed for insertion of a clause saddling Austria
squarely with "full political *and material* responsibility for the war."[29]
This had been at once contested by the British and American delegates
as being manifestly inconsistent with the declared aim of the powers
to treat Austria as a victim of aggression. They had argued that not
only had Austria ceased to exist as a state after the annexation in 1938,
and could not therefore have been responsible in any way for Hitler's
actions in 1939 and afterwards, but to speak of "material" responsibility implied that she would be subject to claims for reparations;
and demands for reparations would hardly square with a professed
desire to reestablish Austrian independence. In the face of Russian
obduracy, the Western Allies agreed to add a phrase to the Moscow
Declaration that read: "Austria is reminded, however, that she has a
responsibility which she cannot evade, for participation in the war on
the side of Hitlerite Germany, and that in the final settlement, account
will inevitably be taken of her own contribution to her liberation."[30]

I had interpreted this sentence as a psychological device to encourage the Austrian people to be more active in opposition to the Nazis;
but to the Russians, obviously, the important clause was the one
speaking of "a responsibility which she cannot evade," and agreement
on that principle gave a certain plausibility to their position at the
Potsdam Conference where they reiterated their claim for reparations
from Austria. It must be remembered that at the time of Potsdam the
Western Allies were not yet in Vienna and the Russians were already
dismantling industrial equipment in eastern Austria under their definition of "war booty."[31] Molotov at Potsdam proposed that reparations

29. Balfour and Mair, *Four-Power Control*, p. 279.
30. *FRUS, 1943*, 1:761.
31. Learning of Russian removals of "German" equipment from Austria, the
British government on April 21 sent instructions to its chargé d'affaires in Moscow
to state: "HMG are sure that the Soviet Government will agree that our common
purpose might well be prejudiced by unilateral action on the part of any occupying
powers in regard to the removal of industrial plant and equipment regardless of
whether or not this was German owned." *FRUS, 1945*, 3:82. The United States
made parallel representations, and on April 25 Kennan reported that they had been
rejected by Vyshinsky, who stated that "the Soviet Government considers that no

from Austria should be fixed at $250 million, payable in goods over a six-year period.[32] This was at once rejected by both the British and American representatives as being incompatible with the Allied pledge in the Moscow Declaration to treat Austria as a liberated country, and Secretary of State Byrnes later pointed out that Austria would require Western assistance through the United Nations Relief and Rehabilitation Administration (UNRRA). The Western powers proceeded from the realization that if Russia continued to remove assets from Austria while that country was receiving aid from the West, this meant in a sense that the West would be indirectly helping to finance Russia's reconstruction without quid pro quo. I believe that this is precisely what the Russians wanted in Austria, and it is also what they got.

Having failed to win approval for Austrian reparations, the Soviet Union managed to obtain Allied agreement at Potsdam that they could satisfy their desire for reparations from Germany by seizing appropriate German foreign assets in Bulgaria, Finland, Hungary, Romania, and eastern Austria. There was no longer any mention of reparations from Austria, but the effect was to be the same. As one commentator put it, "the provision concerning Austria left room for very wide interpretation, and the Soviet Government did not hesitate to apply it in the following months and years to justify *seizures in eastern Austria which would never have been contemplated for a moment by either the British or the Americans, had they realized what was intended.* The issue was to become a central one in future discussions of the Austrian treaty, and the initial failure to resolve it was to place a millstone around the neck of the Austrian economy for the next ten years. . . ."[33] However, the West did agree that German assets in eastern Austria belonged to the USSR. Henceforth the controversy was over a reasonable definition of such assets.

When the Renner government issued its first proclamation to the Austrian people, the Communists insisted that it include a reference to the clause of the Moscow Declaration reminding Austria that it had "a responsibility which she cannot evade." That reference was coupled with a declaration of the willingness of the new government to do what it could to assist the Red Army "although that contribution, regrettably, can only be limited in view of the enfeebled and dispossessed condition of our country."[34]

Believing myself that pursuant to the Moscow Declaration the

---

obstacles should be placed in the way of the urgent removal of trophy equipment which might be used in the war against Germany." Ibid., p. 94.

32. *FRUS, The Conference of Berlin (Potsdam), 1945,* 2:323, 666.

33. Balfour and Mair, *Four-Power Control,* p. 311.

34. *Denkschrift,* p. 74.

future status of Austria might be judged in accordance with an appraisal of its efforts to contribute to its liberation, I drafted a dispatch
in October entitled "Anti-Nazi Resistance in Vienna from 1938 to
1945."[35] It was forwarded to Washington together with my personal
evaluation that the lack of foreign assistance and day-to-day encouragement, the great physical difficulties of underground organization in
Austria (for instance due to the common language and the existence of
a substantial minority of Austrians who considered themselves to be
Germans), and the lack of arms and other physical means of resistance,
combined to make the efforts in Vienna much more respectable than
might appear from mere comparison between the Austrian effort and
that of the occupied countries in the West. In view of those differences
and handicaps, I concluded, the resistance efforts I had analyzed,
although not important in military terms, possessed "great political
significance."

That report did not create any particular reaction in Washington,
which is not surprising since it supported a position that, unknown to
me, the United States had already taken some time before, in the
European Advisory Commission, where the Russians had asserted that
Austria's relatively small contribution to its liberation justified their
economic claims. According to a telegram from the secretary of state
in April, it was the U.S. position that "although in our propaganda we
have consistently exhorted the Austrians to 'contribute to their own
liberation' we do not believe that they can be judged at this time to
have failed to do so . . . considering the grip held by the Gestapo and
the meager aid from outside up to the entry of the Red Army into
Austria this month."[36]

It is not necessary for the purpose of this narrative to go into great
detail about the Russian removals of industrial equipment from Austria,
their seizures of the oil fields and the Danube Shipping Company, and
the establishment of a "state within a state" in the form of their administration of some two-hundred allegedly German properties in
Austria. The inter-Allied discussions of the subject of German assets
were prolonged, sometimes acrimonious, and for a long time incon-
clusive—except for a brief period in 1949 when the Soviets seemed to
fall in with a French proposal that envisaged a cash payment to the
USSR in return for its relinquishment of most, though not all, of its
claims.

The Western position included some excellent arguments—for

35. Vienna dispatch no. 337 of October 18, 1945. National Archives, file
863.00/10-1845.
36. Secretary of state instruction to John G. Winant (U.S. representative on
the European Advisory Commission) dated April 10, 1945. *FRUS, 1945*, 3:58.

instance, reference to the declaration of the United Nations of January 5, 1943, which had reserved the right to declare invalid any transfers of property in occupied territories, whether such transfers had taken the form of "open looting or plunder, or of transactions apparently legal in form, even when they purport to have been voluntarily effected."[37] It was also pointed out that the Russian actions, by handicapping the recovery of Austria, were clearly in contradiction with the spirit of the Moscow Declaration that had spoken of opening "the way for the Austrian people . . . to find that political and economic security which is the only basis for lasting peace."[38] The West also was able to point out that according to the Potsdam agreement, Russian reparations claims (against Germany) were to be satisfied from "appropriate" German external assets, which implied that not every property that was nominally German at the end of the war was necessarily really a German asset. But the Russians had physical possession of the disputed properties, which put them in a rather strong position.

While the aims of the Soviet Union with respect to the claimed German assets in Austria were clear, the methods that were pursued were different at various times. The policy at first was to remove industrial machinery physically from Austria, but after a while it was found that this method was inherently inefficient. (Removal of rolling stock and other readily movable equipment continued, however.) Shortly after Potsdam, the Soviets proposed that their holdings of alleged German assets be taken over by Soviet-Austrian joint stock companies. For instance, the Soviets proposed the formation of a joint oil company, valuing their possession of oil properties and exploration rights at $13.5 million and Austrian assets at only $500,000. The Austrians were to be given five years in which to raise their full share in cash (in U.S. dollars) to complete their half of the investment. Since some of the oil properties had originally belonged to Standard Oil of New Jersey and the Socony Vacuum Company, the United States immediately warned the Renner government against entering any such arrangement, "pointing out that it would have a most unfortunate effect at the present time when assistance to Austria from abroad is so greatly needed."[39]

In the spring of 1946 the Soviet Union suddenly abandoned its

37. *FRUS, 1943*, 1:444.
38. Ibid., p. 761.
39. Vienna telegram no. 165 of September 4, 1945 (National Archives, file 863.5034/9-445), containing report of advice by Erhardt to General Clark on what might be said to the Austrians. The implication was clear that if Austria expected to receive American aid, it had better refrain from any action prejudicing American rights to property that had been expropriated by Germany during the war.

policy of wholesale removals from Austria and adopted a new plan whereby most of the remaining "German assets" were formally placed under a Russian trust and set to work producing goods for Russia. The economic administration that was developed was called USIA (Administration of Soviet Property in Austria) and came to control enterprises producing such commodities as oil, sulphuric acid, rayon, sheet metal, electrical equipment, building materials, and glass. There were also large agricultural holdings. USIA was totally divorced from Austrian law and engaged in exporting, importing, and sometimes selling domestically without regard to Austrian official controls, and even in some instances paying wages (to Communists) that far exceeded the Austrian wage guidelines. Moreover, USIA developed armed brigades for the protection of its plants (called *Werkschutz*) that had ominous implications for the stability of the government, particularly since the Austrian law-enforcement establishment was very poorly armed.[40]

The question of dates now becomes important. The new control agreement was signed by the four powers in Vienna on June 28, 1946. On June 27, one day before that signature, TASS reported that the Soviet Union had issued a directive (Order no. 17) transferring all German property in eastern Austria to the ownership of the USSR. The Western powers immediately protested against this order, and General Clark in a letter to his Russian counterpart noted that

no definition of German property is given. I feel this is unfortunate, since it leaves unsettled the important question of whether Austrian property seized by Germany in Eastern Austria after the *Anschluss* [the annexation in 1938] is to revert to Austrian control. . . . I assure you that my Government adheres fully to the decision of the Potsdam conference providing that no reparations should be exacted from Austria; that Allied claims to German reparations should be satisfied in part from appropriate German external assets. . . . Accordingly, my Government has never questioned the right of the USSR to take over possession and ownership of *bona fide* German assets located in Eastern Austria. However, cases have arisen in which the Soviet authorities have cited the Potsdam Agreement as authority for the seizures of property which had been taken from former Austrian owners by the German Government or German Nationals by forced transfer during the period of German control of Austria.[41]

The Austrian government was up in arms over the Soviet order. The Parliament passed a resolution challenging its validity, and on July

---

40. A report in 1948 noted that at that time only one out of seven policemen in Vienna had a firearm. Winifred Hadsel, "Austria under Allied Occupation," *Foreign Policy Reports* 24, no. 12 (Nov. 1, 1948):137.

41. *FRUS, 1946*, 5:354. The United States military commissioner in Austria (Clark) to the commander-in-chief of the Soviet Central Group Troops (Kurasov). Clark protested against the reported order.

10 the U. S. high commissioner publicly took the same position. On July 11, Chancellor Figl at a special session of the Lower House rejected the Soviet order and recalled the Allied wartime declarations that had pronounced the forced transfers of property in Nazi-occupied countries null and void. It is interesting to note that Ernst Fischer, whom we have encountered earlier as Communist minister of education and who was now one of the party's four deputies in the Lower House, tried to justify the Soviet action by claiming that the Soviets had "delayed the execution of the Potsdam Agreement longer in Austria than in other countries" and that if the Austrian government had been willing to negotiate directly with the USSR, instead of leaving the matter for resolution between the occupying powers, it "could have had a favorable interpretation."[42] He was shouted down by the People's party and Socialist deputies.

On July 26, 1946, the Austrian Parliament enacted a long-pending law nationalizing the largest banks, the coal, lead, copper, iron, and antimony mining industries, the oil, steel, and certain machine and metal industries, electrical and automotive plants, the Danube Shipping Company, and some power installations and transportation firms. Of the over seventy enterprises involved, nearly half were under Soviet control.[43] As soon as the law came before the Allied council, Col. Gen. L. V. Kurasov, the Soviet representative, protested that it interfered with the right of the Soviet Union to dispose of German property in accordance with previous Allied agreements. It was pointed out to him, however, that the law was not a "constitutional" one which under the new control agreement required approval of the council. Whereupon Kurasov declared that the Soviets reserved the right to take such steps as seemed to it necessary for the protection of its interests in the Soviet zone. Since the law would obviously not be permitted to go into effect in that zone, the Austrian government suspended its application for the duration of the occupation.

THE SITUATION IN THE SECOND HALF OF 1946

Although the lamentable story of the dispute over "German assets" did not by any means end with this episode, it is time to look at the situation in Austria in its entirety and to place the political and economic factors in perspective. If any point can be identified when a Cold War broke out between the USSR and the Western Allies in Austria, it probably was *not* after the elections of November 1945 (al-

42. Vienna press telegram to Department of State of July 12, 1946, National Archives, file 740.00119, Control (Austria) 7-1246.

43. Hadsel, "Austria under Allied Occupation," p. 50. Balfour and Mair, *Four-Power Control*, p. 140.

though some cooling of relations became noticeable after that event), but after the Russians came to an open confrontation with the Austrians and the Western occupation powers over the issue of German assets in mid-1946. As one chronicler reported: "The Soviets, who undoubtedly felt that the Americans and British at Potsdam had given them a blank check on 'external German assets,' obviously resented (the) American attempt to 'cancel payment' on the check. . . . The lines were now drawn. The policy differences which had been steadily increasing had now produced a clear, public split in the Allied occupation."[44]

On August 29, 1946, the United States political adviser in Vienna reported to the secretary of state:

Russians now beginning to feel new control agreement of 28 June is tending to let power in Austria slip from their hands . . . Soviet member [of Allied Control Council] introduced six various resolutions all tending to nullify new control agreement by instructing Austrian Government not to implement it until instructed to do so by (unanimous) instructions from AC. *All six were vetoed by western elements.* . . . New control machinery thus strengthens Austrian Government as well as western influence in AC. However, *an unfortunate corollary will be increased reluctance of Soviets to withdraw forces from Austria* as long as Potsdam questions are unsettled and they must rely upon occupation forces to enforce their claims to disputed German assets.[45]

A dispatch later that year characterizing the situation of the various occupying powers noted that

on October 24, 1946, a Soviet diplomatic spokesman in Vienna charged the Western Allies with failure to have a full or sympathetic understanding of Russia's position in Austria. He especially charged the United States with carrying on a propaganda campaign to present the United States as a "ready-to-help angel" and the Soviet as a "devil stripping the land." The Russian spokesman could hardly have expressed more succinctly a widely held Austrian viewpoint in regard to the policies being pursued by these two of the four occupying powers.[46]

CONCLUSIONS

I am on record elsewhere as stating that the Cold War really began just about when World War II ended, between the Yalta and Potsdam conferences, because of the disagreements over Russian policies in Eastern Europe, which in turn were due to the ambiguities in the documents drawn up in Yalta (for instance, the one on Poland and the Declaration on Liberated Europe) and the unwillingness of the United

44. Stearman, *Soviet Union* . . . , p. 47.
45. Vienna no. 1184 to secretary of state, August 29, 1946. *FRUS, 1946,* 5:363-64. Emphasis added.
46. Vienna no. 2079, November 27, 1946, ibid., p. 377.

States to have spheres of influence established in Europe[47] (an unwillingness that did not extend to our own sphere in Latin America).
It would fit in with that general conception if after reviewing the events
in Austria in 1945 and 1946 I were to come to the same conclusion
with respect to the clash between the policies and interests of the USSR
and the United States in that country. However, my conclusion is
that the Cold War did not come to Austria because of any of the
primary factors that were in evidence, for instance, in Germany or
Hungary or Bulgaria, since the Soviet Union pursued different objectives in Austria. Nor did the conflict come into the open at the same
time. As indicated, I think it came into the open only in 1946.

I have tried to show that in my opinion the Soviets did not come to
Austria with a clear political plan, but that their economic objectives—
to draw as much substance out of eastern Austria as possible—had
already become apparent in Moscow in 1943, were reflected in inter-
Allied discussions in early 1945, and were confirmed in Potsdam in
July 1945. I do not believe these Soviet objectives had the purpose of
harming Austria, but rather had to do with the needs of the Russian
economy. The terrible destruction that the Soviet Union had suffered
during the war and its inability to find the necessary resources for
reconstruction—whether from German reparations or from external
loans—accounted more for their behavior in Austria in the early years
of the occupation than did political considerations of a larger scope.

This is not to say that the events in Austria unfolded in isolation
from those in neighboring countries. The Russian actions in Hungary
were watched with growing alarm and consternation in neighboring
Austria. Yugoslav territorial claims were a factor preventing the Soviets
from concluding an Austrian treaty (at least until the ejection of Tito
from the Cominform in 1948). Russian fears about a remilitarization of
Germany found echoes in the Austrian situation. The Western powers
in Vienna cast anxious glances at Berlin, where no national government was operating and where the lines between East and West were
much more tightly drawn, and worried that Vienna might be cut off
from western Austria or that the Soviet Union might proceed to partition Austria at any time. (There were even some American officials,
fortunately none in really important positions, who felt that since
partition was "inevitable," it was better to have it sooner rather than
later. They may well have had some Russian counterparts.)

The Allied disagreements over Eastern Europe, Germany, Greece,
and Iran, which became magnified during this period, certainly were
also reflected in the attitudes of the occupying powers toward each

47. Martin F. Herz, *Beginnings of the Cold War* (Bloomington: Indiana University Press, 1966; paperback ed., New York: McGraw-Hill, 1969), p. 188, both eds.

other in Austria. On the other hand, I can find absolutely nothing in the record, or in my memory, that would suggest that the detonation of atomic bombs in Japan had any effect on events or attitudes in Vienna, whether Austrian, Russian, or American. Later, when Czechoslovakia was taken over and Berlin was blockaded, we—the Western Allies as well as the Austrians—did change our basic attitude because we went through a brief period when we even doubted that an Austrian treaty would be desirable. Our position, as well as that of the USSR in Austria, thus was sometimes fluctuating. But on the whole our policy was sound in supporting the freely elected Austrian government and its claim to a viable national existence free from foreign interference.

Having said this, I wish to state my opinion, or speculation, that while it was politically impossible for us to "ransom" Austria, a deal along those lines would probably have been acceptable to the USSR in the early years of the occupation for the very reasons that I have outlined, that is, because of the apparent primacy of its economic interest in Austria. The Austrians and the Western Allies were agreed that the Russian economic claims on Austria had to be resisted, but we would not have needed to pour as much substance into Austria if we had been willing to "pay" the Russians to leave their zone. Of course, the American mood was totally disinclined to even entertain such a deal—although we came close to it in 1949 when we were discussing the French proposal for a "lump-sum settlement" of the German assets issue (with the payment to be made by Austria), and the Russians got down to bargaining with the Western Allies about the sum. Agreement seemed at hand, except for some relatively minor details. It was a fleeting opportunity, and it was lost because we did not then realize how fleeting it was. Within a few months, the Soviet Union refused to discuss the subject at all, throwing up artificial objections that indicated that it was no longer interested in a treaty; so the negotiations broke down in 1950, and it took an entirely new constellation of events to revive them five years later.

There is little reason to doubt that the Soviet Union would have liked to see the Austrian Communists do well in the 1945 elections, but by the time those elections took place the Soviets should have known from their experience in Hungary that Communist parties do not do well in free elections under Soviet occupation. The Russians certainly supported the Communists in Austria—with money, printing services, transportation, and by the initial inclusion of a Communist minister of interior in the Renner government. But they did not support them nearly as much as they did in East Germany, or other countries occupied by the Red Army. I believe the most obvious explanation for the Russian failure to pull out all the stops in favor of the Austrian Communists is also probably the correct one: They did not desire to incorporate eastern Austria into their sphere of influence and control. Perhaps it was regarded as too small. At any rate the economic purposes of the Soviet Union in its zone of occupation could be accomplished without imposing complete political control over the population.

Having said this, I should add that the Communists in Austria had unusual difficulties to contend with: the renaissance of the two large old political parties—the People's party and the Socialists—occurred to an extent and with a rapidity and élan that few had expected. Those parties were also blessed with leaders who, in retrospect, appear as men of extraordinary stature: the elderly Renner, chancellor of the provisional government and later president, whom both the Russians and the West initially underestimated; the Socialist Vice-Chancellor (later President) Adolf Schaerf; and Leopold Figl, first vice-chancellor, then chancellor, and later foreign minister of the Austrian government. If any of these men had yielded to the temptation to resume the pre-1934 internecine fighting between their parties, or if they had slackened in their opposition to the Communists, or if the Socialists had yielded to Communist appeals for "joint action" or to their splitting tactics, the outcome might well have been different. Yet the greatest handicap of the Communists, in my opinion, was the behavior of the Red Army when it first arrived in Austria, which traumatized the entire country.

LOUIS MARK, JR.

The View from Hungary

INTRODUCTION

Budapest when I arrived at the end of April 1945 was a city in ruins. It had been captured by the Red Army only two months earlier, after a devastating battle with the Germans. An embryonic American legation was already installed in its prewar premises at 12 Szabadsag Ter (Liberty Square), and a tall, energetic, and most capable third secretary, Leslie Squires, was serving as chargé d'affaires. I reported to this legation as a newly assigned Foreign Service clerk, dragging my duffle bag, after a zigzag flight from one military base to another across Newfoundland, North Africa, and southern Italy.

I knew the legation building well from many visits in the 1930s. My father was a well-known Hungarian painter who, between his visit to the United States in 1910 and his death there in 1942, spent about half his time in New York and the other half in Budapest. I was born in New York, had crossed the Atlantic five times by my tenth

Louis Mark, Jr., a native of New York City, was educated in his younger years largely in Hungary. Now a retired Foreign Service officer, he held such positions as Deputy Director (Economic) of Soviet Union Affairs at the State Department, Chief of the Economic Section of the American embassies in Panama and Uruguay, and, much earlier, Marshall Plan Program Officer in West Berlin. In 1945 and 1946 he served for a year and a half in the American legation in Budapest as a Foreign Service clerk. He is a graduate of Columbia University and has a master's degree in economics from the University of California at Berkeley. He wrote his master's thesis on "Postwar Inflation in Hungary."

birthday, and then spent nine years in Budapest, where I completed the usual eight years of gymnasium before returning to New York and earning my A.B. degree from Columbia University in 1940. Thus I had the advantage of considerable local background and bilingual fluency, and a further advantage deriving from my father's profession: Hungarian officials were unable to pigeonhole me in Hungarian social terms, as would have been the case had he been an industrialist, a worker, or a public official.

It was on the basis of this Hungarian background that I had ventured to apply for a position in the legation when it appeared that the East European capitals would shortly be liberated from the Germans. The State Department had intended that I assist the disbursing officer, but to everyone's deep chagrin there was none, so I reported to the Economic Section. I was given the paper work involved in the protection of American property in Hungary, and later (after I had made a mess of running the commissary) I was assigned an increasing amount of reporting and, on a few occasions, bits of negotiating work. As I recall, I was the only clerk who attended the minister's staff meetings and the only one who did some substantive drafting of dispatches.

Everyone was keenly conscious of the presence of Red Army soldiers in Budapest in those days. As I disembarked from the legation's jeep that first day, I saw a Soviet soldier wresting a parcel from a passerby. "Shoot!" yelled one of a pair of Hungarian policemen, reminding his colleague of standing instructions. "You shoot," was the reply of the other policeman, who obviously did not want to get involved with the Russians.

The following day I watched from one of our office windows the unveiling of an heroic monument erected in homage to the Red Army soldier. To Hungarians, however, Soviet soldiers were known less for their heroism than for their practice of "liberating" watches from local citizens. Later, as I passed in front of this large statue, I overheard a passerby remark to the lady on his arm: "Look, darling, the monument to the Unknown Watch Thief!" At a movie I attended, where a newsreel of Yalta was shown, as Stalin was seen whispering to Roosevelt, a loud voice from the audience ad-libbed: "Give me your watch!" There was also a story about the storekeeper who naïvely believed Soviet claims that the Red Army opposed looting. When some Soviet soldiers began loading his goods onto a truck, he stepped out of his store and began shouting "Patrul!" (patrol) to summon Soviet military police. One smiling member of the group thereupon introduced himself—"Ya patrul" (I am the patrol).

There was also a crop of stories, fewer in number, relating kindnesses by individual Soviet soldiers, how they helped people with

food, liked children, and so forth. I recall an industrialist telling me of
his discomfort when a Red Army man kept all too close to him in a
dark street. He decided to offer the soldier some cigarettes. "Cigarette?" he asked meekly. Whereupon the soldier gave him a handful.

Generally speaking, however, the behavior of Soviet soldiers was
brutal, even months after the siege of Budapest was over, and the heat
of battle no longer offered any justification. Although it was hard to
ignore Soviet behavior, we in the legation succeeded fairly well in
keeping our knowledge of their excesses in an airtight compartment in
our minds, separate from high policy, which after all was a different
matter from troop behavior. But while we tried hard to give the benefit
of the doubt to the Russians, disillusionment came quickly, as this
chapter will describe.

When I arrived in Budapest, the hopeful vision I had of the future
course of events in Hungary did not differ in the least from official
American objectives, which, I hoped, would not bring about any conflicts with the Soviet Union. Those of us in the legation wanted to see
the establishment of a peaceful, democratic government in Hungary,
as provided for in the Yalta agreement and embodying President
Roosevelt's Four Freedoms: freedom of speech, freedom of worship,
freedom from want, and freedom from fear. We also recognized that
after fighting a devastating and extremely costly war, the Soviets
had a legitimate desire that countries on their periphery not be hostile.
We agreed to Hungarian reparations payments to the Soviet Union,
Czechoslovakia, and Yugoslavia of a magnitude we then believed to
be consistent with the reconstruction of a viable Hungarian economy.
More generally, we assumed that the future peace and security of the
world would, of necessity, be based on the cooperation of the major
powers, and we went to Hungary determined to make that cooperation effective. We did not feel that any of the American objectives
were contrary to the interests of the Soviet Union. And despite a strong
reaction by Hungarians to the behavior of Soviet troops, there is no
evidence that the majority of Hungarians could have established, or
wanted to establish, a reactionary government that would have been
a threat to the USSR. With the benefit of hindsight, a neutralist government such as was to evolve in Austria might well have developed in
Hungary if the USSR had not interfered.[1]

But Soviet actions made it clear that to them a democratic non-Communist government in Hungary was not acceptable. To them non-

1. In the fateful days of the 1956 Hungarian revolt the government of Imre
Nagy issued a declaration of Hungary's neutrality. This precipitated Soviet armed
intervention, making it clear that Hungarian neutrality was unacceptable to Moscow.
On Austrian neutrality see the chapter by Martin Herz.

Communist meant anti-Soviet. Furthermore, they were determined to obtain total control of the country. At the same time, they attached much importance to democratic appearances, even though these could impress only superficial and far-away observers.

Examples of this Soviet insistence on democratic appearance include the following:

(1) National elections were held in November 1945 without interference at the polls proper, but a coalition government, including the Communists, had to be agreed upon prior to the elections. Following a disastrous showing by the Communists at the polls, the Soviet commander personally dictated the composition of the cabinet. In the months that followed, the Soviets imposed upon the Hungarian people a Communist dictatorship, but always with a façade of democratic or pseudodemocratic procedures.

(2) The Allied Control Council (ACC), consisting of representatives of the Soviet Union, the United States, and Great Britain, went through the motions of holding meetings, but in practice the Soviet chairman, Marshal Klimenti E. Voroshilov, made all the decisions. While orders were issued in the name of the tripartite commission, the Soviets ran the country unilaterally.

(3) The Soviets claimed to look upon the rehabilitation of the Hungarian economy as a purely Hungarian concern and on this basis rejected American proposals for inter-Allied cooperation to halt Hungary's economic disintegration. Yet simultaneously the Soviets exerted constant pressure, through the trade union leadership, for immense wage increases. This encouragement of trade union demands stopped abruptly, however, when a Communist-prepared currency stabilization program was introduced.

The assumption that our objectives might be in harmony with those of the Soviets was to prove entirely unrealistic from the very first day of my arrival in Budapest. All our expectations, with the exception of the tenacity of Hungarians in wanting to live under free institutions, proved to be untenable.

Soon after arriving in Budapest, I walked (since the city was without transportation) to my father's old house and knocked on the door of the janitor's apartment. He received me warmly and insisted that I share with him a large and filling meal. As I soon learned, food was not a problem in Hungary, despite the need to feed Soviet occupation troops, who were believed to number over a million in a country of less than ten million people. Hungary was a predominantly agricultural country, and prices still performed their market function so that the inducement to produce was there. The Hungarian authorities cooperated by not imposing any regulations affecting food (such as price controls, ration coupons, or even restrictions on foreign exchange or gold). This laissez-faire policy, which lasted for several months after the armistice, kept the cities from starving, a prime example of the effectiveness of market forces. While, as a result of wartime destruction and dislocation, fuel and industrial goods were scarce, the availability of food permitted Hungarians to retain both their health and their sense of humor.

The anti-Soviet stories cited above were the mildest of psychological antidotes for the tragedies visited upon the population by the Soviet occupying forces. Robbery, rape, and murder were committed with a light hand and were routinely blamed, in official Soviet explanations, on "deserters" or "persons wearing the uniform of the Red Army." The Soviets, Hungarians concluded, were the representatives of a more primitive civilization, and the implications of this conviction were far-reaching. It was essentially due to this postwar behavior of the Soviet forces that the Communists failed in their efforts, over three decades, to teach Hungarians the Russian language and to inculcate them with Russian culture.

Other factors, deep seated and significant but of lesser importance than Soviet behavior, obstructed rapport between occupiers and occupied. Hungarians are not Slavs, nor do they belong to the Eastern Orthodox church. In addition, every Hungarian schoolchild had been indoctrinated with the idea of "Hungary, the Bastion of the West," which meant that the shock and burden of invasions of Europe from the East, occurring every three hundred years or so, reached as far West as Hungary, there to be stopped at the expense of Hungarian blood— as in the case of the Tartars in the middle of the thirteenth century and the Turks in the sixteenth and seventeenth centuries. Hungarians saw the Soviet invasion as fitting into this historical pattern.

A visible reaction to the invasion was the sudden emergence of ostentatious religiosity. Hungary is about 60 percent Catholic, but this figure includes many nominal Catholics. In 1945 the public became suddenly intensely religious, while the Catholic church and Cardinal Mindszenty became symbols of resistance and a focus for patriotism.

If religion offered an escape from the rigors of Soviet occupation, the press did not. Given police terror, running a censored press offers no problems, but getting the public to read the press output does. With two exceptions the names of all prewar newspapers disappeared. Some of the new names emerge in the following story, making the rounds in Budapest in May 1945. A would-be newspaper buyer asks a news vendor for *Free People.* "No *Free People,*" is the reply. "Then give me *Free Speech,*" says the customer. "No *Free Speech,*" replies the vendor. "Well, what *do* you have?" says the exasperated customer. *"Democracy*—every Thursday."

In cabarets some mild antigovernment jokes survived. But they merely criticized inefficiency, never broad policy, and not, of course, the glorious liberating army. I recall one full-length play, however, in which the Hungarian word for "in the interests of the Party"—PÁR-TÉRDEK—was reversed to read KEDRÉTRÁP. This word entered the vocabulary of the population and denoted the justification for compliance with nonsensical or harmful official measures.

Communist propaganda efforts by press and radio, as far as I could see, were entirely ineffective, while economic favors created only pseudo-Communists. I recall a high-school classmate of mine bringing an intimate friend of his to call on me at the American legation. I noticed that the latter was wearing a hammer and sickle emblem in his lapel and suggested that on a visit to us he should not display it. "Oh, that thing," was the reply, as he took it off and slipped it in his pocket. My classmate explained: "Don't worry, when the situation permits he will change sides so rapidly that you'll blink."

A visiting American friend took advantage of a flat tire to chat with the Hungarian mechanic who came to his aid. After the mechanic had delivered a long tirade against existing conditions and the regime that caused them, my friend asked: "Which of the workers here are members of the Communist party?" He replied: "We all are. Everyone has some fault, but if one is a card-carrying Communist, his faults are overlooked."

SOVIET BEHAVIOR TOWARD THE AMERICAN LEGATION

From the standpoint of the internal operations of the legation—in Foreign Service jargon, "housekeeping"—the Soviets did not hamper us. As late as the latter part of 1945, I recall carrying encoded messages to the telegraph window at the General Post Office in Budapest and paying thousands or hundreds of thousands of pengős for their transmission. I do not recall any delays in their transmission, or in the receipt of messages from Washington.

Several American officers, including Minister Arthur Schoenfeld, resided on the Buda side of the Danube, while the Chancery was on the Pest side. The retreating German army had destroyed all the Danube bridges, and on occasion the temporary wooden bridge constructed by the Russians was closed for the reason or pretext of repairs, but I do not think the minister missed a single day at the office on this account, although, at times, he had to walk across a catwalk spanning the Danube.

The Soviets retained complete control over travel not only of Hungarians, but also of American and British military and diplomatic personnel, even after the German surrender. Gen. William S. Key, chief U.S. representative on the Allied Control Commission for Hungary, strongly objected to this unilateral Soviet policy in a letter to

Minister Schoenfeld on April 9, 1946: "It is humiliating to have to petition our allies to permit entrance into Hungary of official diplomatic or military personnel coming here under orders. . . . I must assume that our authorities at Washington, both military and diplomatic, have satisfactory reason for their implied acquiescence in the present arrangement imposed by the Soviet Government."[2]

I experienced interference with my official travel on the one occasion I left Hungary for a brief trip, even though I had all the permits the Soviets required. This happened in March 1946, some ten months after the German surrender and seven months after Potsdam, by which time more equal American rights in Hungary should have been in effect. A colleague and I were on our way back from Vienna in a legation car with a military driver. At a check point inside Hungary we were arrested and taken to the local Soviet commandant's office. In due course an interpreter was provided from the village who spoke Russian and German in addition to Hungarian. With our documents in perfect order and the Soviets flexing their muscles in this picayune way, I saw no need for any conversation. Our driver said he knew some high school German, so I let him handle it. Finally the Soviet official decided to send us to Soviet headquarters in Budapest under armed guard. I tried to have the car stop first at the American Military Mission, but this would have involved crossing the Danube to Pest, while Soviet headquarters were on the Buda side. The Soviet soldier accompanying us objected to my directing the driver toward the bridge. Around 10 P. M., at a traffic stop, I invited a Hungarian policeman into the car. He would have been delighted to start a fight with the Soviet soldier under American auspices and encouraged me to proceed, but I decided not to let it come to that, and instead our car went on to Soviet headquarters. After some thirty minutes of waiting, we were finally released.

Interference by the Hungarian State Security Police with legation operations occurred when one of our Hungarian drivers was arrested. The driver's daughter came tearfully to my home to report the incident, and I went to security police headquarters accompanied by two adult members of the driver's household. I presented my complaint to the duty officer, a police lieutenant, who, after inspecting his register, firmly stated that our driver was not in the building. He added that there were several other places where our employee might be held, if my information regarding his arrest were correct. Then he asked my

2. Letter from General Key to Minister Schoenfeld, April 9, 1946, in U.S. Department of State, *Foreign Relations of the United States* (hereafter cited as *FRUS*), *1946*, 6 *Europe* (Washington: Government Printing Office, 1955):279.

companions why they thought that he might be in the headquarters building. They answered that their reason for supposing this was that they had followed the two arresting detectives and the legation driver to a side entrance of the building, to which they pointed through the window.

The lieutenant shifted ground then, saying that there might be a number of people in the building who were not under arrest but were there to testify. When his answer to my question whether such a person would be excused for a cup of coffee across the street was negative, I asked him to ascertain whether he was physically in the building in any capacity whatsoever. He courteously complied and ordered a search. When negative results were reported, at perhaps 7 P.M., I asked whether he had objections if I stayed for the night. He offered me a sofa in his office. Finally, at about 11 P.M. the driver was produced. He smiled and said that nothing untoward had happened; he had served as a witness, and he was well.

One of my chief tasks at the legation was to determine what property was American-owned and to see that a placard was affixed to it, thereby placing it under American protection. One day the manager of a medium-sized enterprise that was under the legation's protection appeared in my office and explained that some Soviet soldiers had begun dismantling his plant. He had gone to Soviet Economic Headquarters with our protective placard and had explained the American interest and the absence of any German interest in the firm. (German-owned properties were to pass to Soviet ownership under the Potsdam agreement.) A Soviet official asked how the American interest had been established in the firm, and he was told that it was by a 650,000 pengö investment in the 1930s. (In the 1930s this sum of pengös was worth about $130,000—at the time of this occurrence perhaps a few dollars or less than a dollar.) Thereupon the Soviet official courteously asked him to walk to the cashier's window and receive payment of 650,000 pengös. Obviously, the Soviets were ready to "legalize" their action by "buying out" the Americans for a few dollars. As I recall, the matter was eventually settled by issuing a new letter confirming that the enterprise was under the protection of the United States government.

The property protection case I remember best involved the local plant of the Singer Sewing Machine Company. Its manager came to me to report that on his arrival at the plant that morning he found Soviet soldiers dismantling it. I proceeded by appointment to Soviet Economic Headquarters, where I was received by a group of five officials sitting behind a long table, as if they constituted some kind of a tribunal. There was at least one Muscovite Hungarian among them.[3] I repeated the report from the plant manager and asked why the Soviet authorities had taken possession of a firm under American protection. The answer was twofold: (1) the Soviets do not decide what installations they take over, and act only as "acceptors" when the Hungarian government designates an enterprise for takeover; (2) the Singer Sewing Machine Company was so designated because it was German.

The first point was patent nonsense; we had a steady stream of reports on indiscriminate takeovers, dismantlings, and requisitions. To mention only one area, the Soviets had acquired Hungarian railway cars by simply painting the Soviet insignia on them. I disregarded this point, and asked what made them think that the Singer Sewing Machine Company was German. "Singer is a German name," began the answer. I replied as crisply as I could that the Americans would make no objection to their dismantling the plant if they would state in writing that in their opinion President Roosevelt was a national of Holland. In the stony silence that followed I said that the United States was a country of immigrants, and had provided homes and a higher standard of living to the poor and oppressed from many, many countries, including Germany. The dismantling of Singer was stopped, but for how long following my departure from Hungary, I do not know.

THE ALLIED CONTROL COMMISSION

In the Declaration on Liberated Europe issued at Yalta, Stalin, Churchill, and Roosevelt stated:

> The Premier of the Union of Soviet Socialist Republics, the Prime Minister of the United Kingdom, and the President of the United States of America have consulted with each other in the common interests of the peoples of their countries and those of liberated Europe. They jointly declared their mutual agreement to concert during the temporary period of instability in liberated Europe the policies of their three governments in assisting the people liberated from the domination of Nazi Germany and the peoples of the former Axis satellite states of Europe to solve by democratic means their pressing political and economic problems.[4]

In actual practice, however, concerting policy with Russia in Eastern Europe proved to be impossible. The normal channel for conducting inter-Allied relations in Hungary was the Allied Control Commission, but the Soviet chairman, Marshal Voroshilov, ran things as

---

3. Hungarian Communists who fled to the Soviet Union following the collapse of the first Hungarian Communist regime in 1919, or after being released from jail under the Horthy regime, were called "Muscovites." During the time that I was in Hungary, the Communist party was dominated by General Secretary Mátyás Rákosi and other "Muscovites."

4. *FRUS, The Conferences of Malta and Yalta*, pp. 977-78.

he pleased, often ignoring the American and British representatives. In an article published after the completion of his mission, American Minister Schoenfeld commented: "Some skepticism as to Soviet methods began to be felt in the first weeks following the establishment of my mission in Budapest, four days after V-E day."[5] That there was cause for concern before Schoenfeld's arrival appears clearly from a memorandum of April 19, 1945, by Charles E. Bohlen, then assistant secretary of state in charge of White House liaison. Discussing attempts to ensure that the Soviets inform our representatives on the ACC of directives "prior to their issuance to local governments," Bohlen noted:

> In Rumania we have had informal agreements to this effect, but they have not worked out in practice. In Bulgaria we have had no satisfaction at all. Provision was made in the statutes of the Hungarian Control Commission for such a procedure, but the Soviet authorities, after a good beginning, are not now strictly adhering to it. The result has been that in all three countries ultimate authority rests with the Soviet Government which is at liberty to act either directly, as in the recent Rumanian crisis, or through the Control Commissions.[6]

Thus Soviet conduct on the ACCs was objectionable already in the first period of the occupation, that is, between the signing of the armistice and German surrender; and in the second period of the occupation, after the German surrender, the expected full British and American participation did not materialize. In an ACC meeting on June 5, 1945, General Key stated that "since the First Period of the Armistice was concluded by the cessation of hostilities, the Statutes should be broadened to permit of more active participation by the American and British representatives during the Second Period."[7] This statement, which General Key followed with detailed proposals, produced no result except for the Soviet chairman of the ACC agreeing to seek Western concurrence on "important" subjects.

After the Potsdam Conference, Key received another letter from the chairman submitting the new statute of the ACC in Hungary, which did not differ in substance from the earlier one.[8] However, as Bohlen had already noted in his April 19 memo, "the Department failed to secure Soviet agreement to the inclusion of a reference to the 'second period' (from the end of hostilities against Germany to the conclusion of peace) during which the three Allied governments would have equal participation in and responsibility for the work of the Com-

---

5. H. F. Arthur Schoenfeld, "Soviet Imperialism in Hungary," *Foreign Affairs* 26, no. 3 (April 1948):555.
6. *FRUS, 1945*, 5:835.
7. Ibid., 6:277.
8. Ibid., p. 276.

mission, but reserves the right to reopen this question later."[9] As has been seen, when the question of equal Western participation on the ACC in Hungary was reopened, nothing came of it, and the Soviets continued to run the ACC in unilateral fashion.

SOVIET ECONOMIC POLICIES IN HUNGARY

In this account I put special emphasis on economic matters because, first, I was an economic officer in the Foreign Service, and I paid special attention to the economy when I was in Hungary. Second, the political side of developments in Hungary in 1945-46 has already been told many times, whereas the economic side of the story has been rather neglected.

Soviet refusal to cooperate with their American allies is amply illustrated by their actions regarding the Hungarian economy. This can be shown by presenting a chronology of major American initiatives and Soviet responses:

December 3, 1945. The Hungarian finance minister asked the Allied governments for help; the Soviet chairman declined to accept his note.

December 5, 1945. In an ACC meeting, the American representative recommended establishment of a subcommittee to consider the Hungarian economy; the Soviet chairman refused.

March 2, 1946. The United States raised the same issue in Moscow (Chargé George Kennan to Foreign Minister Vyacheslav Molotov), linking Hungary's economic plight to the burden of Soviet reparations, occupation costs, and so forth.

April 21, 1946. Soviet Deputy Minister Andrei Vyshinsky rejected Kennan's démarche on the grounds that the economy's rehabilitation was within Hungary's competence. He also denied the link with Soviet reparation collections and blamed Hungary's economic difficulties on American failure to return Hungarian property, valued at $3 billion, which had been moved by the Nazis to the American zones of Austria and Germany.

July 23, 1946. The American ambassador to Moscow, Walter Bedell Smith, reiterated that Hungarian transfers to the Soviets were linked to Hungary's economic troubles and showed that the $3 billion estimate by the Soviets of Hungarian property in the American zones was absurdly high. (He left the impression that about one tenth of that amount might be closer to the truth.) Smith noted that the total war damage to Hungarian manufacturing industry had been reliably estimated at $345 million, of which $124 million was due to removals

9. Ibid., 4:836.

by Soviet forces. He further expressed the view that in agreeing to Hungarian reparations the United States had not anticipated that Hungary's national income would be cut in half and that reparations would absorb 24 percent of the national income. He again requested that the three powers get together on the Hungarian economy, as had been agreed to at Yalta.

July 27, 1946. Soviet Vice-Minister of Foreign Affairs V. G. Dekanozov stated that the data cited by the United States were false. He argued that net Soviet reparations taken from the Hungarian economy were almost nominal—some $3.7 million. The Soviets had not removed $124 million in industrial equipment, he said, but only certain military enterprises as booty, with a value not exceeding $11 million. He denied the decline of Hungarian national income by one half. On the contrary, he stated:

In reality the capacity of the industrial enterprises of Hungary curtailed as the result of the war to 60 percent of the prewar level had by the middle of July 1946 risen to 70 to 85 percent in the production of pig iron, rolled metal, and machine building, and to 85 to 90 percent in light industry. If the output of industrial production in Hungary in 1945 constituted 30-35 percent of the prewar level, at the present time the output of production has been brought to 60 percent of the prewar level.[10]

To further illustrate the tone of Soviet statements on the economy, let me recall a Soviet comment on a surplus property credit of $10 million we granted Hungary in February 1946. By this time the disintegration of the Hungarian economy had advanced considerably, and the legation felt that economic recovery was beyond the capacity of the Hungarian authorities unless they got outside aid. But ACC Chairman Voroshilov, meeting informally with his British and American colleagues, cited this loan as evidence that the United States regarded Hungary as a good business risk.[11] This, of course, was absurd, and shows the kinds of argument to which the Soviets resorted to "prove" that Hungary was doing well.

Soviet economic policy in Hungary represented two, sometimes conflicting, purposes: exploiting the Hungarian economy for the benefit of the Soviet Union, and incorporating Hungary into the Soviet empire. The Soviet obstructed the unfolding development of the market economy both by actions normal to harsh victors—including the dismantling of productive capacity—and by arrogating

10. U.S. Department of State, *Documents on American Foreign Relations* (Washington: Government Printing Office, 1946). The quote is from p. 333; the other figures are from pages 332 and 334.

11. *FRUS, 1946*, 6:292, n. 93.

to themselves control over large sectors of the Hungarian economy. In each area there was a difference between admitted and actual behavior.

Direct Soviet Removals

In 1938 Hungarian national income was on the order of $800 million. At the end of World War II it seemed to us in the American legation that Hungary could possibly manage to pay reparations over six years of $300 million, the figure fixed by the armistice. But by early 1947 we recognized that we had overestimated Hungary's reparations potential. In any case, both original and revised estimates became meaningless because the Soviets valued reparations at the lower world market prices (not at higher prewar internal Hungarian prices), charged a 5 percent a month penalty for late deliveries, quartered about a million occupation troops in the country, collected booty on a gigantic scale, and permitted wholesale looting by Soviet soldiers.

Reparations actually taken and computed at prewar Hungarian prices amounted to much more than the $300 million originally agreed to. Arthur Kárász, president of the Hungarian National Bank, spelled this out in careful detail in a confidential memorandum to the British and American missions in November 1945. In it he showed that the projected reparations burden would be almost three times the agreed amount and would be entirely beyond the capacity of the Hungarian economy. Because of dismantlings, reparations, and booty-taking, productive capacity was gravely impaired, and the burden imposed by reparations was staggering. Kárász was made to suffer for telling the truth. At the demand of Marshal Voroshilov, he was removed from all of his official posts, including the presidency of the Hungarian National Bank and his designation as Hungary's principal economic delegate to the proposed Paris Peace Conference.[12]

Soviet Control of Large-Scale Industry

In the summer or early fall of 1945 an official of a Hungarian company told me that his firm was late in making some reparations deliveries, and that he had tried to obtain an extension from the Soviets. To his surprise the Soviet official asked whether his company would like to pay the penalty in shares of stock of the company. This gave us our first inkling that the Soviets intended to obtain positions on the boards of private corporations. By then, unknown to me, larger developments were under way.

---

12. Letter from Kárász to the author, Dec. 1, 1977. See also Stephen Kertesz, *Hungary in a Whirlpool* (Notre Dame, Ind.: University of Notre Dame Press, 1953), pp. 252-54.

The Potsdam agreement transferring German assets in the ex-satellite states to the USSR gave them their trump card for establishing control over large-scale Hungarian industry. Not that German investment was overwhelmingly large in Hungary; by the time of the Hungarian declaration of war it may have been (on a high estimate) about 14 percent to 18 percent of all investment.[13] The loose wording of the relevant clause of the Potsdam agreement enabled the Russians to take German assets without concerning themselves with the liabilities of any company. The Hungarian Supreme Economic Council—dominated in fact though not in form by its Communist members—handed over property to the Soviets under the "German" label with no scrutiny of the nature of German ownership. In a most important instance—that of the Hungarian General Credit Bank—the Soviets obtained a seat on the Board of Directors with only 18 percent of the share capital owned by a French interest and extorted by the Germans during the war. France protested in vain. Not only was this institution Hungary's second largest bank, but it also controlled substantial chunks of industry.

In August 1945, a five-year economic cooperation agreement between the USSR and Hungary was signed in Moscow by Ernö Gerö, minister of commerce and communications (a Muscovite Communist), and Antal Bán, minister of industry (a leftist Social Democrat). The signing occurred without the approval of either the prime minister or the Cabinet, and both the United States and Britain registered protests. The agreement was exclusive, leaving little if anything for agreements with any other countries.

Among other things, this agreement laid the foundation for the establishment of four Soviet-Hungarian "joint" enterprises (so-called fifty-fifty companies), each of which effectively placed a large sector of the economy under Soviet control. Payment by the Soviet Union for these large shares in Hungarian industry did not include any reduction in reparations, let alone any actual resource transfers from the Soviet Union; a part of the Potsdam-based "German assets" proved to

13. "In Hungarian industry foreign interests accounted for 25 percent of the direct portfolio investment; within this total, on the threshold of war, German capital succeeded in obtaining a leading role by means of acquiring Austrian and Czech capital interests." Erik Molnar, ed., *A History of Hungary* (Budapest: Gondolat Könyvkiadó, 1964), 2:424. I have no reason to doubt Molnar's figure as he would have no motive to understate the role of international investment in general and of German investment in particular. The dominant German role (not necessarily meaning ownership of as much as one-half) dates only from the war. I venture as a guess that nonportfolio investment was not likely to have been higher than portfolio investment; further, that as blocks of shares after the *Anschluss* and during the war were ceded to German interests, the ratio of nonportfolio to portfolio investment certainly declined.

be sufficient, so that after settlements, the Soviets still owned out-right, if I remember correctly, over three hundred Hungarian com-panies.

The "joint" enterprises or sectors were petroleum, bauxite, Danube navigation, and civil aviation. In bauxite and aluminum production Hungary ranked third in Europe after the USSR and France, while petroleum production in Hungary was larger than bauxite production. Regarding the Soviet-Hungarian Danube Navigation Company, a Buda-pest wit quipped: "This is a fifty-fifty company, the Soviets will navigate the Danube up and down, and the Hungarians across."

Both British and American officials felt that these agreements, as implemented, constituted a wholesale takeover of Hungarian large-scale industry.[14] One interesting thing in all this activity was that in-stead of outright confiscations, the Soviets chose to assume control by joining the boards of directors of public as well as private corporations, always on the basis of some legal fiction, no matter how transparent.

Hungary's Market Economy

Causes of Hungary's postwar inflation. In the first three months following the armistice, the Red Army increased the supply of Hun-garian currency by as much as 40 percent (adding over four billion pengös to the eleven billion already in circulation).[15] This increase in the money supply was further aggravated by the much faster circula-tion of the distrusted occupation notes than the "good old Hungarian notes," many of which were hoarded, especially in rural areas.

With real wages very low as a result of low productivity and the burgeoning inflationary spiral, the Communist-dominated Council of Trade Unions pressed for enormous wage increases. The council regu-larly claimed to have Soviet support, and certainly there were no disclaimers from any Soviet quarter. An early instance of Soviet inter-vention in wage negotiations reportedly occurred during the siege of Budapest when Soviet troops arriving at the Manfred Weiss machine works ordered an immediate 200 percent wage increase. I have no direct knowledge of the exact link between the Trade Union Council and Soviet occupation authorities, but it was generally believed at that time that such a link existed—possibly through the Communist party—and no businessman was prepared to risk being labeled antisocial by the Soviets for holding out against union demands. That these wage demands were orchestrated from above is indicated by all such demands

14. *New York Times*, Sept. 25, 1945, p. 6. For the U.S. and British protests, see the *New York Times* for Oct. 22 and 23, 1945.

15. In this section I draw heavily on my M.A. thesis, Louis Mark, Jr., "Postwar Inflation in Hungary" (University of California, Berkeley, 1947).

ceasing abruptly with the introduction of the Communist-sponsored stabilization program in August 1946. This turn around in the attitude of the union leadership was indispensable to the success of the stabilization.

While the crushing burdens on the Hungarian treasury are beyond doubt, it was also true that the government did not utilize its taxing powers fully. During the twenty-month-long period of postwar inflation, taxes absorbed only some 2 percent of reduced national income—against a 20 percent ratio before the war—and the administrative breakdown at the time of the armistice cannot account for this twenty-month record. There must have been a gradual strengthening of the taxing apparatus, rather than a *deus ex machina* type of appearance on stabilization day—August 1, 1946—after which the taxing apparatus was quite efficient. The poststabilization tax structure emphasized turnover taxes (à la Soviet), which, as Hungarian experts observed, appeared to many better suited to the difficult prestabilization period. It is clear that the idea of a turnover tax was not new, but that its application was deferred, to be incorporated later into the Communist stabilization program.

During my presence in Hungary, everything led me to believe that the way the inflation and stabilization policies were handled was directly related to Soviet objectives. Two cabinet ministers, including Finance Minister Stephen Vásáry, resigned in protest over Soviet inflationary policies. Arthur Kárász, Hungary's principal economic expert and president of the Hungarian National Bank, was firmly convinced that the Communists deliberately fostered inflation to serve their political ends.[16] The Soviets wished to destroy both the market economy and the middle and upper classes; demonetizing the country achieved both. By undermining the economic structure of the country, they also helped undermine the political structure. And by later introducing a stabilization program, the Communists hoped to gain credit for reviving the economy.

The market economy's losing battle against its demonetization. By late 1945 the Hungarian man in the street had decided that the decline of the pengő's value to zero was a foregone conclusion. Budapest wits depicted the finance minister ordering a 100-million note of beautiful design and telling the artist: "Let it cost what it may—money doesn't count." Indeed, by the end of July 1946, monetary circulation was the equivalent of 460,000 quadrillion pengős, and the purchasing power of this astronomical amount—after price advances had long outstripped printing press capacity—was around $65,000.[17]

16. Dr. Kárász confirmed this in a letter to me in December 1977.
17. It might be more meaningful to say that the purchasing power of the Hun-

As the inflation worsened, price increases outstripped the rapid rise in the money supply so that the economy was being precipitously demonetized. Liquidity is, of course, the lifeblood of any market economy. Between July and October 1945 the money supply contracted from 7 percent to about 1½ percent of the gross national product, while the normal peacetime ratio was 15 to 20 percent. The economy could go in one of two directions: it could contract, or rather collapse, to about a third of its previous size (with the demonetized sector growing), or it could opt out of a market economy by clamoring for comprehensive direct controls. The Hungarian public, both consumers and businessmen, chose yet another road. In a phenomenon unique in the history of inflations, the dollar became the principal medium of payment in the Hungarian economy in October and November 1945, thus doubling the country's eroded money supply. Consumer items, say shoes or sugar, were priced and routinely paid for in dollars.

Even in Germany's hyperinflation after World War I dollars were used for hoarding or accounting units only and did not enter the money stream as a generally accepted medium of payment. (Imagine the difficulty of using Swiss francs or German marks in grocery stores in the United States! This is quite different from holding secret speculative balances in these currencies.) The Hungarian example made clear the preference of the public for an open economy, even though a switch to centrally directed rationing and price controls might have brought substantial short-term relief.

As dollars got into general circulation, it became profitable for the authorities to set up traps in the streets to search passersby. People with a couple of dollars on their persons escaped with light sentences; strangely, larger amounts were rarely found. The public assumed that the police underreported their take, and found ready accomplices in the culprits.

The Communist stabilization program. With the pengö" virtually worthless, the public's initial supplies of the new currency, the forint, were available only for dollars; the monetary authorities could start with a clean slate. The stabilization was a complete success and a feather in the cap of the Communists. It was their program, combining stabilization and economic reorientation. According to the Communist proposals, the economy was to operate under centralized decisions, with a predetermined division of output:

---

garian monetary issue was completely wiped out a few days before stabilization on August 1, 1946. But while pedantic, it is true that a dollar could still be acquired for huge sums of Hungarian issue. For details of this computation see Mark, "Postwar Inflation in Hungary," p. 50, n. 16.

Decisions must embrace not only fiscal matters, but in essence the entire economic life, the entire system of price and wage relations . . . the principal areas of production. . . . The bourgeois experts failed to consider that this grand scale interference is made possible by the strong positions held in the administration by the laboring class. . . . Government expenditures must be secured in the first instance by the introduction of an appropriate system of taxation and its strict enforcement. . . . The Material and Price Office was established in June [1946] to prepare the prices of the principal products . . . as well as for the control of price relationships.[18]

Sufficient taxation and the termination of wage increases appear to have been the ingredients of success in the Communist prescription— a rather conservative formula, especially in view of the overriding importance of indirect taxes in the tax mix.

I learned from a former Smallholder party deputy, who attended a meeting of the Council of Ministers in the summer of 1946, that late in the afternoon, just before adjournment, Communist party General Secretary and Deputy Prime Minister Mátyás Rákosi asked for the floor to make an announcement on a subject not on the agenda. He took some thirty to forty-five minutes to read the Stabilization Program. The non-Communist cabinet members were unprepared, and no discussion ensued. Several former economic policy makers met that night to try to hammer out a politically hard-hitting counterproposal. This group tried to formulate on-the-spot answers to the question of the harm the new program would do to the interests of peasants, workers, and the cause of reconstruction. As far as I could learn, nothing that would "fly" emerged from this meeting, given the prevailing mood of desperation among the participants.

American officials became concerned at an early date with the deterioration of the Hungarian economy and wished to discuss this question constructively with the Soviet authorities. Implicit in this American attitude was our opposition to the excessive Soviet seizures, the various and sundry methods and techniques used to acquire Soviet control over key economic sectors, and the Soviet-supported policies that were undermining the market-oriented economy. Our position was to seek a viable Hungarian economy, which would pay reparations within its means and develop along lines desired by its democratic majority, provided it conformed with the Yalta provisions. No wonder, then, that the Soviets, who had other goals, excluded us and the British from having any effective say in the affairs of the Hungarian economy.

SOVIET INTERFERENCE IN HUNGARIAN POLITICS

Prior to January 1947, Soviet interference in Hungarian politics

18. Molnar, *History of Hungary*, pp. 507-8.

was somewhat indirect. During the early postwar months Soviet influence was chiefly exerted by supporting the Muscovite Hungarians who formed the leadership and hard core of the Communist party, and by limiting the political spectrum to the right only as far as the left-of-center Smallholders party.

There can be no doubt in anybody's mind that Soviet actions were directed to frustrating the Hungarian popular will from the beginning. These actions may well have been in accordance with Stalin's belief, as expressed in his statement at Potsdam, that "any freely elected government would be anti-Soviet and that we cannot permit."[19] But political intervention was not restricted to the elections. Communist leadership was promptly imposed on the trade unions and women's organizations, and youth groups under Communist control were formed in the first weeks of the occupation, in accordance with standard Communist political techniques. Apartment superintendents or janitors, traditionally used as informers by police regimes, found it necessary and easy to switch their party affiliation from the Nazis to the Communists.

A large share of administrative decision making and personnel policy was put in the hands of quadripartite commissions, each consisting of a Communist, a Socialist, a Smallholder, and a trade union representative. In these the left wing tended to predominate, with the Communists in effective charge, exercising power and control beyond what their popular following entitled them to. Similarly, denazification commissions were established with the same kind of membership. If any of the others disagreed with the Communist member, he could count on being branded a reactionary, a designation people sought to avoid. Under this system, the mother of a friend of mine lost her license to run a shop by action of a denazification board, even though her father had committed suicide when the Germans entered Hungary in 1944 and she and her husband had saved the lives of a dozen or more people under the Nazi regime.

The Social Democratic party would have been much more influential than the Communist party in postwar Hungary, except for Soviet interference. Traditionally the majority of Hungarian labor was Social Democratic, and this party had strong organizations in the factories. A good example was given to me by a technical director of the United Incandescent Lamps and Electric Company, one of the largest manufacturing corporations in Budapest.[20] He developed a close personal

19. Philip E. Mosely, *The Kremlin and World Politics* (New York: Random House, 1960), p. 214.

20. When the Soviets dismantled most of it in March and April 1945, they took 700 carloads of machinery, which they counted as war booty.

relationship with the shop steward and other workers when they all conspired together to save the plant from destruction by the retreating Germans (only to see it dismantled two months later by the arriving Soviet troops). The steward, who was the generally acknowledged spokesman for the plant's workers, was a Social Democrat who shortly afterwards became a member of parliament. But his fate was the same as that of many Social Democratic leaders—he was thrown in jail by the Communists. The workers in this factory had expected that the outcome of the political process would be a Social Democratic state with a Communist minority, but their hopes were dashed by Soviet intervention.

The party with the largest following, however, was the Smallholder party. Its leadership remained the traditional one, representing the interests of owner-operators of small and medium farms. Its ranks were swelled, however, by elements, principally businessmen, whose prewar allegiance had gone to liberal and conservative parties. The Smallholders were also infiltrated from the left by crypto-Communists.

The central political events of my stay in Hungary were the Budapest municipal elections on October 7, 1945, and, more important, the national elections on November 4, 1945. (In other Hungarian municipalities and political subdivisions, no elections were held during my tour of duty; the Communists had taken over their administrations as the Red Army entered, and this arrangement proved impenetrable to the other parties.) As I recall, political analysts of the day expected a victory for the Left in the Budapest election, while they were more reserved on the outcome of the national vote. With regard to the Budapest election, Communist and Social Democratic control of the trade unions was expected to be decisive. Moreover, the Soviets got a joint list for the two parties, so that the small size of the Communist vote would be hidden in the combined vote. Predictions along the foregoing lines proved wrong, however, as the Smallholder party won and gained control of the administration of Budapest.

The outcome of the national elections in November was even more astounding. There the Social Democrats succeeded in their desire to keep their list of candidates separate from that of the Communists. The results were (according to most sources) 57 percent for the Smallholders, 17.1 percent for the Communists, and 16.9 percent for the Social Democrats, while the remainder was divided among smaller anti-Communist parties.[21]

These results are all the more noteworthy because, while the Soviets

21. Imre Kovacs, ed., *Facts about Hungary* (New York: Waldon Press, 1958), pp. 57-58, says the Smallholders got 59.9 percent of the vote.

did not interfere with the actual balloting and the counting of the ballots, they did give the Hungarian Communist party heavy support during the campaign—military trucks to transport people to rallies and to the polls, printing facilities for posters and propaganda, direct financial support, and so forth. The American government's (and I believe Britain's) refusal to provide any material support at all to the non-Communist parties was something Hungarians could not understand. It is possible that a certain coolness with which Minister Schoenfeld is remembered by some Hungarians to this day is related to his position on this issue. I do not know how he felt about the matter. His reply that "American diplomatic practice excluded such interference in the internal political affairs of foreign countries"[22] may have sounded formalistic and cold in view of Soviet help to the Communists, but his position represented American policy of the day. Protests against election improprieties, usually initiated by the British, marked the extent of our involvement.

The election results made clear that the Soviets had grossly miscalculated Communist strength. Their error in failing to falsify the results would not be repeated again. In the next elections, held in August 1947, the Communists claimed that they received 22 percent of the vote, the Social Democrats 15 percent, the Smallholders 15 percent, while the remaining 48 percent went to six other parties and some splinter groups. But according to a former American intelligence officer, the true Communist share was only 7 percent.[23]

I cannot fathom the reasons why the Communists and the Soviets believed that the Communist party would make a strong showing in the elections. It may be that the "imported" Hungarian Communists did not want to admit, even to themselves, that communism in Hungary had very weak roots. One theory current at the time was that the lowering of the voting age would add to the Communist vote. (The voting age was changed from twenty-four years for males and twenty-one for females to eighteen for both sexes.) This seems to have backfired entirely. Practically every family had suffered indignities and losses at the hands of Soviet soldiers, and young men whose mothers and sisters had been raped—as well as the victims themselves—did not want to support the party imposed by the conquerors.

The national elections being postponed at American insistence from August to November 1945 may also have improved the chances of the non-Communists since our influence may have momentarily increased following Japan's surrender. While the elections were held, as the Com-

22. Schoenfeld, "Soviet Imperialism," p. 558.
23. Christopher Felix, *A Short Course in the Secret War* (New York: Dutton, 1963), p. 276.

munists desired, during the armistice period, rather than after the anticipated withdrawal of occupation troops, the disintegration of the Hungarian economy by November 1945 was much further advanced than in August. This trend, as a political fact, may have escaped the attention of the Communists in view of the constant wage increases labor had received all along. Yet the illusion of improved economic conditions was losing its force as inflation accelerated. In August prices increased on the average by 2 percent a day; this doubled to 4 percent a day in September, and then rose to 18 percent a day in October! Inflation of this order would hardly cause Hungarians to support the Soviet occupation authorities or their puppets, the local Communists.

In any event, the great victory of the middle-of-the-road parties in the 1945 elections was hollow. The Communists had demanded and received, before the elections, the promise of a coalition government, with strong Communist representation. Nine of the eighteen cabinet portfolios went to the Communists, including (on explicit Soviet command) that of minister of interior, who controlled the police. Four posts each were given to the Smallholders and Social Democrats, and one went to the small Peasant party.

There was much discussion by the public about what the Soviet reaction would be to the terrible defeat the Communists suffered in the 1945 elections. Communist party Secretary Rákosi was ordered to Moscow for consultation following the municipal elections in October 1945 and, according to well-informed Hungarians, Voroshilov went so far as to slap Rákosi in the face.

An anecdote making the rounds at the same time sums up the atmosphere. It has Rákosi calling in his public relations man on the eve of one of his major addresses at a mass rally. "I want 500,000 people to attend," says Rákosi brusquely. The public relations man tries to allege poor communications, lack of transportation, and bad weather to explain why such a turnout cannot be achieved, but Rákosi will brook no excuses. On the morning of the speech, he raises his demand to an attendance of one million. A million people actually do turn up and Rákosi, surprised and pleased, calls in the public relations man to ask how he did it. "Well, at your first request, for an audience of 500,000, I started a rumor that Cardinal Mindszenty was going to speak. But you know the Cardinal would not draw a million people. So when you gave the second order, I spread the rumor that Rákosi was going to be hanged."

CONCLUSIONS

As its dispatches to Washington show, the American legation maintained sufficient contact with Hungarians to be well informed on all

important trends in Hungarian public life. Our officers had the necessary diplomatic, political, and economic skills, and several of them
spoke Hungarian or Russian. The gathering of information was not
hard, and, mostly by word of mouth, we obtained all the facts we
needed; indeed, knowledgeable Hungarians were eager to confide in
us. Doing so was, however, against the wishes of the Soviets, and
therefore, we could not effectively use such information in negotiations. The confidential memorandum President Kárász of the Hungarian
National Bank prepared for us and the British in November 1945 was
an act of personal courage. Some others were equally brave; they were
motivated by a hope for American action, which we could not take.
A Soviet colonel supervising the dismantling of a large Hungarian
plant described our weakness succinctly: when a plant official called a
modest American interest in the concern to his attention, he answered:
"Where do you see any American troops?"

Initially, American officials did not foresee any need for conflict
with Soviet authorities. We did not regard democratic, non-Communist
governments and parties as being necessarily anti-Soviet. We thoroughly
appreciated the Soviets' need for security along their borders, and
would have joined with them in opposing the emergence of any political trend, which, even under extreme conditions, might have posed a
threat to the Soviet Union. We were convinced that democratic regimes
in Eastern Europe by themselves could not possibly endanger the
Soviet Union as long as the German question was taken care of. We
would even have acquiesced in a dominant Communist role in Hungary,
if the Hungarian people had freely opted for such an arrangement. But
this was, of course, purely theoretical, since Hungarian attitudes at all
times precluded such a possibility. On a more practical level, we would
have had no problem with the emergence of a Social Democratic regime
such as the one that appeared in Finland, had that been what Hungarians wanted.

Soviet behavior indicated that in Soviet-occupied Hungary we could
not look forward to the realization of even our minimal aspirations,
for which we had expended our blood and treasure, notwithstanding
explicit agreement among the four Allies to secure these aspirations and
our willingness to make adjustments in deference to Soviet desires.
Indications were clear that rapport with the Soviets was not to be had—
that is, that our relations were moving toward a complete impasse,
later called the Cold War. Our only course was to abandon hopes for
even a bankruptcy quota in our war aims.

The Russian attitude was made obvious when they frustrated the
outcome of free elections by imposing a cabinet that violated the
expressed preferences of the electorate, when they established joint

Soviet-Hungarian enterprises on a scale so large as to preclude similar arrangements between Hungary and other countries, and when they vetoed consideration by the ACC of Hungary's economic rehabilitation. Our protests document a long and bitter process of disillusionment, in which our officials on the scene saw their initial hopes and efforts disappointed, month by month and year by year.

Washington attitudes and actions were in line with, but were attenuated versions of, legation recommendations. As early as June 1945, as we have seen, General Key was complaining that Washington support could not be enlisted in such an elementary matter as the free movement into, out of, and within Hungary by U.S. occupation personnel. The question of why the United States failed to press effectively at the Washington-Moscow level for the achievement of our minimum objectives in Hungary cannot be answered explicitly in these pages. It is obvious, however, that the administration had to view developments in Hungary (and in other Eastern European countries) in the context of its over-all policy, which was based on the hope for Four Power cooperation. Not until the evidence was overwhelming that we could not solve key problems (especially the German problem) through Four Power cooperation, did we change our policies. Up to that point the Hungarian experience was part of the process of educating American officials, but it was not of sufficient importance to alter our basic approach to the Soviets. The change in approach began with Secretary Byrnes's Stuttgart speech in 1947 and became firmly established in our response to the Berlin blockade in 1948.

While in those early years Hungarians felt that we did far too little on their behalf, and Soviet reactions indicated that we were trying to do much more than was actually possible, the decades that followed produced more differentiated situations and thus scope for more nuanced policies. More than thirty years have passed, during which I was not in any way involved in American policy toward Hungary. My impression as a distant observer is that Hungarian strivings toward a social transformation that would involve the assimilation of Western democratic values did not find much response in effective American actions. Hungarians sought a new regime and neutrality between East and West by their revolt in 1956, and, standing alone, they were unsuccessful. Since then, through sustained, quiet effort Hungary has succeeded in gaining a certain degree of independence in shaping its economic, social, and cultural life. Until very recently, however, our preoccupation with our own relations with the Soviet Union seems to have relegated the question of encouragement of liberalizing trends in Hungary to secondary importance.

JOHN A. ARMITAGE

The View from Czechoslovakia

My interest in postwar relations between the United States and the Soviet Union and in a Foreign Service career coincided. During the last year of the war, I was serving in the navy on an over-age cruiser in the North Pacific. Operating in the cold semi-Arctic waters off the Aleutian Islands, we shelled the thinly defended Kurile Islands and went after Japanese merchant shipping in the Sea of Okhotsk, along the Siberian Coast. We had constant but arms-length liaison with Soviet ships and aircraft operating in the area, and this rather tenuous involve-

Born in Greeneville, Tennessee, in 1919, John A. Armitage received a Bachelor of Science degree from the University of Tennessee and an M.B.A. from Northwestern University and attended the Russian Institute at Columbia University. He joined the Foreign Service in September 1947 and served as Third Secretary and Vice Consul in the American embassy in Prague from December 1947 to January 1950. Since then his positions have been related mainly to the Soviet Union. They have included two tours in Moscow, one assignment in the Office of Soviet Union Affairs, and another as Chief of the East European Service of the International Broadcasting Service (Voice of America). His most recent assignment (1973-77) was Deputy Assistant Secretary of State with responsibility for the Soviet Union and Eastern Europe. Mr. Armitage also served twice in Tehran and once in Bern, Switzerland. He was Director of the Office of United Nations Political Affairs from 1970 to 1973. He received the Meritorious Honor Award in 1966 and attended the National War College in 1962.

In 1959-61 he accompanied then Vice-President Nixon on his trip to the Soviet Union, and Soviet leader Khrushchev on his visit to the United States, and was in the official party of President Kennedy for the meeting with Khrushchev in Vienna.

ment with the Soviet Union stimulated my latent concern over future Russian-American relations.

In the prewar years I had shared fully the insular outlook of many Americans. For me, as for them, the war had markedly altered my perspectives and created at least the beginnings of a consciousness that the world had difficult problems with which the United States would have to be involved. I recall the early months of the Nazi assault on the Soviet Union in the summer of 1941. Earlier, during my school years in east Tennessee, Europe had seemed remote and distant, but when the Nazi armed forces advanced, apparently irresistibly, into the Soviet Union, my father daily charted the battle lines on a large map. When the Nazis invested Smolensk and it subsequently fell, we had the feeling that our future as well as that of Europe had been dealt a severe blow. We looked on the Soviet soldiers as defenders against the Nazi threat to our own way of life. This sympathy for identification with the Soviet Union was doubtless politically naïve and indiscriminate, but it was a deeply felt and widely shared sentiment among Americans like myself. Until the war's end, the problem of Allied military victory weighed much more heavily in our concerns than did any future problems of shaping the postwar peace.

We had been aware of Tehran and Yalta, and later Potsdam, but for most of us it was the decisions concerning the conduct of the war that commanded our attention. If we thought of political problems at all, it was likely to be in terms of how affairs could be managed so that there would be no threat of a resurgent Nazi Germany. How could we avoid a repetition of the two world wars that had wreaked such havoc on Europe, including Russia, and which necessitated American participation in fighting far from our shores?

With me the thought persisted that we needed to know more about the Soviet Union because it was the Soviet Union we would wrestle with over the answer to that question. I probably assumed, perhaps incorrectly, that others were as ignorant of Russia as I was. I enrolled in an armed services correspondence course in the Russian language while still aboard the old cruiser, and as soon as the navy released me in 1946, I entered Columbia University's newly formed Russian Institute.

The next year and a half in the institute was an exhilarating experience. The faculty was outstanding. Classmates were sharp, probing, intensely interested. Discussion was constant, animated, challenging, and immensely informative. Much of it focused on Soviet domestic development. We learned in fascinating detail of the ambitious goals and plans to which the Soviet peoples had devoted their prewar efforts. We were deeply impressed with the accomplishments—the spread of literacy and education, the build-up of industry, the development of

medical care, and the extension of culture to the masses of the population. And, although the government had not admitted that twenty-
five million Soviet citizens had lost their lives during the war, we were
deeply moved by the magnitude of Soviet sacrifices in a war against our
common enemy. We were conscious of the immense task the Soviet
people faced in repairing the almost incalculable damage and devastation brought about by the war. As war veterans, many of us could identify and sympathize with Soviet veterans returning, war-weary, to the
backbreaking job of restoring the shattered Soviet economy.

At the Russian Institute an element of doubt about the prospects
of postwar cooperation with the Soviet Union began to creep in during
our discussions of Soviet internal developments. For most of us, the
Soviet regime's harsh repression of its own peasantry in the collectivization drive, with the loss of millions of lives, could not be justified
or rationalized as an unfortunate but necessary price of progress. These
doubts were reinforced by our study of the purges of the 1930s and the
arbitrary procedures by which millions were doomed to labor camps,
both before and after the war. While these were internal matters, we
began to question how our country could find a basis for dealing with
Stalin's regime when that regime could handle its own people only by
mercilessly suppressing and subjugating them.

Nonetheless, we reminded ourselves that the Soviet Union was a
country of great natural resources and immense area, and that this
presumably meant that there were no inexorable pressures driving the
Soviet Union to external expansion. We thought that there were no
serious bilateral disputes over which our two countries contended.
We assumed that, with an appreciation of each other's needs, accommodation should be possible in spite of the polar differences in our beliefs
and ideals. But on what terms?

The future of Germany was clearly the central European question.
The Soviet Union's need for assistance in rebuilding its devastated
economy was apparent, but we were deeply disturbed by the Soviet
unwillingness to consider that their almost boundless demands for
reparations could create the conditions for another Hitler.

Also disturbing was Professor Philip E. Mosely's account of the
great difficulties American officials had had in their abortive efforts to
organize democratically functioning political systems in Eastern Europe.[1] His description of how the Soviet army had been utilized to
destroy democratic parties and install Communist parties in power
was both eye-opening and frightening.

1. Professor Mosely had been adviser to the American delegations at the
Moscow Conference, the Potsdam Conference, and the meetings of the Council
of Foreign Ministers in London and Paris, besides serving as U.S. Representative
on the Commission for the Investigation of the Yugoslav-Italian Boundary.

But it was the sad fate of the Poles, for whom Americans have particular sympathy, that produced the greatest reaction among those of us at the Russian Institute. We studied the process by which their country was communized: the smashing of the strong anti-Nazi, non-Communist underground forces, the Soviet army's imposition of Communist control in police and governmental organs, and the perversion of judicial and political processes to destroy democratic leaders and parties. Soviet actions in Poland seemed equivalent to a "war" against all those not subservient to the Kremlin.

The signs of disturbing Soviet behavior were not confined to Europe. During 1946 and early 1947 developments around the southern periphery of the Soviet Union also raised questions among students and faculty regarding Soviet policies and intentions. Soviet troops remained in northwest Iran beyond the date they were committed to withdraw, and supported the formation of Communist-dominated regional governments defying the shah; only stiff Western opposition and some adroit Iranian diplomacy induced Stalin to pull out his forces. Meanwhile, Stalin treated Turkey like an enemy state, laying claim to several of its eastern provinces and mobilizing Soviet forces along the border to add military threat to his diplomatic pressures.

Developments in Greece also produced vigorous discussions at the institute. Some students considered the Greek government reactionary and were inclined to excuse the Communist revolt in Athens in the early postwar days as a legitimate expression of the popular will. As the Communist guerrilla operations against the government continued and the British announced their inability to provide further support to the Greek government, the differences among the students intensified. Supporters of the Communist insurrection justified the Soviet and Yugoslav assistance to the guerrillas, judging it to be as valid as the British help to the government. Others of us maintained the right of legitimately constituted governments to defend their authority. We granted the possible imperfections of the existing government, but found it far preferable to the Soviet-imposed, Communist-dominated governments in Eastern Europe. In any case, Communist rejection of free elections convinced us that what was at stake in Greece was a Soviet-backed challenge to free political institutions outside the reach of the Soviet army. The Communists had taken the fight to the free world, and the "war" was "cold" only to those not directly involved in the fighting. When President Truman announced his decision to support Greece and Turkey and said "I believe that it must be the policy of the United States to support free peoples who are resisting attempted subjugation by armed minorities or by outside pressures,"[2]

2. Harry S. Truman, *Memoirs* (Garden City, N.Y.: Doubleday, 1956)2:106.

he had the warm support of most of us. We believed that the gauntlet had been thrown down by the Soviets; ours was the honorable response.

The announcement of the Truman Doctrine impelled us to restudy a key speech that Stalin had given in February 1946. That speech had been viewed at the time by all but the most prescient students of Soviet affairs as a call to the Soviet people to bend their efforts to the staggering task of economic reconstruction. Rereading it in the light of subsequent developments, it seemed to convey marching orders to all who followed Moscow's dictate. Stalin's message seemed to be that wartime collaboration had nothing to do with postwar Communist relations with the capitalist world. Reconstruction was needed so that the Soviet Union could more effectively carry on the struggle with the "imperialist powers"—and since Germany, Italy, and Japan had been defeated, the "imperialist powers" could only mean the Western democracies led by the United States. If this were so, Stalin had declared "Cold War" whether we had come up with the term or not. The only questions left for U.S. policymakers were what kind of risks Stalin would run in pursuit of his policy and under what circumstances he would pull back to avoid endangering the Soviet homeland.

It was with thoughts like these that I entered the Foreign Service in September 1947, eager to go to Moscow and take part in exploring these pressing questions. I soon learned that Moscow could not be a first post for new Foreign Service officers, so I applied for assignment to Prague, Czechoslovakia. The government there still contained democrats as well as Communists, and it seemed an ideal place to observe and assess Soviet policy.

Assignments for new Foreign Service officers were not customarily made until a few weeks in advance, but I started to read up on Czechoslovak history and foreign relations in optimistic anticipation. Meanwhile, I wondered if the seemingly inexorable seizures of power by the Communist parties in other·Eastern European countries did not bode ill for Czechoslovakia's future. Was there any reason to anticipate that its fate would differ from that of its neighbors?

History at least suggested some substantial ground for believing so. The Czechs and Slovaks did not have historical reason to hate the Russians as did the Poles, or to harbor deep-seated animosity and disdain for them as did the Hungarians. Unlike Poland and Hungary, Czechoslovakia had never been invaded by Russian troops to suppress movements for national independence. In addition, the common Slavic heritage, foreign to Hungarians or Romanians, was a source of pride and shared identity to both Czechs and Slovaks. Here, it would seem, was a basic empathy on which the Russians could build and rely.

This empathy had found concrete expression in Czechoslovakia's policies toward the USSR in the 1920s and 1930s. Although Czechoslovakia's democratic traditions were alien to Soviet Communist values, Czechoslovakia's "George Washington," President Thomas Masaryk, and his chief colleague, Foreign Minister Eduard Beneš, had steadfastly and consistently based their foreign policy on the hard-headed assessment that good relations with the Soviet Union were essential to Czechoslovak security. Masaryk, earlier than most Western statesmen, had recognized the staying power of the Bolshevik regime and cautioned against Western intervention in the Russian Civil War. A commercial treaty with clear political overtones was negotiated with the Soviet Union as early as 1922. After Hitler came to power, Beneš had worked hard, but without success, to put together an Eastern pact consisting of the Soviet Union, Czechoslovakia, the Baltic states, and Poland to oppose the Nazis. When Germany invaded Russia in June 1941, most Westerners were pessimistic about the Soviet capacity to resist the Nazis, but Beneš, now president of the goverment in exile, hastened to conclude a treaty with the Soviet Union less than a month after the Nazi attacks. He followed it with a formal Treaty of Alliance in December 1943. A close collaborator of Beneš stressed the significance of this treaty, saying "it provided the Soviet Union with an assurance that Czechoslovakia will participate in the creation of no hostile blocs which might seriously imperil the interests of Soviet security."[3]

As the war drew to a close, Beneš went far to reinforce those historic assurances and to convince Stalin of his commitment to the closest possible relations. He had been operating a fully functioning Czechoslovak government in London, intending that it should return directly to Prague as soon as it was liberated and exercise political authority until elections could be held. After receiving a letter of support from Stalin in January 1945, Beneš abandoned this plan. Instead, he went to Moscow in March, agreed to new negotiations on the composition of the postliberation government, and agreed also to return to Czechoslovakia from the East, in the wake of the Red Army. He accepted an interim government in which the Communists were given key positions of influence and power, and he approved a political program to be proclaimed when the new government first began operations. This program provided for the closest collaboration with the Soviet Union, not only in bilateral matters but on questions concerning Germany, reparations, and the organization of peace. It prescribed the nationalization of key sectors of the Czechoslovak economy and,

3. Hubert Ripka, *East and West* (London: Lincolns-Prager, 1944), p. 38.

though providing for political rights and early elections, accepted the
formation of national committees at local, district, and provincial
levels—along the lines of the soviets in the USSR. In sum, it committed
Czechoslovakia to a political course substantially influenced by and
presumably acceptable to the Soviet Union.

When, contrary to wartime Soviet assurances, Stalin annexed
Ruthenia, the easternmost section of Czechoslovakia, Beneš yielded
without protest. He seemed to have done his utmost to assure Stalin
of his determination not to allow divisive issues to arise between
Czechoslovakia and the Soviet Union.

Beneš's posture had a measurable effect on the attitude within
the Department of State toward Czechoslovakia. I do not recall having
been shown any definitive policy paper covering Czechoslovakia—
I'm not sure that there was one. But the general view seemed to be that
Czechoslovakia already hewed very close to the Soviet foreign policy
line and that, indeed, it could not hew more closely even if the Communists took over the government. There was some desire in the State
Department to provide support to the private sector of the economy,
the political base of the democratic parties, but such support was limited because of the reluctance of the Czechoslovak government to settle
certain financial issues between the two countries.

In discussions I had with other new officers in the department, we
asked ourselves how the Czechs and Slovaks assessed the U.S. attitude
toward their country, and we concluded that they had rather mixed
impressions drawn from three major developments. First was the
failure of Gen. George Patton's army to liberate Prague in May 1945.
Patton's forces had reached Pilsen, some sixty miles from the highly
symbolic capital city, well before the Soviet forces approached Prague.
But, in accordance with Allied agreements designed to avoid blunder-
ing encounters between American and Soviet forces, Patton had halted
his advance and Soviet troops had been given the honor of liberating
Prague. Second, an announced raid by Czechoslovak pilots in the
British Air Force to support the uprising of Czechoslovak resistance
forces in Prague was canceled by higher authorities. These actions,
possibly explicable on military grounds, were interpreted by Czechoslovaks as deliberate political acts, signaling limited Western interest in
Czechoslovakia and tolerance of strong Soviet influence in the country.
Many Czechoslovaks probably concluded that the spirit of prewar
Munich, when the British and French had left them at the mercy of
the Nazis, still prevailed in the West.

On the other hand, however, there was the third event: President
Truman's initiative in getting the Red Army out of Czechoslovakia.
He had written Stalin on November 2, 1945, saying: "I should . . .

like to propose to you that the Red Army be withdrawn simultaneously with our forces."[4] Stalin had replied promptly that Truman's proposal "can only be welcomed" and agreed that the withdrawal would "be completed by the first of December."[5] The mutual withdrawal took place accordingly. The presence of the Soviet army had been used in Czechoslovakia as a cover behind which to infiltrate Communists into influential political positions and to impede the revival of democratic parties. I believe that Czechoslovaks had seen in Truman's action a clear expression of U.S. interest in their future.

As I reviewed our postwar economic actions in Czechoslovakia, I thought that the ordinary man in the street might be somewhat confused. Right after the Nazis left, milk, fat, powdered eggs, canned goods, and other products from the United Nations Relief and Rehabilitation Administration had poured into Czechoslovakia, relieving much human misery and helping to revive the economy. The UNRRA administrator had been a Russian but "Aunty UNRRA" was considered by the Czechs and Slovaks to be an American relation. Later, an Export-Import Bank credit of $50 million was extended, but then withdrawn in part when Czechoslovak delegates to an international conference loudly seconded Soviet charges of U.S. "economic imperialism." Also clouding American-Czechoslovak economic relations was that much property belonging to American citizens had been nationalized without compensation. I judged that Czechoslovaks probably felt that the United States could be of considerable economic help, but that their government would first have to respect American interests and American dignity.

The question that engaged me most deeply, however, as I prepared for my hoped-for assignment was this one: Would the Soviets tolerate the continued existence of a democratic Czechoslovakia? Or would the democratic political parties and processes be stamped out there as they had been in the other East European countries?

Up to mid-1947, the signs seemed reasonably propitious. Stalin had withdrawn the Soviet army and permitted relatively free elections when he could have done otherwise. Klement Gottwald, the leader of the Communist party and, since 1946, the prime minister, assured his fellow countrymen that the Communists could be depended upon to follow the rules of the democratic political process. The Communist party utilized its positions in key ministries and in regional and local governments to weaken its political opponents, but the democratic

4. U.S. Department of State, *Foreign Relations of the United States* (hereafter cited as *FRUS), 1945,* 4 (Washington, D.C.: Government Printing Office 1968):507.

5. Ibid., p. 508.

parties contended vigorously, and legal bounds were respected, if tested, by the Communists. The nationalization program, a subject of sharp disputes among the parties, had been ended without the Communists being able to extend it further. Beneš told American Ambassador Laurence Steinhardt in 1947 that there "had been no direct intervention by the Soviet Government in Czechoslovak affairs other than the Soviet request for the signature of the recent Czechoslovak-Polish treaty."[6] (This overlooked the active Soviet intervention that had occurred when the Red Army swept across Czechoslovakia in 1945.) The Communists' announced objective of a 51 percent majority in the next election was generally judged to indicate an intent to abide by democratic rules. In addition, the food situation had improved considerably, and the government had agreed on a realistic two-year plan for economic development. There seemed grounds for optimism.

The situation had its worrisome aspects, of course. The Communists had moved into dominant positions in mass organizations like the trade unions as well as in the police and the armed forces, and these positions gave them considerable capability to resort to nonlegal means if they decided to do so. And there was an external shadow in the failure of the Council of Foreign Ministers (consisting of the United States and the United Kingdom, France, and the USSR) to reach significant agreement at their March meeting in Moscow. The ministers had discussed mainly the problem of postwar Germany, and lack of agreement on Allied treatment of Germany boded ill for agreement on the smaller Eastern European countries.

Further disturbing signs began to appear in Czechoslovakia in mid-1947. After the government, including the Communists, had accepted an invitation to discuss the Marshall Plan in Paris on July 12, its leaders had gone to Moscow and had been peremptorily informed by Stalin that he would consider its participation in the Paris meeting an anti-Soviet act. The brutal manner in which Stalin handled the matter struck me as signifying to the Czechoslovaks an ominous message: Stalin had seen the Marshall Plan as a powerful projection of American economic influence into Europe and was drawing a political line on the continent; those who did not unequivocally side with the Soviet Union would be considered no longer as friends, but enemies. The American embassy in Prague reported that people regarded Stalin's actions as an ultimatum and muttered, "It's just like Munich." One could only surmise how sharply Stalin had spoken to Gottwald about his failure to read correctly Soviet interests in Eastern Europe and what courses of action he was given to follow in Czechoslovakia to best serve those interests.

Over succeeding weeks a number of domestic developments re-

6. *FRUS, 1947*, 4:200.

ported by the embassy suggested to me that Gottwald had taken Stalin's interjection as a signal and was moving toward political warfare against the democratic parties. The grain harvest in 1947 had proven catastrophic but, instead of seeking ways to alleviate tragic hardships, the Communists made a demagogic proposal for an unrealistic "millionaires' tax," which would have done little to improve the situation but which they sought to use to undermine the democratic parties. In early September bombs were discovered in packages intended for three prominent non-Communist ministers, including Minister of Justice Prokop Drtina and Foreign Minister Jan Masaryk, the son of the founder of the Republic; evidence pointed to a minor Communist functionary. The next day the Communists announced what proved to be a sub rosa deal by which the Social Democratic party pledged to work as a bloc with the Communists. In the following weeks, the Communists tried to discredit the strong Slovak Democratic party by alleging an extensive antistate conspiracy involving high party leaders, and the Communist-dominated trade union then demanded a reconstitution of the Slovak governing Board of Commissioners. It seemed to me that Communist tactics had changed to virtual political war against their fellow parties in the National Front.

The democratic parties fought back vigorously. All stood firmly against the "millionaires' tax." The Slovak Democrats reacted to the Communist attacks with determination and firmness, retaining strong positions on the Slovak Board of Commisioners and deflecting a Communist effort to mobilize partisans as a separate armed force. The Social Democrats held a congress and voted out their fellow-traveling chairman, Zdenek Fierlinger. I wondered whether the Communists would accept these setbacks and keep their activities inside the already strained legal limits. I could not quarrel with Ambassador Steinhardt's statement that these developments would soon oblige the Communists "to make a basic policy decision as to whether they should continue their efforts to take over government by a semblance of legal means or whether they should resort to means employed in other countries now under Soviet domination."[7]

Beneš did not think the Communists would use force. He told Steinhardt that he thought "a turning point had been reached. While he anticipates the Communists will make at least two more efforts between now and elections in May to intimidate, even to terrorize, the non-Communists and thus to influence the outcome of the elections, he did not believe that further efforts will precipitate a more acute crisis than those just passed through."[8]

7. Ibid., p. 245.
8. Ibid., p. 249.

It was difficult for me to share Beneš's optimism. Ominous local events coincided with a more broadly ominous international event. In September 1947, Stalin had called into being a new international Communist body, the Cominform, and his henchman, Andrei Zhdanov, launched the new organization with a resounding call to intensified class struggle by the Communist camp, led by the Soviet Union. My impression after the Marshall Plan announcement that Stalin had drawn the line between friends and foes—and left no room in between— seemed to find emphatic confirmation in the establishment of the Cominform and the accompanying call to arms. Was it not highly likely that Gottwald had gotten strict marching orders to bring Czechoslovakia solidly into the Communist camp? And after the roasting he must have gotten after his initial acquiescence in Czechoslovak participation in the Marshall Plan, would Gottwald not feel obliged to prove himself to Stalin? It seemed a likely bet that Stalin was bringing the "Cold War" to Czechoslovakia with a determination to control the course of events.

It was at this juncture that I got the chance to observe the situation on the ground. My assignment to Prague came through, and I arrived there on December 27, 1947—in the midst of the Christmas vacation period.

To a newcomer the visible things in Prague in the first few weeks gave a impression of surface calm. The difficult food situation struck me right away when I discovered that this long after the war's end many food items, including meat, sugar, fats, and even bread, were still obtainable only with ration coupons. But on the immense public square named for "good king Wenceslaus," people went purposefully about their business, or frequented the many cafés, or strolled and window shopped at stores where goods were not plentiful but adequate. In the kiosks one could buy not only the international edition of the *New York Herald Tribune* but also the *London Times, Le Monde,* or the *Neue Zürcher Zeitung.* I was told that the funds for U.S. cultural programs in Czechoslovakia had been sharply cut in 1947, but in front of the interesting windows of the U.S. Information Service crowds gathered thickly enough to block the sidewalk. Inside, the library did a land-office business; the demands for informational and pictorial materials were intense. And I soon found Czechs more than willing to make my acquaintance and to talk on all manner of subjects until the late hours.

I began to sense some of the tension when I saw translations of *Rude Pravo* and other Communist newspapers. If Gottwald's orders had, as reported, reduced the abuse of the U.S. and American life in the press, previous issues must have been vituperative indeed. And the way the Communist organs tore into the democratic party leaders sounded close to verbal warfare. I soon learned that the strident press battle between the Communist and non-Communist newspapers and journals was closer to the true state of things than the surface calm.

Meanwhile, the international situation had grown more and more strained. At the meeting of the Council of Foreign Ministers in London in December 1947 the exchanges between Foreign Minister Molotov and Secretary of State Marshall had become sharp and pointed, with the Soviet minister often charging the United States with leading a crusade against the Soviet Union. It seemed more and more likely that European questions on which East and West were divided would be resolved by contention rather than by negotiation. In this context, Stalin's position in opposing Czechoslovak participation in the Marshall Plan kept coming back to remind Czechoslovaks of the limited nature of their choices. I recall attending a number of festive balls organized by Czechoslovak-American Friendship Societies. They had an atmosphere of "whistling past the graveyard" as these friendly people reminded me that they were the only remaining democracy in Eastern Europe.

Alongside this conviviality, however, political events appeared to be rushing almost irresistibly toward a climax. Every issue appeared to move quickly beyond its substantive examination to a political test of wills. The Communists seemed to be smarting from their setbacks. We heard that a secret poll done for them had predicted that they would lose about 10 percent of their strength in the coming elections.

The Communists saw to it that there was no lack of issues. Several of these were ostensibly economic, though they had clear political ramifications. The Communist minister of finance put forward a plan for centralizing administration of the nationalized banks and giving the Communists extensive control over them. The Communist minister of domestic trade exploited a textile shortage to begin eliminating private textile wholesalers, thereby weakening these supporters of the democratic parties. The Communist minister of agriculture advanced proposals that would have curtailed private farms—and the non-Communist strength in the countryside. On these economic issues, the democratic parties could not count on the support of the Social Democrats.

However, the Social Democrats did join the other democrats to defeat a Communist attempt to minimize proposed salary and pension increases for the civil service, a significant locus of democratic strength. The Communists were furious, and Antonín Zapotocký, the Communist trade union leader, threatened to convoke a nationwide Congress of the union's unit committees. It was to meet on February 22, a fateful day.

But the issue on which the political battle was most decisively joined was the question of the control and operation of the police and intelligence agencies under the Communist minister of the interior, Václav Nosek. The investigation of the assassination attempt against the three National Socialist deputies had ground on and on until January 21, when Minister of Justice Drtina laid before the cabinet carefully assembled evidence that a Communist deputy had concealed in his home a cache of arms, which he had conspired to use for political purposes. In the face of this evidence, the Communist party had the deputy waive his parliamentary immunity, and he was arrested. Public reaction was pronounced against the Communist-dominated Ministry of the Interior, which had tried to quash the investigation. Shortly thereafter, Drtina's ministry documented another gross misuse of police power by revealing that a much-publicized case of antistate espionage had been a fabricated conspiracy directed by specified police agencies.

The democratic leaders had long been disturbed by the increasing transformation of the police into fully controlled Communist instruments. With evidence accumulating of Communist intent to employ the police in Prague as they had in Slovakia, the democrats were alarmed at reports of the replacement of non-Communist officials by trusted Communists. Hence, at the meeting of the cabinet on February 13, 1948, Drtina presented a detailed report of the systematic communization of the police apparatus. In the embassy we heard that he also reported to the cabinet that the Communist commander of the security police had ordered the replacement of eight key non-Communist divisional police commanders by reliable Communists. These were the only officials who could distribute arms to the police. Hence, all of the non-Communist ministers supported Drtina's proposal that these changes be suspended until February 24, when the cabinet was to make a decision on the establishment of a special commission to investigate the charges.

The Communists reacted with violent press attacks against the "reaction" and laid stress on the upcoming meeting of the trade union unit committees as an expression of the will of the people, that is, more representative than the elected parliament! The non-Communist parties, except for the Social Democrats, seemed to conclude that the mass meeting would come forth with radical proposals for reorganizing the economy and replacing effective non-Communist officials in the National Front. Their apprehensions increased on February 19 when Soviet Deputy Foreign Minister Valerian Zorin, baggy pants and all, arrived in Prague unannounced. Whatever his actual role in subsequent events, we in the embassy felt that his presence would be interpreted by the Czechoslovaks as an indication that the Soviet Union was closely following developments and that anything the Communist party did would be done with Soviet knowlege and support. Given Czechoslovakia's geographical position and the presence of the Red Army in neighboring countries, Zorin's presence hung menacingly over the unfolding crisis.

That crisis came to a head on February 20. When the Communist minister of the interior refused to obey the cabinet decision regarding the police, the twelve non-Communist ministers of the National Socialist, Slovak Democrat, and Catholic People's parties submitted their resignations. The Social Democratic ministers equivocated by leaving the decision to the party's executive committee. There was electricity in the air, and all of us in the diplomatic corps knew that the issue was now fully joined. Would the Communists yield on the police issue? Would President Beneš back the resigning ministers? Would the Communists operate within democratic ground rules?

The weekend began on Saturday, February 21. It was damp and cold, with some snow flurries, but the Communists swung into action anyway. A "spontaneously" assembled crowd gathered on the Old Town Square, in the center of which stands the formidable statue of Jan Hus. (Ironically, its base is encircled with inscriptions extolling truth.) Prime Minister Gottwald harangued them, denouncing the "reactionary" ministers who sought to disrupt the government and calling on Beneš to accept their resignations so that new ministers who would "follow the socialist road" could be appointed to replace them. The crowd applauded, some loudly, some dutifully, some not at all. Then Gottwald urged them to form action committees wherever they worked. The crowd sensed an ominous overtone in this injunction but soon dispersed. There was a tautness in the weekend atmosphere that could not be missed, but there was no sense of panic.

We heard at the embassy that Beneš had taken the position that all ministers should remain on the job. He was receiving ministers and leaders from all parties, but Gottwald seemed to be seeing him more than anybody else. I heard that Beneš had refused to give him a free hand to replace the resigned ministers with more pliant ones. But Beneš had also passed the word that the Communists would be fully represented in any government he appointed. That was the message he gave to the workers' delegation that insisted on seeing him after the town square meeting and that they were to pass on to the thousands who had sent him form telegrams, prescribed by the Communist party.

On Sunday the Communists staged the Congress of Trade Union Unit Workers, 8,000 strong. We heard that Gottwald and Zapotocký were wildly applauded when they continued their attacks on the "reactionary" ministers. But there were non-Communists among the union delegates, and the resolution demanding far-reaching nationalization of industry and commerce and further collectivization of agriculture had to be passed by shouted vote. The congress also threatened a general strike if the Communist demands were not met and scheduled a one-hour protest strike for Tuesday, February 24.

In the embassy we began to hear disquieting rumors that Gottwald had gotten together a full slate of ministers, including fellow travelers from the non-Communist parties, and that arms were being secretly passed out to selected cadres. Most of the resigning ministers had gone out of Prague to elicit support from the provinces and to test the mood of their followers. We also heard that they, alone of the ministers, had not yet been received by President Beneš.

On Monday, February 23, the alarm signals mutiplied. Men in blue workmen's jackets appeared at key intersections in the vicinity of the embassy, wearing red armbands and with rifles slung on their shoulders. I recall the yellowish, shiny appearance of the rifle stocks, which we judged to indicate they were of recent issue. And the action committees that Gottwald had called for seemed to spring up everywhere. We first heard reports that they had moved into the offices of the resigning ministers and prevented their entering their own offices. Then we began to get accounts of the appearance of action committees in all sorts of organizations. When a friend told me that one was running things even in the ping-pong club, I concluded that every group in the country was being directed by them. The radio had sounded for the past two days as if there were no point of view other than the Communist one; now non-Communist newspapers became hard to find or failed to appear at all. We heard that the non-Communist party offices had been searched by the police, and some said that arrests had been made. The Communists and their sympathizers seemed to be everywhere.

Someone in the embassy's political section told me that a Nationalist Socialist leader had called and reported that the resigning ministers had finally been received by Beneš that afternoon. The president had flatly assured them that he would stand firm and negotiate only with the authorized representatives of the parties and that he would not be a party to the installation of a puppet government. Beneš further maintained that he had consistently taken that position in his conversations with Gottwald. Somehow, Beneš's words did not sound fully reassuring in the face of the mobilized forces of the Communists.

That evening a colleague and I went out to see what was going on in the streets. We passed several of the militia men with armbands but were not stopped. We strolled toward the president's castle, which is not far from the embassy. And, finally, we saw a crowd of students filling the streets. We fell in with them and learned that they were a large group that had just come from the castle where Beneš had received a delegation of their members. The students said he had assured them that constitutional procedures would be observed, that he would be true to the Masaryk tradition. The group was on its way back to a much larger crowd that had assembled in the square near the historic Powder Tower to hear its report. We went along. As the group entered the square, it faced a phalanx of police-manned tommy guns mounted on tripods. Two groups of additional police with rifles were splitting the student crowd in two to disperse it. The students would begin singing the national anthem, "Where Is My Home?" and the police would stand still. But that could last only so long. The dispersal tactic worked, assisted by the students' failure to located a properly operating loudspeaker, and my friend and I had the unusual and disconcerting experience of being pushed around by Communist rifle butts. Sadly, this was the only mass manifestation of opposition to the Communists' power play that Prague saw that week.

Tuesday things moved, inexorably it seemed, downhill. We heard again that Gottwald had succeeded in lining up a list of cabinet members including straw representatives of all the parties—plus Gen. Ludvik Svododa, the minister of defense. So much for possible army resistance! Arrests continued and grew in numbers. The action committees were in full swing. The Communist-led protest strike went off, briefly but successfully, and demurring workers lost their jobs. We heard that the courageous Social Democratic minister of the food industry, Václav Majer, had thrown out bodily the first two action committee thugs who tried to oust him from his own office but had had to yield to the subsequent reinforcements.

Wednesday, Gottwald saw Beneš once more and rejected the president's plea that he negotiate with the resigning ministers. Gottwald submitted his own full list of cabinet nominees, which now included Jan Masaryk. Reportedly, he also produced a list of a majority of the members of the assembly who were committed to support his Communist-dominated cabinet. Beneš promised an answer. It was then that the aged and ailing president made his fateful decision. Late that afternoon he handed Gottwald's cabinet list back to him with his (Beneš's) signature affixed. The Communist coup was complete.

Next day a pall hung over Prague. I remarked to a friend that it was as if a thick blanket of fine dust had settled down on the lovely capital, snuffing out the vitality of what had been a vibrant city.

Two weeks later a prominent life was snuffed out. Jan Masaryk's body was found beneath the window of his apartment. Shocked, all of

Prague sought to find out whether it was murder or suicide. There was "evidence" to support either conclusion. But tragic as the foreign minister's death was, it seemed right that the respected name of Masaryk, son of the man who founded the democratic Czechoslovak republic, should not be associated with a regime that had trampled Czechoslovak democracy in the dust.

The shattering collapse of democracy in Czechoslovakia was a rude shock to the Western public, for Czechoslovakia's tradition of democracy was widely respected. If Western nations could find no way to prevent the tragedy, they could not leave it unremarked. Urgent consultations brought agreement on a joint U.S.-British-French statement, issued on February 26: "The Governments of the United States, France and Great Britain . . . note that, by means of a crisis artificially and deliberately instigated, the use of certain methods already tested in other places had permitted the suspension of the free exercise of parliamentary institutions and the establishment of a disguised dictatorship of a single party under the cloak of a Government of national union. . . ."[9]

Sadder and possibly wiser, I pondered with other embassy officers the significance of what had happened. There had not been the slightest reason for Stalin to believe that Czechoslovakia, then or in the future, would allow itself to be used in any way that threatened the Soviet Union. I had been struck by the lack of any word critical of the Soviet Union in any non-Communist newspaper or journal. Hubert Ripka, the most adroit tactician among the democrats, had written a book during World War II whose sole purpose was to underline the absolute necessity of Czechoslovak cooperation with the Soviet Union. And the entire history of the Czechoslovak Republic, in good times and bad, had underscored the nation's complete understanding of that imperative.

But for Stalin, independent buffer states in Eastern Europe were not enough. His penchant for Soviet security demanded not only that Eastern European governments be friendly but that they be completely dominated. Not only were the territories of these countries to be denied to potential enemies, they were to be used to project Soviet military power to the middle of Europe—and halfway through Germany. Herein lay the roots of the Cold War. For if Soviet power thrust its way toward Western Europe, there was in the postwar years only U.S. power to oppose it. Czechoslovakia was only the symbolic and convincing example of Stalin's Cold War. Even if U.S. power were manifest only in the Marshall Plan program to put Western Europe

9. *FRUS, 1948,* 4:738.

on its feet and in the resistance to impoverishing and destabilizing Germany, Stalin's reaction was to clamp the Communist yoke on Czechoslovakia, to bring the Cold War to Prague.

Certainly the United States had done nothing in Czechoslovakia to provoke the Soviet-Communist take-over. The agreement by the Americans to let the Russians liberate Prague and other acts had suggested that the United States had accepted that Czechoslovakia was in the Soviet sphere of influence. In the complex situation of a coalition government with influential Communist leadership, we had found no way to support the democratic forces effectively. Ambassador Steinhardt had felt that the need for economic assistance from the United States would persuade Stalin and the Czechoslovak Communist leaders to tolerate the democratic parties and institutions. He had come back from Washington on February 19 with authorization to pursue the possibilities of American credits and a commercial treaty. This had been too late and too uncertain to affect the fast-moving events at that time, but it seems doubtful that earlier and more decisive economic moves by the United States would have changed things. Stalin's angry reaction to Czechoslovak flirting with Marshall Plan participation seems convincing on that score.

What did we feel were the lessons of Czechoslovakia for other countries in which Communist parties might contest for power? Looking back, we understood why the democratic leaders decided to force the police issue rather than allow themselves to be fragmented and beaten into submission by Communist use of the police power. But we could not understand why they had not tried to strengthen Beneš's hand by demonstrating that the majority of the people were behind them; the students had seemed pitifully alone. However, this did not seem to have been decisive.

The key question seemed to be: Why hadn't Beneš called on the army for support? We decided that, in the immediate sense, he could not because he had not established working access to reliable commanders. But why not? He was the commander-in-chief according to the constitution, and the prewar lines of authority ran straight from the president's office to the Armed Forces command. We could not find out for sure, but were left to conclude that from his meeting with Stalin in 1945, Beneš had never taken steps to ensure the army's loyalty and availability. Why not? Maybe for fear of offending Stalin and risking depletion of the democratic forces before the return to Prague? Perhaps. But, then why not after the return? We were not sure, but the answer seemed to lie in the political character of the people, in the Czechoslovak dispostion to rely upon diplomacy in the belief that small nations had no other weapon, and in the indisposition to think in terms of ultimate force and the willingness to employ it. And that had proved a fatal error when dealing with Stalin, whose bottom line was: "How many divisions does he command?"

Given the increasingly sharp and bitter differences between the Western powers and the Soviet Union, had "February" been inevitable? At some point, we thought, probably so. But we kept looking at the Finnish situation and decided that, in the absence of the Red Army, it need not have been. In an analogous situation, and subject to strong Soviet pressures on both its foreign and domestic fronts, Finnish democratic leaders had felt themselves constrained to yield to the Soviet Union on many points, including foreign policy and freedom of operation for the Communist party. But the Finns had also realized that their army and police must not fall under Communist control. In May 1947 they dared to throw out the Communist minister of Interior—and the Soviets did nothing. The lesson seemed to be that when Communist parties go for control of the army and the police— or separate armed militia—the fate of non-Communist parties is at stake. At that point the Communists are implementing Stalin's Cold War against democratic and any other political forces who refuse to go along with them. If the non-Communists manage to retain control of those instruments of power, they can contend with the Communists; if they lose it, their fate is in the Communists' hands. We reasoned that here was the heart of what the United States' "containment" policy was designed to forestall. Here was the American response to the Cold War Stalin seemed to be intent upon—and we thought it both a correct and a necessary policy.

The Communists'—and Stalin's—campaign against the democratic political parties in Czechoslovakia had been won. In the succeeding months I was to witness the intensified campaign that Communists in power wage against their own people. Unchallenged but still insecure in their illegitimate power, the Communists set out systematically to subjugate all who might see things differently from them. At the embassy we felt it most palpably in the treatment accorded our Czechoslovak employees. One example is illustrative. Not long after the Communist take-over Dagmar, a secretary in the embassy's public affairs section, and Luboš, a translator, began to be harassed by police agents. The police hinted that their quite legitimate work with Western media representatives somehow represented antistate activity and that their continued association with the embassy was suspicious. Later, they were called in for police questioning. And finally they were both arrested, charged with espionage—which was errant nonsense—and sentenced to terms of eighteen and twenty years, respectively. It was a cruel and unjust way for the government to pass the message to its citizenry that association with Americans was hazardous. Czechs who had been close to members of the embassy and who had felt free to discuss political developments now became progressively reluctant to meet us, and finally gave up altogether. It was heartrending for me to witness the struggles between their consciences and their need to conform in order to provide for the welfare of their families.

The church—both Catholic (the majority) and Protestant (the minority)—soon began to feel the repressive hand of the government. The state began to intrude in church affairs with petty regulations, with restrictions on church finances, with interference in the selection of the clergy, and with controls over the training of divinity students. Word was passed regarding the line between the acceptable and the forbidden in sermons. Tension between the Catholic church and the government mounted steadily, although in Czechoslovakia the proportion of Catholics is much smaller than in Poland or Hungary.

The tension soon focused on Archbishop Josef Beran, the highest Catholic official, and it came to a head, ironically, on the traditionally joyous feast day of Corpus Christi. I was out of town, but friends went to the service at the cathedral on Hradčany Hill. The first dissonant note, which brought a sense of foreboding, came from the contrast between the little girls in their white dresses and the police who were controlling access to the church. Nonetheless, the cathedral was packed when the archbishop entered. As he approached the pulpit, there was some uneasy movement in the front rows. A ripple of tension ran through the worshippers as they realized that the movement came from the jostling of members of the political police, who had brought their forbidding presence into the House of God itself. In a firm and unhesitating voice the archbishop delivered a sermon that used the familiar "render unto Caesar" injunction to make clear the duty of the faithful to hold fast to "that which is God's." As he descended from the pulpit the plainclothes policemen clustered around the steps and, forming a tight cordon, walked the archbishop behind the altar. Audible gasps from the audience conveyed the awareness of what was happening. The archbishop did not return for the remainder of the service. The people sensed—correctly—that it was his last sermon, and their weeping was most devastating because it was mostly silent.

They were to weep again in September when, weakened by the remorseless contest with the Communists, President Beneš died. And the Communists were to reveal again their secret fears by the elaborate precautions they took to prevent his funeral from becoming a political demonstration.

Three months before Beneš's death the Communists had solidified their power through fraudulent elections. On election day my friend and I sallied forth and, rather foolishly, went into several polling places to observe the balloting. Voters had a choice of the chosen candidate or a blank ballot—but if they chose the blank ballot, they had to deposit it in a basket pulled out from behind its screen and placed in full view of an obvious observer who recorded those who used that basket. Somehow the travesty of the Communists following democratic procedures in form while emptying them of any substance brought home with extraordinary force the gulf that separated us from the Russians.

Embassy operations were progressively hampered and restricted; informational activities were steadily curtailed; the American library and downtown office with the display windows were closed down. Officers were expelled on spurious charges, with forty-eight hours to depart, leaving us to pack and ship their effects. The number of visas granted for embassy officials and employees was constricted, reducing our numbers until by early 1950 only seven officers, including military attachés, remained. Tedious regulations were put into effect to absorb our time and hamper our movement and operations. Those of us still left in the embassy soon came to feel more like the inmates of a beleaguered fortress than part of a governmental establishment promoting relations between the two countries involved. The chill of the Cold War came in daily doses from a government determined to convey its hostility toward us.

This Cold War waged so implacably against us, and against the Czechoslovak people, left us convinced that the United States would have to muster force to oppose those who initiated it. We were convinced also that finding a way to contain and channel our differences without allowing them to degenerate into a hotter conflict would be a long and arduous task.

KARL MAUTNER

The View from Germany

The 82nd Airborne Division, in which I served, moved to Berlin on July 26, 1945. Once in the city, my detachment of linguists was put to work organizing a displaced persons (DP) camp. Down on the working level, we were too busy then and later with day-to-day tribulations to bother much about foreign ministers' conferences, summit consultations, Trieste, the civil war in Greece, or big power politics generally. But, ironically, it was there at the working level, especially in working for the Berlin Military Government, that we discovered the facts of life about the East-West confrontation long before the higher echelons seemed to. Those "worm's-eye" experiences, reported up the line, eventually helped convince governments that the battle for Berlin would have to continue long after the end of the war, or we risked facing a Soviet-dominated Europe. You might say we midwifed the Cold War there in Berlin.

Karl Mautner was born in Vienna in 1915 and attended the Handelsakadamie and the University of Vienna. He emigrated to the United States in 1940 and became a citizen in 1942. He served in the United States Army from 1941 to 1947, entering as a private and rising to the rank of major. From 1947 to 1958 he was U.S. Liaison Officer to the Berlin City Government, representing first the U.S. Military Government and then the Department of State. He was assigned to Washington's Berlin Task Force from 1961 to 1963. From 1963 to 1965 he was Chief of the Political Section in the American embassy in Khartoum, the Sudan, and was International Affairs Officer with NASA from 1965 until his retirement in 1975. In 1976 he was elected to the Washington, D.C., Chevy Chase Advisory Neighborhood Commission, and in 1977 he became its chairman.

THE WAR COMES TO AN END

It must have been on April 30, 1945, when our division crossed the Elbe River some sixty miles upstream from Hamburg. Thereafter, the German resistance collapsed, and we moved through road-choking hordes of German refugees, liberated Dutchmen, Frenchmen, Ukrainians, and Belgians, to meet the Russians just east of Ludwigslust, Mecklenburg. The westward-moving refugees were full of horror stories about Russian behavior that we mostly discounted as Goebbels propaganda designed to drive a wedge between us Allies. Having some idea what the Germans had done in Russia, we weren't particularly sympathetic listeners. We captured a group of German generals who berated us for not trying to stop the Eastern menace being turned loose upon Europe. That, too, was obviously propaganda! Admittedly, we were low-level combat troops whose main interest was getting the war over with. Those of us of European background had little difficulty suppressing thoughts that all might not be pure propaganda, particularly after we liberated a concentration camp. There the piles of emaciated corpses had to be buried, the survivors fed and registered, and dispatched to the rear, that is, to the west. No one wanted to go east even if they came from there, which seemed rather strange. More Goebbels?

After meeting the Russians, and after the obligatory vodka-saturated celebration, we ourselves began to grasp the reason for the refugee's horror stories and began to understand the panic driving people westward—away from the Russians. The most fearful—strangely enough—were liberated Soviet P.O.W.'s who were in terror of being liberated by their compatriots. We figured they must have been people who had collaborated with the Germans and who were trying to escape the punishment they deserved. Looking back on those days, it still surprises me how little we actually knew about our Russian allies. I suppose we assumed they were more or less like us, although maybe a bit rougher. Nor can I say that we gave it much thought.

Shortly after V-E Day, the local population began to tell us that the American units were to be pulled out of the area and the Russians would take over in Mecklenburg. We were besieged by people begging us to stay, or to give them papers to cross the Elbe, requests that officers of company or battalion level had no power to grant. Besides, we had no idea where the occupation zones were to be, and, consequently, we tried to calm the worried inhabitants for whom we felt neither official nor personal sympathy. The local concentration camp effectively quashed any such feelings.

At the end of May, the 82nd Division was relieved by British units, moved back to base camp in France, and set to work preparing for our designated occupation of Berlin—beginning almost immediately, we thought. But the Soviets obviously had no desire to expedite our arrival; they saw Berlin as a political prize to be exploited, looted, and secured before the Western Allies were permitted to enter in fulfillment of the European Advisory Commision agreements of September 12, 1944. It was not until July, and then only after we made our withdrawal from a large part of today's East Germany, that the Russians allowed us to move into the sectors of Berlin allocated to the Western Allies. (Mecklenburg, Saxony, Thuringia, and other parts of today's GDR, including Leipzig, had fallen to U.S. and British forces.)

ON TO BERLIN

On July 24, the 82nd Airborne officially moved up the Autobahn to Berlin. An advance military government party under Col. Frank Howley had been permitted to come in on July 4 and had begun to set up the administrative arrangement. The eight boroughs of the U.S. sector, with their individual city halls, were taken over from the Soviets and placed under American control. Control up to a point. The Soviets had carefully staffed each of the city halls with "anti-Fascists" of their choosing, and they were by now well entrenched. The "Gruppe Ulbricht," German Communists brought in from Moscow at the end of April, had worked quickly. After we arrived it took months and often longer to gain real control of civil affairs in the western sectors and to install "anti-Fascist" officials of our choice. Let nobody be mistaken: our criteria were rigid; identifiable Nazis were absolutely barred no matter how eager they might be to collaborate, or how efficient and experienced as administrators they might have been. The Soviet occupiers were much less squeamish. They acted on the principle that anybody could be used, if useful. Nazi backgrounds did not matter, as long as the individual was under their control and did their bidding.

My initial duties involved organizing the registration of non-German refugees, the displaced persons or DP's. Extended interviews with them gave us a closer look at what the Soviets were doing in the areas surrounding Berlin and in the Soviet- and Polish-occupied parts of Germany, an area almost completely inaccessible to the Western Allies. The picture we got, while admittedly one-sided, was increasingly depressing.

If even the non-German refugees encountered cruel treatment from the Soviets, how much worse it must have been for the millions of Germans driven from their homelands! The Potsdam agreement spoke of a "humane transfer of population," but the Soviets and the Poles expelled the German population from western Poland in a ruthless, inhumane manner. Even our non-German DP's, who had little sympathy for the Germans, were full of tales of gruesome incidents that, often as not, entangled them in the indiscriminate trek of disease, hunger, and terror engulfing the millions forced to move westward.

Outside our official duties, my colleagues and I could not help but observe the permeating, almost obsessive terror with which the Berlin women regarded the Soviets. Among Berlin women "The Russians" were almost the only subject of conversation. The stories were endless; about rapes, the contempt for human life, the occasional episode of surprising human decency, and the vagaries of survival under Russian occupation. It was no longer Goebbels, we knew now. But all those thin, anxious, hungry women, old ladies and young girls, working at clearing up rubble with their bare hands and a few awkward tools? Some revenge was understandable, but why did all those women keep streaming from the Soviet sector into the Western sectors every night for months to stay with relatives, friends, or just with anybody? Well, those were the Russians, as we soon learned.

WINTER 1945-46: POLITICAL DEVELOPMENTS

The winter of 1945-46 was long and cold. The suffering in bombed-out Berlin was intense, but so it was all over Europe. Our interest in the local suffering was based more on practical than on humanitarian considerations. It was a question of allocating enough food and fuel and distributing it fairly to get the city services functioning and prevent chaos, disease, and unrest.

Being German-speaking I gradually became attuned to the political developments in the city and became increasingly aware of the struggle to rebuild the newly enfranchised pre-Hitler parties. We had as yet little direct contact with the Berlin politicians themselves, but the stories of the Soviet maneuvering to aid or harass people in these parties were coming more and more to our attention. Former German citizens in the U.S. Military Government who had political connections from the past began getting firsthand reports, especially from old friends in the Social Democratic party (SPD), the party with the greatest support in Berlin. Although I was not immediately connected with military government or civil affairs, I became involved on the fringes when the Social Democrats came under intense Soviet pressure, beginning in December 1945, to merge with the Communists into a unified socialist workers' party—an ancient dream for many old-time German socialists. Yet memories of the vicious infighting within the Left during the 1920s and 1930s made many Social Democrats dubious about the fate of the SPD in such a merger—particularly with the Soviet army standing behind the Communists. The Social Democrats in Berlin wrestled with their consciences for weeks as the pressure intensified. On the

American side, we were officially neutral (and for the most part ignorant); it was something for the Germans to decide and did not concern us. There was little if any official American help for those trying
to buck the Soviet tide—no food packages, no additional ration cards,
coal, transportation, or cigarettes (the real currency of the day). Only
occasionally some low-level officials who had begun to understand
would act on their own to supply assistance, usually without the knowledge of their superiors (the British Labour government provided some
support).

Social-Democratic functionaries had to contend with German
Communists brought back from Moscow, with socialists convinced by
or bought off by the Soviets, and with those idealists who wanted the
merger for purely ideological reasons—all of whom had the full support
psychologically, materially, and physically of the Soviet occupation
forces. Those who opposed the merger had little to fight with but
conviction and guts. They attended endless meetings in East Berlin
(where the Soviets before our arrival had carefully located all party
headquarters). Some of the West Berliners never returned from those
sessions, simply disappearing for years or indefinitely. The others had
to walk or bicycle back for miles in the early morning hours (risking
Russian looters en route) after waiting out the end of every meeting
since the Communists regularly tried to delay voting until after most
participants had left.

Our respect began to grow for those dogged political personalities, often survivors of concentration camps or prisons, and for their
iron determination to create a better Germany. And when finally the
Berlin SPD, led by a group of West Berliners, made the historic decision
on March 31, 1946, not to merge with the Communists, we really
began to take note on the official level. But the Social Democrats in
the Soviet zone were far more vulnerable to the enormous pressure
being exerted on them, and they eventually accepted the shotgun marri-
age. Thus the Socialist Unity party (SED) came into being. Those
Social Democrats became a Greek chorus for the Communist regime in
East Germany, despite vastly outnumbering the Communists in the
SED. In Berlin as a whole, however, the SPD had a new lease on life.[1]

It may be that the Berlin Social Democrats' refusal to be swallowed
up marked the turning point for U.S. relations with the Berliners. In

1. Details of this referendum can be found, inter alia, in Elmer Plischke,
Development of Government and Administration of Berlin (U.S. High Commission
for Germany, Historical Division, 1952), p. 153; Arno Scholz, *Null Vier, Ein
Jahrgang zwischen den Fronten* (Berlin: ARANI, 1962), pp. 306 ff.; W. Phillips
Davison, *The Berlin Blockade: A Study in Cold War Politics* (Princeton: Princeton
University Press, 1958), p. 40.

any event, from then on the realization gradually filtered up to the higher echelons of military government that not all Germans should be treated as enemies, that those Germans—epitomized by most Berliners— who wanted to build a democratic state needed and deserved our backing, and that what was developing in the Soviet zone was a new and ominous dictatorship. In Berlin at least, the Cold War had begun.

FIRST ELECTIONS AND THE ALLIED KOMMANDATURA

In the meantime, the Allied Kommandatura, consisting of four sector commandants and their staff (American, Russian, British, and French) moved toward the first postwar elections in Berlin, to be held on October 20, 1946. The kommandatura operated on a four-power basis with a rotating chairmanship. It functioned under a handicap that eventually proved fatal—all decisions had to be unanimous. At its first meeting on July 11, 1945, it was agreed that all measures enacted by the Soviet administration between Berlin's fall on May 2, and the date of that meeting (July 11) would remain valid unless altered by unanimous decision. Consequently, personnel changes, if they concerned someone the Soviets had already appointed, proved almost impossible to effect; ration card and other regulations and their implementation could not be altered; energy allocations, public safety measures, organization permits, office requisitions, building materials, and thousands of other measures affecting the city as a whole were frozen by the Soviet veto power. The Western commandants were able to act unilaterally within their own sectors, but the city-wide apparatus was controlled by those the Soviets had appointed, as well as by the rules and regulations promulgated in the first two months. Nevertheless, preparation for the elections moved along under kommandatura auspices, and the emerging election modalities and law were reasonably democratic ones, based initially on the existence of the four political parties already authorized: the Social Democrats (SPD), the Communists (KPO), the Christian Democrats (CDU), and the Liberal Democrats (LDP). The Soviets evidently hoped that the Communists, now running under the mantle of the Socialist Unity party (SED) in all of Berlin, would garner substantial defections from the Social Democrats at least in their sector and would win the elections. They remembered that before 1933 several of Berlin's working-class districts had strong Communist majorities.

Despite massive support through newsprint allocations, food packages, facilities for election rallies, and so forth, from the Soviet military authorities, and despite brutal harassment of their opponents, the SED still came in a weak third. The Social Democrats won a resounding victory, while the Christian Democrats came in second. (The vote was split as follows: SPD, 48.7 percent; CDU, 22.2 percent; SED, 19.8 percent; LDP, 9.3 percent.) The Soviets evidently were as surprised as they had been by the outcome of earlier elections in Austria and Hungary. It is still a matter of astonishment how they managed to deceive themselves so badly.

THE FIRST ELECTED CITY GOVERNMENT: TRIALS AND TRIBULATIONS

In January 1947, a newly elected city government replaced the one appointed by the Soviets in May 1945. That same month I was offered the job of American liaison officer to the mayor and the city assembly.

When the new assembly chose the city executive, according to the kommandatura-approved temporary constitution governing Berlin, it picked as lord mayor an imposing bald-headed, old-time SPD functionary named Dr. Otto Ostrowski. He had three deputies (an SPD woman, a CDU man, and an SED man) and a cabinet made up of a number of councilors—the *magistrat*—from all four parties. In many ways, it did not matter at first who was actually designated councilor (department chief) since the previously installed department deputies remained, and most were active Soviet collaborators. The department offices were all located in the Soviet sector, as was the city hall. Only slowly were the elected officials of the non-SED parties able to establish some authority. Removal of their deputies was impeded by the Soviet representatives' insistence that such removals required unanimous approval.[2] Moreover, Ostrowski did not live up to his imposing Mussolini-like appearance. His support for his embattled colleagues was weak—he claimed to be "neither an Ostrowski nor a Westrowski"—and his own party soon forced him to resign when he attempted to make deals with the SED. The assembly then voted to replace him with the remarkable Ernst Reuter. Reuter had been a prisoner of war in 1917 in Russia, joined the Bolsheviks and helped found the Volga German Republic. Later he returned to Germany and, disillusioned with communism, rejoined the SPD. The Nazis ousted him as mayor of Magdeburg, and he spent the war years in exile in Turkey.

The Soviets had never forgiven Reuter his defection from communism. They blocked approval of his election in the kommandatura, despite the doubtful legality of their right to veto such an election. The issue was escalated to the Allied Control Council (the military governors of the four occupation zones of Germany) where, in the name of Allied solidarity, the western side acquiesced to the Soviet veto. The City Assembly refused to elect anyone else and the SPD deputy

2. *Report by the Office of Military Government*, Berlin Sector, July 1, 1945 to September 1, 1949, p. 15.

mayor, frail Louise Schroeder, took over as acting lord mayor, with the CDU deputy mayor, Dr. Ferdinand Friedensburg, substituting during her frequent illnesses.

THE LIAISON OFFICERS' TASKS

The work of the liaison officers was altered by the new situation. All four Allied representatives occupied pompous offices in the city hall, and all four were now busy keeping their fingers on the pulse of the new government where before they had merely transmitted orders. I had the advantage of being junior to my colleagues and so seemed more approachable to the Germans. In addition, I had an Austrian-acquired fluency in German, represented the Western power that really counted (even if it did not always seem attuned to ground-level realities), and had splendid backing from Col. (later General) Frank Howley, director of the Berlin military government, to whom I reported. The combination made it possible to breach the rigid code that, according to my predecessor's instructions, required the mayor to call on the liaison officers and practically stand at attention. I took to visiting Mayor Louise Schroeder in her office and, even more, was soon able to persuade a chivalrous Colonel Howley to call on that sweet old lady, whose physical frailty masked an indomitable will and shrewd intelligence. The other Western liaison officers and their superiors followed suit. After the favorable publicity Howley garnered, they could hardly do otherwise. My own entrée was made. (The Soviet liaison officer tried to outbid us by bringing Frau Schroeder a freshly caught fish wrapped in a copy of *Pravda!*)

But from then on it was the U.S. Liaison Office that received the complaints, proposals, suggestions, and perhaps the bulk of the confidences. We were alerted to many a unilateral step taken by the Soviets—or their German collaborators—to move things of value from West to East, or undermine elected or other non-Communist officials who were too energetic. We were quickly advised of Soviet attempts to sabotage the successful management of the city's many problems. It became increasingly clear that Moscow did not want a well-run city if if it were well run by non-Communists.

One of the earlier episodes I recall was insignificant, but typical of the relentless, single-minded Soviet pursuit of every advantage, no matter how minor—"slicing salami" as we later called it. On June 26, 1947, one of the city councilors came in to complain that the Soviets had ordered the Archives of Contemporary History, a valuable collection of news clippings and documents, to be crated and removed to some locality deep in the Soviet zone. The order was obviously illegal since only the Allied Kommandatura could issue orders affecting a city-wide institution. Unfortunately the West's objections came too late; the files had already disappeared and the magistrat had to function without them.

A more serious blow came late in June 1947 through the inexperience or naïveté of a newly appointed U.S. commandant, Gen. Cornelius Ryan, who later redeemed himself by a courageous stand during the McCarthy hearings.[3] The deeply entrenched Communist deputy in the Department of Education, Ernst Wildangel, had been waging a persistent campaign of sabotage against his elected Social Democrat superior, Siegfried Nestriepke. The department was a natural battleground since both the SPD and the Communists had strong ideological commitments. The Soviet attacks against Nestriepke were routine weekly events in the kommandatura's Education Committee and were brushed off just as routinely. Soviet General Aleksandr Kotikov, commandant of the Soviet sector of Berlin, however, saw a chance to test a new U.S. commandant and, during a formal kommandatura session suddenly launched an attack on Nestriepke, claiming he had disobeyed Allied orders, was inefficient, truculent, and so forth. General Ryan, to the horror of Howley sitting next to him, and to the shock of us aides behind, immediately proposed that such a man should be removed from office. The French, who had never liked Nestriepke, quickly agreed; Kotikov praised this proposal as a good gesture to restore discipline, and the British general, also new on the job, nodded consent. Nestriepke was therefore fired! The blow to the newly elected government was serious, especially since the Soviets then tried to use the Reuter precedent to force unanimous approval of a successor. We recovered a little by winning the point that no approval was needed, but it was an expensive lesson and one that had to be learned again and again: The Russians never relaxed; they took advantage of every weakness and tested every opportunity.[4]

Around the same time in June 1947, Economic Councilor Gustav Klingelhofer learned that the Soviets were unilaterally extending to all of Berlin an order by Marshal Vasilii Sokolovskii, military governor, Soviet zone, to ship all available ferrous scrap to the USSR. The rubble of devastated Berlin contained immense amounts of scrap. Since the Soviets controlled the railroads and also dominated many second-

3. He should not be confused with the author of *The Longest Day* and other best-selling books on World War II.

4. *Berlin, Behauptung von Freiheit und Selbstverwaltung 1946-1948* (Berlin: Heinz Spitzing Verlag, 1959), p. 260 (this publication details the episode as officially reported but erroneously described General Ryan as the British commandant); Frank Howley, *Berlin Command* (New York: G.P. Putnam's Sons, 1950), p. 141.

echelon officials in the Western sectors, the preparations were well
underway before Klingelhofer got wind of it. He informed the Western
liaison officers and made a speech on the subject in the assembly, an
act of courage at that time. In this case, our superiors were able to stop
the forcible and illegal export of vast quantities of scrap from the
Western sectors.

Throughout the summer of 1947 the petty harassments mounted,
non-Communist party chairmen were summoned to Soviet headquarters
to receive orders not to discuss the case of Reuter's aborted electon in
public gatherings or the assembly, and warned that disobedience would
be considered punishable "anti-occupation activity." The CDU chairman,
Walter Schreiber, was no longer permitted to attend meetings at CDU
headquarters in East Berlin because of his "anti-Soviet" attitude. A
British military government official was refused admittance to a CDU
conference by Russian officers, a clear breach of the four-power agreements. SPD meetings in the Soviet sector were banned or the scheduled
meeting place suddenly became unavailable. Unilateral orders were sent
to city councilors interfering with their work. The elected borough
mayors in East Berlin (all SPD) were increasingly harassed. Mrs. Ella
Kay, mayor of Prenzlauer Berg (Soviet sector) was dismissed on the
grounds that she was "incapable of providing the people with firewood
for the coming winter." In fact, she had been allocated a parcel of
forest some fifty miles distant for cutting wood, but when the labor
force was assembled in Berlin and the tools collected (no mean feat in
those days), the Soviets withdrew the trucks allocated to her and left
the group stranded.

The Soviets also tried to intimidate the Berlin assembly. The deputy
of my Russian colleague, Major Otchkin, threatened to hold Assembly
Chairman Dr. Otto Suhr responsible for any "anti-Soviet" statements
made in the assembly. Suhr refused to place a gag on the assembly but
he was obviously shaken when he told me about the Soviets' "friendly"
admonition.

At one point, the Soviets attempted to repeat their Nestriepke coup
by accusing Lord Mayor-elect Reuter (who was then city councilor
for utilities) of deviously providing preferential heating gas rations to
several hundred SPD friends. The kommandatura dutifully summoned
Reuter to a hearing. Reuter admitted he had issued preferential rations
to SPD officials newly elected or advanced to important positions,
having taken the same number away from Communists who had been
arbitrarily given these privileges in the prior administration. Reuter was
not fired.

More sinister things happened at the university—the venerable
Humboldt University located in East Berlin. Several non-Communist

student leaders disappeared or were officially arrested, and professors lost their jobs. Communization of the faculty, administration, and curricula advanced rapidly, and western-oriented students were pressured to conform or get out. The elected student government could no longer function. The situation deteriorated to the point where the three non-Communist parties in the assembly voted to establish a "free university" in West Berlin. No physical plant was available in West Berlin, however, so the scheme remained on paper for some time. (On April 24, 1948, Gen. Lucius D. Clay, military governor of the U.S. zone, authorized the creation of the new university, today's Free University, and provided financial, logistical, and directional assistance. Even then, the first classes met in cellars and other makeshift quarters by candlelight.)

The Soviets even used potatoes to harass the non-Communists. At the height of the 1947 potato harvest, several trainloads of potatoes suddenly and without warning arrived in the American sector from surrounding areas that by agreement were to supply potatoes to all of Berlin. This normally welcome event quickly took on a less welcome cast with the realization that the central storage facilities were in East Berlin, under Soviet control. The weather was rainy, and the dumped potatoes were piled yards high and unprotected on U.S. sector sidings. The Soviet press immediately unleashed a vicious campaign charging that the Americans were indifferent to the fate of the starving Berliners and were deliberately letting potatoes rot, that the SPD food affairs councilor was inefficient and an American tool to boot. The harassed councilor, Paul Füllsack, suggested to me that there was an empty factory hall near the sidings in the U.S. sector that the U.S. forces had requisitioned in July 1945, to store and repair tanks. Couldn't we let him have the hall? Getting things derequisitioned from the army wasn't all that easy, but Howley got the hall within two days, and we could register a small, but satisfying success. In addition, we had the potatoes!

Meanwhile, the assembly continued to work on a new constitution, which the kommandatura had mandated for submission during the spring of 1948. A draft was approved by the assembly despite SED opposition in April 1948, and submitted to the kommandatura. It provided for new elections late in 1948, elections that the Soviets were by now determined should not take place.

THE PRESSURE INCREASES

Throughout the winter of 1947-48, the Soviet-controlled "mass organizations"—of women, youth, victims of fascism, war invalids, labor unions, and so forth—grew increasingly militant, supported in their activities by the eastern police, by logistical assistance, money, and unvarnished terror. SPD members, journalists, and students continued to disappear (some came back from Siberia in the mid-1950s); the kommandatura machinery stagnated more and more; vituperation replaced strained conviviality at meetings of the four occupation powers. Interestingly enough, the lowest level—our working level—was the primary target of the new stress-producing pinpricks. Long before they seemed to understand on the lofty level of General Clay and his colleagues—not to mention Washington—we realized what was going on and could not help but see the Soviet game clearly, since we were exposed to it daily. So the Czechoslovak coup in February 1948 came not so much as a surprise but somehow as a relief since now at last the eyes of those who still wanted to "get along" with the Russians had to be opened. We had learned early that compromising with the Soviets "to get along" only meant they would up their demand.

In January 1948 the Soviets began interfering seriously with the rail deliveries from Berlin to the West, justifying it by accusing us of encouraging the looting of East Germany.[5] Trips into the Eastern zone by West Berliners now suddenly required documentation that was almost impossible to obtain. Trucks were stopped and searched on the borders between East and West Berlin. On April 5, 1948, East German police under Soviet supervision put up road signs directing traffic between Soviet headquarters in Karlshorst (East Berlin) and Potsdam by a route that by-passed West Berlin. On April 22, all construction material and equipment belonging to West Berlin contracting firms working in East Berlin or the Soviet zone was seized without compensation. (The SED deputy, Starck, made these arrangements behind the back of the SPD city councilor for building and housing, Paul Bonatz.) On April 29, non-Communist city officials living in the Eastern sector had their telephones cut off.

Soviet control over the Berlin police (ostensibly under four-power jurisdiction) was tightened even more. The Soviets in 1945 had installed Paul Markgraf, a highly decorated Nazi officer, captured at Stalingrad, as police president. Although the city assembly voted no-confidence in him following his failure to act when the Soviets kidnapped a West Berlin journalist, Markgraf remained in office with Soviet backing. In the spring of 1948, he even reappointed as his deputy Hans Seidel, a man the kommandatura had previously dismissed from the police force for Nazi activities and a criminal record. The city authorities continued to compile a file of incriminating facts on Markgraf, but with little effect.

---

5. Davison, *Berlin Blockade*, pp. 64 ff., is a good account of the accelerating attempts to strangle the city.

In the meantime, matters came to a head at higher levels. The Allied Control Council ceased to function on March 20, 1948, when Marshal Sokolovskii walked out, removed his staff, and unilaterally declared the council no longer in existence. His official pretext was the Western move to coordinate administrative and economic policies in the Western zones.

Meanwhile, Soviet obstruction of the access routes to Berlin got nastier. Military trains were periodically stopped or diverted; ever new documents were demanded of transiting Allied personnel and new controls were instituted. The American and British aid stations half-way along the Autobahn to Berlin were closed on Soviet insistence. Canal traffic was obstructed for days. In response to the difficulties on the train, the United States for a time began to send some passengers and military provisions by air, but freight airlifting was discontinued when the train traffic became normal for a time. On April 5, 1948, a British passenger plane was rammed by a Soviet fighter and crashed, killing fourteen passengers.[6] The Berlin kommandatura still continued to function for several months after the control council ceased operation, but there, too, Soviet officials gradually began walking out of various committee meetings. Finally, on June 16, 1948, the acting Soviet commandant, Alexei Yelisarov, stalked out of the building after a sixteen-hour long confrontation with Howley and the other commandants.

CURRENCY REFORMS

On June 18 the Soviets stopped all rail and ship traffic between Berlin and the West, and shortly thereafter all highway traffic, citing technical reasons as a pretext. That was the day the Western powers introduced a new currency in the three Western zones—the long needed currency reform that triggered West Germany's rapid economic recovery. Berlin was not included in the currency reform. Strong remonstrations by city officials that excluded Berlin from the currency reform would inevitably lead to its absorption in the Soviet zone were brushed off by the Western commandants. When on June 23, Marshal Sokolovskii issued order No. 111 declaring a currency reform for his zone and Berlin, thus claiming jurisdiction over all of Berlin, the Western commandants declared the order invalid in their sectors.

An emergency session of the city assembly called that afternoon to discuss the problem was broken up by a mob of "spontaneous demonstrators" brought in openly on Soviet trucks. On leaving the building, SPD delegate Jeannette Wolff, a Jewish concentration camp survivor, was one of several members pummeled by the bully boys, who also

6. Ibid., p. 65.

rocked my car and spat on it as I left. A police commissioner who intervened and actually dispersed the mob was dismissed by Markgraf on Soviet orders the same evening. Electricity from the Soviet sector, where the only important Berlin power plant not dismantled by the Soviets was located, was cut off. All remaining ground traffic in and out of the city was stopped. On June 25, the Allied authorities reconsidered, and included West Berlin in the Western currency reform. The Soviet-sponsored mark remained valid within the city, but its exchange value immediately dropped. An airlift to supply the Western military garrisons had already begun. General Clay now ordered supplies for the German population to be flown into Berlin as well. The airlift was on! Berlin was blockaded. All the needs of three million people—food, coal, drugs, milk, even eventually some Christmas trees— now had to be supplied by air or there would be no supplies at all.

The conviction that the Soviets intended to force us out of Berlin had of course given rise to considerable anxiety in the Western community. Pessimistic assessments of our chance—and our willingness— to withstand the mounting pressure had been circulating for some time. An article by James O'Donnell in *Newsweek* a year earlier (August 11, 1947) had depicted an imaginary humiliating exodus of Americans under Soviet prodding and had occasioned a furious reaction on the part of General Clay. That brash piece of journalism, did, however, serve to alert higher officials to the prevailing atmosphere of doubt and probably contributed to the decision to stand firm when the time came. And now the time had come.

A SUMMER OF DOUBTS AND DISTRESS

The city itself was not yet split, however. The central administration was still officially intact. But during the summer of 1948, Soviet "liaison officers" set up desks in the Education and Food Department councilors' offices to "assist them" in their tasks. They made the councilors' work impossible, so those departments moved their offices to West Berlin, and most of their staff followed. Acting Mayor Frau Schroeder, frail and ailing, was plagued with midnight calls from the Soviet liaison officer who would order her to report immediately to the "Commandant of Berlin," where she was then handed Russian language documents that, as often as not, were of no particular import. Special food rations were offered to West Berliners who would register in East Berlin, but even in the worst part of the blockade winter less than 2 percent of West Berliners availed themselves of this opportunity. Administrative regulations barred West Berlin newspapers from East Berlin.

Then the police crisis came to a head. When Markgraf continued to defy assembly and magistrat orders to account for his actions, especially those of June 23, he was declared dismissed. The city authorities, with Western support, then appointed an old SPD police commissioner of pre-Nazi days, Dr. Johannes Stumm, as Markgraf's successor. When Markgraf refused to move aside, Stumm took up his duties in West Berlin and hundreds of pro-Western officers purged in East Berlin joined Dr. Stumm's force. (If they lived in East Berlin, that meant leaving behind possessions and apartments. Many did.) Thus, in August 1948 we were faced with two police forces, the clearest indication of where things were drifting.

On August 23, when the members of the city assembly arrived at the city hall for a regular meeting, they found the hall packed with hoodlums brought in Soviet trucks for a "spontaneous" demonstration. The chairman thereupon postponed the meeting until the next day, when the same thing happened again. The session was then further postponed until September 6. Long before the scheduled meeting time on that day, demonstrators were all over City Hall, packing every stair and hallway like sardines. My French colleague, Victor Ziegelmeier, attempted to fight his way into his office but was stuck on the stairs for over four hours. The assembly chairman, blocked in his own office, finally announced that the assembly could no longer conduct business in an orderly fashion in the Soviet sector and would henceforth meet in the Technical University in the British sector. Before the mob slowly dispersed, a group of pro-Western policemen and newspaper correspondents were chased through the building. Some were beaten or arrested, and others took refuge in the French Liaison Office and the office of my secretary. There they were barricaded in by East sector police and Soviet soldiers. A U.S. lieutenant who was at the city hall at that time was locked in with twenty policemen and my secretary until the next day when Soviet soldiers broke down the door and took the policemen away in handcuffs. As for those in the French Liaison Office, a day later General Kotikov personally gave the French commandant, Gen. Jean Ganeval, his word that the men would be given safe conduct to the French sector. But the convoy taking them there was stopped by Soviet soldiers, who arrested them and took them to prison. Some returned several months later, others only after several years. General Ganeval never spoke to General Kotikov again.

DETERMINED RESISTANCE ASSURED

While the Western and Soviet officials negotiated in Moscow throughout the summer seeking a solution to the crisis, the tension in Berlin increased, although the morale of West Berliners rose with each new record of tonnage flown in by the airlift.

At the beginning of September, the negotiators in Moscow finally agreed to instruct the Allied military governors to meet again for the first time since Sokolovskii's walkout in March and consider a proposed accommodation on Berlin. The city fathers, who feared a compromise at the expense of the Berliners, called on the population to demonstrate its willingness to stick out a blockade rather than be integrated into the Soviet orbit. September 9, 1948, has always seemed to me one of the real milestones in the East-West conflict. Despite meager rations, lack of transportation, and short notice (no radios because of electricity blackouts), a crowd of 300,000 filled the rubble-strewn field near the Brandenburg Gate to hear speeches by Reuter and other city leaders. When excited youngsters climbed the Brandenburg Gate and tore down the red flag, one was killed and several wounded in a Russian fusillade, while others were arrested. The big crowd, however, remained orderly and marched to the Allied Control Council building to demonstrate to the Western military governors that they were prepared to hold out, winter or no winter, blockade or no blockade. The message evidently got through to the Western generals who this time did not give in to Soviet demands, as those negotiating in Moscow had come close to doing.

From then on, the end of a unified Berlin was obvious. One after the other, the remaining functions of the elected officials in the city hall were sabotaged, and the offices were forced to move to West Berlin, often having to leave behind files and invaluable, hard-to-get paper supplies and typewriters. (I must admit to seeing to it that a good many such items reached West Berlin surreptitiously.) Hundreds of minor non-Communist employees found themselves suddenly dismissed when someone backed by a Soviet official appeared at their desks to take over.

Then, finally, on November 30, several hundred delegates from the various Communist East sector mass organizations met at the Opera House, announced that the city assembly had ceased to exist since it no longer met at the city hall, declared their own convention to be the legitimate representative of the population, and "elected" as mayor an SPD renegade, Fritz Ebert (son of the first Weimar president). The next morning, the acting lord mayor, Dr. Friedensburg, knowing the risk he was running, still went to the city hall to go to his office. He was refused entry by East sector police brandishing carbines. My colleagues and I witnessed the incident, reported to our headquarters, and were ordered to close down our offices and leave. The police and the bully boys attempted to harass us, too, but stopped after our energetic intervention with the Soviet liaison officer.[7]

7. *New York Times*, Dec. 3, 1948.

The city was now split. East Berlin had an appointed Communist government, West Berlin a democratically elected one, albeit in the unenviable position of facing a blockade and a long winter with uncertain flying weather.

NEW ELECTIONS

The new Berlin constitution submitted to the kommandatura in April had specified elections in all of Berlin in late 1948, and the date decided on was December 5, 1948. The elections, of course, never took place in East Berlin. In West Berlin, however, they were held on schedule. A full 86.3 percent of the population voted, giving the SPD 65 percent, the CDU 19 percent, and the LDP 16 percent of the votes. Reuter was again chosen as lord mayor. The Allied Kommandatura reconvened on a tripartite basis, leaving a seat open for the Soviets, and recognized Reuter. There were now indeed two quite separate and different Berlins.

A Berlin military government report of September 1949 stated: "In this city, international politics often appear first as local politics and then inflated to international politics, problems for the great capitals of the world."[8] This was indeed a true statement, one that we learned the hard way.

CONCLUSIONS

Looking back now and pondering whether we could have done things better had we been more knowledgeable or more understanding of our Soviet allies, I think I must conclude we probably could not have acted much differently. The circumstances, the political climate, our respective national mentalities and perspectives all argued against either us or the Soviets behaving otherwise.

Despite the dubious record of what the Soviets had done to Poland, the Baltic states, and Finland between 1939 and 1941, we met the Russians in Germany with a relatively open mind in 1945. They had more than acquitted themselves in the bloody struggle just concluded and we were ready to cooperate to "make peace work." But we soon discovered that their understanding of cooperation was quite different from ours, and their plans for postwar Germany and Berlin did not square with our idea of "democratic development." Even if their paranoia about security was understandable, we soon saw that security meant for them lots of real estate and total domination of it. Sitting in the Berlin enclave, deep inside Soviet-occupied territory, we and the Berliners were the ones who had tangible reasons to feel insecure, and the Soviets gave us no reason for feeling otherwise.

8. *Report by the Office of Military Government*, Berlin Sector, September 1949, p. 121.

That too puzzled us. After all, we had no territorial ambitions and had squelched any our Western allies may have had. We firmly expected the occupation to be only a short-term affair, just long enough to ensure that the German menace had finally been laid to rest. And we went about demobilizing our wartime army almost immediately.

But daily encounters with calculated Soviet pressure designed to make our position in Berlin untenable eroded our friendly attitudes in short order. At the working level, we had initially been willing to compromise, but grew to resent being constantly pushed to the wall where we had rights of our own. Then too, there was the gradual realization that we had become responsible for several million people who were now dependent on our protection. That added a human and tangible factor to the politics involved. Our abandoning Berlin would have meant disaster for them, danger for the rest of Germany, and the subsequent impact on the Europe of those days could have been disastrous for us also.

In short, we learned on the job that if we intended to stay in Berlin, we were going to have to dig in our heels and get tough in our turn. But it wasn't a gun-brandishing militancy that developed. No one as far as I recall even remotely raised the idea of exploiting our nuclear monopoly in connection with Berlin. Our proselytizing was directed at the American higher-ups who—we thought—didn't seem to realize that a firm stance was all that was needed. We were convinced the Russians had no intention of fighting a war over the city; they just wanted us to leave quietly. Those upper echelons, of course, had the "big picture" to worry about; we didn't. But the airlift decision showed that they had gotten the message.

One can argue that being more conciliatory might have made the Soviets more responsive in some areas, or that a more generous attitude on economic arrangements or reparations might have eased some of their concerns about our intentions. Maybe it would have, but it would not have basically altered their opposition to our presence in Berlin, or their efforts to undermine it once they found we were staying. And that, in turn, set the switches for their policy toward all of Germany.

Our responses, one might say, just developed naturally. There certainly was no master plan. "Containing" Soviet activities was a common-sense reaction of those on the spot trying to do a job conscientiously but without much in the way of guidelines from on high. We could have been better coordinated on occasion, clearer about objectives, less contentious, or more consistent. But no matter what the style, a Cold War over Berlin was inevitable as long as we insisted on staying there and making it possible for the West Berliners to decide their own fate.

RICHARD T. DAVIES

The View from Poland

I took the oath as a Foreign Service officer on my twenty-seventh birthday, May 28, 1947, and entered the basic officer course at the Foreign Service Institute a few days later. Some time in July, members of my class were given their overseas assignments. I was assigned to the embassy at Warsaw.

During July and August, I spent as much time as I could on the Polish desk, reading the files, following the reports from Warsaw on current developments, and talking with desk officers about Poland and our policy toward it.

I was surprised to find so little attention being paid in the State Department to developments in Eastern Europe. In the Bureau of European Affairs, the focus was upon what was happening in—and feared for—Western and Mediterranean Europe. The Truman Doctrine and the Marshall Plan had been proclaimed earlier in the year and U.S. policymakers were understandably engrossed in applying the new

R. T. Davies is a retired Foreign Service officer of the class of Career Minister who served two tours of duty in Poland. He was Vice-Consul and then Third Secretary (Political Officer) in Warsaw in 1947-49 and Chief of Mission in 1972-78. His other overseas assignments included service in Moscow, 1951-53 and 1961-63, on the International Staff of the North Atlantic Treaty Organization in Paris, 1953-55, in Kabul, 1955-58, and as Consul General in Calcutta, 1968-69. His Washington assignments included a detail to the United States Information Agency as Assistant Director for the Soviet Union and Eastern Europe, 1965-68, service on the Planning and Coordination staff of the Department of State 1969-70, and as Deputy Assistant Secretary of State for European Affairs 1970-72.

policies. In July, George F. Kennan's article, "The Sources of Soviet Conduct," appeared in *Foreign Affairs*, leading some of us younger officers to believe that, after all, there was some inclination at the upper levels of the department to be more energetic in counteracting Soviet aggressiveness in the arena where it was most acute. Mr. Kennan called not only for containment of Soviet expansion, but added: "The United States has it in its power . . . to promote tendencies which must eventually find their outlet in either the break-up or the gradual mellowing of Soviet power." He concluded by calling upon the American people to "[accept] responsibilities of moral and political leadership that history plainly intended them to bear."

Kennan's appeal came at the end of a whole chain of Soviet acts that, to us in Washington, clearly added up to a planned effort to expand Soviet power. Following the manipulation of governments in Eastern Europe, the attempt to set up Soviet-style governments in the Iranian provinces of Azerbaijan and Kurdistan, and demands for Turkish territory and a greater voice in the Straits regime, the Soviet leadership in early 1947 seemed intent upon reproducing in Germany the political institutions that were being used in Eastern Europe to create "people's democracies," that is, Soviet puppet governments. In Austria, Soviet policy seemed at best to envisage truncating the restored state and turning it into an economic dependency of the USSR. And, most dramatically, the Greek civil war appeared to grow out of an attempt to install a Communist government by force of arms, with Soviet and Yugoslav support.

In 1945 I had been in the army in occupied Germany and was responsible for a small camp containing displaced persons from Soviet Ukraine. These people told us Americans how deeply they abhorred communism and how intent they were on resisting repatriation. They asked why the Americans, who said they were for democracy and against totalitarianism, were not now preparing to deal with "the greatest totalitarian regime of all time." They warned us that, if we delayed, Stalin would seize the most favorable moment to occupy all of Germany and Western Europe. When these D.P.'s learned that a Soviet repatriation mission was to visit the camp, they disappeared overnight, leaving not one Ukrainian to be shipped back to the USSR.

When I was assigned to Warsaw, therefore, I expected to find my senior colleagues in the department working on plans to counter Soviet subversive efforts in Eastern Europe and to mobilize the anti-communism of the peoples of Eastern Europe against the Communists. Instead, I found a mixture of resignation and fatalism. I asked whether, for example, we were planning to seek closer links with the Polish Socialist party (PPS). I was told that, in Poland, the game had been lost when the Soviets and Polish Communists stole the election of January 19, 1947, awarding their government bloc 87 percent of the seats in the Diet (Sejm) and excluding from power the highly popular Polish Peasant party, which represented the dwindling hopes of Poles for a measure of independence from Soviet control. In the Office of Eastern European Affairs, the Polish Socialist party was regarded as no more than a Communist tool. As for the Catholic church, traditionally a bastion of Polish nationalism, it was beset by the Communists and adjudged hardly a viable institution for political purposes. The American constitutional principle of division of church and state, moreover, made political activity by church leaders an unpalatable concept.

The more I read about Polish-Soviet relations and the events of 1939-45, the more apparent it became that the Poles were the most anti-Communist, anti-Soviet, and anti-Russian people in Eastern Europe and the more disappointed I was that we had no plan to help them maintain some measure of independence from Soviet domination.

I studied the historical origins of Polish-Russian enmity, which had, of course, not begun in 1939, but went back centuries, to the days when Poland was the dominant power in Eastern Europe and one of the principal obstacles in the way of Muscovy's effort to unite the Russian lands. The culmination of this rivalry was the infamous Third Partition of 1795, when the ancient historic state of Poland was destroyed. Russia got the lion's share, including Warsaw, and pursued policies of russification that led to recurrent insurrections, each of which became the occasion for bloody suppression and renewed efforts to break the Polish spirit.

I also read how, after World War I, Poland, like the phoenix, had been reborn from the ashes. The Bolsheviks, then in the first flush of revolutionary fanaticism, attempted to promote a Communist revolution among the Poles during the Polish-Soviet War of 1920. The attempt failed completely, however; few Poles felt any attraction to bolshevism, especially when imported on Russian bayonets. The Poles won the war and, in the subsequent Treaty of Riga, took full advantage of Soviet weakness by annexing territories that had first come to Poland in the sixteenth century. In these eastern lands, most of the townsfolk and landlords were Polish, but the great majority of the population was Ukrainian or Byelorussian, thus giving Moscow ethnic grounds to claim them as irredenta. The claim was activated in 1939, when Stalin and Hitler, as pictured in David Low's classic cartoon, shook hands over the smoking ruins of Poland, effectively obliterating it from the map of Europe.

The Stalin-Hitler pact and its consequences, including the Fourth Partition, were events I had experienced vicariously as a sophomore at

Columbia College in New York City and as a frequent participant in the free forums of Columbus Circle and Union Square. This period, with the Nazi blitzkriegs and the intervening "phony war," was a living school of international politics to those, like myself, who were trying to understand a world gone mad.

It was not, however, until I began in 1947 to study the details of Poland's fate between the totalitarian giants that I learned how overwhelming were the grounds for Polish hatred of the Soviets. Not only had Stalin's treaty with Hitler enabled the Nazis to invade Poland, it also allowed the Soviets to seize the eastern parts of Poland, incorporate them into the adjacent Soviet republics, and begin deporting leading Poles to prisons and forced-labor camps in the USSR. This was that "dark side of the moon" of which the Western world caught only glimpses during the war. An early glimpse was provided by reports that Henryk Erlich and Wiktor Alter, leaders of the Jewish social-democratic labor union in Poland, the Bund, had been executed in Russia.

I remembered that in April 1943 the question marks and ellipses surrounding the initial Soviet occupation of Poland were horribly dispelled by the announcement that the Nazis had discovered mass graves, containing the bodies of thousands of Polish officers, in the Katyn forest near Smolensk. The Polish government in exile in London, led by Gen. Władysław Sikorski, asked the International Red Cross to investigate and determine the truth of the German charge that the officers had been murdered by the Soviets. Nine days later, the Soviet government broke relations with the Polish government, incensed at the latter's refusal to accept at face value its protestations that the officers had been killed by the Nazis. The murder of these officers was enough in itself to have poisoned Polish-Soviet relations for many years.

I knew that the Poles also had good cause to hate the Soviets for refusing to come to the aid of the Warsaw uprising. On August 1, 1944, the Homeland Army (A.K.), the main underground military organization of the Polish people, launched an attack designed to drive the German units out of Warsaw. Encouraged by reports that the Soviet army was about to begin its assault on left-bank Warsaw (it already held the right bank) and by Moscow broadcasts in Polish appealing to the people of Warsaw to rise up, the Homeland Army, supported by the population of the city, began a struggle that was to last over two months. Despite appeals from the Polish government in exile, from the commander of the Homeland Army, and from the British and American governments, the army of Soviet Marshal Konstantin Rokossovsky rendered no effective aid to the struggling city. Everything led to the conclusion that Stalin had not only incited the people in Warsaw to rise against the Germans, but had then acted in such a way as to prolong the fighting until nearly a quarter of the city's population, including many of the effectives of the 40,000-man Warsaw units of the Homeland Army, had been killed.

In my State Department researches, I learned that already during the war Stalin had taken steps toward the formation of a Communist puppet government. As early as December 1941, even as the Wehrmacht was threatening Moscow, Stalin had sponsored the meeting at Saratov of a group of pro-Soviet Polish Communists and leftists to bring pressure on General Sikorski, who was in Moscow for negotiations. In January 1942, there followed the establishment of the Polish Workers' party (PPR), a revived version of the disbanded and decimated Polish Communist party, without the word "Communist," which was so unpopular among the great mass of Poles. Finally, in March 1943 members of the group that had met at Saratov fifteen months earlier established the Union of Polish Patriots. Together with the small Communist underground in Poland, the union formed the basis for the Polish Committee of National Liberation, which was proclaimed on July 22, 1944, near Lublin. The Lublin committee began acting as a provisional government in Polish territory west of the Curzon Line, as it was occupied by the Red Army and the Soviet-controlled Polish army commanded by Gen. Zygmunt Berling. The territories east of the Curzon Line were, of course, reintegrated into the contiguous Soviet republics.

In January 1945, the Soviet government unilaterally recognized the Lublin committee as the interim government of Poland. It was equally arbitrary in setting the de facto boundaries of Poland, not only in the east, but also in the west, placing under Polish administration lands that before 1939 had been part of Germany.

As I prepared to leave for Warsaw, I read again about the Yalta Conference, at which the Big Three had continued the wartime practice of issuing resounding declarations of general principles. In the Declaration on Liberated Europe, they undertook to "assist the people in any European liberated state . . . to form interim governmental authorities broadly representative of all democratic elements in the population and pledged to the earliest possible establishment through free elections of governments responsive to the will of the people. . . ."[1]

Contrary to this principle, however, the British and Americans accepted a Soviet proposal that took the Lublin "government" as the basis for formation of an interim government that they might be able

1. U.S. Department of State, *Foreign Relations of the United States, 1945, The Conferences at Malta and Yalta* (Washington, D.C.: Government Printing Office, 1955), p. 977.

to recognize after it had been "reorganized" to include some non-Communist Poles. The implementation of this vague formula was left to a commission of three, but Soviet obstructionism prevented the commission from fulfilling its mandate. Finally, in May 1945, President Truman sent Harry Hopkins to Moscow with instructions to break the deadlock.

Hopkins was in poor health. He had little or no knowledge of Polish affairs and no adviser with such knowledge, and he accepted Soviet proposals that envisaged minimal changes in the composition of the Lublin government. The Polish Government of National Unity, formed after his visit, included the former premier of the London government, Stanisław Mikołajczyk, as second deputy premier and minister of agriculture and land reform, together with four other Peasant party ministers and one independent Socialist. Arrayed against these five non-Communists, however, were fourteen ministers from the Lublin government. Nonetheless, on July 5, 1945, the United States and Britain recognized the new government.

This provisional government was pledged to hold "free and unfettered elections as soon as possible," and Stalin had said at Yalta that the elections could take place within a month. Pushing for free elections was the principal mission of Ambassador Arthur Bliss Lane, who arrived in Poland in July 1945. He has told the story of this period in his book, *I Saw Poland Betrayed,*[2] while Mikołajczyk in his memoirs, *The Rape of Poland,*[3] has dealt with the machinations of the Soviets and the Polish Communists as seen from inside the government. The elections were finally held, not after one month, but after twenty-three months, and they were not free.

In my reading, I learned why free elections were impossible in the Poland of 1945-47. First, the country was occupied by Soviet troops, while the Berling army was controlled by Soviet and Polish Communist officers. Second, the Ministry of Public Security (the police), modeled closely on its Soviet counterpart, was controlled by the Communists, who used it to suppress the Peasant party and other independent political forces. Third, most of the media and important sectors of the economy and social life were controlled by the Communists and their allies. Censorship kept essential information from the people and distorted the facts of political life. Getting a job or, in the case of the peasantry, getting seed, fertilizer, and farm implements depended upon one's "political reliability."

The cables from our Warsaw embassy that I read in the State

2. Indianapolis: Bobbs-Merrill, 1948.
3. New York: Whittlesey House, 1948.

Department reported that the pattern of intimidation, police interference, manipulation, terror, and just plain murder intensified as the
general election of January 19, 1947, approached. Afterward, the
United States and Britain protested that the election had not been free
and thus did not fulfill the provisions of the Yalta and Potsdam agreements. But there was no effective follow-up to these protests. Early in
March, Ambassador Lane returned to Washington for consultations,
avowedly as a result of the January election, and did not return to
Warsaw, but diplomatic relations were not broken.

Shortly before my assignment to Warsaw, Stanton Griffis presented
his credentials as U.S. ambassador to Bolesław Bierut, the chairman
of the Council of State and ceremonial chief of state. When Griffis
called on the foreign minister, Zygmunt Modzelewski, before the
presentation, the minister confirmed Poland's intention to accept the
invitation to attend the Paris conference on the Marshall Plan. Only
hours after the presentation ceremony, however, Griffis was called to
the Foreign Ministry to be told that the Poles would not be going
after all—a decision obviously imposed on them, as on the other Eastern
European countries, by the Soviet leadership. Understandably, Ambassador Griffis felt that he and the Iron Curtain had descended on
Poland simultaneously.[4]

Thus it was clear to me, even before I left Washington, that the
Polish Communists, on orders from Moscow, were betraying the interests of the Polish people for the sake of the Cold War that Stalin
was waging against the West.

At the end of August 1947, I sailed for Gdynia on the M.S. *Batory,*
the flagship of the Polish Ocean Lines. When I got to Warsaw, I was
assigned to the citizenship unit of the consular section. Thousands
of claimants to American citizenship besieged our offices. Many were
young people from the traditional areas of emigration in southern and
southeastern Poland. Their parents had brought them back to Poland
in the 1930s as the fathers were thrown out of work by the American
depression. The difficulty of our task lay in establishing the validity of
each claim. Having returned to Poland as children, most of our appli-
cants spoke no English and many had only a vague notion of where
in the United States they had been born and lived. Those still in touch
with relatives in the States had no trouble obtaining copies of birth
or baptismal certificates, but it was a different matter for those who,
during years of war and dislocation, had lost touch.

What impressed me, though, was the desperation with which these

4. Stanton Griffis, *Lying in State* (Garden City, N.Y.: Doubleday, 1952),
pp. 161-62.

would-be refugees from the Cold War were trying to get out of Poland. By 1947, the agricultural economy was reviving and there was enough food in the villages to ensure that no one starved, so economic hardship was not the principal motivation. It was, rather, fear of communism and the Russians, of agricultural collectivization and atheistic doctrine, of occupation by a power that, unlike the Nazis, might spare the body, but only if it could possess the soul.

Outside the embassy offices there was in Warsaw plenty to engage the attention and engross the energies of junior members of the diplomatic and consular corps. We were living in a city that had undergone appalling destruction, so that hardly a building in left-bank Warsaw was intact. It was rumored that a delegation of Soviet architects that visited Warsaw in 1945 recommended that the city be rebuilt fifteen or twenty kilometers up or down the river. If Warsaw were to be rebuilt where it had stood in 1939, the work of removing the rubble and clearing sites for reconstruction would double the cost and time required to build a new city elsewhere.

There was never a chance that the people of Warsaw would accept any such recommendation. As soon as possible, they returned to the ruins and reestablished themselves somehow, anyhow, in cellars, shanties, or lean-tos they constructed out of the city's debris. It was not surprising at night to see a light coming from the upper story window of an otherwise apparently gutted building, betraying the aerie of a family that had found parts of a floor and ceiling still intact between two walls, had somehow enclosed the space between them, and now, like squirrels in a tree, scurried up and down ladders to get in and out of their precarious home. On summer days in the Old City, the smell of decaying corpses was heavy. Uncounted victims of the last days of the uprising still lay under the rubble.

Without machinery or trucks, the people of Warsaw had organized themselves to begin the effort of reconstruction. With such tools as they had they were cleaning and reclaiming brick, clearing the rubble from sites on which new buildings would rise or old ones would be faithfully rebuilt. Most people had only one suit of clothes or one dress, which they wore to work. After work, they went directly from the shop or office to a site where they helped clean and stack bricks and loaded them into long farm wagons, pulled by gaunt horses.

All the inhabitants of this city—itself reminiscent of what we imagined the landscape of the moon must look like—were survivors of the multiple holocausts of World War II. The people of Warsaw had survived ordeals that lasted longer and posed more dangers than those of most other Europeans. I felt strongly that, after all their sufferings, they deserved better than to have an alien government imposed upon them by Moscow. I felt, too, that, as a self-proclaimed champion of democracy and opponent of totalitarianism, the United States bore a heavy moral responsibility for what was happening to Poland and the Poles.

In the late 1940s, Warsaw's night life had the febrile quality generated by people who find themselves able to relax after long periods of stress and are intent on indulging their lust for life after prolonged deprivation. The consumption of hard liquor was constant and high, and candles burned at both ends. The prevailing philosophy was eat, drink, and be merry, for tomorrow, who knows?

Aping their Soviet masters, the Polish Communist leaders conducted a constant cold war against the United States in the press and through police harassment. Westerners were the targets of the unceasing psychological aggression of the Communist media, full of "anti-imperialist" propaganda to which the Office of Security (Urząd Bezpieczeństwa, or U.B.) tried by its unceasing activity to lend substance. The U.B. spent a lot of time following embassy officials and foreign journalists and browbeating their Polish employees and acquaintances, striving—usually daily—to get reports on the activities and political views of Western employers or friends. It was easy to fall into a siege mentality and develop symptoms of paranoia. One American official was unable to get out of bed one morning and face another day in the office; he had to be sent home, a victim of psychological shell shock. Other foreigners were entangled by the U.B. in compromising relationships with Poles of the opposite—or, even worse, the same—sex.

As a result, the community of non-Communist foreigners, diplomats, journalists, officials of relief agencies, businessmen, visiting firemen, and their Polish associates constituted a kind of political demimonde, set apart both from official society and from contact with the man in the street by the common knowledge that those Poles who associated with foreigners ran the risk of being branded and perhaps even put on trial as "agents of imperialism." This demimonde was at the same time invested with a kind of glamour. The overwhelming majority of Poles felt ideological solidarity with these officially proclaimed pariahs. If they had a chance, most Poles would have liked nothing better than to associate with the outcasts. As to the outcasts themselves, membership in this club evoked a kind of esprit de corps, a bravura feeling that one was running risks that were all the more exciting because they were so poorly defined, and a bravado on the part of the more defiant members, who delighted in playing games with the U.B. by trying to lose their shadows or by providing known agents with misinformation.

The atmosphere of intrigue was heightened by the secrecy with which both Polish and Soviet Communists operated and by the constant stream of hyperbole, innuendo, slander, and outright lies that issued from Communist media instruments. Often, it seemed, this must be a nightmare that had somehow turned into real life.

The Communist penchant for mystification was illustrated in the founding of the Communist Information Bureau, or Cominform, that occurred a couple of weeks after I reached Moscow. The Communiqué on the Informational Conference of the Representatives of Certain Communist Parties was both undated and devoid of venue. It said that, "at the end of September, an informational meeting took place in Poland with representation from" nine parties, those of the Soviet Union, the Eastern European states (with the exception of Albania), France, and Italy. Journalists and diplomats in Warsaw trying to cover this story were assured by Communist spokesmen that the initiative for the meeting had come from the Polish Communists. It was nonetheless apparent that the scheme had been born in Moscow, where the Comintern had been dissolved only four years earlier. It was also alleged that the proposal to establish a permanent body, the Communist Information Bureau, had come from the Polish representative, the secretary-general of the Polish Workers' party (PPR), Władysław Gomułka. Later, Gomułka's opposition to the whole idea of the September conference and the establishment of the bureau would be cited as proof of his "nationalistic, Titoistic deviation."

Since Poles will talk under nearly every imaginable circumstance, we soon learned that the delegates had met at Szklarska Poręba, a remote resort in the Sudeten Mountains. Beyond that, details on the circumstances surrounding the meeting were hard to get. What was quite apparent, however, was that the Cominform was a more modest revival of the Comintern and would be an instrument for tightening Moscow's control over what were coming to be called the Eastern European satellites. The inclusion of the French and Italian Communist parties—the only ones in the West that had a mass character—and Andrei Zhdanov's charge to them to defend their countries against the "expansionist plans of American imperialism" appeared to us to reveal Soviet hopes that France and Italy might soon become Communist also.

The foundation of the Cominform gave a significant impetus to the formalization of the division of Europe into two blocs, or "camps" to use Zhdanov's term. More, it appeared to me as evidence that the Soviets were following a master plan designed to establish their domination of all of Europe. I feared that if he thought he could get away with it, Stalin would turn the Cold War being waged against us into a Hot War for the conquest of Western Europe.

In October, we were electrified by the news that Stanisław Mikołajczyk had escaped from Warsaw and by the story of his trip on foot
and by jeep through western Poland and the Soviet occupation zone
of Germany. Second Secretary M. Williams Blake left the embassy
shortly thereafter, before his tour of duty was completed, and there
was a good deal of speculation, both in diplomatic circles and the
Western press, that Mikołajczyk's departure had not been accomplished
without foreign assistance. Ambassador Griffis managed matters well,
however, and few in the embassy knew the true story until five years
later. In his book, *Lying in State,* Griffis told how Mikołajczyk had
been taken to Gdynia in an embassy truck and escorted aboard an
American ship bound for England.[5] The driver of the truck was Gren-
fall L. Penhollow, who ran the embassy motor pool. But of all this we
knew nothing at the time.

Mikołajczyk's escape was the signal for other Peasant party leaders
and those most closely associated with the West to try to get out of
Poland. Some of them—such as the vice-chairman of the Peasant party,
Kazimierz Bagiński, and the outstanding wartime underground leader,
Stefan Korboński—made it; others did not and were arrested.

Mikołajczyk's escape also signaled an intensification of the Cold
War in Warsaw through increased harassment of Poles who associated
with Westerners. My secretary in the consulate, Sofia Michałowska,
failed to come to work one morning. When a trusted local employee
went to her flat, he found it under police seal. Neighbors said she had
been taken away in the middle of the night. She spent nearly ten years
in prison. Our senior local consular employee, Czesław Lemański,
tried to get his family out across the "green border," as the illegal
escape route to Berlin was called, but was captured and imprisoned
until 1956. And nearly all our Polish employees told us that the U.B.
had redoubled its attempts to get them to report on the activities and
political reactions of American personnel.

Despite the increased repression, Poles from every walk of life
continued to astound us with their courage. They were well aware of
the risk they ran in continuing to associate with foreigners, but they
refused to be intimidated. Many continued to visit the United States
Information Service (USIS) library on Pope Pius Street, although,
when they left the building, they were liable to be taken to the police
station a block away, where they were identified, interrogated, and
warned not to return.

In April 1948, Walter Schwinn, the director of USIS, decided to
clean out his warehouse, in which a good deal of cubage was taken up
by thousands of copies of a trial issue of a Polish-language magazine,

5. Ibid., pp. 173-74.

Ameryka, the distribution of which the Ministry of Foreign Affairs had
disapproved. He ordered that a stack of these magazines be put on a
table in the hallway of the USIS office for visitors to take if they
wished. They certainly did wish. Before long, there was a line a block
long and it was necessary to replenish the supply. Mr. Schwinn got
rid of most of the magazines and was reprimanded by the foreign ministry for endangering public order. Meanwhile, boys who helped themselves to multiple copies were hawking them in the streets at fancy
prices. The militia (i.e., the uniformed police) succeeded in confiscating
some, but few Poles were deterred from joining the line in front of
USIS by the knowledge that some of them were bound to be picked
up, shaken down, grilled, and warned by the police. (Once they went
off duty, the militiamen themselves were not above selling the copies
they had confiscated.)

Early in 1948, the embassy's internal-political officer, Tom Dillon,
was transferred to Bern and I was assigned to replace him. During a
brief overlap, Tom introduced me to as many of his sources as, by that
time, were prepared to run the risk of associating with officers of the
American embassy. It was surprising how many of them still were.

When I moved from the consulate to the chancery, I also helped
edit the daily English-language bulletin on the Polish press, published
by the American and British embassies, upon which those resident
foreigners who did not read Polish relied for their knowledge of what
was in the press. This work forced me to learn more Polish more
rapidly, and immersed me in the never-never land of the Communist-
controlled press. The principal organizer of that press was Jerzy Borejsza, a long-time member of the Polish Communist party who specialized
in agitprop work. When the outstanding Polish poet, Czesław Miłosz,
defected and wrote a roman à clef, *The Seizure of Power,* he depicted
Borejsza in the character of Baruga: "a catcher of souls, a patron, a
Maecenas," who "was never entirely natural." "Every word Baruga
uttered had a tactical aim."[6]

Certainly, nearly every word in the Communist-controlled press had
a tactical aim in the strategy of the Cold War. The formula was simple.
About the Soviet Union, nothing bad. Everything that happened there
was presented as a boon to all mankind, consciously conceived as such
by the Soviet Communist party. About the West, and particularly the
United States and Great Britain, nothing good. Everything that happened there was presented as though it had been consciously plotted by
the capitalists and their tools, the politicians, to hurt the working
people or the "socialist states," or both. Moreover, the propagandists

6. New York: Criterion Books, 1955, p. 170.

tried, whenever possible, to make sure that there was a grain of truth at the heart of each lie, so that if the reader were able to strip off the husk of mendacity he found the kernel of plausibility, however distorted, and had to admit that "there is something to it, after all." The Cold War was an assault on the hearts and minds of the Polish people.

With the flight of Mikołajczyk and his associates, the Polish Peasant party had been eliminated as significant opposition. The Communists moved next against the Socialist party. It had taken about two years to destroy the Peasant party. Practice makes perfect, however, and the elimination of the PPS as a separate organization took just one year.

At the Wrocław Congress of the PPS on December 14, 1947, Gomułka called for the "establishment of one working-class party" and "accelerating this process" of merging the Socialist and Workers' parties. The Socialist party's leading ideologist, Professor Julian Hochfeld, had prepared for consideration at the congress a plan of platform principles, which provided a theoretical justification for the continuing existence of two working-class parties. The plan envisaged measures of workers' control over the means of production not unlike those that later came into being in Titoist Yugoslavia. It called for "liquidating dictatorial ways and means of wielding power," for popular election of central and local representative bodies, for freedom of conscience, press, assembly, and organization, and for increasing civil rights and liberties generally. "The scope of civil rights and liberties," Hochfeld wrote prophetically, "is of a distinctly functional character in relation to the prosperity and living standard of a nation."[7] Such principles were neither here nor there in the eyes of the Communists, who continued relentlessly to press the Socialists for merger.

In November 1948, I attended the show trial of Kazimierz Pużak, the prewar secretary-general of the Polish Socialist party, and of other leaders of the party's wartime underground organization. The trial was blatantly political. One of the defendants was accused of having belonged to a military detachment that, in 1919-20, had fought the Red Guards, a Communist-sponsored guerrilla group in Silesia. The purpose of the trial was to impart to leaders and members of the PPS who opposed the merger with the PPR the warning that they, too,

7. "R," "The Fate of Polish Socialism," *Foreign Affairs* 28, no. 1:125-42. Reprinted in *The Soviet Union, 1922-1962: A Foreign Affairs Reader*, ed. Philip E. Mosely (New York: Praeger, 1963), pp. 269-70. Hochfeld's plan was submitted to the Congress in draft. A translation of the draft was sent to the Department of State under cover of a dispatch from the Warsaw embassy early in 1948. I have been unable to find a copy of the dispatch in the diplomatic records maintained at the National Archives in Washington.

might be tried for their "right-wing tendencies." This trial was yet another in a whole series of applications, staged by the Polish Communists, of the technique invented in the USSR and brought to its highest point in the Moscow trials of the 1930s. Its lesson was not lost on the leaders of the PPS.

Thus, in December 1948, just a year after the Wrocław PPS Congress, the two parties became one at a merger congress, held in Warsaw, which created the United Polish Workers' party (PZPR). As had been the case with its Communist progenitor, the PPR, the name of the new party omitted the word "Communist" in the hope that, sooner or later, the people whom it professed to represent could be convinced that it was in truth their party.

In the spring of 1949, Hamilton Fish Armstrong, the editor of *Foreign Affairs,* visited Warsaw to gather material for his book, *Tito and Goliath,*[8] a pioneering effort to explain the background and significance of the Soviet-Yugoslav rift. He asked me to write an article on the strategy and tactics used by the Communists in destroying the PPS. The article, "The Fate of Polish Socialism," appeared in the October 1949 issue of *Foreign Affairs.*[9] It describes in detail the "salami tactics," as we saw and understood them at the time, used to eliminate the Socialist party.

Meanwhile, in January 1949, the Chinese Communists had entered Peking. Polish Radio broadcast the Soviet song "Moskva-Pekin" over and over. Those non-Communist Polish intellectuals who prided themselves on being "realists" and "pragmatists" argued that the triumph of communism in China proved Stalinism was the wave of the future. And the Polish media provided endless articles to the same effect, contending that the rallying of a third of mankind under the "banner of Marxism-Leninism" demonstrated the truth of the doctrine and "the irreversible march of mankind towards socialism."

Ordinary Poles hoped merely that the shortage of meat, which had developed suddenly in the fall of 1948, would now end. One of the popular explanations of the shortage was the hypothesis that the Soviets were sending the meat east to help feed the Chinese Communist armies. In fact, the shortage was probably the result of growing fears of collectivization in the Polish countryside, prompted by the arrival there of increasing numbers of Communist "cadres" or "activists." These dehumanizing terms for PPR members conveyed both the sense of an irresistible machine and of unquestioning obedience on the part of those so designated.

8. New York: Macmillan, 1951.
9. "R," "Fate of Polish Socialism," pp. 125-42.

Little attention has been given to the fact that, in Poland, the Cold War concealed a Hot War. As Susanne Lotarski points out, "To consolidate their power, the Communists had to wage a civil war which lasted more than two years and resulted in the loss of over 17,000 lives."[10] Some 4,000 of those were members of the PPR. The collectivization drive, which began to gather momentum after the destruction of the Peasant party, could be accomplished only at the cost of more Communist sacrifices. Almost every day in the party newspaper there were one, two, or three brief obituaries: "Comrade N., a member of the KPP since 1928 and of the PPR since 1944, was killed yesterday by fascist bandits near the village of Z. He gave his life while performing his duty to Party and State." The Polish peasant had received his land during the hastily decreed land reform that followed the establishment of the Lublin government and had no intention of putting it in the hands of a "cooperative," as the proto-collective farms were called in Poland.

In Warsaw, together with some Americans and other members of the foreign colony, I lived on Filtrowa Street. One morning, we woke to find the street cordoned off and many uniformed and plainclothes police patrolling it. A few houses away, we heard, an officer of the Homeland Army had been arrested. Later, we learned that he had had in his house the card files on members of the A.K. throughout Poland. In the round-ups that followed, many of these were arrested and imprisoned.

Thus the Communists methodically pursued the strategy of "divide and rule," isolating in turn each actual or potential center of opposition, preventing it from combining with other non-Communist groups, and using every means, fair or foul—mostly foul—to destroy it. Efforts by leaders of the Peasant party and the moderate Socialists before the January 1947 election to establish joint lists of candidates in certain districts were "unmasked" by the Communists as "hidden machinations of the agents of imperialism." Similar divisive tactics were practiced before December 1948 on the internal factions and tendencies within the Socialist party, to weaken it and set its leaders to fighting among themselves.

We saw these tactics of the Cold War in action and were able to talk about them with those against whom they were employed. It was difficult to discuss them with the Communist tacticians, who, by and large, remained inaccessible to Western diplomats and journalists. When we compared these developments with what was going on in neighboring states, we concluded that a master plan, devised in the Kremlin,

10. Thomas T. Hammond, ed., *The Anatomy of Communist Takeovers* (New Haven: Yale University Press, 1975), p. 341.

was in operation. The goal, we believed, was Communist domination of the entire European subcontinent.

We found further evidence to support this view in the Communist seizure of power in Czechoslovakia in February 1948. President Eduard Beneš had been the most faithful non-Communist ally of the Soviet government and a steadfast proponent of the closest alliance between the East European states and the USSR. That, however, was not enough to satisfy Stalin. To feel secure, he had to have a government and a socioeconomic system in each of the Eastern European states that imitated the Soviet model.

Like Beneš, many of the non-Communist Polish political leaders I knew accepted the necessity of friendly relations with the USSR. I remember discussing this with one of the independent Catholic deputies in the Sejm. "Look," he said,

the Nazis came in here and hunted us down like rabbits. They were going to destroy the Poles as a nation. We were next on the list after the Jews, gypsies, Jehovah's Witnesses, mental defectives, and physically handicapped, and they had already begun to kill us in droves. When one German soldier was killed by the underground, 10, 50, or 100 Polish hostages were seized in the street and shot on the spot. And how many Poles died in the concentration camps? No one knows.

It will be impossible for two or three generations, at the very least, for us Poles to reach a point at which we can meet a German and shake hands with him without shuddering. Is this the man who killed my father, my brother, my cousin? Did the father of this German take Jewish or Polish babies by the leg and dash their brains out against the wall? Is this German related to one of the people at Auschwitz, Buchenwald, or Dachau who operated the furnaces, or the factories, or the railroads which took millions to their deaths?

The Soviets came and were very brutal, there is no doubt of that. We will never forget Katyn, the Molotov-Ribbentrop Pact, or the hundreds of thousands who never came back from the USSR. But, while the Soviets are indifferent to whether this individual or that is "liquidated," their theory does not call for the extinction of the Poles, as a lower race. At least they are prepared to see the Polish nation survive as a nation.

So Comrade Stalin does not need to fear that we are going to repeat the folly of the 1930's and try to balance between the USSR and Germany. We can never again contemplate allying ourselves with Germany or being neutral towards it.

The only thing we ask is to have our own political system in Poland, which truly represents our people's views. The Poles are individualists and are not made for Communism. If Stalin tries to fit us into the Soviet mold, he will not win increased security for the Soviet Union, but, quite the contrary, will create a potentially explosive situation in Poland.

Another Catholic leader who felt this way was Monsignor Zygmunt Kaczyński, editor of *Tygodnik Warszawski,* the newspaper of the Warsaw archdiocese, and the secretary of the Polish episcopate responsible for contacts with foreign diplomats and journalists. He had been a chaplain with Polish units in the tsarist army during World War I and, after the February Revolution, became one of the leaders of the organization of Poles in Russia. After the Bolshevik coup d'état of November 1917, he was one of the group of Poles who negotiated with Lenin to convince him that the infant Soviet government's wisest move would be to support the reestablishment of an independent Poland.

I once asked Monsignor Kaczyński what he thought would be the most important thing a Polish government could do if, by some miracle, Soviet domination were to be removed overnight. He answered, "Establish a Soviet-Polish Friendship Society." I said with some surprise that such a society already existed. Monsignor Kaczyński acknowledged this, but said that it could not realize its objectives, since it was correctly regarded by all Poles as simply an instrument of the occupying power. "What we need," said Monsignor Kaczyński, "is a society that will work to educate Poles about their Russian, Ukrainian, and Byelorussian neighbors as peoples with their own distinct histories, cultures, and national interests. We have to live together in this Europe and some day we have to understand each other, not as objects to be dominated or fought against, but as neighbors with whom we can cooperate."

I said to Monsignor Kaczyński that many Poles had expressed to me the belief that only through World War III could Poland regain its independence. He laughed ruefully and said that World War III would be fought with atomic weapons. "Following such a war," he said,

there will probably be no Polish people left, since we lie between the two principal protagonists. Perhaps those who speak in this fashion are right about the inevitability of World War III. Perhaps they are right about that being the only way in which the Soviet Union could be compelled to withdraw behind its borders. But I am afraid they are wrong when they talk about this as a way to achieve Polish independence, because there would probably be no Poles left on this Polish soil to take advantage of that opportunity for independence.

Monsignor Kaczyński used to give me searching critiques of the activities of the Polish and Soviet Communists. With relish, he noted that, as the only person in Poland who had negotiated with Lenin, he was undoubtedly the best qualified to advise the PPR leadership. "Unfortunately," he would add, "these Stalinists are too dogmatic to seek advice from a companion of Lenin." (Some time after I left Warsaw, Monsignor Kaczyński was arrested. He died in prison.)

In June 1948, the Soviet authorities in East Germany instituted the famous blockade of Berlin, and the Western Allies responded with their equally famous airlift. To us in Warsaw, West Berlin was directly, personally important since we got supplies for our embassy commissary from the military post-exchange system there. And Berlin was a place

where we could go to get away from the ubiquitous U.B. and the incessant harping of the Polish media on American "imperialism," "capitalism," and "racism." Although parts of occupied Berlin were as
badly destroyed as left-bank Warsaw, enough remained to constitute a
semblance of the great prewar capital. Above all, it was the West.

We now found it amusing, when we visited Berlin, to listen to our
colleagues there talk about being "in the front lines of the Cold War"
and "in the forefront of the fight for freedom." We couldn't help
wondering where that left those of us who were stationed in Warsaw,
over three hundred miles to the east, not to mention the members of
our embassy in Moscow.

Also in June 1948, came the expulsion of Yugoslavia from the
Cominform. Yugoslavia had been the most orthodox of the Eastern
European countries, and had gone the furthest in introducing Soviet
forms and policies. Yet Communist orthodoxy was not enough to
satisfy Stalin. The cardinal sin of the Yugoslav leaders was that they
had resisted Soviet efforts to penetrate the Yugoslav government and
party apparatus and had refused to remove officials who were not
slavishly pro-Soviet. Stalin was determined that he, not Tito, would be
the boss in Yugoslavia.

If there had ever been any doubt about Stalin's insistence upon the
adoption of Moscow-style "socialism" everywhere in the Soviet sphere
of influence, it had been removed by the Prague coup. The Cominform
communiqué expelling the Yugoslav party now made it evident that
even that was not enough. Not only must the government and the
socioeconomic system be modeled on those of the USSR; they must
also be subject to direct Soviet control through the introduction of
Soviet personnel into the apparatuses of party and government.

Not long after the Cominform's denunciation of Tito, rumors began
to circulate in Warsaw that Gomułka was in trouble on similar grounds.
We in the embassy had noted with interest that Gomułka had not attended the Cominform session at which the expulsion of the Yugoslav
party was announced. Moreover, Gomułka was no longer making public
appearances.

Party and government spokesmen in Warsaw professed surprise at
the questions of Western journalists about Gomułka's whereabouts. He
was sick, they said at first. Then the story became more elaborate,
until, eventually, it involved a stroke (or, in another version, a heart
attack) and a prominent Swedish brain surgeon was said to have been
in Warsaw.

To us in the embassy, however, the evidence that Gomułka was in
trouble seemed convincing, despite its circumstantial character, and we
reported it in July, together with our assessment that the rumors were
probably accurate. The report was read in Washington with greater

credence than had been given initially to the report of June 18 from
Belgrade, by Charles G. Stefan and his colleagues in our embassy, about
the Soviet-Yugoslav rift. Once one crack had appeared in the monolith,
it was no longer unthinkable that there might be others.

Finally, in September, Gomułka's heresy became public knowledge;
he was relieved of his post as secretary-general of the Workers' party
and replaced by Bierut. For the time being, Gomułka remained a member of the Central Committee and continued to go through the motions
as vice-premier of the government and minister of recovered territories.

Meanwhile, I attended the first of the Soviet-initiated "peace" con-
gresses, the World Congress of Intellectuals in Defense of Peace, which
was held in Wrocław in August 1948. The congress opened with a
savage attack on the West by the secretary-general of the Union of
Soviet Writers, Aleksandr Fadeyev. Among other things, Fadeyev accused "the American expansionists and their agents in Europe" of
"wanting to wield their truncheons over the whole world." "The
Americans," he said, "together with the imperialists of Britain, France,
and Italy, want to put all mankind in handcuffs and turn the whole
planet into a police station under American supervision." He likened
T. S. Eliot, Eugene O'Neill, John Dos Passos, Henry Miller, Jean-Paul
Sartre, and André Malraux to "hyenas and jackals," and accused them
of writing "aggressive propaganda."

This congress was a lineal descendant of those interwar meetings
whose most adroit organizer had been the talented German Communist,
Willi Muenzenberg. The would-be Muenzenberg of the Wrocław congress was Jerzy Borejsza. Manipulating the pathos of the exceptional
losses suffered by Poland and its distinction as the first nation to be
submerged in the fighting of World War II, Borejsza convinced a number of dignitaries from the West to come to Wrocław. Among those at
the congress were Irène Joliot-Curie and her husband, Professor Frédéric
Joliot, of France, and Dr. Julian Huxley of Britain, the secretary-general of UNESCO. A group of Americans, including O. John Rogge, a
former assistant attorney general of the United States, had been travel-
ing in Europe to participate in ceremonies honoring the late mayor of
New York City, Fiorello H. La Guardia, and had come to Poland to
attend the naming of a school in La Guardia's honor. With some trepi-
dation, the group had submitted to the urging of their Polish hosts and
had come to Wrocław, only to find themselves billed as the American
delegation to the congress. There were other Americans there, such as
the sculptor Jo Davidson, who had taken up residence in Paris to
avoid the inquiries of the Committee on Un-American Activities. But
these Stalinists or fellow travelers kept their distance from the group
honoring La Guardia, who were Democrats or Socialists.

Walter Schwinn, accompanied by Ed and Terry Symans, and I were sent to observe the proceedings, as was Grant Purves of the British embassy. Initially, we were permitted to enter the Wrocław Polytechnic where the congress met, but on the afternoon of opening day, we were barred from the hall. I still have a yellowed cutting from the Warsaw daily, *Życie Warszawy*, showing us sitting on the steps in front of the Polytechnic. The headline is "Only for Intellectuals," and the caption reads: "Entry into the hall in which deliberations of the World Congress of Intellectuals are taking place is permitted only for members of the delegations and the press. But, since they were eager to listen, even if only outside the door, the Anglo-Saxon diplomats spent long hours at the gates of the Congress."

Whatever else might be said about this text, it exaggerated in implying that journalists were welcome. One, at least, the *New York Times* correspondent in Warsaw, Sydney Gruson, had been denied credentials because in an advance story he had written that the congress would be turned into "a sounding board for support of Russian policies against the United States and Great Britain." And so it was.

The congress was carefully organized and crudely manipulated to produce the planned impression: that the intellectuals of Europe condemned "Anglo-American imperialism" and blamed the U.S. and British governments for starting the Cold War. But the heavy-handedness of Fadeyev and other Soviet-line speakers rapidly produced a reaction. Julian Huxley protested that "nearly everything has been destructive and nothing has been constructive" at the congress. A respected American educator, Dr. Bryn J. Hovde, director of the New School for Social Research in New York City, finally succeeded, despite all the obstacles put in his way by the congress's presidium, in obtaining time to reply to the repeated attacks on the United States. At the end of a slashing counterattack, Dr. Hovde concluded, "My own people can only judge itself terribly threatened and unite in preparation for the worst."

Crowds of Polish students gathered every day at the Polytechnic to see the prominent people attending the congress and ask them to autograph reproductions of the dove of peace, drawn for the congress by Picasso. Among the La Guardia group was Yaroslav Chyz, a Ukrainian-American who worked for the Common Council on American Unity in New York, supplying ethnic newspapers in the United States with materials on American history, politics, and economics. Mr. Chyz spoke perfect Polish, and when the delegates came out of the Polytechnic at the end of the first day's session, the waiting Polish students asked him for his autograph. He told them in Polish that he was just a rank-and-file member of the American delegation, and recommended they approach some of the better known delegates. When the students heard him speak Polish, they began questioning him about life in the United States. As a result of his work with foreign-language newspapers,

Chyz was a gold mine of information on every aspect of American life and had all the relevant statistics at the tip of his tongue. Shortly, about fifty young Poles had crowded around him and he was holding an impromptu seminar on the sidewalk, which lasted over an hour. When he finally broke away, I warned him that some of Borejsza's goons had been listening to what he had been saying. Chyz laughed and said, "I was in prison under the Tsar and under Piłsudski. To make my record complete, I only need to be in prison under the Communists."

By the next afternoon, the word had obviously gotten around among Wrocław's university students. Mr. Chyz's sidewalk seminar now numbered a hundred or more, each of them trying to get his or her question in. Mr. Chyz again was lucid in his replies, which carried great conviction. He had been answering questions for about twenty minutes when ten of Borejsza's men, spotted in different places in the crowd, began shouting provocative questions at him, one after the other, giving him no chance to reply. "How many blacks did you Americans lynch last year?" "What about the persecution of progressive political leaders, like Henry Wallace and Paul Robeson?" "Why is every American city nothing but one vast slum, full of starving blacks and unemployed whites?" "Why are there so many millions who cannot find a job?" As Chyz patiently tried to tackle each of these questions and was cut off by the next, the goons started shouting at him, "So you can't answer?" and "Why don't you answer?" Finally, the chief goon shouted at him, "You had better be careful about spreading Fascist propaganda in our country. That is a crime for which people are sent to prison."

This was too much. Raising his voice for the first time, Chyz shouted back, "I know you, wearing the trench coats and the fedoras. You are the same people who arrested me for anti-Tsarist activity before the first World War and the same people who arrested me in the '20s for defending the rights of the Ukrainians. I sat [i.e., in prison] under Tsar Nicholas and under the Marshal [Piłsudski], and I am quite prepared to sit again, under Stalin."

At this, the young people turned on Mr. Chyz's tormentors, telling them to shut up and leave him alone. The goons were taken aback and retreated to consider their next step or, more likely, to get fresh instructions from Borejsza. Mr. Chyz explained to the students that it would be better for all concerned if they parted at that point. Each student now insisted upon obtaining Mr. Chyz's autograph on whatever clean scrap of paper he or she could find, and the goons permitted this assembly-line signing of autographs to take place. Following it, there were hearty farewells on both sides and the quondam Ukrainian nationalist left his admiring Polish pupils.

As its final act, the Wrocław congress adopted a resolution establishing in Paris an International Committee in Defense of Peace, consisting of Communist sympathizers from the West and cultural apparatchiki from the USSR and the Eastern European countries. A number of the Americans and Britons attending the congress issued dissenting declarations. Nevertheless, the "peace movement," another Soviet weapon in the Cold War, had been born.

In April 1949, the foreign ministers of Belgium, Canada, Denmark, France, Great Britain, Iceland, Italy, Luxemburg, the Netherlands, Norway, Portugal, and the United States met in Washington to sign the North Atlantic Treaty. From our vantage point in Warsaw, it was high time. Beginning in January 1948, the Soviet Union and the Eastern European states had signed with each other a series of bilateral treaties of friendship and mutual aid, supplementing those concluded by the USSR during the war with Czechoslovakia, Poland, and Yugoslavia. This alliance system was directed against the West, which obviously needed to unite in its own defense.

Meanwhile, Gomułka was gradually removed from power. At the Merger Congress in December 1948, he had been reelected to the Central Committee, but when the new government was subsequently formed, he lost his posts as vice-premier and minister of recovered territories and was named merely second deputy chairman of the Supreme Control Chamber, the principal auditing body of the Polish government. Gomułka, a leader of the Communist underground in Poland, was replaced as secretary-general of the party by Bolesław Bierut, a former Comintern employee and Soviet citizen. Similar changes in the leadership were imposed by Moscow throughout Eastern Europe. For example, in 1949 László Rajk, a Hungarian party leader, was accused of "Titoism," tried, and executed. In Warsaw, we thought it would only be a matter of time before Gomułka was given the same treatment. Stalin, we saw, was determined to remove any potential Titos and replace them with officials who would be slavishly obedient to him. Moreover, by the application of terror, even against the most loyal Communists, he was intent on reducing Eastern European party leaders to the level of Pavlovian conditioned response that he had achieved among his subordinates in Moscow.

On the morning of November 7, 1949, Polish Radio broadcast a communiqué announcing that Bierut had asked the Soviet government to permit Soviet Marshal Rokossovsky, now alleged to have been born near Warsaw, to return to his "homeland" and assume a leading role in the Polish government. Up to that point, no one had ever hinted that Rokossovsky's connection with Poland antedated World War II. Everyone knew simply that he and his Soviet army had sat on the right bank of the Vistula while the German SS put down the Warsaw uprising of

1944. Now, according to the commentary on the radio and in the PZPR newspaper, *Trybuna Ludu,* Rokossovsky was a "Polish eagle who has returned to his nest."

That morning, as I traveled to the office by tram and bus, the people were untypically silent; they seemed to be avoiding each other's eyes. When I reached the chancery, our receptionist was in tears. In many ways, this was the worst debasement to which Stalin could have subjected the proud Polish spirit. The title of marshal of Poland, which had been borne by the founder of modern Poland, Piłsudski, was now to receive its ultimate degradation through bestowal on a Soviet military leader, the product of the army that had imposed an alien system on Poland. Polish subjection to Soviet domination would be symbolized to all the world by placing a Soviet officer in command of the Polish army.

When the Sejm began its proceedings later that morning, I was in the diplomatic gallery. For the government, Premier Cyrankiewicz presented three draft bills in a speech pronounced in a monotone, during which he did not once raise his eyes from the papers he was reading. The three bills were to make Rokossovsky a citizen of Poland, to make him marshal of Poland, and to make him a member of the Council of State, minister of defense, and commander-in-chief of the Polish army.

Each bill had to receive three readings before it could become law. In the first of the nine votes, all but two of the members of the PZPR rose to vote "aye." Seated in the middle of the group of PZPR deputies, Gomułka was ostentatiously reading *Trybuna Ludu.* He never got up or looked up throughout the nine votes. Next to him, his friend and ally, Zenon Kliszko, also retained his seat throughout the voting. The deputies of the Peasant party, bearded men wearing kneeboots, also refused to vote for the bill. The ushers hurried up the aisles and whispered urgently to these stubborn peasants. As each vote was taken, one or two of them rose hesitantly, shamefacedly, some with tears rolling down their cheeks and their broad shoulders shaking. As the ninth of the series of votes was hurried through, only Gomułka, Kliszko, and one of the peasant deputies remained in their seats, defending their ideas of that thousand-year-old Poland that was almost driven from the chamber that day.

As the marshal of the Sejm finished announcing the passage of the third bill, the door to the gallery to my left opened and Bierut entered. Behind him, resplendent in a gleaming new uniform bearing the insignia of marshal of Poland in silver thread, came Rokossovsky, his *konfederatka*—the distinctive four-cornered Polish military cap—under his arm. A fine figure of a man, about six feet two inches in height, handsome, with the white-blond hair often seen among Poles and Byelorussians, Rokossovsky might have stepped straight off the page of an illustrated manual called "Uniforms of the Armies of the World."

As the pair took their places in the front row of the gallery, most of the deputies rose and a hesitant, subdued clapping began. Again, the peasant deputies had to be encouraged to stand up, and few joined in the applause. Again, the single peasant deputy, Gomułka, and Kliszko kept their seats. Following this spectacle, Bierut and Rokossovsky withdrew. The marshal of the Sejm signaled the conclusion of the session. The deputies filed out in silence, many of them openly weeping.

Immediately after Rokossovsky's installation as Soviet viceroy, the Central Committee of the PZPR met and expelled Gomułka and his closest colleagues from the Central Committee of the party. The consolidation of Polish Stalinism had now been achieved.

A month later, I left Poland to return to Washington. With me, I took two strong impressions.

On the one hand, I had watched the inexorable progression of what I could only regard as a carefully devised Soviet scheme to take over Poland and turn it into a replica of a union republic of the USSR in everything but name. From Warsaw I had observed the application of analogous schemes to the other countries of Eastern Europe. George Orwell's *Nineteen Eighty-four* had just been published. I read it with a morbid shiver of recognition. This, I thought, explained how men become puppets in the hands of a tyrant. If the tyrant's plan had succeeded so brilliantly in Eastern Europe, who could doubt that it was also meant to be applied elsewhere? In Eastern Germany, the same kind of scheme was being implemented. And the danger that it would sooner or later be extended to Western Europe seemed clear.

In their letters to Tito and Kardelj, Stalin and Molotov expressed regret that the Soviet army had not reached Italy and France. If it had, they wrote, the Communist parties of France and Italy would have assumed power, as their counterparts had in Eastern Europe. We asked ourselves when and under what circumstances Stalin would feel that it was feasible to move west of the Lübeck-Trieste line.

On the other hand, I had been deeply impressed by the devotion with which the Poles were rebuilding their country despite their rejection of the new ruling class and its Soviet masters, by the stubborn nationalism typified by Gomułka and the peasant deputy who were prepared to run any risk rather than vote to make a Soviet soldier marshal of Poland, and by the deep piety of the people, who, deprived of representative political institutions, were turning more and more to the church as the living vehicle of the Polish national idea.

I recalled the words of Rousseau: "Poles! If you cannot prevent your neighbors from devouring your nation, do your best to make it impossible for them to digest it." But it seemed unlikely they could succeed in the face of all the techniques of persuasion, compulsion, and terror so effectively employed by the most powerful totalitarian state of our time.

When I got back to Washington, I was debriefed by working-level officers dealing with U.S.-Polish and U.S.-Soviet affairs, but did not see any policy-level officials. Nor did I have any indication that anything we had written from Warsaw during my two years in the embassy's political section had had an effect on U.S. policy. The attention of the State Department's policy makers was directed toward Western and Mediterranean Europe, just as it had been when I left for Warsaw in 1947.

In conclusion let me add a few observations about the Cold War.

On June 6, 1944, the Western Allies landed in Normandy, and Operation Overlord, the invasion of occupied France, began. In *Tides of Crisis: A Primer of Foreign Relations,* Adolf A. Berle, Jr., wrote:

> Such evidence as is available strongly suggests that the Soviet Union there-upon [i.e., following the invasion] reviewed its foreign policy: probably in June or July of 1944, though possibly somewhat later. Decision seems to have been taken at that time to close out the relationship of war cooperation and to play a lone hand against the field. The decision was secret, and much of the evidence rests on the fact that the Soviet Union quietly withdrew from a number of the negotiations then proceeding to organize post-war Europe.[11]

From Moscow, Ambassador Harriman and his deputy, George F. Kennan, sent reports in the summer of 1944 that made it clear that, having gotten what he wanted out of his allies, Stalin was now preparing to "become a world bully," as Harriman put it.[12] The first significant demonstration of the new policy was Stalin's refusal to render aid to the Warsaw uprising or to permit British and American planes carrying such aid to land on Soviet airfields. Stalin thus initiated the Cold War in the middle of 1944. At first he proceeded with his customary craftiness and guile, concerned not to alarm his allies more than he could help.

In the summer of 1945, in a conversation with Edgar Snow, Maksim Litvinov complained, "Why did you Americans wait 'til right now to begin opposing us in the Balkans and Eastern Europe? You should have done this three years ago. Now it's too late. . . ."[13] In a letter to

11. New York: Reynal & Co., 1957, pp. 105-6.
12. W. Averell Harriman and Elie Abel, *Special Envoy to Churchill and Stalin, 1941-46* (New York: Random House, 1975), p. 344.
13. Edgar Snow, *Journey to the Beginning* (London: Gollancz, 1959), p. 357;

Charles E. Bohlen written at the time of the Yalta Conference, George F. Kennan said, "We have consistently refused to make clear what our interests and our wishes were, in eastern and central Europe. We have refused to name any limit for Russian expansion and Russian responsibilities, thereby confusing the Russians and causing them constantly to wonder whether they are asking too little or whether it was some kind of trap."[14]

The Cold War began because, after the mortal fright he had had from the near-success of the Nazi attack, Stalin was determined to push the boundaries of the Soviet sphere as far to the West as he felt he could without provoking effective American and British counteraction. For their part, Roosevelt and Churchill were determined to avoid a situation in which their war-weary peoples would be asked to confront the second totalitarian power immediately upon the heels of the defeat of the first. In addition, the end of the war in Europe would still leave Japan to be dealt with, and Stalin's help was considered necessary if a large expenditure of American lives were to be avoided.

Churchill was at least prepared to suggest opening a front in the Balkans. Roosevelt, however, gave little or no thought to what would have to be done if a serious attempt were to be made to realize the promises of the Atlantic Charter.

This was evident as early as March 1942, when, during his visit to Washington, General Sikorski tried to obtain American support for an Eastern European confederation. In a memorandum he wrote on March 7, Roosevelt said that Sikorski "should be definitely discouraged on this proposition. This is no time to talk about the post-war position of small nations, and it would cause serious trouble with Russia."[15] As it turned out, the right time for the discussion of the postwar position of small nations never came. And Roosevelt's military strategy never reflected any effort to realize the high-sounding principles of the Atlantic Charter or the Declaration on Liberated Europe. These remained rhetorical statements, for the practical effectuation of which the American president appears never to have planned. Thus, at Yalta, Roosevelt told Stalin that American troops could participate in the occupation of Germany for no more than two years.[16] Similarly, in

---

cited in Vojtech Mastny, *Russia's Road to the Cold War: Diplomacy, Warfare, and the Politics of Communism, 1941-1945* (New York: Columbia University Press, 1979), p. 283.

14. Charles E. Bohlen, *Witness to History, 1929-69* (New York: W. W. Norton, 1973), p. 175.

15. U.S. Department of State, *Foreign Relations of the United States, 1942,* 3, *Europe* (Washington, D.C.: Government Printing Office, 1961): 113 f.; cited in Mastny, *Russia's Road*, pp. 56-57.

16. Winston S. Churchill, *The Second World War*, 6, *Triumph and Tragedy*

March 1945 General Eisenhower decided on military grounds not to push forward toward Berlin, but to turn south toward Bavaria. This left Berlin open for Soviet capture.

Would there have been a difference in postwar developments if American troops had penetrated to the Oder, as they did into the Czech lands, and if they had maintained those positions while negotiations over the shape of the postwar Polish government were taking place? Presumably, there would. As late as the spring of 1944, Stalin appears to have been prepared to support a genuine coalition government in Warsaw, containing representatives of the London government and of the Polish émigrés in the United States, as well as Communists, left-Socialists, and left-Populists from within Poland and from the émigrés in the USSR.[17] If he were considering supporting such a government in the absence of effective Western pressure, presumably the application of pressure would have found him no less ready to do so.

But this sort of outcome would have been dependent upon a very different approach to postwar planning by the American president, whose principal goal was not a world of coequal, independent states, regardless of their size, strength, or weakness, but rather the establishment of the United States, the Soviet Union, and Great Britain as the three gendarmes that, he thought, would maintain world order and guarantee the peace.

In Warsaw in 1947-49, I saw the third phase of the Cold War. The first phase, from the summer of 1944 to the end of the war, was one during which Stalin felt out the Western Allies to determine how far west his troops could go without alarming them. This was a delicate period for him, since he feared that the Western Allies might combine with the Germans and turn against him. After all, this was what he had done in 1939 and would gladly have done again after Stalingrad, as Professor Vojtech Mastny makes clear in his brilliant study of Soviet wartime policy, *Russia's Road to the Cold War.*[18]

The second phase, which in Poland lasted from the end of the war to January 1947, was one of transition, during which Stalin was content to tolerate a regime that included non-Communists and even non-Socialists. Ever cautious, Stalin was still concerned not to alarm his western partners unnecessarily. In Poland, an important test was the referendum of June 30, 1946, which was held to justify postponing still further the general election that, at Yalta, Stalin had said could take place within a month. The results of the referendum were blatantly

(London: Cassell & Co., 1954): 308.

17. Mastny, *Russia's Road*, pp. 167-82.

18. Ibid., pp. 73-85.

falsified. When the Western Allies took no effective counteraction, Stalin knew it was possible with impunity to take the next bite of the salami. The result was the rigged election of January 19, 1947.

The third phase was that of the consolidation of Stalinism and the elimination from power not only of non-Communists, but of all those, Communists included, who were not prepared to follow slavishly the policies laid down in Moscow.

The fourth phase lasted from 1950 to 1953. This was the period of full Stalinization, of the "deep freeze," which ended only with Stalin's death. It was succeeded by the fifth phase, the thaw of 1953-56, which in Eastern Europe culminated in the Hungarian revolution and the "Polish October" and, in East-West relations, brought the first hesitant steps toward détente.

Between January 1947 and October 1956, events in Poland played no significant role in the Cold War, which was waged on other battle-fields: Greece, China, Berlin, Korea, and Indochina, among others. The imposition of Communist rule in Poland and the rest of Eastern Europe was important because it served as a vivid warning of what could come elsewhere—in Germany, Austria, and even Western Europe—if the West failed to agree on common policies of defense.

In writing about Poland's importance in the eyes of the U.S. govern-ment, some commentators contend that, as a result of the large Polish-American electorate, the U.S. government was particularly sensitive to conditions in Poland. There are two noteworthy episodes that can be cited in this connection, and both belie the claim. One is President Roosevelt's desire at Tehran not to be associated with any agreement on Poland's future frontiers because of his concern about the Polish-American vote in the 1944 elections. One would have thought that, for that very reason, he would have been interested in proposing and de-fending a process of fixing Poland's borders, which involved consulting the views of the Polish people. The second instance was the espousal by John Foster Dulles of "liberation" or "roll-back" during the presidential campaign of 1952. These slogans were designed to appeal to the East European ethnic vote and especially to the largest of its elements, the Polish-Americans. That this was political hokum was revealed within the first year of President Eisenhower's administration, when the people of East Berlin rose against the Soviet occupation forces and the United States did nothing although we had tested the hydrogen bomb and the USSR had not. The hollowness of these slogans was demon-strated again in 1956 during the Hungarian revolution.

In writing about the Cold War, some revisionist historians propound the view that it resulted in part from American efforts to maintain an "open door" for American trade in Eastern Europe. In his recent re-

view article, "The Cold War Revisited,"[19] Arthur M. Schlesinger, Jr.,
demonstrates the groundlessness of this claim. In the light of my own
postwar experience, I can only confirm that it is quite wrong. Those
few American businessmen who showed any interest in Poland in 1947-
49 did so because they were forlornly seeking compensation for property nationalized by the Communist government, not because they
thought there might be trade opportunities there. Of these, there were
few indeed.

Other revisionists have written about American "atomic diplomacy." In my experience in the Poland of the late 1940s, the U.S.
atomic monopoly was invoked only when angry anti-Communist
Poles demanded we drop the bomb on Moscow. "You betrayed Poland
at Yalta," our more hotheaded friends would say. "Now you must
atone for that betrayal by destroying the perfidious Reds and setting us
free." Our more reasonable acquaintances asked why we could not at
least use the threat of the bomb as a means of compelling Stalin to
observe the obligations he had assumed in the Declaration on Liberated
Europe. But at that time thoughts like these hardly appear to have
been seriously entertained by responsible American leaders—even when
the people of Eastern Germany rose in 1953 and began to stone the
tanks of the Soviet occupying forces.

Tempted by Western division, irresolution, and indifference to the
fate of the small nations of Eastern Europe, Stalin began the Cold War.
We could only have avoided this if we had absorbed the lessons of the
Molotov-Ribbentrop pact and the Nazi-Soviet alliance and acted in such
a fashion as to inhibit the ability of the Soviets to expand beyond their
borders of 1939. Our provision of Lend-Lease supplies was a potential
weapon in such an effort. But the real lever was the scheduling of Overlord and the even more fundamental question of whether the Second
Front in the form of a frontal invasion of France was desirable at all.
In reaching decisions on these issues, the American government was
guided almost solely by domestic political and military considerations,
to the exclusion of international political ones. Thus, in its naïveté, it
unwittingly connived at the initiation of the Cold War, leaving unful-
filled the noble sentiments of the Atlantic Charter, the Declaration on
Liberated Europe, and the United Nations charter. The chasm thus
opened between American ideals and expediency is still unbridged, and
the problems of America's moral obligations to the nations of Eastern
Europe still unresolved.

19. *New York Review of Books*, Oct. 25, 1979, pp. 46-47.

THOMAS T. HAMMOND

Conclusions

America, Russia, and Eastern Europe, 1941–1946

The issue that, more than any other, led to the Cold War was the issue of Eastern Europe. It was particularly the controversies between Russia and the West over the fate of the small countries stretching from Finland to Greece that gradually, month by month and year by year, brought about the worsening of relations between East and West that came to be known as the Cold War.

Why was this so? Because Russia and the West had contradictory goals for Eastern Europe.

SOVIET GOALS IN EASTERN EUROPE

Soviet goals in Eastern Europe were mainly two, military security and economic exploitation. The first was stated eloquently by Stalin himself in an argument with Churchill at Yalta:

> The Prime Minister has said that for Great Britain the question of Poland is a question of honor. For Russia it is not only a question of honor but also of security . . . not only because we are on Poland's frontier but also because throughout history Poland has always been a corridor for attack on Russia. . . . During the last thirty years our German enemy has passed through this corridor twice. . . . It is not only a question of honor but of life and death for the Soviet State.[1]

What Stalin said about Poland was also true to a lesser extent about other countries of Eastern Europe; all of them had, at one time or

---

1. U.S. Department of State, *Foreign Relations of the United States* (hereafter cited as *FRUS*), *1945, The Conferences at Malta and Yalta* (Washington: Government Printing Office, 1955), pp. 679-80.

another served as steppingstones to Russia by various conquerors—
the Swedes, the Turks, the French, and the Austrians, as well as the
Germans. Stalin was determined that these invasion routes be blocked
so that no great power could ever use them again. To ensure this the
governments of the East European countries would have to be friendly
toward the USSR. But, since most of the peoples of this area were anti-
Russian and anti-Communist, this meant that friendly governments in
many of these countries could probably not be freely elected democratic ones, but would have to be imposed Communist ones. Stalin did
not want to take chances. He calculated that the best way to make sure
that he could maintain control of Eastern Europe was to do what Russian emperors and empresses had done in the past—to set up satellite
states and hand-pick their rulers. Whereas Catherine the Great had
placed one of her former lovers on the throne of Poland, Stalin would
choose Bolesław Bierut, "an obscure official of the Comintern, little
known even among Polish Communists."[2]

Thus Stalin's interest in Eastern Europe was not theoretical. It was
primarily a matter of immediate, vital, national security—the defense of
the USSR from future armed attacks through the establishment of a
protective belt of satellite states. Nor was it mainly a matter of ideological commitment to the cause of world revolution. Stalin imposed
communism on Poland not because he thought it would bring happi-
ness to the Polish proletariat, but because he thought it would bring
benefits to the Soviet Union.

Aside from military security, Stalin also looked upon Eastern
Europe as an area for economic exploitation. Russia had been terribly
devastated by the war with Germany, and Stalin wanted everything he
could grab from the countries he liberated—machinery, raw materials,
petroleum, even whole factories—whether they were simply seized as
war booty or taken as reparations sanctioned by the Allies. (Later,
however, after he had firm control of these countries, he helped them
to build up their own economies.)

AMERICAN GOALS IN EASTERN EUROPE

In comparison with Russia's, America's interests in Eastern Europe
were comparatively weak, sentimental, idealistic, and theoretical.
Whereas Eastern Europe was right next door to Russia, it was many
thousands of miles away from American shores. It was of little importance to American security. There was some American investment in
Eastern Europe and some trade, but not enough to matter much.

2. Adam Ulam, *Expansion and Coexistence* (New York: Praeger, 1968),
p. 376.

As far as American domestic politics were concerned, there were quite a few American voters with East European backgrounds, but only the Poles were numerous enough to constitute much of a voting bloc. However, the Polish vote was of significance not only in presidential elections, but also was vital for some members of Congress, notably Senator Arthur Vandenberg of Michigan, a key Republican in matters of foreign policy. Both Roosevelt and Truman were concerned about the Polish vote, and they urged Stalin to moderate his policies toward Poland to help them politically. Unfortunately, this may have given Stalin the impression that this was the only reason for their concern about Poland.

Americans and American leaders also had some sentimental attachments to Eastern Europe. Poland was known as the country of great men like Kościuszko, Chopin, and Paderewski, and also as the heroic victim of the German and Soviet invasions that started World War II. Finland was loved by Americans as "the only country that paid its war debts" and as "plucky little Finland," which had resisted the Soviet invasion of 1939-40. Czechoslovakia was looked upon with affection by some Americans because it had succeeded in functioning as an American-style democracy between the wars, and had been the helpless victim of the Munich Pact. In addition, Thomas Masaryk, the "George Washington" of Czechoslovakia, had married an American, and their son Jan had many friends in the United States. The president of Czechoslovakia, Eduard Beneš, was also widely known and respected as a democratic statesman and a foe of fascism.

Some of the countries of Eastern Europe were also looked upon by Americans as shining examples of the principle of "self-determination of peoples." Indeed, it was mainly in regard to Eastern Europe that Woodrow Wilson had proclaimed this principle and had tried to implement it in the peace treaties after World War I. Several of the states of Eastern Europe had been created, or re-created, in accordance with this principle—Finland, Estonia, Latvia, Lithuania, Poland, Czechoslovakia, and Yugoslavia—and Wilson had played a leading role in championing their cause. Just as the American states had fought for their independence from the British Empire, so these states had fought for their freedom from the Russian, German, Austro-Hungarian, and Ottoman empires. It was only natural that men like Roosevelt and Hull, who had served in Washington during the Wilson era, should have shared his paternalistic concern for these small states, which were constantly being threatened by powerful neighbors. During World War II they had fallen victim to Hitler, and Americans thought it would be tragic if, on their liberation from German domination, they should fall under foreign rule once more.

It has often been said that generals always fight their wars on the basis of the lessons derived from the previous war, and the same can be said of statesmen. Both Roosevelt and Hull naturally thought of World War II and the forthcoming peace settlement in terms of their experiences during and after World War I. They had been indoctrinated early in the Wilsonian aspirations to "make the world safe for democracy" and to fight "a war to end all wars." After World War I they had shared in the disillusionment over disclosure of the secret treaties, the injustices of the Paris peace settlement, the Senate's rejection of the League of Nations, the triumph of isolationism, and the calamitous descent of another Armageddon. Roosevelt and his colleagues were imbued with a determination not to let this happen again. This time the peace settlement would be just, and therefore long lasting. This time no secret territorial agreements would be allowed during the war, and the Wilsonian principle of self-determination would be implemented. Plebiscites would be required for all territorial changes so that the people themselves could decide which country they wished to belong to. This time a new League of Nations would be structured in a realistic way, the United States would participate actively, and the league, therefore, would be able to preserve the peace.

These fine principles were held dear not only by Roosevelt and other officials, but also by very many of the American people. Such beliefs were further strengthened by Roosevelt's "Four Freedoms" speech of January 1941, the Atlantic Charter of August 1941, and other such statements. The American people needed to believe that the war was being fought for high principles. If American soldiers were to travel across the ocean to fight and die in towns and atolls they had never heard of, they had to have a reason. The reasons given them by the Roosevelt administration were to defeat the Axis, restore peace, wipe out tyranny, establish democracy, and promote the self-determination of peoples.

Another American attitude toward Eastern Europe (one shared by both Roosevelt and Truman) was fear of involvement, lest the United States be drawn into war again. Americans knew that both world wars had started in Eastern Europe, and many felt that the safest course was to avoid foreign entanglements, particularly in areas not vital to American interests. For example, in February 1944 Roosevelt wrote Acting Secretary of State Edward R. Stettinius, Jr., that "I do not want the United States to have the post-war burden of reconstituting France, Italy and the Balkans."[3] There was a widespread view that Eastern

3. Maurice Matloff, *Strategic Planning for Coalition Warfare, 1943-1944* (Washington: Department of the Army, 1959), p. 491. See also Henry L. Stimson and McGeorge Bundy, *On Active Service in Peace and War* (New York: Harper, 1948), p. 609 and n. 6 for a similar statement by Stimson to Truman.

Europe consisted of small, squabbling states, and that the United States should not get involved in their petty and trouble-making affairs.

THE CONFLICT BETWEEN SOVIET AND AMERICAN GOALS

The contradictions between American goals and Soviet goals in Eastern Europe were not acute during the early years of the war, for many reasons. First, both Russia and the United States were busy fighting the enemy, and deciding the terms of the peace was not so pressing when one was not even sure of winning the war. Second, American leaders sometimes tended to assume that since such goals as "self-determination" were so obviously just, all countries would accept them. Third, Stalin made statements during the war that seemed to indicate that he shared these goals. For example, on July 3, 1941, he said: "Our war for the freedom of our country will merge with the struggle of the peoples of Europe and America for their independence, for democratic liberties."[4] Much more explicit was the statement in Stalin's speech of November 6, 1941:

> We have not and cannot have such war aims as the seizure of foreign territories, the subjugation of foreign peoples. . . . We have not and cannot have such war aims as imposing our will and our regime on the Slavs and other enslaved peoples of Europe who are awaiting our aid. Our aid consists in assisting these peoples in their liberation struggle against Hitler tyranny and then setting them free to rule on their own land as they desire. No intervention whatever in the internal affairs of other peoples![5]

Roosevelt could hardly have made a better statement himself on the self-determination of peoples! And Stalin could hardly have made a statement more diametrically opposed to the policies he would actually carry out.

The underlying contradictions between American and Soviet goals in Eastern Europe were also obscured in the early years of war by Stalin's adherence to the Atlantic Charter, which Roosevelt and Churchill issued in August 1941, and which said in part: "First, their countries seek not aggrandizement, territorial or other; Second, they desire to see no territorial changes that do not accord with the freely expressed wishes of the peoples concerned; Third, they respect the right of all peoples to choose the form of government under which they will live. . . ."[6]

4. J. V. Stalin, *The Great Patriotic War of the Soviet Union* (New York: International Publishers, 1945), pp. 15-16; cited in William Hardy McNeill, *America, Britain, and Russia: Their Cooperation and Conflict, 1941-1946* (London: Oxford University Press, 1953), p. 77.

5. McNeill, *America, Britain, and Russia*, pp. 78-79n.

6. *FRUS, 1941* 1:368. The Soviet Union, along with several other states, indicated its adherence to the Atlantic Charter in September 1941; *FRUS, 1941*

One may doubt the strength of Stalin's devotion to the Atlantic Charter, as well as the sincerity of his two statements above, and still understand why he said such things. In 1941 the Soviet Union was fighting for its survival, and Stalin probably would have been willing to say almost anything to win the aid of the United States and Britain. Indeed, Stalin drastically transformed the nature of Soviet propaganda during the war to please his newfound allies and encourage them to give him the support he needed.[7]

And Stalin continued to say and do things to camouflage his true intentions and reassure his allies. The most famous example was his dissolution of the Communist International in May 1943, an act that was probably designed in part to convince the West that he had abandoned the traditional Soviet policy of spreading communism to other countries.

Still, the United States should have known better than to believe Stalin when he said that the Soviets "have not and cannot have such war aims as the seizure of foreign territories, the subjugation of foreign peoples." For one thing, Russia had for centuries been expansionist, and there was no reason to believe that Stalin had abandoned such policies. Indeed, as recently as the period of the Nazi-Soviet Pact Stalin had annexed the three Baltic states, as well as parts of Finland, Poland, and Romania. And even in December 1941, when German troops were at the gates of Moscow, Stalin began pressing Britain and America for official recognition of these annexations.

ROOSEVELT'S AND HULL'S UTOPIAN PRINCIPLES

But while Stalin was concerned about solidifying his claim to annexed territories, Roosevelt and Hull were largely absorbed with lofty principles. Harry Hopkins once said of Roosevelt: "You and I are for Roosevelt because he's a great spiritual figure, because he's and idealist, like Wilson. . . . Oh—he sometimes tries to appear tough and cynical and flippant, but that's an act. . . . You can see the real Roosevelt when he comes out with something like the Four Freedoms. And don't get the idea that those are any catch phrases. *He believes them!* He believes they can be practically attained."[8]

1:378. The USSR, however, added a qualification to its statement of adherence, and Churchill declared that it did not apply to the British Empire. Martin F. Herz, *Beginnings of the Cold War* (Bloomington: Indiana University Press, 1966), pp. vii–viii.

7. For further examples. see McNeill, *America, Britain, and Russia*, pp. 76–79.

8. Robert Sherwood, *Roosevelt and Hopkins*, rev. ed. (New York: Grosset & Dunlap, 1950), p. 266. Roosevelt had, of course, a large slug of realism in his makeup also. According to his biographer, James MacGregor Burns, Roosevelt was

Roosevelt's Wilsonian idealism was embodied first of all in his belief that a new (but improved) League of Nations would solve the problems of the postwar world. Both he and Hull thought that if only they could establish a United Nations organization and also preserve Russian-American unity, peace would be assured. This view was reflected in Hull's behavior at the Moscow Conference of October 1943, when he gave top priority to obtaining a Soviet promise to participate in a future United Nations; every other question he considered relatively unimportant. When Averell Harriman suggested to Hull that he pressure Molotov on the Polish problem, Hull replied: "I don't want to deal with these piddling little things. We must deal with the main issues."[9] The contrast between Hull's idealistic faith in a future United Nations and Stalin's realistic reliance on a ring of satellite staes shows up clearly in Hull's memoirs, where he said: "I could sympathize fully with Stalin's desire to protect his western borders from future attack. But I felt this security could best be obtained through a strong postwar peace organization."[10]

Closely related to Roosevelt's and Hull's devotion to the idea of a United Nations organization was their opposition to spheres of influence. In their view, spheres of influence (except for the U.S. sphere of influence in Latin America) led to the denial of the rights of small states, while balance of power politics led to war. Instead of states dividing up into spheres of influence and power blocs, they should all be united in a world organization where every nation's rights would be protected and war would be outlawed. Hull's naïveté on this point is revealed in the highly optimistic speech he made to Congress upon his return from the Moscow Conference in 1943: "As the provisions of the Four Nation Declaration are carried into effect, there will no longer be need for spheres of influence, for alliances, for balance of power, or any other of the special arrangements through which, in the unhappy past, the nations strove to safeguard their security or to promote their interests."[11] With Hull holding views like this, it is not surprising that he objected when Churchill proposed in 1944 that, since Soviet armies were rapidly approaching the Balkans, the area should be divided tem-

---

"a combination of a realist and an idealist. . . . He was a short-run opportunist and a long-run idealist." Speech by Burns at the American consulate in Munich, April. 27, 1969; notes taken by the present author.

9. W. Averell Harriman and Elie Abel, *Special Envoy to Churchill and Stalin, 1941-1946* (New York: Random House, 1975), p. 236.

10. Cordell Hull, *The Memoirs of Cordell Hull* (New York: Macmillan, 1948), 2:1170. Roosevelt's notion of the "Four Policemen" makes it clear that he did not want a powerless United Nations in which all countries would be equal.

11. Ibid., pp. 1314-15.

porarily into Soviet and Western "zones of responsibility." As a result, Churchill had to make his famous "percentages agreement" with Stalin on the sly, not informing Washington of all the details.[12]

Another Wilsonian principle that affected Roosevelt's and Hull's policies lay in their belief that all territorial settlements should be postponed until after the war. This belief was also, of course, a result of their memories of the peace settlement after World War I, when Wilson discovered that the secret treaties signed by the European Allies during the war made it impossible in several areas to apply the principle of self-determination. Roosevelt and Hull were determined not to let that happen again. Instead, territorial decisions would be deferred until the end of the war, when all such matters could be settled in a just and comprehensive way, rather than in a piecemeal manner. As Hull put it in his memoirs, "Our attitude had been predicated on our general policy not to recognize any territorial changes that had been made in European frontiers since the outbreak of the war, and not to enter into any territorial commitments that might hamper the proceedings of the post-war peace conference."[13] Thus, for example, when the Soviets tried, in late 1941 and early 1942, to get the British to guarantee the territories that Russia had acquired as a result of the Nazi-Soviet Pact, the American leaders protested strenuously, and this provision was left out of the Anglo-Soviet treaty of May 1942.[14]

AMERICA'S "POLICY OF NO POLICY" TOWARD EASTERN EUROPE

The American principle of postponing territorial decisions until after the war meant, in practice, almost a "policy of no policy" toward Eastern Europe. While the Americans clung to the noble principle of "no predetermination" and refused to make deals, Stalin proceeded to train East European Communists for the job of taking over the govern-

12. Excellent analyses of the percentages agreement may be found in Herz, *Beginnings of the Cold War*, pp. 117-20; Vojtech Mastny, *Russia's Road to the Cold War* (New York: Columbia University Press, 1979), pp. 207-12, and R. L. Wolff, *The Balkans in Our Time* (Cambridge, Mass.: Harvard University Press, 1956), pp. 251-64. For details from the British side and the changes made by Eden and Molotov, see Llewellyn Woodward, *British Foreign Policy in the Second World War* (London: H. M. Stationery Office, 1962), pp. 306-8. Of course neither Roosevelt nor Hull ever registered any objection to the American sphere of influence in Latin America. Hull argued, however, that the U.S. had exercised "self-restraint" in Latin America, while other countries, perhaps including Russia, could not be depended upon to behave in such a manner. Hull, *Memoirs*, 2:1644

13. Hull, *Memoirs*, 2:1168.

14. Philip E. Mosely, "Hopes and Failures: American Policy toward East Central Europe, 1941-1947," in *The Fate of East Central Europe*, ed. Stephen D. Kertesz (Notre Dame, Indiana: University of Notre Dame Press, 1956), p. 53.

ments of Eastern Europe, and at the same time the Red Army, which would determine the fate of most of the countries in the area, continued its march toward Eastern Europe. While the United States postponed decisions, the future of Eastern Europe was being largely predetermined by Soviet military and political actions.[15]

At times America's "policy of no policy" seemed to be not simply a matter of postponing decisions regarding Eastern Europe, but of being indifferent toward the area, or of not wanting to get involved. Indeed, on many occasions the United States seemed to go out of its way to indicate that Eastern Europe was of little interest. For example, when Greek officials asked that American troops, as well as British ones, take part in the liberation of Greece, the request was refused.[16] Similarly, when Hull was in Moscow in October 1943, he largely ignored Eastern Europe, thereby forcing Anthony Eden to carry the ball on matters affecting this area. When the question of the Yugoslav and Polish governments was brought up. Hull even went so far as to suggest that Eden and Molotov discuss the matter and reach agreement, thereby giving the impression that he cared little about the fate of these countries.[17]

Roosevelt behaved in similar fashion at Tehran, leaving it to Churchill to reach agreements with Stalin about Eastern Europe, while FDR sat and listened, committing himself only by his silence. A year later it was Churchill again who negotiated the percentages deal with Stalin, despite protests from Washington that any such arrangement might lead to spheres of influence, and hence was bad. And when the British and the Soviets negotiated an armistice agreement for Bulgaria in October 1944, the American representative was present only as an observer.[18]

Commitments regarding Eastern Europe were opposed especially by American military leaders. In the fall of 1943 the Joint Chiefs of Staff indicated that the United States should assume no responsibilities "in the area of the Balkans including Austria [sic]," and it was not until many months later, in December 1944, that they finally agreed to the idea of the United States taking over an occupation zone in Austria.[19] General Eisenhower, like most of the American military leaders, was inclined not only to ignore postwar political considerations, but to resent any suggestions that political factors should be

15. The classic account of the "policy of no policy" is the one by Mosely, "Hopes and Failures," pp. 51-74.

16. Ibid., p. 59.

17. Ibid., pp. 64-65. Mosely was an adviser at the Moscow conference.

18. Lynn Etheridge Davis, The Cold War Begins (Princeton: Princeton University Press, 1974), p. 168. The representative was Harriman.

19. Mosely, "Hopes and Failures," pp. 62-63.

considered in military planning. Eisenhower once said that he would be "loath to hazard American lives for purely political purposes,"[20] thereby displaying his ignorance of the fact that wars are, of course, fought precisely for political purposes. And it was Eisenhower who decided that Gen. George Patton's army should halt at Pilsen, in western Czechoslovakia, and should refuse to liberate Prague, which Patton could easily have done.[21] This event, more than anything else, convinced the Czechoslovak people that the United States had abandoned their country to the tender mercies of the Russians. It may also have provided Moscow with additional evidence that the United States was not vitally interested in Eastern Europe.

ROOSEVELT'S CHANGE IN ATTITUDE TOWARD THE SOVIETS

During the early years of the war Roosevelt seems to have been rather naïvely optimistic about Stalin's intentions toward Eastern Europe. For example, he once said: "I think the Russians are perfectly friendly; they aren't trying to gobble up all the rest of Europe or the world. . . . They haven't got any crazy ideas of conquest."[22] According to William Bullitt, Roosevelt brushed away warnings about the dangers of dealing with Stalin with the following comment: "I just have a hunch that Stalin is not that kind of man. Harry [Hopkins] says he's not and that he doesn't want anything but security for his country, and I think that if I give him everything I possibly can and ask nothing from him in return, *noblesse oblige,* he won't try to annex anything and will work with me for a world of democracy and peace."[23]

But if Roosevelt initially had hopes that Stalin wouldn't "try to annex anything" after the war, he later came to realize that Stalin was determined to regain, at the very least, the territories he had seized under the Nazi-Soviet Pact. Moreover, as the war progressed it became clear that Russia would eventually be in a position to take these territories, and perhaps more. When Anthony Eden talked with Roosevelt in March 1943, the president appeared resigned to Stalin reannexing the Baltic states, although Roosevelt hoped that plebiscites would be held for the sake of American public opinion. He felt that if Poland were

20. Mastny, *Russia's Road,* p. 274.

21. The present author heard Eisenhower defend his decision at a banquet of the faculty of the history department at Columbia University in the fall of 1949. See Ivo Duchacek, "Czechoslovakia," in *Fate of Central Europe,* ed. Kertesz, pp. 202-4, and Mastny, *Russia's Road,* pp. 275-78.

22. John L. Gaddis, *The United States and the Origins of the Cold War, 1941-1947* (New York: Columbia University Press, 1972), p. 6.

23. William C. Bullitt, "How We Won the War and Lost the Peace," *Life* 25 (Aug. 30, 1948):94.

given East Prussia and part of Silesia, this would more than compensate her for the loss of the lands east of the Curzon Line. He also said that Russia had a right to get some territories from Romania and Finland.[24]

Similarly, in September 1943, Roosevelt told Cardinal Spellman that "the European people will simply have to endure the Russian domination in the hope that—in ten or twenty years—the European influence would bring the Russians to become less barbarian." He also indicated that he thought Germany and Austria would become Communist, even if the Red Army did not intervene, while Austria, Hungary, and Croatia would become Soviet protectorates. The president declared that he could not prevent Stalin from taking these territories and that it would be better, therefore, to acquiesce gracefully. He would attempt to get Stalin to promise to limit his expansion to some particular line, but he was not hopeful that Stalin would do so.[25]

Thus by the spring of 1943 Roosevelt had reconciled himself to Stalin taking back the territories that he had acquired during 1939-41. But what about the rest of Eastern Europe—and Western Europe? Roosevelt hoped to keep Stalin from expanding too far by using a variety of tactics. He would try appealing to Stalin "on the grounds of high morality."[26] He would try to persuade Stalin to be generous with his neighbors. He would warn Stalin that world public opinion would be shocked if he engaged on a program of expansion.[27] He would ease Stalin's fears about military security by agreeing to the dismemberment of Germany. If necessary, he would put pressure on Stalin by promising or withholding economic aid.[28] And, finally, Roosevelt placed exaggerated hopes on his ability to charm Stalin. As he wrote to Churchill in 1942, before he had even met Stalin: "I think I can personally handle Stalin better than either your Foreign Office or my State Department. Stalin hates the guts of all your top people. He thinks he likes me better, and I hope he will continue to do so."[29]

At the Tehran Conference Roosevelt worked hard to charm Stalin, even going as far as to tease Churchill. Roosevelt also went along with

24. Memorandum by Hopkins on the Roosevelt-Eden conversations, March 15, 1943, in Sherwood, *Roosevelt and Hopkins*, p. 710, and *FRUS, 1943*, 3:13-18; Anthony Eden, *The Reckoning* (Boston: Houghton Mifflin, 1965), pp. 430, 432.

25. Robert I. Gannon, *The Cardinal Spellman Story* (Garden City, N.Y.: Doubleday, 1962), pp. 222-24; cited in Mastny, *Russia's Road*, p. 108, and Gaddis, *United States and Origins*, p. 136.

26. Hull, *Memoirs*, 2:1266.

27. Gaddis, *United States and Origins*, p. 136.

28. Ibid., pp. 196-97.

29. Davis, *Cold War Begins*, p. 29.

Stalin on every issue related to Eastern Europe. On Poland, Roosevelt told Stalin that he agreed to the necessity of moving both Polish borders further to the West, but added that he could not formally participate in any such decision because of the large number of Polish-American voters in the United States. Regarding Finland, neither Roosevelt nor Churchill objected when Stalin insisted that Finland would have to restore the areas that Russia had seized in 1940, pay reparations, and give Russia either Hangö or Petsamo.[30] As far as the Baltic states were concerned, Roosevelt seems to have accepted that they would be reannexed by the USSR, but he politely suggested to Stalin that plebiscites be held. "The big issue in the United States," he said, ". . . would be the question of referendum and the right of self-determination." Roosevelt also pointed out that there were a large number of Estonian, Latvian, and Lithanian voters in the United States.[31]

Thus in regard to Poland, Finland, and the Baltic states Roosevelt may have given the impression that he was content to let Stalin violate the principle of self-determination, but hoped that the annexations would be carried out in a manner as inoffensive as possible to American voters. However, this is not the same thing as saying that Roosevelt was indifferent to the fate of these countries. He did care about them, and he really believed in the principle of self-determination. But he also needed Stalin's cooperation in defeating the Axis and in establishing a peaceful postwar world. And since he gave in on Stalin's violations of self-determination regarding Poland, Finland, and the Baltic states he was perhaps reluctant to accept additional violations later on.

It is also important to note that the territories that Roosevelt agreed, either explicitly or implicitly, to let Stalin annex were all territories that Russia had some legitimate claim to—either an ethnic claim (as in eastern Poland and northern Bukovina), or an historic claim (as in Finland, the Baltic states, and Bessarabia). Thus Stalin's demands for these territories were not based simply on conquest.

American leaders were aware of Stalin's desire to improve the military security of the Soviet Union along its East European frontiers, and they were sympathetic toward this desire—up to a point. Until Yalta or shortly thereafter, they were so eager to keep Stalin's friendship that they gave him the impression he could do almost anything he wished in Eastern Europe (other than Greece) to guarantee Soviet

30. Winston S. Churchill, *The Second World War* (Boston: Houghton Mifflin, 1948-1953), 5:362, 396-400; *FRUS, 1943, The Conferences at Cairo and Tehran*, p. 594.

31. *FRUS, 1943, Tehran*, pp. 594-95.

security. But trouble arose when it turned out that Stalin wanted much more than American statesmen thought was essential to make his country secure. Averell Harriman, who was the American ambassador in Moscow at the time, expressed this view as follows: "What frightens me is that when a country begins to extend its influence by strong arm methods beyond its borders under the guise of security it is difficult to see how a line can be drawn. If the policy is accepted that the Soviet Union has a right to penetrate her immediate neighbors for security, penetration of the next immediate neighbors becomes at a certain time equally logical."[32] It was on this issue—where the line should be drawn—that the Cold War broke out. How far into Eastern Europe would Soviet domination extend, and how would this domination be exercised?

YALTA

Aside from the question of the territories that Russia would annex, there was also the equally important question of the fate of the independent states in Eastern Europe. Here the key question was the kind of governments these states would have, the amount of influence the Soviet Union would exercise upon them, and the role of the local Communists in those governments.

In the early years of the war this had not been a matter of dispute among the Allies because all of Eastern Europe was occupied by the Germans, and the formation of postwar governments seemed far away. When the Big Three met at Yalta, Roosevelt was still hopeful that, although Russia' would reannex the lands acquired under the Nazi-Soviet Pact, the principle of self-determination would apply in the rest of Eastern Europe. This hope received concrete expression in the Declaration on Liberated Europe that he presented to the conference and that was adopted with little discussion. It said in part:

> The establishment of order in Europe and the rebuilding of national economic life must be achieved by processes which will enable the liberated peoples . . . to create democratic institutions of their own choice. This is a principle of the Atlantic Charter—the right of all peoples to choose the form of government under which they will live. . . .
>
> The three governments will jointly assist the people in any European liberated state or former Axis satellite state in Europe where in their judgment conditions require . . . (c) to form interim governmental authorities broadly representative of all democratic elements in the population and pledged to the earliest possible establishment through free elections of governments responsive to the will of the people; and (d) to facilitate where necessary the holding of such elections.[33]

32. *FRUS, 1944,* 4:993; cited in Mastny, *Russia's Road,* pp. 212-13.
33. *FRUS, 1945, Yalta,* p. 972.

It is difficult to say just what Roosevelt, Churchill, and Stalin secretly thought about this declaration. Some have suggested that Roosevelt did not really mean what the declaration said, and certainly did not expect Stalin to live up to it, but was merely engaging in his usual practice of composing pretty phrases for American public opinion. James F. Byrnes. for example, later claimed that FDR had presented the declaration to reassure those in the United States who were worried about the trend toward the establishment of spheres of influence in Eastern Europe.[34]

There is considerable evidence to dispute this view, however. When the Russians violated democratic principles in Romania, for example, Roosevelt seemed surprised and angry, and he protested to Stalin. He referred to the Declaration on Liberated Europe and added: "I frankly cannot understand why the recent developments in Romania should be regarded as not falling within the terms of that agreement."[35] He also felt very strongly that Stalin's behavior toward Poland was a violation of the Declaration on Liberated Europe and of the specific agreements made at Yalta regarding Poland. He told Stalin: "I must make it quite plain to you that any . . . solution which would result in a thinly disguised continuance of the present Warsaw regime would be unacceptable and would cause the people of the United States to regard the Yalta agreement as having failed."[36] And in his speech to Congress after his return from Yalta, Roosevelt claimed that the Declaration on Liberated Europe had stopped the trend toward the establishment of spheres of influence in Eastern Europe, which "if allowed to go on unchecked . . . might have had tragic results."[37]

In the weeks after Yalta, State Department officials also indicated that they took the declaration seriously. For example, Charles Bohlen, in referring to American pressure for free elections in Bulgaria, stated: "Since such action is not only permissible but becomes an obligation under the Yalta Declaration on Liberated Europe, we are unable to comprehend why the invocation of the Declaration should be cause for

34. Gaddis, *United States and Origins*, pp. 163-64; McNeill, *America, Britain, and Russia*, p. 559.

35. Roosevelt to Stalin, April 1, 1945, in *Correspondence between the Chairman of the Council of Ministers of the U.S.S.R. and the Presidents of the U.S.A. and the Prime Ministers of Great Britain during the Great Patriotic War of 1941-1945* (Moscow: Foreign Languages Publishing House, 1957), 2:202 (hereafter cited as *Correspondence*).

36. Ibid., pp. 202-3.

37. Samuel I. Rosenman, ed., *The Public Papers and Addresses of Franklin D. Roosevelt* (New York: Harper, 1950), 13:579; cited in Gaddis, *United States and Origins*, pp. 164-65.

misunderstanding. The American people fully expect that the Declaration will be given reality in the treatment of liberated and ex-enemy peoples."[38] Similarly, Secretary of State Stettinius sent a message to Georges Bidault, the French foreign minister, which said in part: "Far from regarding the Declaration on Liberated Europe as QUOTE window dressing UNQUOTE, we are making and will continue to make every effort to give it reality. These efforts have the full support of the American press and public opinion."[39]

Churchill probably felt differently from Roosevelt about the Declaration on Liberated Europe, mainly because of his percentages agreement with Stalin, which had put Romania, Bulgaria, and Hungary, at least temporarily, in a Soviet sphere of responsibility. In his memoirs Churchill indicated that this restrained him from protesting over Stalin's actions in Romania: "If I pressed [Stalin] too much he might say, 'I did not interfere with your action in Greece; why do you not give me the same latitude in Romania?' "[40] The percentages agreement also inhibited Churchill from protesting about Soviet intervention in Bulgaria and Hungary, but did not prevent him from trying to salvage something in Yugoslavia, where Stalin had agreed to 50 percent British influence. However, the percentages deal said nothing about Poland, and Churchill protested vigorously about Stalin's antidemocratic moves in that country.

Whatever Churchill may have thought about the Yalta declaration secretly, he took it seriously in public. As he told Roosevelt, "I have based myself in Parliament on the assumption that the words of the Yalta declaration will be carried out in the letter and the spirit. Once it is seen that we have been deceived, . . . a very grave situation in British public opinion will be reached."[41]

What did Stalin think of the Declaration on Liberated Europe? It is quite possible that he looked upon it as merely fancy rhetoric that Roosevelt had put forward to please the American public. But even if he thought that Roosevelt took the declaration seriously, Stalin had the right to interpret the words according to their usual Soviet meaning, rather than to accept Roosevelt's interpretation.[42] As Harriman commented:

38. Memo of April 19, 1945, *FRUS, 1945,* 5:835.
39. Message of March 24, 1945; cited in Davis, *Cold War Begins,* p. 272.
40. Churchill, *Second World War,* 6:420.
41. Cable of March 8, 1945, *FRUS, 1945,* 5:147-48.
42. Harriman believed at the time and later that Stalin at Yalta intended to permit free elections in Eastern Europe because he overestimated Communist strength; only later, after the Communists lost their second election in Hungary, did Stalin change his mind. Harriman and Abel, *Special Envoy,* p. 414. This explanation

We must recognize that the words "independent but friendly neighbor" and in fact "democracy" itself have entirely different meanings to the Soviets than to us. Although they know of the meaning of these terms to us they undoubtedly feel that we should be aware of the meaning to them. We have been hopeful that the Soviets would accept our concepts whereas they on their side may have expected us to accept their own concepts, particularly in areas where their interests predominate.[43]

Stalin may have assumed that the percentages agreement was still in effect. In addition, he may have reasoned that, since the Western powers were doing as they pleased in Italy and Greece (and soon would do the same in Japan), he could do as he pleased in Eastern Europe. He probably believed that, since Eastern Europe was crucial to Soviet security, the West should give him a free hand. He was prepared to recognize Western spheres of influence—in Western Europe and Latin America, and later Japan—in exchange for a Soviet sphere of influence in Eastern Europe. He wrote Churchill that he understood "how important Belgium and Greece are to the security of Great Britain," so why didn't Churchill understand the importance of Poland for Russia?[44]

WHY ROOSEVELT DID NOT LET STALIN HAVE EASTERN EUROPE

Stalin probably thought it quite unreasonable that the Americans and the British were telling him what to do and what not to do in Eastern Europe. He might well have said to Roosevelt and Churchill something like this:

I'm not interfering in the British Empire, the Western hemisphere, or Western Europe. So why do you stick your noses into my garden? Eastern Europe is vital to me but not to you. Many of these peoples joined the Germans in attacking us and devastating our land, but we liberated them from the Nazis at the cost of millions of Soviet lives. Why then do you try to prevent us from taking steps to ensure that Eastern Europe never again serves as an invasion route against Russia? You have your spheres of influence, so why can't I have mine? You are doing as you wish in Italy and Greece, so why can't I do as I wish in Eastern Europe?

This in effect was what Stalin said to Roosevelt and Churchill during their various negotiations. Why didn't Roosevelt agree?

First of all it might be pointed out that some Americans, including George Kennan, felt that a Soviet sphere of influence in Eastern Europe

---

seems to the present author quite implausible. For one thing, it ignores Stalin's statement at Potsdam, quoted below, to the effect that free elections in Eastern Europe would produce anti-Soviet governments.

43. Harriman to secretary of state, April 6, 1945, *FRUS, 1945*, 5:822; cited in Davis, *Cold War Begins*, p. 216.

44. *Correspondence*, 1:331.

was inevitable. This being the case, he argued, it was idle for us to
protest against it, or to be a party to any deals concerning it. "It made
little sense," he said, "to go on arguing with Stalin and Molotov about
the composition of a future Polish government, as though there were a
real chance of genuine Polish independence."[45] Kennan pointed out
to Harriman in December 1944, that "the Soviet government has never
ceased to think in terms of spheres of interest. They expect us to support them in whatever action they wish to take in those regions, regardless of whether that action seems to us or to the rest of the world to
be right or wrong. . . . They would be equally prepared to reserve
moral judgement on any actions which we might wish to carry out,
i.e., in the Caribbean area."[46] What Kennan proposed as the best
means for preserving peaceful relations with Russia was "a reasonable
balance of power and understanding on spheres of influence."[47]

I continued . . . to be an advocate—the only advocate, I suppose, in the higher
echelons of our government service—of a prompt and clear recognition of the division of Europe into spheres of influence. . . . I remained convinced that it was
idle to hope that we could have any influence on the course of events in the area to
which Russian hegemony had already been effectively extended. . . . This being
so, I saw no reason why we should go out of our way to make things easier for the
Russians . . . either by aid programs . . . or by sharing moral responsibility
for what they were doing.[48]

This was not Roosevelt's view, however. He rejected Stalin's bid for
a sphere of influence in Eastern Europe for a number of reasons:

First of all, Roosevelt the Wilsonian was opposed to spheres of influence on principle. He and Hull favored instead a world organization
that would supposedly make spheres of influence impossible and un-
necessary. When Roosevelt returned from Yalta, he naïvely told Congress that the Yalta Declaration on Liberated Europe had ended a
tendency toward the establishment of spheres of influence.[49]

Second, Congress and the American public opposed any spheres of
influence deal with Stalin. Roosevelt remembered the defeat that
Woodrow Wilson had suffered on the League of Nations, and he was
determined that this time the United States would join. The Senate
would never approve membership, however, if it experienced the same

45. George F. Kennan, *Memoirs, 1925-1950* (Boston: Little, Brown, 1967),
p. 215.

46. Ibid., p. 222.

47. Ibid., p. 250.

48. Ibid., p. 253. See the memo by John D. Hickerson in *FRUS, 1945, Yalta*,
pp. 93-96, for a similar view. For Harriman's dissent, see Harriman and Abel,
Special Envoy, pp. 414-15.

49. Rosenman, *Public Papers and Addresses*, 13:570-86.

disillusionment with the peace settlement that had occurred in 1918-20. Roosevelt feared that if Russia imposed a blatant sphere of influence on Eastern Europe, with or without American approval, Congress and the people would return to their former isolationist sentiments, and the prospects for a peaceful world would disappear.

A third reason why Roosevelt did not want to agree to Stalin's plans for Eastern Europe was his gradual realization of just what a Soviet sphere of influence would be like. What Stalin seemed to want was not just *influence* in the East European countries, but *total domination,* with Western influence completely eliminated. The United States was willing for Russia to be predominant in Eastern Europe, but it did not see why Britain and the United States should be totally excluded. This view was expressed in the State Department's briefing book for Yalta, which said: "It now seems clear that the Soviet Union will exert predominant influence over the area in question [Poland and the Balkans]. While this Government probably would not want to oppose itself to such a political configuration, neither would it desire to see American influence in this part of the world completely nullified."[50] The point is well summed up by J. L. Richardson: "Due to the special character of the Soviet system, its demand for security could be satisfied only by far greater infringements on the independence of the countries of Eastern Europe than other great powers have chosen to impose on states in their security region."[51] In other words, Roosevelt's long-standing opposition to spheres of influence was further strengthened as he became aware that what Stalin had in mind was much more than a traditional sphere of influence, but involved the establishment of subservient satellite states, ruled by Communists whom Stalin had personally selected and placed in power.

Perhaps another reason why Roosevelt refused to let Russia have a free hand in Eastern Europe was his failure to comprehend that free elections in some of these countries would probably result in anti-Soviet regimes. At Yalta Roosevelt said he wanted "a Poland that will be thoroughly friendly to the Soviet [Union] for years to come."[52] Yet he demanded free elections in Poland, apparently not realizing that these two goals were probably contradictory. The debate over Russia's desire for "friendly" governments along its border was not resolved under Roosevelt; it continued under Truman, and it is still fought over by historians today. As George Kennan says in his chapter, "What was wanted by Moscow in the way of governing personalities in those

50. *FRUS, 1945, Yalta,* p. 235.
51. "Cold War Revisionism: A Critique," *World Politics* 24, no. 4 (July 1972): 589.
52. *FRUS, 1945, Yalta,* p. 678.

Eastern European countries was something far more than, and different from, 'friendly' and also different from 'nonreactionary.' . . . What was wanted at that time in the occupied territories . . . were not independent 'friendly' political figures, but subordinates, tried and trusted agents of Soviet power."

At Potsdam, after Roosevelt's death, Stalin put the issue bluntly when he said: "A freely elected government in any of these [East European] countries would be anti-Soviet, and that we cannot allow."[53] Stalin's statement has been repeated many times, and Western writers have generally accepted it as being correct, but it is not. Both Finland and Austria have had free elections ever since World War II, but neither has chosen an anti-Soviet government. Free elections in Czechoslovakia in 1946 gave the Communist party a plurality and resulted in a government headed by a Communist prime minister. Since both Bulgaria and Yugoslavia had strong Russophile traditions, it seems doubtful that free elections in those countries would have resulted in anti-Soviet regimes. As for Hungary, free elections there in 1945 did not produce an anti-Soviet government, but hatred of Russia and communism among Hungarians might have changed this as soon as the Soviet armies of occupation left the country. The most serious threats to Russia, however, were posed by Poland and Romania, where anti-Russian and anti-Communist sentiment was strong and where territorial disputes intensified the traditional antagonism.[54]

Roosevelt apparently was not aware of these electoral complexities; he failed to see the contradiction between Soviet security and free elections. Indeed, he seems to have been rather ignorant about Eastern Europe generally. He wanted good relations with Russia, and he seemed not to understand that this goal conflicted with his other goal of democratic regimes. The more Roosevelt pressured Stalin for democracy in Eastern Europe, he more he endangered the prospects of Soviet-

53. Philip E. Mosely, *Face to Face with Russia.* Headline series no. 70. (New York: Foreign Policy Association, 1948), p. 23. Mosely was present at Potsdam when Stalin made this statement.

54. Some authors assume the Western powers wanted to set up anti-Soviet regimes in Eastern Europe and opposed any government that was leftist or friendly toward the USSR. The record does not support this view. Both the United States and Britain abandoned their support for the Polish exile government, partly because they felt it was incapable of working with the Soviets. Similarly, the West did not oppose the Czechoslovak government formed in 1946 by Prime Minister Klement Gottwald, a Communist, because the Communists had won a plurality in free elections. As Louis Mark observes in his chapter on Hungary, the United States would have opposed the formation of anti-Soviet regimes in Eastern Europe because it knew that no such regime was likely to survive in the postwar era and because it wanted lasting peace in Europe.

American cooperation during and after the war. Stalin's dilemma was the opposite of this: the more he pursued his goal of creating a ring of puppet states, the more he threatened harmony between East and the West.[55] Neither side ever resolved their mutual dilemmas. As long as Roosevelt lived, he tried desperately to maintain good relations with Russia, but he also protested against Soviet actions in Eastern Europe. Stalin, meanwhile, established his domination over Eastern Europe with single-minded determination, even when he knew this was antagonizing Roosevelt.

Roosevelt and the other members of the American delegation left Yalta in a highly optimistic mood. They had concluded that Stalin was a reasonable man who would cooperate with the Western Powers in establishing a just and lasting peace. But within just a few weeks these hopes received a series of jolts. Soviet actions in Eastern Europe, especially in Poland and Romania, seemed to be in obvious conflict with what had been agreed upon at Yalta. As one author has described it:

> In the remarkable swing from ostensible harmony to hostile competition, within a mere six weeks, the ambiguous results of the Yalta summit had set the stage. The Western statesmen had contributed their share by rushing agreements for agreements' sake without taking proper care to impress on Stalin how far they really would let him go. . . . But it was Stalin who . . . held the main responsibility for the subsequent breakdown. He knew well that the integrity of the Yalta accord depended on his behavior in eastern Europe.
>
> Since his determination to subdue his new eastern European subjects did not differ before and after the conference, Stalin did not deliberately wreck Yalta. Yet he wrecked it all the same—by first underestimating his partners' opposition and then overestimating it when their response began to show that he and they had misjudged one another. He had shown his ability to retreat before, and he could have chosen to conciliate again.[56]

During his last days Roosevelt seems to have had difficulty in maintaining a uniformly optimistic attitude toward relations with Russia. Shortly before his death he told Anne O'Hare McCormick he had found out that Stalin's word was not to be trusted.[57] At about the same time he told Anna Rosenberg Hoffman: "Averell [Harriman] is right; we can't do business with Stalin. He has broken every one of the promises he made at Yalta."[58] Roosevelt was also shocked and dismayed when Stalin accused him of duplicity regarding the American attempt to

---

55. For similar views see McNeill, *America, Britain, and Russia,* p. 535, and Gaddis, *United States and Origins,* pp. 133-34.

56. Mastny, *Russia's Road,* pp. 264-65.

57. Harriman and Abel, *Special Envoy,* p. 444.

58. Arthur Schlesinger, Jr., "Origins of the Cold War," *Foreign Affairs* 46, no. 1 (October 1967):24 n.

arrange the surrender of the German army in Italy. When Stalin virtually called him a liar, Roosevelt wired back: "Frankly I cannot avoid a feeling of bitter resentment toward your informers, whoever they are, for such vile misrepresentations of my actions or those of my trusted subordinates."[59]

The following day, on April 5, Churchill cabled Roosevelt that he had been "astounded" by Stalin's "insulting" message, and added, "I deem it of the highest importance that a firm and blunt stand should be made at this juncture by our two countries in order that the air may be cleared and they realize that there is a point beyond which we will not tolerate insult."[60]

Roosevelt replied to Churchill the following day: "I am in general agreement with your opinion . . . and am pleased with your very clear strong message to Stalin. . . . We must not permit anybody to entertain a false impression that we are afraid. Our Armies will in a very few days be in a position that will permit us to become 'tougher' than has heretofore appeared advantageous to the war effort."[61]

On the other hand, Roosevelt continued to hope for the best and tried to minimize the conflicts with the Russians. In his last message to Stalin, on the day he died, Roosevelt referred to the dispute over the negotiations with the German armies in Italy as a "minor misunderstanding."[62] And in his final cable to Churchill he said: "I would minimize the general Soviet problem as much as possible, because these problems, in one form or another, seem to arise every day, and most of them straighten out, as in the case of the Berne meeting. We must be firm, however, and our course thus far is correct."[63]

Thus Roosevelt died with ambivalent feelings about Russia. He had learned that Stalin could not be trusted. He had become very angry when Stalin, in effect, called him a liar. He felt he had to be "tougher" with the Russians. But he was still optimistic that the various problems in East-West relations could be straightened out.

TRUMAN, BYRNES, AND THE EAST EUROPEAN PROBLEM

This same ambivalence is evident in Truman's policies. Like Roosevelt, he was shocked and angered by the things the Soviets were doing in Eastern Europe. Unlike Roosevelt, however, he expressed his

59. *FRUS, 1945*, 3:746.

60. Document quoted from *FRUS* by Francis L. Lowenheim in *New York Times*, March 27, 1972, p. 35.

61. Ibid. Roosevelt's message was found at the Roosevelt Library at Hyde Park. Professor Lowenheim was the first to publish it.

62. Harriman and Abel, *Special Envoy*, pp. 439-40.

63. Churchill, *Second World War*, 6:454.

feelings in blunt language. He talked "tough" to Molotov when the latter visited Washington shortly after Roosevelt's death.[64] He talked bluntly on other occasions, as, for example, at some of the sessions of the Potsdam Conference.[65]

But talk is cheap. When it came to actions, Truman saw, as Roosevelt had, that there was no way he could prevent Eastern Europe from falling under Soviet domination short of going to war. And, like Roosevelt, he also realized that good relations with the USSR were necessary for the establishment of a stable postwar world. As he wrote in his diary, "I want peace and I am willing to work hard for it; to have a reasonably lasting peace, the three great powers must be able to trust each other."[66] With such goals in mind, he held back from any real confrontation with Stalin.

Although Truman soon resigned himself to the domination of Eastern Europe by the Soviet Union, he still hoped to preserve some degree of democracy in these countries. One of the few bargaining chips he had for obtaining concession along this line was the withholding of diplomatic recognition from Moscow's client states. Both Moscow and the states themselves were very eager to obtain such legitimization. Yet in country after country Truman traded away this bargaining chip in return for paper promises. He granted recognition to Poland on July 5, 1945, after the Polish government had been reorganized to include five non-Communist ministers—a cosmetic change that left the Communists in complete charge through their control of the police and the armed forces, as well as most of the other branches of the government. To Romania he granted recognition after just two non-Communist ministers had been added to the government—a change even more meaningless than the one in Poland. In Bulgaria the Soviets agreed to add two non-Communists to the cabinet, but when this was not done the United States recognized the government anyhow. In Yugoslavia the American ambassador reported that the elections of November 1945 had not been free and recommended that *de jure* recognition be withheld, but the State Department granted recogni-

64. Harriman later said that he "was a little taken aback . . . when the President attacked Molotov so vigorously." Harriman and Abel, *Special Envoy*, p. 453.

65. Truman sometimes used even blunter language in his private journal. On January 27, 1952, he wrote himself a memo in which he talked of threatening Russia and China with all-out war, including the destruction of Moscow and Peking and other cities, as well as "every manufacturing plant in China and the Soviet Union." *New York Times*, Aug. 3, 1980, p. 20.

66. Truman Diary, May 22, 1945; quoted in Gaddis, *United States and Origins*, p. 232.

tion nonetheless.[67] In effect the United States swapped a Soviet sphere of influence in Eastern Europe for an American sphere of influence in Western Europe and Japan.

Another bargaining chip that the United States had was the atomic bomb. Byrnes hoped that American possession of the bomb would frighten the Soviets and force them to make concesssions in Eastern Europe. He left for the London Conference of Foreign Ministers in September 1945 with, as he said, "the implied threat of the bomb in his pocket," expecting that it would make Molotov more manageable.[68] But Molotov was more difficult than ever, perhaps because of fear of the bomb. As Byrnes told Stettinius, "they were at a deadlock on most everything they discussed. They were getting nowhere and it was most discouraging."[69]

Averell Harriman, who was American ambassador in Moscow at the time, speculated that Molotov's stubbornness and aggressiveness was due to the Soviets' renewed feelings of military insecurity and "capitalist encirclement" resulting from American possession of the atom bomb. On November 27, 1945, he advised Secretary Byrnes as follows: "With victory [in World War II] came confidence in the power of the Red Army and in their control at home, giving them [the Soviet leaders] for the first time a sense of security. . . . Then, suddenly, the atomic bomb appeared and they recognized it as an offset to the power of the Red Army. This must have revived their old feeling of insecurity. . . . This attitude partially explains Molotov's aggressiveness in London."[70]

The attempt to use the atom bomb as an *implied* threat failed completely, perhaps because the Soviets knew that the United States would not use the bomb to get its way about Eastern Europe. There is no evidence that the United States ever used the bomb as an *explicit* threat. There was some talk in Washington about swapping the secret of the bomb to the Russians in exchange for concessions in Eastern Europe, but nothing was ever attempted along these lines.

Far from taking a strong stand in Eastern Europe, Byrnes re-

67. Davis, *Cold War Begins*, pp. 354-57.

68. Diary of Henry L. Stimson, Aug. 12-Sept. 3, 1945, p. 3.

69. Calendar Notes, Sept. 28, 1945, pp. 12-13, Edward R. Stettinius, Jr., Papers, Bx. 247, University of Virginia Library.

70. Harriman and Abel, *Special Envoy*, p. 521. Elsewhere in his memoirs Harriman says: "The increasingly unilateral nature of Soviet policy became more marked after the London conference. George Andreychin [a Bulgarian-American friend] . . . attributed the change primarily to the atomic bomb. The ruling group in the Kremlin . . . had been shocked to learn that America's possession of the bomb once again exposed Russia's comparative weakness. It was to conceal this weakness . . . that the Russians now were being so aggressive." Ibid., p. 519. For further comments on the "atomic diplomacy" question, see Thomas T. Hammond, " 'Atomic Diplomacy' Revisited," *Orbis* 19, no. 4:1403-28.

peatedly acted with caution. For example, in Bulgaria one of the American representatives told the Soviet authorities that the United States wanted a postponement of the elections scheduled for August 26, 1945. When Byrnes heard of this, he immediately sent the American diplomat a reprimand.[71]

Byrnes was similarly cautious on Romania. When King Michael went "on strike" in an effort to oust the Soviet-imposed government of Petru Groza, Byrnes ordered the American representatives in Bucharest not to support the king, for fear that Moscow might be antagonized:

Principal concern of US Govt at present juncture is, as you know, to keep the road open to a solution of Rumanian political crisis which will be acceptable to all three Allied Govts. We hope no action will be taken which might seem to give ground for Soviet suspicion that crisis was brought about by "Anglo-American intervention." Contact with Rumanian political leaders should be avoided at present stage.

In this connection we do not think that any advice or assurances should be given to the King regarding his present difficult position vis-a-vis Groza and Soviet officials or regarding contingencies which may arise with respect to this political future or personal position . . . though you may apprise him of this Govt's hope that measures which might further provoke Soviet officials will be avoided.[72]

All in all, one would have to conclude that Truman and Byrnes did very little in 1945 and 1946 to preserve freedom in Eastern Europe, except, of course, to make protests. But there was not much else they could do. The Red Army occupied most of the area, and the Soviets gave full support to the local Communists. Both Truman and Byrnes did make efforts to give the democratic elements in Eastern Europe at least a fighting chance. But their interest in this area of the world was not very strong, and they soon tired of their efforts. Eastern Europe became a nuisance, a source of endless wrangling with Molotov and Stalin, so they rid themselves of these troublesome issues in return for cosmetic concessions that could be presented to Congress and the American people as evidence that the Yalta agreements had been implemented. Both of them were eager to get on with the job of completing the peace settlement so that America could forget about the war and enjoy "peace" once more. It was not until the Greek Communists, with outside Communist support, resumed their armed rebellion in 1946 that Washington finally took concrete, meaningful action in the form of the Truman Doctrine, and, as a result, Greece was saved from

71. *FRUS, 1945*, 4:305, 308-9. See also the chapter above by Cyril Black. As it turned out, the Soviets, surprisingly, agreed to postpone the elections, and Byrnes was pleased. The postponement made no difference in the end, however, since elections were held under conditions of terror in November, with predictable results.

72. *FRUS, 1945*, 5:594.

communism. Soon thereafter came the Marshall Plan, which presumably helped to save Western Europe from communism.

But the Truman Doctrine and the Marshall Plan worked because neither Greece nor Western Europe were occupied by the Red Army. Elsewhere in Europe the possibilities for American action were severely limited. Still, within those limitations, the American and British leaders tried to save some semblance of democracy in Eastern Europe, and they deserve some credit for their efforts. As Harriman put it:

It was absolutely necessary for Roosevelt and Churchill to do everything they possibly could to provide an opportunity for the peoples of Eastern Europe to develop governments that would be friendly to, but not the creatures of, Moscow. If they had failed to make the effort, they would have been condemned by history as having willfully sold out these countries. This was an honest attempt to build an orderly relationship with the Russians and there was a certain amount of give and take on our part in the hope of achieving orderly settlements. The fact that we tried and failed left the main responsibility for the Cold War with Stalin, where it belongs.[73]

THE AUTHORS AND THEIR CONCLUSIONS

What about the views of the authors of the preceding chapters regarding the start of the Cold War? What light do they cast on the reasons why Soviet-American relations deteriorated? What conclusions did they reach regarding the behavior of Soviet officials and the Communist leaders of Eastern Europe? What common elements did they see in Soviet objectives, Soviet strategy and tactics, Soviet attitudes, Soviet methods, and Soviet treatment of American representatives? What sort of experiences did they have in dealing with the Russians?

The usual (though not uniform) pattern of experiences that the authors had was something like this:

Initially most of them were not at all hostile toward the Soviet Union and Soviet citizens, but on the contrary felt quite friendly toward our wartime allies. This may have been due in part to none of them (except George Kennan) ever having been involved previously in the rather frustrating and annoying task of dealing with Soviet officials. Although the authors probably all entertained serious doubts about the Soviet system, most of them shared the generally pro-Soviet sentiments that engulfed the American people during the war. They felt that Russia and the West had cooperated reasonably well during the war, and they assumed that this cooperation would continue after the war, even though some conflicts would probably arise.[74]

73. Harriman and Abel, *Special Envoy*, pp. 414-15.
74. Hugh De Santis in his book, *The Diplomacy of Silence: The American*

Ambassadors Kennan and Davies were exceptions. Kennan had dealt with the Soviets for a long time, and he had no illusions about them. As he explains in his chapter, he had learned "by painful experience over a number of years that the Soviet regime was not an easy one for us to have good relations with," and he saw "no reason to expect or to hope that our relations with the Soviet regime would be any better after the war than they had been before—if anything, rather the contrary." As he saw it, "the seeds of further conflict and misunderstanding" were "built into the situation." As for Ambassador Davies, he had administered a camp for Soviet displaced persons in Germany in 1945, and they had told him about life in the USSR and their fear that Stalin intended to expand the Soviet sphere of influence as far to the west as he could.

But most of the authors tended to share the widespread optimism regarding the future of Soviet-American relations that was felt by President Roosevelt and many of his advisers, as well as by the American public. And even Kennan, despite his memories of many years of frustrating encounters with the Russians, "did not want bad relations with the Soviet Union." On the contrary, he says, "I had devoted fifteen years of my life to the hope of achieving something better." Thus all of the authors, Kennan included, were quite ready to work with Soviet officials and hoped that this could be done in an amicable way.

When the authors came into actual contact with Soviet officials, they were disappointed. They found the Soviets to be unreasonable, stubborn, secretive, bureaucratic, uncooperative, dictatorial, and generally difficult to deal with. In those former Axis satellites that were now under occupation by the Red Army (Bulgaria, Hungary, and

---

Foreign Service, the Soviet Union, and the Cold War, 1933-1947 (Chicago: University of Chicago Press, 1980), has traced the development of the attitudes toward the Soviet Union of thirty American foreign service officers, including one of the contributors to this book, George Kennan. It is interesting to note that his conclusions about the views of his thirty diplomats apply equally well to most of the ten Americans represented in the present volume. He writes (p. 2): "Impressed by the Russian military effort during World War II, the apparent 'democratizing' movement within the USSR signalled by developments such as the dissolution of the Comintern and the success of the Moscow-Teheran conferences of 1943, they had believed their Russian ally would join the United States in constructing a postwar world of peace and harmony. By the winter of 1944-45, however, as Soviet armies planted themselves in Eastern Europe, they began to question anew the Kremlin's motives. Gradually, trust gave way to suspicion and fear, friendship disintegrated into antagonism, and their expectations of postwar cooperation eventually collapsed into the pile of wartime rubble."

and Romania), Soviet officials tended to treat the Americans as inter-
lopers who really did not belong in those countries at all, but whose
presence was reluctantly tolerated. The Allied Control Commissions were
bossed in unilateral fashion by their Soviet chairmen, who frequently
issued orders in the name of the ACCs without even bothering to
consult their American and British counterparts (as described by Professor Black and General Schuyler).

The Soviets, moreover, were slow to grant permission for American
planes to land, for American officials to travel about the country, or
for Americans to arrange such things as the bringing in of supplies or
the setting up of communications facilities. When approached regarding
such matters, Soviet officials seemed unnecessarily arrogant and arbi-
tary, almost as if they were deliberately trying to antagonize their
American colleagues.

While the authors were irritated by the treatment they received
from Soviet officials, they were much more alarmed by Soviet acts
against the local populations. They heard countless stories about rape
and pillage by the Red Army (as described by Louis Mark, Karl Mautner, and Ambassador Martin Herz). Aside from the spontaneous looting
by ordinary Soviet soldiers, they observed the organized looting by
Soviet officials of whole factories, including factories owned by American corporations.

More important, the authors (except Herz in Austria) witnessed
the various steps by which Soviet officials and their local collaborators
imposed Communist regimes on these countries. Despite Soviet agreement at Yalta to cooperate in the holding of free elections and the
formation of democratic governments, the authors saw that the Soviets
and the native Communists were using every means at their disposal to
destroy the democratic parties, terrorize the population, and ensure
the establishment of minority dictatorships dominated by Communists.
The authors found that many democratic activists (including some they
knew personally) were arrested, intimidated, tortured, or killed. Some
democratic leaders had to flee for their lives (like Dr. Dimitrov in
Bulgaria, as described by Professor Black). Democratic political parties
were harassed, their meetings broken up, their newspapers closed down,
and their offices taken over (as described by John Armitage and others).

Most disturbing of all to the authors were what these events seemed
to tell them regarding Soviet foreign policy. First of all, it appeared that
Stalin had made up his mind to achieve complete control of as many as
possible of the countries of Eastern Europe—not just a sphere of Soviet
influence, but total domination, with American influence and American
economic relations completely eliminated. Furthermore, Stalin seemed
not to care if this domination was carried out in such a blatant manner

that American officials (and American public opinion) were thereby antagonized. In other words, Stalin's policies in Eastern Europe appeared to be based on the assumption not that the United States would continue to be an ally after the war, but that it would be a foe.[75]

Some of the authors, including Ambassador Davies, were also worried about the future of Western Europe. After Stalin had established his dominion over Eastern Europe, what would restrain him from moving further west? Would he, with the aid of Communists in Italy, France, and elsewhere, march his armies all the way to the Mediterranean and the English Channel? Or would he help the local Communists subvert these countries from within? It was fears like these that led to the Marshall Plan, NATO, and the hardening of the Cold War.

GREECE

Greece was an exception to almost everything said above about Soviet policies in Eastern Europe. As Professor McNeill points out, in Greece during his tour of duty from November 1944 to June 1946, the USSR never gave "direct or unambiguous support to the Greek Communist cause." More than that, Soviet officials consistently advised

---

75. De Santis, *Diplomacy of Silence*, p. 9, presents the following thesis: "The diplomats' perceptions of events in Eastern Europe after 1944 were colored by their ingrained cultural values and beliefs, by historical memories of Bolshevik propaganda as well as Nazi behavior in the region, and by the psychological effects of social-environmental influences. It is my contention that these factors blurred their memory of interwar Eastern Europe and narrowed their vision of Soviet objectives, which . . . were not globalistic, as American diplomats believed, at least for the immediate postwar period, but rather cautious and limited in both strategy and tactics. . . . These Foreign Service officers, . . . socially and culturally conditioned to a particular view of the world, misperceived Soviet intentions." De Santis assumes it is a self-evident, incontrovertible fact that Soviet postwar objectives were "cautious and limited in both strategy and tactics," but he does not prove this and, indeed, makes no attempt to prove it. He also fails to take into consideration the possibility that his own opinion regarding Soviet objectives may derive from his being "socially and culturally conditioned to a particular view of the world." He tries to evaluate the objectivity of the diplomats, but has no standard against which to measure their objectivity other than his own opinions. De Santis also devotes considerable attention to the background of the thirty diplomats, who were mostly white, Angol-Saxon Protestants from upper-middle-class families, and had attended the best schools. This, he argues, made them more anti-Soviet than they otherwise would have been, but he presents no evidence to support this contention. It seems likely that if all thirty had been from quite different American backgrounds, they would have been just as horrified by the policies the Soviets pursued in Eastern Europe. The great majority of the American public—not just the elite—viewed Soviet actions in 1945–47 with alarm and drew conclusions regarding Soviet objectives similar to those of the professional diplomats.

the Greek Communists to cooperate with the British, the Americans, and the Greek government, rather than try to seize power. When the Communist-dominated EAM rose in rebellion in Athens at the end of 1944, the local Soviet representative gave "no encouragement whatever" to EAM or the Greek Communists, "either before or after the outbreak of hostilities."

Why was the Greek case so different? Because as Mr. McNeill says, Stalin had agreed with Churchill in 1944 that Greece would be a British "sphere of operations." And, as Churchill admits in his memoirs, Stalin adhered loyally to their agreement, at least during the months that McNeill was in Greece. As far as McNeill knows, the Soviets did nothing in Greece during this period to contribute to the start of the Cold War.

As to whether the Soviets instigated or supported the resumption of Communist-led civil war in 1946, that is another question, one that Mr. McNeill does not deal with since he was not a witness to those events. President Truman declared in his memoirs that: *"Under Soviet direction . . .* Greece's northern neighbors—Yugoslavia, Bulgaria, and Albania—were conducting a drive to establish a Communist Greece."[76] This was the common American assumption at the time, but it was probably mistaken. Milovan Djilas, who was one of Tito's chief lieutenants in 1946, told the present author that the Greek Communists renewed the civil war on their own initiative, after getting promises of support from Yugoslavia, but probably without even informing Moscow.[77] According to Djilas, Stalin gave very little aid to the Greek rebels and later demanded that the insurrection be ended.[78] However it is possible that Stalin originally favored the resumption of the civil war in 1946 and only later came to oppose it, either because he thought it had no chance of succeeding, or because it seemed likely to increase Tito's power and influence. In any case, it is understandable that Truman assumed Stalin was behind the Communist insurrection of 1946 because the Communists in Greece, Yugoslavia, Bulgaria, and Albania all spoke and acted in public at the time as if they were absolutely loyal, and even subservient, to Moscow.

76. Harry S. Truman, *Memoirs* (Garden City, N.Y.: Doubleday, 1956), 2:98 (emphasis added).

77. Private interview with Djilas in Belgrade, June 1969. George Kousoulas also presents evidence that the decision by the Greek Communist party to resume its armed struggle for power "was made mostly on the Party's own initiative and even in the face of Soviet reservations." Kousoulas, "The Greek Communists Tried Three Times—and Failed," in *The Anatomy of Communist Takeovers*, ed. Thomas T. Hammond (New Haven: Yale University Press, 1975), pp. 302-6.

78. Milovan Djilas, *Conversations with Stalin* (New York: Harcourt, Brace & World, 1962), pp. 181-82.

Regardless of what he did subsequently, in 1944-45 Stalin seems to have done nothing in Greece to help bring about the Cold War. During 1946-49, however, the American belief that he was responsible for the resumption of the Greek civil war helped to intensify the Cold War and led to the Truman Doctrine. Americans assumed that Stalin was behind the Greek guerrillas for two reasons: (a) they knew he had supported Communist takeovers in most of the countries of Eastern Europe, and (b) they thought he was still able to dictate to Communist parties throughout the world, including the one in Greece.

"Atomic Diplomacy"

One of the chief issues in the debate about the origins of the Cold War has to do with accusations that the United States used "atomic diplomacy" against Russia. This view was popularized by Gar Alperovitz in his book, *Atomic Diplomacy: Hiroshima and Potsdam: The Use of the Atomic Bomb and the American Confrontation with Soviet Power.* He argues as follows: "Shortly after taking office Truman launched a powerful foreign policy initiative aimed at reducing or eliminating Soviet influence from Europe. . . . I believe new evidence proves not only that the atomic bomb influenced diplomacy, but that it determined much of Truman's shift to a tough policy aimed at forcing Soviet acquiescence to American plans for Eastern and Central Europe."[79]

The contributors to this volume give no support at all to this contention. If Truman adopted a new, "tough" policy regarding Eastern Europe, based on the atomic bomb, one would think that leading American officials stationed in the area would have been aware of it. Yet if "atomic diplomacy" were being practiced by the U.S. government, they were quite unaware of it. Where the authors comment on the atom bomb, they are unanimous in saying that, as far as they know, the bomb was not a factor in East European developments.

For example, Cyril Black says: "To the best of my recollection, the atom bomb played no role in U.S. policy toward Bulgaria. . . . I have seen no evidence that U.S. possession of the bomb had any influence on Bulgarian or Soviet thinking." Apparently Alperovitz has greatly exaggerated the role of the atom bomb in American diplomacy.

American Economic Interests and the Open Door

Another issue in the Cold War debate has to do with American economic interests. Some of the revisionist authors have argued that the Cold War was caused mainly by American capitalism. That is, they say that the conflict between Russia and the United States was

79. *Atomic Diplomacy* (New York: Random House, 1965), p. 13.

due in large part to the attempt to preserve an "open door" for American economic interests in Eastern Europe—to keep this area open for American trade, investment, and economic exploitation (see chap. 1).

The contributors to this volume do not provide any evidence to support such arguments. They do point out that American officials in Eastern Europe tried to protect American-owned properties from confiscation or looting by local governments or Soviet officials, but they make it clear that economic considerations played only a minor role in American policies in Eastern Europe. George Kennan specifically rejects the economic argument, that is, the suggestion "that American statesmen of those years were prejudiced against the Soviet Union because they were representatives of American capitalism, lusting for the economic subjugation of Russia and Eastern Europe." The notion, writes Kennan, that such men as Roosevelt, Hopkins, Harriman, Hull, Truman, and Eisenhower "would be suspected of being tools of Wall Street, and of being animated in their approach to the Soviet Union by a desire for the economic subjugation of Eastern Europe, is a suggestion of such absurdity that I cannot really treat it seriously."

The Influence Exercised by American "Witnesses"

As noted above, most of the contributors to this volume initially shared the widespread American friendliness felt during the war toward our Soviet ally. Frustrating, irritating, and unpleasant contact with Soviet officials changed these attitudes in most cases, however. Since Soviet officials and their collaborators were treating the people of Eastern Europe with undisguised brutality, the initial friendliness of the American officials was replaced by hostility. In other words, they gradually acquired what came to be known as "Cold War attitudes."

All of this was, of course, reflected in the dispatches that the authors and their colleagues sent back to Washington. The State Department was flooded with messages from Europe telling about the things that the Russians and their Communist friends were doing, most of them bad.[80] In addition, some of the Americans stationed in Europe returned to Washington for consultations with high officials. For example, General Schuyler flew back from Romania and had an interview with President Truman on May 2, 1945. He told the president that if "the Soviets were able to get away with their program [in Romania and Bulgaria] . . . they would be encouraged to try the same game in every other country in Europe as far as they could penetrate."[81] Later

80. For examples, see the volumes for 1944-48 of *FRUS*.
81. Joseph C. Grew, *Turbulent Era* (Boston: Houghton Mifflin, 1952), 2: 1454-55; cited in Paul D. Quinlan, *Clash over Romania: British and American Policies toward Romania, 1938-1947* (Los Angeles: American Romanian Academy of Arts and Sciences, 1977), p. 132.

Schuyler told a colleague that the president had been "greatly moved" by his report, that Truman "felt strongly on the Roumanian crisis," and that, as a result, "there would be a stiffening of attitude on America's part towards Russia."[82]

Professor Cyril Black also had an opportunity to report directly to a top official about Soviet activities in the Balkans. Together with Mark Ethridge he composed a report on Soviet policy in Romania and Bulgaria that they delivered personally to Secretary of State Byrnes in December 1945, shortly before Byrnes left for the meeting of the Council of Foreign Ministers in Moscow.

Of course American leaders and the American public heard about Communist actions in Eastern Europe not only from diplomats, but also from journalists. American policies were influenced not only by what was reported in official dispatches and interviews, but also by the news media. Day by day and month by month the press was filled with an endless stream of reports of democratic leaders being arrested, charged in kangaroo courts, and jailed or executed; of propaganda trials similar to the notorious Moscow trials of the 1930s; of Communist bully boys intimidating voters and breaking up democratic political meetings in a manner reminiscent of the Nazis; of private property being confiscated arbitrarily and without compensation; of Soviet soldiers looting and raping on a wholesale scale; and of people being thrown in prison simply because they were friendly toward the West. American officials in Eastern Europe, such as the authors of this volume, were aware not only of what was happening in the countries where they were stationed, but knew of similar events in other countries and saw a general pattern of Soviet behavior. As Ambassador Martin F. Herz put it, "When I was in Vienna, I was influenced not only by what the Communists were doing in Austria but also by the news, day by day, about the destruction of the Smallholders Party in Hungary, the splitting of the Hungarian Socialists, and the wholesale accusations against their enemies made by the Communists in Romania, etc."

Why did the Cold War begin? We are convinced that one of the most important reasons, perhaps the most important reason, was Soviet policy in Eastern Europe. American officials (and journalists) were witnesses to Soviet intervention, by armed force and otherwise, in one country after another to help install undemocratic Communist regimes. They saw this happen in East Germany, Poland, Czecho-

82. LeRougetel to Foreign Office, May 26, 1945, F.O. 371/48541, and Sir Llewellyn Woodward, *British Foreign Policy in the Second World War* (London: H.M. Stationery Office, 1971), 3:589-90; quoted in Quinlan, *Clash over Romania*, p. 132.

slovakia, Hungary, Bulgaria, Romania, and Yugoslavia, not to mention
North Korea. (Estonia, Latvia, and Lithuania had been invaded and
annexed earlier, in 1940.) Not only did the Soviet Union intervene in
these countries, but in some cases it did so in a very ruthless, bloody
fashion.

American witnesses to these events were disturbed by what they
saw and they reported their observations back to the United States.
Similar reports told of Soviet efforts to gain control of northern Iran
though the establishment of two puppet states, the Kurdish People's
Republic and the Autonomous Republic of Azerbaijan.[83] When the
Communists in Greece attempted to overthrow the Greek government in 1946, President Truman concluded, erroneously but understandably, that this was simply one more step in Stalin's plan to expand
Soviet hegemony wherever he could. The threat to Greece, combined
with Soviet pressure on Turkey, led to the Truman Doctrine, which led
in turn to the Marshall Plan. By then the policy of "containment" was
in full swing. When the North Korean army invaded South Korea, that
was also interpreted as part of Stalin's grand design to spread communism throughout the world, and American troops were sent to
Korea to fight against the Communists. The Cold War had become a
hot war.

To end with the simplest, shortest statement of our conclusions:
We feel that Soviet acts in Eastern Europe and Germany, as interpreted
and reported by Americans on the spot, were a major contributing
factor, perhaps the main contributing factor, to the start of the Cold
War.

83. For details see the chapter by Rouhollah K. Ramazani in *Anatomy*, ed.
Hammond, pp. 448-74.

Index

PUBLICATIONS ON RUSSIA AND EASTERN EUROPE OF THE SCHOOL OF INTERNATIONAL STUDIES

1. Peter F. Sugar and Ivo J. Lederer, eds. *Nationalism in Eastern Europe*. 1969. 487 pp., index.
2. W. A. Douglas Jackson, ed. *Agrarian Policies and Problems in Communist and Non-Communist Countries*. 1971. 485 pp., maps, figures, tables, index.
3. Alexander V. Muller, trans. and ed. *The* Spiritual Regulation *of Peter the Great*. 1972. 150 pp., index.
4. Ben-Cion Pinchuck. *The Octobrists in the Third Duma, 1907-1912*. 1974. 232 pp., bibliog., index.
5. Gale Stokes. *Legitimacy through Liberalism: Vladimir Jovanović and the Transformation of Serbian Politics*. 1975. 280 pp., maps, bibliog., index.
6. Canfield F. Smith. *Vladivostok under Red and White Rule: Revolution and Counterrevolution in the Russian Far East, 1920-1922*. 1975. 304 pp., maps, illus., bibliog., index.
7. Michael Palij. *The Anarchism of Nestor Makhno, 1918-1921: An Aspect of the Ukrainian Revolution*. 1976. 428 pp., map, illus., bibliog., index.
8. Deborah Hardy. *Petr Tkachev, the Critic as Jacobin*. 1977. 339 pp., illus., bibliog., index.
9. Tsuyoshi Hasegawa. *The February Revolution: Petrograd 1917*. 1981. 652 pp., maps, tables, illus., appendixes, bibliog., index.
10. Thomas T. Hammond, ed. *Witnesses to the Origins of the Cold War*. 1982. 318 pp., index.
11. Bogdana Carpenter. *The Poetic Avant-Garde in Poland 1918 to 1939*. Forthcoming.